Geo-Economics and Power the 21st Century

CW00833776

Starting from the key concept of geo-economics, this book investigates the new power politics and argues that the changing structural features of the contemporary international system are recasting the strategic imperatives of foreign policy practice.

States increasingly practise power politics by economic means. Whether it is about Iran's nuclear programme or Russia's annexation of Crimea, Western states prefer economic sanctions to military force. Most rising powers have also become cunning agents of economic statecraft. China, for instance, is using finance, investment and trade as means to gain strategic influence and embed its global rise. Yet the way states use economic power to pursue strategic aims remains an understudied topic in International Political Economy and International Relations. The contributions to this volume assess geo-economics as a form of power politics. They show how power and security are no longer simply coupled to the physical control of territory by military means, but also to commanding and manipulating the economic binds that are decisive in today's globalised and highly interconnected world. Indeed, as the volume shows, the ability to wield economic power forms an essential means in the foreign policies of major powers. In so doing, the book challenges simplistic accounts of a return to traditional, military-driven geopolitics, while not succumbing to any unfounded idealism based on the supposedly stabilising effects of interdependence on international relations. As such, it advances our understanding of geo-economics as a strategic practice and as an innovative and timely analytical approach.

This book will be of much interest to students of security studies, international political economy, foreign policy and International Relations in general.

Mikael Wigell is Senior Research Fellow at the Finnish Institute of International Affairs and Adjunct Professor in International Political Economy at the University of Tampere, Finland.

Sören Scholvin is Research Fellow at the Institute of Economic and Cultural Geography, University of Hanover, Germany.

Mika Aaltola is Director of the Global Security Programme at the Finnish Institute of International Affairs. He also works as Professor of International Relations at Tallinn University, Estonia.

Routledge Global Security Studies
Series Editors: Aaron Karp and Regina Karp

Global Security Studies emphasizes broad forces reshaping global security and the dilemmas facing decision-makers the world over. The series stresses issues relevant in many countries and regions, accessible to broad professional and academic audiences as well as to students, and enduring through explicit theoretical foundations.

Nuclear Terrorism
Countering the Threat
Edited by Brecht Volders and Tom Sauer

Nonproliferation Policy and Nuclear Posture
Causes and Consequences for the Spread of Nuclear Weapons
Edited by Neil Narang, Erik Gartzke and Matthew Kroenig

North Korea, Iran and the Challenge to International Order
A Comparative Perspective
Patrick McEachern and Jaclyn O'Brien McEachern

Stable Nuclear Zero
The Vision and its Implications for Disarmament Policy
Edited by Sverre Lodgaard

US Grand Strategy in the 21st Century
The Case for Restraint
Edited by A. Trevor Thrall and Benjamin H. Friedman

US National Security Reform
Reassessing the National Security Act of 1947
Edited by Heidi B. Demarest and Erica D. Borghard

Geo-Economics and Power Politics in the 21st Century
The Revival of Economic Statecraft
Edited by Mikael Wigell, Sören Scholvin and Mika Aaltola

For more information about this series, please visit: www.routledge.com/Routledge-Global-Security-Studies/book-series/RGSS

Geo-Economics and Power Politics in the 21st Century

The Revival of Economic Statecraft

Edited by
Mikael Wigell,
Sören Scholvin
and Mika Aaltola

LONDON AND NEW YORK

First published 2019 by Routledge

2 Park Square, Milton Park, Abingdon, Oxfordshire OX14 4RN
52 Vanderbilt Avenue, New York, NY 10017

Routledge is an imprint of the Taylor & Francis Group, an informa business

First issued in paperback 2019

British Library Cataloguing-in-Publication Data
A catalogue record for this book is available from the British Library

Library of Congress Cataloging-in-Publication Data
Names: Wigell, Mikael, editor. | Scholvin, Sèoren, editor. |
Aaltola, Mika, editor.
Title: Geo-economics and power politics in the 21st century : the revival of economic statecraft / edited by Mikael Wigell, Sèoren Scholvin, and Mika Aaltola.
Description: Abingdon, Oxon ; New York, NY : Routledge, 2018. | Series: Routledge global security studies | Includes bibliographical references and index.
Identifiers: LCCN 2018012150| ISBN 9780815397304 (hardback) | ISBN 9781351172288 (e-book)
Subjects: LCSH: International economic relations–Political aspects. | Balance of power–Economic aspects. | Geopolitics–Economic aspects. | International relations–Economic aspects.
Classification: LCC HF1359 .G4695 2018 | DDC 337–dc23
LC record available at https://lccn.loc.gov/2018012150

ISBN: 978-0-8153-9730-4 (hbk)
ISBN: 978-0-367-48049-3 (pbk)

Typeset in Times New Roman
by Wearset Ltd, Boldon, Tyne and Wear

Contents

Figures

Tables

Contributors

Mika Aaltola is Program Director of the Global Security Research Programme at the Finnish Institute of International Affairs (FIIA) and Professor of International Relations at Tallinn University, Estonia.

Pavel K. Baev is a Research Professor at the Peace Research Institute Oslo (PRIO). He is also Senior Non-Resident Fellow at the Brookings Institution, Washington, DC, and Senior Associate Fellow at the Institut Française des Relations Internationales (IFRI), Paris.

Braz Baracuhy is Deputy-Director for Policy Planning at the Office of the Brazilian Foreign Minister, Brasília.

Christian O. Fjäder is a Senior Visiting Research Fellow at the Finnish Institute of International Affairs (FIIA) and Director of Policy, Planning and Analysis at the National Emergency Supply Agency, Finland.

Bart Gaens is a Senior Research Fellow at the Global Security Research Program and Project Director for the Center on US Politics and Power at the Finnish Institute of International Affairs (FIIA) in Helsinki. He is also Adjunct Professor at the University of Helsinki, and Specially-Appointed Associate Professor at the University of Osaka.

Mikko Huotari is Head of Program at the Mercator Institute for China Studies (MERICS), Berlin.

Hans Kundnani is Senior Transatlantic Fellow at the German Marshall Fund and Associate Fellow at the Institute for German Studies at Birmingham University.

Juha Käpylä is a Senior Research Fellow in the Global Security Research Programme at the Finnish Institute of International Affairs (FIIA), Helsinki.

Mikael Mattlin is a Senior Lecturer in International Politics and Adjunct Professor at the University of Turku, Finland. He is also Non-Resident Senior Fellow at the China Policy Institute, Nottingham University and Associate Research Fellow of the European Research Centre on Contemporary Taiwan at Tübingen University.

Kari Möttölä is a Professorial Visiting Scholar at the Network for European Studies, University of Helsinki.

Smruti S. Pattanaik is a Research Fellow at the Institute for Defence Studies and Analyses, New Delhi, India.

Martha Lucía Márquez Restrepo is an Associate Professor at the Political Science and International Relations School of the Javeriana University and Director of the Pensar Institute, Colombia.

Paul Rivlin is a Senior Fellow at the Moshe Dayan Center for Middle East and African Studies, Tel Aviv University and Visiting Professor at the Interdisciplinary Center Herzliya, Israel.

Niklas Rossbach is an Analyst at the Swedish Defence Research Agency, Stockholm.

Sören Scholvin is a Research Fellow at the Institute of Economic and Cultural Geography at the University of Hanover and Associate Research Fellow at the German Institute of Global and Area Studies, Hamburg.

Ana Soliz Landivar is a Research Fellow at the GIGA German Institute of Global and Area Studies, Hamburg.

Mikael Wigell is a Senior Research Fellow in the Global Security Research Programme at the Finnish Institute of International Affairs (FIIA), Helsinki and Adjunct Professor at the University of Tampere, Finland.

1 Geo-economic power politics

An introduction

Sören Scholvin and Mikael Wigell

Power politics by economic means

States increasingly practise power politics by economic means. Whether it is about Iran's nuclear programme or Russia's annexation of Crimea, Western states prefer economic sanctions to military force. In spite of sabre-rattling vis-à-vis North Korea, the Trump presidency also highlights this trend: the 2017 National Security Strategy of the United States differs from previous strategies in its emphasis on economic statecraft, stating that 'economic security is national security' (White House 2017, p. 17). A central means for President Trump in trying to persuade others to follow US policies appears to be the deployment of economic sticks. A recent example is Trump threatening to withdraw economic aid over the question of recognising Jerusalem as Israel's capital, as reported by the *Washington Post* (20 December 2017).

Other major powers put more emphasis on economic carrots: China is using finance, investment, and trade as means to build alliances and gain influence in countries across Africa, Asia, and Latin America (Holslag 2016; Khanna 2016; Yu 2015). Brazil and South Africa have also become cunning agents of economic statecraft, using state-owned banks and state-owned enterprises to create asymmetric relations with neighbouring countries in order to maintain (sub)continental spheres of influence (Bond 2004; Flynn 2007; McDonald 2009). Oil-rich states, especially Qatar and Saudi Arabia, deploy chequebook diplomacy to wield influence in regional affairs (Blackwill and Harris 2016). Russia is leveraging its energy resources to cement political alliances and drive wedges within counter-alliances. Its clever manipulation of energy flows is causing divisions in the European Union's approach to Russia in general, and the Ukraine crisis in particular (Vihma and Wigell 2016; Wigell and Vihma 2016).

Yet, the way states use economic power to pursue geostrategic aims remains an understudied aspect of contemporary international relations. Departing from the key concept of geo-economics, this collaborative book project aims to shed light on this alternative form of power politics. It shows how power and security are no longer simply coupled to the physical control of territory, but also to commanding and manipulating the economic ties that bind states together. By making use of the leverage provided by the asymmetric vulnerabilities inherent in these economic interconnectivities, geo-economics provide a way for states – one different from territory-based geopolitics – to conduct power politics. Indeed, as the chapters in this volume show, the ability to wield economic power forms an essential means in the grand strategies of major powers.

Hence, while competition appears to be once again the predominant driver of international relations, the means used by states to engage in this strategic competition are not predominantly military, as often assumed in academic debates (e.g. Mead 2014). Recent years have also laid bare the limitations of the liberal interdependence paradigm. In the aftermath of the Cold War, there was a central belief that as the world grew economically more interdependent, states would come to abandon power politics in favour of more cooperative foreign policies and integration into the liberal, rule-based world order (e.g. Ikenberry 1998; Mandelbaum 2002). These convictions remain attractive to many scholars (e.g. Ikenberry 2011). Yet, what we have been witnessing for the past few years is the simultaneous increase in interdependence and strategic competition, even conflict (Haass 2017; Wright 2017). It is a trend that resembles earlier periods of time, such as the late nineteenth century, when Germany and Russia emerged as continental powers with the potential to control the entire Eurasian landmass. Back then, Halford Mackinder (1904), in a famous speech delivered at the Royal Geographical Society in London, highlighted the importance of economic factors and technological progress for geostrategic ends, such as railway lines connecting Asia and Central Europe for access to natural resources.

We argue that the strategic competition of today is largely driven by economic means. This is well demonstrated by the efforts of the Obama administration to advance two economic mega-communities – the Trans-Atlantic Trade and Investment Partnership, and the Trans-Pacific Partnership – so as to boost US hegemony, cement the trans-Atlantic partnership and limit China's power, as analysed by Kari Möttölä in Chapter 7 of this book. And while there is, except for the case of Russia and arguably also China, little evidence of any military balancing amongst non-Western powers against the United States, we observe efforts of soft balancing – that is, balancing through non-military, including economic, means (Flemes 2010; Pape 2005). Instead of challenging Western powers militarily, rising powers form alliances, such as BRICS, in order to build alternative economic structures – a 'world without the West' (Barma, Ratner and Weber 2014).

The BRICS Bank is only one of many emerging economic institutions routing around the Western-led order. The analyses by Mikko Huotari (Chapter 10), Mikael Mattlin and Bart Gaens (Chapter 11), as well as Mikael Wigell and Ana Soliz Landivar (Chapter 12) all show how China is using its growing financial leverage, setting up institutions such as the Asian Infrastructure Investment Bank, to foster closer diplomatic ties with countries around the world and to embed its global rise. Regionally, most major powers still attempt to build their own spheres of influence but instead of conquering territory, they often attempt to bind these regions to themselves economically. For example, the Eastern Partnership of the European Union and China's New Silk Road initiative clash with

Russian aspirations to uphold its historical sphere of influence in Eurasia (Kaczmarski 2017; Raik and Saari 2016; see also Chapter 4 in this volume). This clash is about the projection of economic power. It constitutes geo-economic power politics.

The objective of *Geo-economics and Power Politics in the 21st Century* is, thus, to shed light on geo-economics, challenging the simple accounts of a return to traditional, military-driven geopolitics, while not succumbing to any unfounded idealism based on the supposedly stabilising effects of interdependence on international relations. In his classical but often-overlooked study *National Power and the Structure of Foreign Trade* (1945), Albert Hirschman showed how international trade relations were used as an instrument of German power. By exploiting asymmetric trade relations, Germany transformed trade into a geostrategic tool. The contributions to this volume derive from that insight. They advance our understanding of geo-economics as a strategic practice and as an analytical approach within the field of international relations (IR).

The rise of geo-economics since the early 1990s

In a seminal article, Edward Luttwak (1990) used the term geo-economics to describe how in the post-Cold War international system the main arena for rivalry amongst states would be economic, rather than military. He (1993) elaborated further on these ideas in a book published three years later. With the Soviet threat to Europe and the United States almost gone, Luttwak did not see any likely interstate military confrontation in the near future. In a similar vein, Huntington observed how '[…] in a world in which military conflict between major states is unlikely[,] economic power will be increasingly important in determining the primacy or subordination of states' (1993, p. 72). Hence, in the view of these early geo-economists, the end of the Cold War did not equal any 'end of history' (Fukuyama 1992). Instead, they foresaw a transformation of the way conflict was being played out – 'with disposable capital in lieu of firepower, civilian innovation in lieu of military-technical advancement, and market penetration in lieu of garrisons and bases' (Luttwak 1990, p. 18). In the new geo-economic era, states would still be pursuing adversarial goals but through economic instead of military means.

Luttwak's ideas quickly fell out of fashion, though, as the 'new global order' proclaimed by President George H. Bush (1991) and the Washington Consensus seemed to have entrenched a more cooperative international system in which all major powers bought into globalisation and the hope for a long period of economic growth, creating mutual benefits that would lessen the chances of serious conflict. The realist assumptions inherit in the early geo-economics paradigm did not appear useful for this liberal era, in which economic integration and cooperation, not conflict, had become the most dominant features of international relations.

However, while the 1990s and even more so the 2000s saw a rapid increase of economic interdependence on the international scale, so did the challenges and risks, many of which are geo-economic in nature. As noted, interdependence is often asymmetric, meaning that it entails sources of power in bargaining relationships. Risks that result from interdependence – and affect states asymmetrically – include disruptions in global supply chains and illicit trade flows, as well as the use of asymmetric vulnerabilities as strategic leverage (Aaltola *et al.* 2014, World Economic Forum 2016). These vulnerabilities are propelling economic security to the centre of the global agenda for the foreseeable future, and thus for geo-economic calculations to become paramount in the concerns of both major and minor powers in their strategic calculus, as Christian Fjäder argues in his contribution to this book (Chapter 3).

The concept of geo-economics has thus become increasingly fashionable in scientific and semi-scientific debates. Yet, as Mattlin and Wigell (2016) observe, it is striking how many scholars use the term geo-economics as a catchword without defining it clearly, or at least taking into consideration how others use it. The following overview highlights how different contemporary understandings of geo-economics are, and how difficult it would be to bring them together under a common frame. We start with authors who have an understanding of geo-economics that is roughly compatible with Luttwak's and then proceed to varieties of geo-economics that have little in common with Luttwak's conceptualisation, or are outright incompatible with it. Afterwards, and building on these former approaches, we present our own understanding of geo-economics, which constitutes the basis for the individual analyses in this volume.

Geo-economics in the tradition of Luttwak

Since the end of the Cold War, numerous scholars have studied geo-economic phenomena, explicitly or implicitly drawing on Luttwak's seminal article. Hudson *et al.* (1991), for example, define geo-economics as strategies of territorial control that are economically motivated and carried out by economic means, most importantly investment and trade. Hsiung (2009) understands geo-economics as a shift from military to economic security concerns, especially with regard to China's new role in global politics. Mattlin and Wigell (2016) suggest that geo-economic strategies are typical for non-Western powers – Brazil, China and India – because they rely on non-military means in their soft balancing vis-à-vis the United States.

In their aforementioned articles, Vihma and Wigell examine the way Russia has attempted to project power into its neighbourhood, not only by military means but also through economics, demonstrating the different strategic natures of geo-economics and geopolitics and the way they may undermine each other's effectiveness when applied simultaneously. The very broad research on how China has gained access to raw materials and political influence through partnerships with developing countries and on how Germany has imposed its preferences in the European Union by leveraging its market power also stands in the Luttwakian tradition, even if the term geo-economics is not always used in according publications (e.g. Alves 2015; Kärkkäinen 2016; Kundnani 2011;

Scholvin and Strüver 2013). Another relevant topic is the impact that unconventional oil and gas resources in North America have had on US foreign policy, for example with the world power losing interest in sub-Saharan Africa, which was projected to become a politically reliable provider of oil and gas in the immediate post-9/11 period (Andreasson 2015).

Several chapters in this book take up these critical issues. Niklas Rossbach analyses the impact of the shale gas revolution on the United States, focussing on how the new resource endowment contributes to US power, and how it influences its foreign political grand strategy (Chapter 9). Hans Kundnani argues that Germany, in particular with regard to the Eurozone, pursues a strategy of 'neoliberal geo-economics', using markets to impose its political preferences (Chapter 5). Pavel Baev looks at the Russian pivot to the east, and the way it has focussed on using the export of hydrocarbons as strategic leverage (Chapter 6).

However, despite what Luttwak expected, geo-economics has not entirely replaced military means of statecraft. Economic and military instruments coexist, being used by states depending on what they consider adequate for the specific challenges they are facing. Blackwill and Harris therefore suggest that 'for today's most sophisticated geo-economic actors, geo-economic and military dimensions of statecraft tend to be mutually reinforcing' (2016, p. 9). Unfortunately, labelling states that refer to military means as geo-economic actors is an example for the often-confusing terminology that unfortunately marks the state of the art. While this introduction is meant to clearly define geo-economics, and distinguish between geo-economics and geopolitics, the volume also addresses the co-occurrence of economic and military means in power politics, particularly in the chapters by Braz Baracuhy (Chapter 2), Paul Rivlin (Chapter 8) and Sören Scholvin (Chapter 15).

Other researchers also conceptualise geo-economics and geopolitics – the latter being understood as the pursuit of strategic objectives by military means – as overlapping strategies. In his study of the competition between China and India, Scott (2008) points out that the control over sea-lines of communication is essential to geo-economics and geopolitics; so is access to vital resources. Grosse (2014) analyses China's domestic capital accumulation and broader economic development, arguing that increasing economic bases of national power enable the People's Republic to change the structures of the global economy according to its preferences. Whereas Scott clearly distinguishes between geo-economics and geopolitics, Grosse proposes that geo-economics is the merger of economic and geopolitical goals, and implies that there are hybrid strategies of economic and military power projection. Huntington (1993) similarly suggests that states that increase their economic bases of power are likely to gain advantages in technology and thus become stronger in military terms.

The terminological muddle becomes particularly apparent in an article by Sanjaya Baru, the former Director for Geo-economics and Strategy at the International Institute of Strategic Studies. Baru (2012) defines geo-economics as the mutual interplay of economics and geopolitics: economic developments, for example the declining economic power of a specific state, have geopolitical impacts; geopolitical change such as territorial conquest influences economics. Yet elsewhere in the same text, geo-economic power appears as a status that derives from successfully applied economic power, as Baru argues that Japan turned into an economic power in the 1980s, but 'it never became a geo-economic power, having failed to convert its newfound economic clout into military and political power' (2012, p. 51). From an analytical perspective, it is problematic that only successful policies qualify as geo-economics. Apart from that, if applied economic power turns a state into a geo-economic power (as a status), or constitutes geo-economic power (as a practice), what is the difference between a geo-economic and a geopolitical power, considering that Baru defines geo-economics as the mutual impact of economics and geopolitics? And why do, according to the above quote, geo-economic powers refer to military means? Should one rather not speak of a geopolitical power whenever the military is vital for power politics?

The volume *Connectivity Wars* (2016) suffers from similar problems. In its introduction, Leonard argues that there are three new arenas in which conflicts amongst states are now being carried out: economics, international institutions and infrastructure. Key to understanding international relations in the twenty-first century is interdependence: 'the very things that connected the world are now being used as weapons' (2016, p. 15). This leads to tactics by which state A seeks to make state B dependent on itself – through economic relations, institutional affiliations and infrastructures – in order to gain political leverage. Although this concept seems convincing, the defining features of geo-economics addressed by Leonard do not say anything specific about how power is used. For example, bombing airports and power plants, which are infrastructures, is not geo-economics. Building hub airports on which entire continents depend, and establishing power stations that guarantee the electricity supply of neighbouring countries is geo-economics. Beyond that, Leonard does not explain what the geo in geo-economics is about, turning geo-economics into an overly broad and somewhat semi-scientific form of international political economy.

Blackwill and Harris fail to properly explain the geo-dimension, too. They try to distinguish between geo-economics and geopolitics, arguing that the latter 'explain[s] and predict[s] state power by reference to a host of geographic factors (territory, population, economic performance, natural resources, military capabilities, etc.)'. Geo-economics, meanwhile, is 'a parallel account of how a state builds and exercises power by reference to economic factors' (2016, p. 24). First, economic factors somewhat confusingly appear in both definitions. What is more, economic performance and military capabilities are not geographical factors. Unless one maintains that everything is geographical because everything is located somewhere, geographical factors are limited to place-specific features – a mountain range that serves as a natural barrier against military invasions, or vast energy resources that constitute the fundament for economic prosperity, for instance. Whenever such factors are taken into consideration in explanations of foreign policy and international relations, it can reasonably be argued that geo-economics and geopolitics (instead of economics and politics) are analysed. Before returning to these thoughts, the next section provides an overview of approaches to geo-economics that do not stand in the Luttwakian tradition.

Non-Luttwakian approaches to geo-economics

Some publications that may run under the label of geo-economics are much less related to power politics than Luttwak's own work, or not at all. Scholvin and Draper (2012), as well as Scholvin and Malamud (2014), concentrate on the impact of material structures in the geographical space on Brazil's and South Africa's respective regional economic relations. Käpylä and Mikkola (2016) explain that geographical conditions induce states to cooperate in the Arctic, because open confrontation would risk everyone's economic objectives. As a side note, this concept of geo-economics – geographical conditions shaping economic outcomes – equals the understanding of geopolitics historically held by geographers, who thought of geopolitics as political outcomes shaped by geographical conditions (Scholvin 2016).

Others relate geo-economics to the rise of new actors that matter for economic and political dynamics beyond the national scale. For instance, Barton (1999) argues that while the era of geopolitics was about hegemonic states and stability in international relations, the era of geo-economics is marked by highly flexible non-state actors and borderless transnational relations. Mercille (2008) suggests that while businesspeople act according to a geo-economic logic, the logic behind the actions of politicians is geopolitical. From a slightly different perspective, Cowen and Smith (2009) suggest that the assemblage of territory, economy and people under the authority of nation-states – key criteria of the era of geopolitics – is being recast, mainly because territorial borders have lost the defining role they used to play for the economy and society. The era of geo-economics is marked by global production being more and more segmented, which comes along with the rise of transnational enterprises as key actors. Security threats such as terrorism are also not bound to territorial borders.

Defining geo-economics via its particular territorial logic, Cowen and Smith furthermore reason that geo-economics was crucial to international relations long before the end of the Cold War: the rise of the United States to global powerhood in the early twentieth century was about free trade, or rather 'the accumulation of wealth through market control' (2009, p. 42). The United States arguably neglected territorial control, which was essential to the geopolitical strategies pursued by the European great powers of these days. Smith (2005) accordingly suggests that the imperial liberalism pursued during the presidencies of Woodrow Wilson, Franklin D. Roosevelt and George W. Bush is a geo-economic project; albeit one that depends on the US military as some sort of global police force.

Another branch of research is characterised by defining geo-economics by its ends (and not by its means). Coleman (2005) and Sidaway (2005) investigate flows of finance and trade, taking into consideration political aspects behind them. For Youngs, geo-economics revolves around 'the use of statecraft for economic ends' (2011, p. 14). O'Hara and Heffernan (2006) understand geo-economics as being about the natural resources that a region contains, and the politics of controlling and exploiting these resources. However, as Blackwill and

Harris (2016) point out, defining different types of power politics by their respective ends is not convincing: if a library is destroyed by cruise missiles, one would not speak of cultural warfare; if a factory is destroyed the same way, one would not call this economic warfare. What matters for classifying acts of aggression is the means used by the aggressor.

Whereas these approaches share a meta-scientific basis with the Luttwakian tradition, constructivist geo-economics fundamentally differs from all the articles and books referred to so far. Generally speaking, constructivists understand geo-economics as discourses. We have provided an overview of constructivist approaches to geo-economics elsewhere (see Scholvin and Wigell 2018). Considering that constructivism does not matter to the contributions to this volume, we will not repeat this overview here. While acknowledging that constructivist approaches have enriched the academic debate, we would like to point out three weaknesses of corresponding research. First, constructivists start with the assumption that geo-economic policy advice and research is ideological, meaning intended misinformation that serves disguised interests (Dalby 1990; Ó Tuathail 1998). This universal suspicion tends to lead to conclusions that are hard to fathom – at least for readers who do not share the sometimes very partisan political convictions held by constructivist scholars.

Second, constructivists have interpreted geo-economics as a securitising discourse. The concept of securitisation, as developed particularly by the Copenhagen School of IR, highlights how security risks often become appropriated – or even discursively constructed as threats – so as to legitimise extraordinary counter-measures (e.g. Buzan, Wæver and de Wilde 1997). For example, Morrissey suggests that the grand strategy of the United States in the Middle East has revolved around 'the discursive identification and positing of the Persian Gulf as a precarious yet pivotal geoeconomic space' (2011, p. 874). He argues that it is this perpetual scripting of the region as being 'pivotal for the effective functioning and regulation of the global political economy [that] legitimizes a strategic argument for the necessity of military interventionism' (2011, p. 879). Morrissey does not find it necessary to analyse whether the Persian Gulf might actually hold a special relevance for the global economy. When seeing nothing but discourses, analysts fail to capture material structures that influence international relations and are beyond the control of those who shape discourses.

Third, constructivists usually keep quiet about the fact that the alternative interpretations that they advance implicitly are – at least from their own constructivist perspective – neither better/more correct nor worse/less correct than the discourses that shape geo-economic practices. As Vihma notes, the curious absence of the author in the text 'protects the critical scholar against charges that he himself [or she herself] has misread political events or history' (2017, p. 12). And while analytical suspicion serves an important function, the warning against geo-economic thought that constructivists make by arguing that geo-economics helps to mask neoliberal agendas and securitisation projects raises the question of whether such considerations should limit the scholarly agenda.

Geo-economics as an analytical framework and strategic practice

In our understanding, geo-economics is both a strategic practice and an analytical framework. As an analytical framework, geo-economics stands in the tradition of IR realism, which emphasises how competition for relative power drives state behaviour. Luttwak accordingly wrote that states 'are inherently inclined to strive for relative advantage against like entities' (1990, p. 19). Yet, geo-economics transcends IR realism insofar as it recognises that geographical features that are particular to places and spaces shape international relations (and foreign policies) – not only the distribution of power amongst states. These geo-elements are seen as determinants of national power, as best demonstrated by Chapter 9 and 14 of this volume.

Geo-economics as a strategic practice – or practical geo-economics – refers to the application of economic means of power by states so as to realise geostrategic objectives, or more formally, as 'the geostrategic use of economic power' (Wigell 2016, p. 137). The geo-dimension in geo-economics means that the economic bases of national power must have decisive geographical features: resources being located at specific places, or sea-lines of communication taking specific routes, for example. Alternatively, the objective of geo-economic strategies must be geographically delimited, as in the case of a sphere of influence that a hegemon controls by keeping its neighbouring countries economically dependent on itself.

All chapters in this book adhere to this definition of geo-economics. It is probably best exemplified by the contributions by Martha Márquez and Smruti Pattanaik. Márquez analyses how Venezuela – during the era of Hugo Chávez – applied its own domestic oil abundance to exert political influence in Latin America and the Caribbean, advancing a regional project directed against the hegemony of the United States (Chapter 13). Pattanaik explains the use of economic means of power in the Indian–Pakistani rivalry in Central and South Asia, meaning in a clearly delimited region that India and Pakistan seek to control (Chapter 14). These means – most importantly transport corridors to Afghanistan and to the post-Soviet republics in Central Asia – also have a clear geographical dimension.

Defining geo-economics and particularly its geo-dimension this way, we partly detach ourselves from Luttwak's seminal article. Luttwak argued that the global flows of capital, data, goods and people penetrating sovereign state space do not mean that states change the territorial character. States regulate the economy in numerous ways, for example by collecting taxes and providing public goods such as transport infrastructure. Being territorially bound, states aim at nationally best outcomes instead of outcomes that would be best for the global economy as a whole. For Luttwak, this territoriality and the resulting competitive behaviour of states constitute the geo-dimension in geo-economics. He proposed that 'the international economy [is] affected by that fraction of its life that is geo-economic rather than simply economic in character' (1990, pp. 22–23).

Yet, in our world of global flows and interconnectivities, the strategic imperatives of state practice are changing. All states increasingly depend on these fluid circulations of capital, data, goods, and people for their national security and welfare. States have to secure a steady access to positive flows – for example commercial and financial flows or technology networks – and ensure their resilience vis-à-vis negative flows such as narcotics trade. States remain security providers but they increasingly need to provide security by controlling these flows in addition to their national territory; and it is economic means of power – not military force – that in most cases appear suitable for this task (Brattberg and Hamilton 2014).

Given a frequent confusion of terms, we consider it necessary to stress that practical geo-economics is not a simple revival of mercantilism, at least not in Luttwakian terms. Comparing the logic of geo-economics to the logic of mercantilism, Luttwak pointed out that mercantilist states used military means as a supreme force to achieve their goals. The Portuguese dominated spice trade with India in the early sixteenth century because they had sunk the dhows of their economically superior Arab competitors. British piracy from the 1650s to the 1730s was effective against Spain's economic supremacy in trade with the Americas. The United States forced Japan to open its domestic market to imports by sending a navy squadron into Tokyo harbour in July 1853. In the era of geo-economics, military power does not trump economic power anymore: nobody would sink foreign export car ferries to support domestic manufacturers or deliver import-restricted high-tech hardware by airborne assaults to customers in need of them.

What is more, Luttwak (1990, 1993) – and also Huntington (1993) – concentrated on domestic policies that they considered characteristic of states that sought to increase their economic bases of power. These policies aim at strengthening a state's own domestic economy through the selective provision of incentives and disincentives to domestic and foreign companies. The contributors to this volume conversely analyse how geo-economic power is applied, shedding light on the way power politics in international relations is being pursued in contemporary circumstances of interdependence. We therefore think that this book does not only advance empirical knowledge on geo-economic state practices, but it also offers realist (and, in some chapters, institutionalist) approaches and concepts for geo-economics as an academic discipline – a discipline that merits more recognition in the pluralist canon of IR.

References

Aaltola, M., Käpylä, J., Mikkola, H. and Behr, T. (2014) *Towards the Geopolitics of Flows: Implications for Finland*, FIIA Report No. 40 (Helsinki: The Finnish Institute of International Affairs). Available at: www.fiia.fi/en/publication/towards-the-geopolitics-of-flows, accessed 10 January 2018.

Alves, A. C. (2015) 'China and Brazil in Sub-Saharan African Fossil Fuels: A Comparative Analysis', in Scholvin, S. (ed.), *A New Scramble for Africa? The Rush for Energy Resources in Sub-Saharan Africa* (Farnham: Ashgate), pp. 33–51.

Andreasson, S. (2015) 'British and US Strategies in the Competition for Energy Resources in Sub-Saharan Africa', in Scholvin, S. (ed.), *A New Scramble for Africa? The Rush for Energy Resources in Sub-Saharan Africa* (Farnham: Ashgate), pp. 13–31.

Barma, N., Ratner, E. and Weber, S. (2014) 'Welcome to a World without the West', *National Interest*, 12 November. Available at: http://nationalinterest.org/feature/welcome-the-world-without-the-west-11651, accessed 9 February 2018.

Barton, J. R. (1999) ' "Flags of Convenience": Geoeconomics and Regulatory Minimisation', *Tijdschrift voor Economische en Sociale Geografie*, 90, 2, pp. 142–155.

Baru, S. (2012) 'Geo-economics and Strategy', *Survival*, 54, 3, pp. 47–58.

Blackwill, R. D. and Harris, J. M. (2016) *War by Other Means: Geoeconomics and Statecraft* (Cambridge, MA: Harvard University Press).

Bond, P. (2004) 'The ANC's "Left Turn" and South African Sub-imperialism', *Review of African Political Economy*, 102, pp. 599–616.

Brattberg, E. and Hamilton, D. (2014) 'Introduction', in Brattberg, E. and Hamilton, D. (eds), *Global Flow Security: A New Security Agenda for the Transatlantic Community in 2030* (Washington: Center for Transatlantic Relations), pp. v–vii.

Bush, G. H. (1991) 'Address Before a Joint Session of the Congress on the State of the Union', 21 January. Available at: www.presidency.ucsb.edu/ws/?pid=19253, accessed 30 November 2017.

Buzan, B., Wæver, O. and de Wilde, J. (1997) *Security: A New Framework for Analysis* (Boulder, CO: Lynne Rienner).

Coleman, M. (2005) 'U.S. Statecraft and the US–Mexico Border as Security/Economy Nexus', *Political Geography*, 24, 2, pp. 189–205.

Cowen, D. and Smith, N. (2009) 'After Geopolitics? From the Geopolitical Social to Geoeconomics', *Antipode*, 41, 1, pp. 22–48.

Dalby, S. (1990) *Creating the Second Cold War: The Discourse of Politics* (London: Pinter).

Flemes, D. (2010) 'Brazil: Strategic Options in the Changing World Order', in Flemes, D. (ed.), *Regional Leadership in the Global System: Ideas, Interests and Strategies of Regional Powers* (New York: Routledge), pp. 93–112.

Flynn, M. (2007) 'Between Subimperialism and Globalization: A Case Study in the Internationalization of Brazilian Capital', *Latin American Perspectives*, 34, 6, pp. 9–27.

Fukuyama, F. (1992) *The End of History and the Last Man* (New York: Avon Books).

Grosse, T. G. (2014) 'Geoeconomic Relations between the EU and China: The Lessons from the EU Weapon Embargo and From Galileo', *Geopolitics*, 19, 1, pp. 40–65.

Haass, R. (2017) *A World in Disarray: American Foreign Policy and the Crisis of the Old Order* (New York: Penguin Books).

Hirschman, A. (1945) *National Power and the Structure of Foreign Trade* (Berkeley: University of California Press).

Holslag, J. (2016) 'Geoeconomics in a Globalized World: the Case of China's Export Policy', *Asia Europe Journal*, 14, 2, pp. 173–184.

Hsiung, J. C. (2009) 'The Age of Geoeconomics, China's Global Role, and Prospects of Cross-strait Integration', *Journal of Chinese Political Science*, 14, 2, pp. 113–133.

Hudson, V. M., Ford, R. E., Pack, D. and Giordano, E. R. (1991) 'Why the Third World Matters, Why Europe Probably Won't: The Geoeconomics of Circumscribed Engagement', *Journal of Strategic Studies*, 14, 3, pp. 255–298.

Huntington, S. P. (1993) 'Why International Primacy Matters', *International Security*, 17, 4, pp. 68–83.

Ikenberry, G. J. (1998) 'Institutions, Strategic Restraint, and the Persistence of American Postwar Order', *International Security*, 23, 3, pp. 43–78.

Ikenberry, G. J. (2011) *Liberal Leviathan: The Origin, Crisis and Transformation of the American World Order* (Princeton, NJ: Princeton University Press).

Kaczmarski, M. (2017) 'Non-Western Visions of Regionalism: China's New Silk Road and Russia's Eurasian Economic Union', *International Affairs*, 93, 6, pp. 1357–1376.

Käpylä, J. and Mikkola, H. (2016) 'The Promise of the Geoeconomic Arctic: A Critical Analysis', *Asia Europe Journal*, 14, 2, pp. 203–220.

Kärkkäinen, A. (2016) 'Does China Have a Geoeconomic Strategy towards Zimbabwe? The Case of the Zimbabwean Natural Resource Sector', *Asia Europe Journal*, 14, 2, pp. 185–202.

Khanna, P. (2016) 'The Era of Infrastructure Alliances', in Leonard, M. (ed.), *Connectivity Wars: Why Migration, Finance and Trade Are the Geo-economic Battlegrounds of the Future* (London: European Council on Foreign Relations), pp. 103–108.

Kundnani, H. (2011) 'Germany as a Geo-economic Power', *Washington Quarterly*, 34, 3, pp. 31–45.

Leonard, M. (2016) 'Introduction: Connectivity Wars', in Leonard, M. (ed.), *Connectivity Wars: Why Migration, Finance and Trade Are the Geo-economic Battlegrounds of the Future* (London: European Council on Foreign Relations), pp. 13–30.

Luttwak, E. N. (1990) 'From Geopolitics to Geo-economics: Logic of Conflict, Grammar of Commerce', *The National Interest*, 20, pp. 17–23.

Luttwak, E. N. (1993) *The Endangered American Dream: How to Stop the United States from Becoming a Third-World Country and How to Win the Geo-economic Struggle for Industrial Supremacy* (New York: Simon & Schuster).

Mackinder, H. (1904) 'The Geographical Pivot of History', *The Geographical Journal*, 23, 4, pp. 421–437.

Mandelbaum, M. (2002) *The Ideas that Conquered the World: Peace, Democracy, and Free Markets in the Twenty-First Century* (New York: Public Affairs).

Mattlin, M. and Wigell, M. (2016) 'Geoeconomics in the Context of Restive Regional Powers', *Asia Europe Journal*, 14, 2, pp. 125–134.

McDonald, D. A. (ed.) (2009) *Electric Capitalism, Recolonising Africa on the Power Grid* (Cape Town: HSRC Press).

Mead, W. R. (2014) 'The Return of Geopolitics: The Revenge of the Revisionist Powers', *Foreign Affairs*, 93, 3, pp. 69–79.

Mercille, J. (2008) 'The Radical Geopolitics of US Foreign Policy: Geopolitical and Geoeconomic Logics of Power', *Political Geography*, 27, 5, pp. 570–586.

Morrissey, J. (2011) 'Closing the Neoliberal Gap: Risk and Regulation in the Long War of Securitization', *Antipode*, 43, 3, pp. 874–900.

O'Hara, S. and Heffernan, M. (2006) 'From Geo-Strategy to Geo-economics: The "Heartland" and British Imperialism Before and After Mackinder', *Geopolitics*, 11, 1, pp. 54–73.

Ó Tuathail, G. (1998) 'Introduction', in Ó Tuathail, G., Dalby, S. and Routledge, P. (eds), *The Geopolitics Reader* (London: Routledge), pp. 103–113.

Pape, R. A. (2005) 'Soft Balancing Against the United States', *International Security*, 30, 1, pp. 7–45.

Raik, K. and Saari, S. (2016) *Key Actors in the EU's Eastern Neighbourhood: Competing Perspectives on Geostrategic Tensions*, FIIA Report No. 47 (Helsinki: The Finnish Institute of International Affairs). Available at: www.fiia.fi/en/publication/key-actors-in-the-eus-eastern-neighbourhood, accessed 9 February 2018.

Scholvin, S. (2016) 'Geographical Conditions and Political Outcomes', *Comparative Strategy*, 35, 4, pp. 274–283.

Scholvin, S. and Draper, P. (2012) 'The Gateway to Africa? Geography and South Africa's Role as an Economic Hinge Joint between Africa and the World', *South African Journal of International Affairs*, 19, 3, pp. 381–400.

Scholvin, S. and Strüver, G. (2013) 'Tying the Region Together or Tearing It Apart? China and Transport Infrastructure Projects in the SADC Region', in du Pisani, A., Eramus, G. and Hartzenberg, T. (eds), *Monitoring Regional Integration in Southern Africa 2012* (Stellenbosch: TRALAC), pp. 175–193.

Scholvin, S. and Malamud, A. (2014) 'Is There a Geoeconomic Node in South America? Geography, Politics and Brazil's Role in Regional Economic Integration', ICS Working Paper, N 2/2014. Available at: www.ics.ul.pt/publicacoes/workingpapers/wp2014/wp2014_2.pdf, accessed 9 February 2018. .

Scholvin, S. and Wigell, M. (2018) 'Power Politics by Economic Means: Geo-economics as an Analytical Approach and Foreign Policy Practice', *Comparative Strategy*, 37, 1, pp. 73–84.

Scott, D. (2008) 'The Great Power "Great Game" Between India and China: "The Logic of Geography" ', *Geopolitics*, 13, 1, pp. 1–26.

Sidaway, J. D. (2005) 'Asia–Europe–United States: The Geoeconomics of Uncertainty', *Area*, 37, 4, pp. 373–377.

Smith, N. (2005) *The Endgame of Globalization* (London: Routledge).

Vihma, A. (2017) 'Geoeconomic Analysis and the Limits of Critical Geopolitics: A New Engagement with Edward Luttwak', *Geopolitics*, 23, 1, pp. 1–12.

Vihma, A. and Wigell, M. (2016) 'Unclear and Present Danger: Russia's Geoeconomics and the Nord Stream II Pipeline', *Global Affairs*, 2, 4, pp. 377–388.

Washington Post. (2017) 'U.S. Threatens Countries with Loss of Aid over U.N. Vote on Jerusalem', *Washington Post*, 20 December. Available at: www.washingtonpost.com/world/national-security/us-threatens-countries-with-loss-of-aid-over-un-jerusalem-vote/2017/12/20/3ddacadc-e5bc-11e7-833f-155031558ff4_story.html?utm_term=.3607d559bae2, accessed 9 February 2018.

White House. (2017) 'National Security Strategy of the United States of America', *The White House*, December. Available at: http://nssarchive.us/wp-content/uploads/2017/12/2017.pdf, accessed 10 January 2018.

Wigell, M. (2016) 'Conceptualizing Regional Powers' Geoeconomic Strategies: Neo-Imperialism, Neo-Mercantilism, Hegemony, and Liberal Institutionalism', *Asia Europe Journal*, 14, 2, pp. 135–151.

Wigell, M. and Vihma, A. (2016) 'Geopolitics Versus Geoeconomics: The Case of Russia's Changing Geostrategy and Its Effects on the EU', *International Affairs*, 92, 3, pp. 605–627.

World Economic Forum. (2016) 'The Age of Economic Coercion: How Geo-politics is Disrupting Supply Chains, Financial Systems, Energy Markets, Trade and the Internet', *World Economic Forum*. Available at: www3.weforum.org/docs/WEF_Age_of_Economic_coercion.pdf, accessed 14 January 2017.

Wright, T. J. (2017) *All Measures Short of War: The Contest for the 21st Century and the Future of American Power* (New Haven, CT: Yale University Press).

Youngs, R. (2011) 'Geo-economic Futures', in Martiningui, A. and Youngs, R. (eds), *Challenges for European Foreign Policy in 2012: What Kind of Geo-economic Europe?* (Madrid: Fundación para las Relaciones Internacionales y el Diálogo Exterior), pp. 13–17.

Yu, L. (2015) 'China's Strategic Partnership with Latin America: A Fulcrum in China's Rise', *International Affairs*, 91, 5, pp. 1047–1068.

2 Geo-economics as a dimension of grand strategy

Notes on the concept and its evolution

Braz Baracuhy[1]

Introduction

The study and practice of geo-economics – broadly understood as the use of economic means of power to achieve strategic objectives, involving a clear geographical dimension (see Chapter 1 of this volume) – have been rediscovered in recent times. This should not come as a surprise. Just like in other instances of the past, the revival of geo-economics appears to be associated with particular moments of power transition in the international system. Not by accident has the rise of a multipolar system of economic power created ideal conditions for a renewed interest in geo-economics. Leading think tanks such as Chatham House, the Council of Foreign Relations, the European Council of Foreign Relations, the International Institute for Strategic Studies as well as the Finnish Institute of International Affairs have carried out extensive research on the topic. The supposed shift from geopolitics to geo-economics, which is one of the major motivations behind this volume, has been nicely demonstrated by the renaming of the Agenda Council on Geopolitical Risks of the World Economic Forum into the Agenda Council on Geo-economics in 2014.

This chapter explores the field of geo-economics from a conceptual and historical perspective. The first section defines geo-economics, distinguishes it from geopolitics, and discusses different contemporary facets of the concept, emphasising the role of geo-economics as a key dimension of grand strategy. The second section outlines the historical evolution of geo-economic studies, showing their links to the discipline of geopolitics. This evolution is divided into four generations: classical geo-economics, which emerged at the beginning of the twentieth century, a second generation from the 1970s and 1980s, a third generation from the 1990s, and contemporary approaches. In the conclusion of this chapter, I argue that geo-economics and geopolitics should be seen together under the framework of geostrategy. I also make the case for paying more attention to geo-economics in research on international relations.

Geo-economics in the context of grand strategy

Geo-economics and geopolitics are two sides of the same coin. Although different in their instrumental and operative logics, they are both expressions of the geostrategic competition among great powers, acquiring relevance and meaning in foreign policy. The prefix 'geo' indicates a clear geographical or spatial feature of what would otherwise simply be economics, politics and strategy: a sphere of influence that great powers seek to control, for example. Grand strategy – 'the intellectual architecture that lends structure to foreign policy' (Brands 2014, p. 1), relating available means to larger objectives of the state in the international system – unifies geo-economics and geopolitics. In other words, in a grand-strategic design of foreign policy, the competition among powers can be pursued geo-economically and geopolitically. Thus, two conceptually distinct yet interrelated and often simultaneous types of strategies are available to states:

- Geopolitical strategies – the geostrategic use of political power. In these strategies, political leaders pursue geostrategic objectives by employing diplomatic and military means, as well as intelligence capabilities.
- Geo-economic strategies, which, according to Wigell, are 'the geostrategic use of economic power' (2016, p. 135). Therein political leaders pursue geostrategic objectives through the control over markets, resources, and rules that shape international economic interaction.

Grand strategy identifies and gives coherence to foreign-policy objectives. These objectives find their expression when being implemented in geographical space, as power capabilities and instruments are strategically and tactically deployed by states in pursuit of their interests. Taken together, geo-economic and geopolitical power projections define the strategic morphology of the world map.

The Asia-Pacific region provides a good example of geo-economics and geo-politics being applied simultaneously. By launching the 'Pivot to Asia' strategy in 2011, the United States under the Obama administration moved into the 'gates to the heartland', using an expression coined by Nicholas Spykman. The idea was for the United States to reorient its foreign-policy focus towards the Asia-Pacific region, rebalance its military assets, and reinforce its traditional diplomatic partnerships. Under Obama, this strategy had a crucial geo-economic component – the Trans-Pacific Partnership (TPP). Though abandoned by the Trump administration, the TPP was a US-led initiative that sought to regain a solid preponderance for the United States in regional rule-making for trade (see also Chapter 7 in this volume). Aspiring to be more than a traditional free trade agreement, the TPP was designed to regulate investment and standards beyond borders, and to create a favourable business environment for transnational corporations and their value chains. The underlying factor for the geostrategic rebalancing in the Asia-Pacific region – both geo-economically and geopolitically – is the rise of China and its central role in investments and trade, which has led to asymmetric interdependences among some of the regional countries.

Seen by the time of its inception as a reaction to the TPP, China's geo-economic strategy of One Belt–One Road – tapping resources, building infrastructures, and creating economic interdependences in the heartland of Eurasia – echoes Halford Mackinder's classical geopolitical formulation. In his article *The Geographical Pivot of History* (1904), Mackinder touched upon a central anxiety of international politics: the fear that Eurasia's massive territory and resources could be organised under the control of a single continental power, which would be in a position to project power and influence globally, unmatched by sea powers. Mackinder foresaw three potential candidates well positioned for redrawing that geopolitical balance of power: Germany, Russia and China. He argued that a Chinese expansion towards Eurasia's heartland 'would add an oceanic frontage to the resources of the great continent, an advantage as yet denied to the Russian tenant of the pivot region' (1904, p. 437). Kaplan (2017) and Nye (2017), among others, have recently restated this idea.

Geo-economic power projection results from the available economic capabilities of a state. Economic power provides geostrategic leverage in the context of economic interdependences among countries. Economic power is based on three components: markets, resources, and rules that shape international economic interaction. Relevant features of markets are the economic weight of the respective state and its growth expectations, market access, international flows of investment and trade, and resulting interdependences. Resources cover the access to and control of financial, natural, and technological resources. Rules refer to the ability to shape the institutions and regimes that define the international economic order. In different compositions, these components are the fundament of different forms of power, ranging from financial and investment power to resource-supplying power to sanctioning power. Geostrategic competition among great powers is at play whenever such forms of economic power refer to a geographically defined objective – shaping the Asia-Pacific region through a new set of rules, for instance. To avoid a common misunderstanding: although economic diplomacy and economic statecraft are essential for successful geo-economics, they are not identical. Economic diplomacy and economic statecraft lack a geographical dimension.[2]

The term geo-economics gained notoriety with a publication by the geostrategist Edward Luttwak in 1990. His article *From Geopolitics to Geo-economics* (1990) reflects the anxiety about Japan's increasing economic power, supposedly challenging the hegemony of the United States. Luttwak suggests that geo-economics has replaced geopolitics, becoming the key strategy in the international arena. The United States should adapt its foreign policy accordingly. Notwithstanding his importance in forging the term geo-economics, Luttwak's prescriptions rather re-edit an old toolkit of mercantilist practices. Moreover, geo-economics as a foreign-policy practice is older than Luttwak's article implies. Further below, I show that geo-economics and geopolitics both originated at the beginning of the twentieth century, and, as noted, interest in the two sides of geostrategic competition has always reappeared when shifts in the international balance of power occurred.

Contemporary perspectives on geo-economics vary. Common among most of them is the notion of geo-economics as a phenomenon at the confluence of economics and geopolitics. Scholars who take this viewpoint portray geo-economics as an area of studies close to or identical with International Political Economy, the intersection of economics and international politics. Baru, for instance, proposes that geo-economics is about studying 'the geopolitical consequences of economic phenomena' and 'the economic consequences of geopolitical trends'. He argues that

> both the notion of 'trade follows the flag', that there are economic consequences of the projection of national power, and the idea that 'the flag follows trade', that there are geopolitical consequences of essentially economic phenomena, would constitute the subject matter of geo-economics.
>
> (2012, p. 2)

In the same vein, Grevi states that 'geo-economics encompasses both the conversion of economic assets into political influence and the mobilisation of political power to achieve economic goals through a mix of competition and cooperation' (2011, p. 28). Blanke and Kaspersen (2015), highlighting a new scenario of risks to global businesses, suggest that 'we can no longer talk about geopolitics and economics in isolation; instead we must generate a deeper understanding of geo-economics'.

This overlap of economics and geopolitics is not new. A state's economy provides the horizon of possibilities for the projection of power for geopolitical ends. States cannot keep their political power – from military forces to diplomatic and intelligence machines – without an underlying economic basis. There is indeed a quite dense literature on how the economic conditions of states affect their political power and, as a consequence, their international standing. The famous historian Paul Kennedy surveys five centuries of international history in *The Rise and Fall of the Great Powers*, concentrating on the relationship between economics and political power. He demonstrates that 'there is a causal relationship between the shifts which have occurred over time in the general economic and production balances and the position occupied by individual powers in the international system' (1987, p. xxii). Another example is Zakaria's (1999) study of the importance of budgetary appropriation for converting economic wealth into political power.

From a systemic point of view, the interaction between (geo)politics and international economic relations also has a long tradition. Economic phenomena, such as the 2008 financial crisis, have always received attention with regard to their impact on geopolitics (e.g. Burrows and Harris 2009). Economic globalisation – the process of growing economic integration and interdependences among states through flows of investment and trade – relies on the configuration of diplomatic and military power. 'The pattern of trade', O'Rourke suggests, 'can only be understood as being the outcome of some military or political equilibrium between contending powers' (2009, p. 8). The international economy requires a favourable international power equilibrium, which provides order and stability to the day-to-day operations of economic relations, making sure, for example, that there are efficient financial institutions, and that trade itself is rule-based and that trade routes are safe. Even scholars who adhere to pure raw-power capabilities in international relations recognise the relevance of rules for the international economy, being convinced that these rules are made by the most powerful states. Waltz, for example, notes in this sense that 'the international economy, like national economies, operates within a set of rules and institutions that have to be made and sustained' (2000, p. 53).

In spite of this conceptual proximity to economics and (geo)politics, geo-economics is, in my understanding, distinct because of an underlying logic of integrating geostrategic ends and economic means into a coherent grand strategy. The relationship between geostrategic ends and economic means that character-ises geo-economics can only be fully understood in the context of the grand-strategic calculus of ends and means. Geo-economics adds a new dimension to the competitive logic of great-power relations. As Blackwill and Harris define it, geo-economics is 'the use of economic instruments to promote and defend national interests, and to produce beneficial [...] results' (2016b, p. 20). This means that geo-economics does not substitute geopolitics, as Luttwak argues. Rather, geo-economics and geopolitics are distinct yet related and com-plementary types of geostrategy. The French scholar Yves Lacoste, who has shaped academic geopolitics for decades, accordingly points out that 'géopoli-tique et géoéconomie se complètent parfaitement' (1997, p. 40).

Great powers pursue grand strategies in the international system, as defined by the geographic limits and reach of their times. The balance of power, as a structural feature, encompasses the overall distribution of power. For analytical purposes, it is helpful to distinguish two dimensions of this overall distribution of power, linking the international system and the grand strategies of great power: the distribution of political power for geostrategic use composes the geo-political structure; the distribution of economic power for geostrategic use com-poses the geo-economic structure.

The geo-economic power structure can decouple from geopolitical power structure, having consequences for grand strategy and the configuration of the international system. The globalisation process of the 1990s was essentially based on the post-Cold War convergence of geo-economics and geopolitics, meaning the hegemony of the United States in both spheres. The North Atlantic was the economic centre of the world. The globalisation process spread out of that core to encompass the whole world through investment and trade. As a political institution, the G7 reflected the global distribution of economic power. In the early 1990s, the G7 generated 55 per cent of the world economic output, and were responsible for 53 per cent of global exports. The United States, inter-twining the major European powers and Japan as economic partners, had a clear leading role within the G7, constructing and sustaining a rule-based system that smoothed innovation, investment, production, trade and, as a consequence, eco-nomic growth.

Geopolitically, globalisation benefited from the post-Cold War unipolar power architecture, having the United States as the undisputable hegemon.

Acting in concert with its allies, the United States enjoyed pre-eminence in projecting its power worldwide. This unipolar situation safeguarded, for instance, sea-lanes of communication, which are so vital to the global economy. Wright coined the term 'unipolar concert' to describe that the relationship among great powers in the 1990s 'rested on US unipolarity and hegemony as well as the collective willingness [of the other great powers] to work within it' (2015, p. 10).

By the end of the 2000s, a structural divergence between the global distribution of economic and political power became apparent, decoupling geo-economics and geopolitics. A multipolar economic power structure took shape in terms of innovation, investment, production, trade, and, of course, economic growth. The centre of economic gravity had moved away from the North Atlantic towards other regions, especially the Far East. Established poles of economic power and major geo-economic actors – France, Germany, Great Britain, Japan and the United States – now coexist with new poles of economic power that have become increasingly active in terms of geo-economics: Brazil, China and India among others.

Although the international political structure has remained predominantly unipolar, it has come increasingly under pressure because of geo-economic transformations. China in particular has gradually translated its economic success into diplomatic and military capabilities, a trend that could well lead to a bi-multipolar political power structure in the future. Territorial disputes in the China Seas increasingly impact sea-lanes of communication, causing geopolitical friction already today. Perhaps more importantly from a geostrategic point of view, the new poles of economic power are decoupled from the United States in terms of diplomatic commitments and security arrangements. By implication, economic interdependences no longer coincide with security arrangements, as they did for Germany and Japan in the Cold War era. Therefore, 'US dominance in the international security arena no longer translates into effective leverage in the international economic arena' (Mastanduno 2009, p. 123).[3]

Four generations of geo-economics

Instead of further speculating on the future of geo-economics as a foreign-policy practice, I would now like to provide an overview of the evolution of geo-economics as an academic discipline, which has always had a strong policy orientation. It is a misconception to see geo-economics naturally evolving from geopolitics, as Luttwak suggested in his seminal contribution to the field. The two types of geostrategic analysis and practice share the same intellectual roots. Geo-economics is deeply connected with geopolitics in its classical origins, and therefore it is important to clarify what geopolitics is.

The term is not univocal in the international literature, and its history is charged with controversies, as Schuman (1942) explains in detail. The Swedish political scientist Rudolf Kjellén introduced the neologism geopolitics in 1916. Ever since then, the subject has essentially dealt with the relationship between geographic space (geo) and power (politics). How such a relationship operates has been highly disputed. One way to approach geopolitics is to examine which of the two factors has the preponderant explanatory weight: geographical space or power being the defining factor of foreign policy. In the first case, geopolitical traditions range from different variants of classical geopolitics, which was strongly materialist, to the immaterial representations of geography that frame foreign-policy ideas according to present-day post-structuralists. The second case is probably best exemplified by Brzezinski's *The Grand Chessboard: American Primacy and Its Geostrategic Imperatives* (1997). Brzezinski identifies Eurasia as the arena for great-power competition in the post-Cold War era, and stresses the outstanding relevance of Central Asia, which he pictures as the most conflict-laden and militarily and politically instable part of the world. What happens in Central Asia derives from the power wielded by the United States and its challengers.

Even within the geo-oriented literature there are considerable differences. Whereas German scholars such as Karl Haushofer and Friedrich Ratzel advanced social-Darwinist models of the expansion of states, Anglo-Saxon adherents of geopolitics like Mackinder, Spykman and also Alfred Mahan were interested in location as a key factor and the dynamics between military power and technological progress that shaped the geopolitics of their time (Scholvin 2016). Under the current conditions of the international system, classical elements of geopolitics are renewed: the distinction between continental and sea powers, the strategic importance of Eurasia in general and chokepoints such as the Strait of Hormuz in particular, and the relevance of raw materials.

In historical perspective, the challenge of rising powers in an evolving international system has consistently brought attention to geo-economics. In fact, classical geopolitics and contemporary approaches that make up this tradition – John Mearsheimer's (2001) reference to 'the stopping power of water', for example – overlap with geo-economics, which I divide into four generations. The first generation, which I call classical geo-economics, is so close to classical geopolitics that Mackinder should actually be seen as a representative of both. The shifting balance of power in Europe in the late nineteenth century and its geostrategic repercussions were central drivers of classical geo-economic thinking. Germany and Russia, being emerging continental powers that could potentially control the entire Eurasian landmass, were seen as a threat to the British Empire and its global hegemony, which was based on sea power. Mackinder highlighted the importance of economic factors and technological instruments for geostrategic ends. The strategic importance of railways connecting Asia and Central Europe for access to natural resources and military purposes is a major feature in Mackinder's 1904 speech at the Royal Geographical Society. James Fairgrieve's *Geography and World Power* (1915) and *The Gateways of Commerce* (1921), co-authored with Ernest Young, are two other examples of studies in classical geopolitics that could also be labelled geo-economics. The first book is about geographical conditions shaping civilizations throughout history. The second book derives geostrategic imperatives for Britain from the global distribution of resources and economic production.

The first generation of geo-economics also includes Albert Hirschman's classical study of Germany's geostrategy before World War II. In *National Power and the Structure of Foreign Trade*, Hirschman showed how international trade relations were used as an instrument of German power. By exploiting asymmetric trade relations, Germany transformed trade into a geostrategic tool. According to Hirschman, 'a system of international trade can very easily be exploited for purposes of national power policy' (1980, p. x). Because of this potential for strategic use, he advised that 'a textbook for the modern prince should indeed contain, in addition to Machiavelli's classic chapters, extensive new sections on the most efficient use of quotas, exchange controls, capital investment, and other instruments of economic warfare' (1980, p. ix).

The practical linkages between economics and geopolitics were not absent in the minds of the architects of the post-Second World War order. The Bretton Woods System, the Marshall Plan, and the process of economic integration in Europe demonstrate how geo-economics went along with geopolitics: the permanent military presence of the United States in Europe and the foundation of the North Atlantic Treaty Organisation. It is revealing that the Containment Strategy – a role model of geopolitics – and the Marshall Plan, which was geo-economics in practice according to my understanding of the term, were geared towards the same geostrategic objective: limiting Soviet influence in Europe.

The second generation of geo-economics emerged in the 1970s and 1980s under the conditions of a relative economic decline of the major Western powers due to various factors ranging from oil price shocks to a deep crisis of the Bretton Woods System to the trauma of the Vietnam War. Important transformations of the global economy were taking place with the expansion of transnational corporations from Europe and North America to other parts of the world, the deepening economic integration in Europe, and the economic diplomacy of the G7. It was in this context that scholars of international relations, most importantly Robert Keohane and Joseph Nye (1971, 1977), resumed studies of economic asymmetries as sources of power. International regimes for finance and trade were also examined with regard to their relevance for power in international relations (e.g. Krasner 1976). Cooper noticed 'the intrusion of trade problems into "high foreign policy"' (1972, p. 18). He argued that the Bretton Woods System was successful in suppressing the political elements of financial and trade negotiations, encapsulating them into technical discussions within an institutional framework. Rosecrance anticipated the coming commercial competition among states in *The Rise of the Trading State* (1986).

The third generation of geo-economics appeared in the 1990s with the power transition at the end of the Cold War. These studies, including Luttwak's famous article, focussed on policy advice for the United States with regard to two challenges: how to deal with the economic competition of a rising Japan, and how to navigate the process of economic globalisation in a unipolar world. The central argument in these publications was the importance of economic power for the rise and fall of great powers. In addition to the competition with Japan, the expansion of market democracy during the presidency of Bill Clinton, economic regionalism, negotiations on free trade, new trade issues such as intellectual property rights and the reshaping of the multilateral system with the establishment of the World Trade Organisation marked these debates. Luttwak and also the French scholar Pascal Lorot emphasised that military power had lost its pre-eminence in international relations. Strongly contradicting the optimism voiced by Francis Fukuyama in *The End of History?* (1989), Lorot and Luttwak represented those who were convinced that competition and conflict among states would continue to reign in the post-Cold War world, albeit in the shape of geo-economics – 'the admixture of the logic of conflict with the methods of commerce' (Luttwak 1990, p. 19).

More recent publications by Lorot and Luttwak are useful to understand what geo-economics is not. In a study on China, Luttwak (2012) distinguishes between economic protectionism and geo-economics. Lorot also goes beyond trade instruments, and defines geo-economics as 'l'analyse des stratégies d'ordre économique – notamment commercial – décidées par les États dans le cadre de politiques visant à protéger leur économie nationale [et] à aider leurs "entreprises nationales"' (1997, p. 14). A careful reading reveals that both authors identify geo-economics with economic policy or, to be more precise, with a type of commercial and industrial policy, mercantilist in nature that has also been discussed as state capitalism (e.g. Bremmer 2008). This original confusion is relevant, because this identification of geo-economics with a type of economic policy – using national power for economic goals via interventionism in the economy, for example through protectionism – can still be traced in academic and policy debates.

Geo-economics, of course, is not a synonym of mercantilism and state capitalism. Lorot's and Luttwak's thinking ended up being included in the literature on competitiveness, popular in the 1990s, and target of much criticism. Paul Krugman, for instance, opposes the idea of states competing just like companies do. He points out that authors using the competitiveness label are actually talking about productivity and protectionism. This way, Krugman identifies an issue of political economy: certain interest groups appropriate the term competitiveness, seeking protectionism and diverting attention from the true causes of economic productivity. In Krugman's own words, 'the major nations of the world are not in any significant degree in economic competition with each other'. Yet he admits that 'there is always a rivalry for status and power – countries that grow faster will see their political rank rise' (1994, p. 35). This shows how geo-economics differs from protectionist policies.

The challenge for geo-economics – translated from foreign-policy analysis and policy advice into foreign-policy practices – is to align good economics and good foreign-policy. Geo-economics as a practice has to be conscious of the long-term foreign-policy interests that it serves, and, at the same time, promote or at least avoid hurting the country's economic interests so as to win the support of key domestic interests groups (Bergsten 2016). Even though I do not have enough space here to elaborate further on this issue, I would like to stress that I doubt that the policy advice given by the proponents of the third generation of geo-economics leads to positive economic outcomes.

The fourth generation of geo-economics revitalises many elements from classical geo-economics – so much so that it could perhaps be branded 'neo-classical geo-economics' – obviously within a new context of shifting balances of power: the geopolitical consequences of economic phenomena, economic interdependences and their use for geostrategic purposes, and the strategic relevance of Eurasia. This generation of geo-economics has gained traction due to the 2008 financial crisis, and the crisis of the Euro zone, as well as the consequences that both crises have had for the economic power and related role in international politics of major European powers and the United States. The key topics of according studies are:

- emerging economies (most importantly Brazil, China and India) (e.g. O'Neill 2011),
- China's 'One Belt–One Road' strategy (e.g. Zhao 2015 and Chapter 4 in this volume),
- the new balance of economic power on the global scale and its consequences for global governance, especially the BRICS as a new bloc and the changing roles of the G7 and G20 (e.g. Baru and Dogra 2015; Grevi 2011),
- currency internationalisation, sovereign wealth funds, new development banks such as the Asian Infrastructure Investment Bank and the New Development Bank, and other forms of financial South–South cooperation (e.g. Burrows and Harris 2009; Kirshner 2005; Wheatley 2013 and Chapters 10 and 11 in this volume),
- Russia's use of its energy resources for geostrategic ends (e.g. Wigell and Vihma 2016),
- global supply chains from a perspective of international relations and power (e.g. Aaltola *et al.* 2014; Khanna 2016), and
- Germany's geo-economic strategy in Europe (e.g. Kundnani 2011 and Chapter 5 in this volume).

Conclusion

The four generations of geo-economic studies share, as an underlying process, economic power transitions in the international system. Authors from the four generations have consistently highlighted the interrelationships between economics and geopolitics. In a world of competing states, geo-economics and geopolitics are two complementary dimensions of the foreign policy of great powers. The renewed importance of the study and practice of geo-economics – geostrategic competition by wielding economic power – reflects the contemporary moment of power transition in the international system. Although scholars who stand in the tradition of Luttwak would disagree, I suggest that states, pursuing the strategic pursuit of their interests in the international arena, must combine geo-economics and geopolitics in their respective grand strategies.

Geo-economics makes use of economic tools. Economic factors – markets, resources and rules – are the fundament for gaining influence in geostrategic competition among states, including the shaping of the institutional framework that governs the international economic order. In scholarly work, particularly in international relations and grand strategy, geo-economics deserves much more attention, being an autonomous field of study that addresses a particular type of foreign-policy practices. However, this autonomy should be seen as relative. As shown above, geo-economics and geopolitics refer to different instruments but – as particular types of geostrategic competition – they should be seen as constitutive of a broader understanding that deals with the power configuration of the international system and its consequences for great-power rivalry.

Geo-economics and geopolitics ultimately share the same grand-strategic objective: the geostrategic positioning of states in the international arena. They are both about managing and shaping the strategic environment in which great powers operate for the pursuit of their respective interests. Spykman used to remind his students at Yale that each foreign ministry operates according to a geopolitical map of the world. It would certainly not go unnoticed for him, under the current conditions of the international system, that there are also geo-economic maps of the world that guide foreign ministries in their decision making – or, perhaps, grand-strategic maps that bring geo-economics and geopolitics together.

Notes

1 The views expressed in this chapter are personal. They do not necessarily reflect those of the Brazilian Foreign Ministry. The author would like to thank Sören Scholvin, Mikael Wigell, Elizabeth Bradley, and Charles Hill for their helpful comments on earlier versions of the text.
2 Blackwill and Harris (2016a) and Youngs (2011), among other scholars, use geo-economics as a synonym of economic statecraft though. The same conception marks statements by politicians. Hillary Clinton, for example, characterised the geo-economic strategy of the United States vis-à-vis the Asia-Pacific region in general and China in particular as economic statecraft:

> that is why I have put what I call economic statecraft at the heart of our foreign-policy agenda. Economic statecraft has two parts: first, how we harness the forces and use the tools of global economics to strengthen our diplomacy and presence abroad; and second, how we put that diplomacy and presence to work to strengthen our economy at home.
> (www.state.gov/secretary/20092013clinton/rm/2011/10/175552.htm)

3 The decoupling of geo-economics and geopolitics does not have to last though. Present trends in great-power geostrategy indicate a recoupling. As Zoellick (2016) observes,

> the 20th century demonstrated that conflicts in East Asia can threaten the United States, but also that US security can underpin Asia's prosperity. The United States now needs to create an economic and security network in the Asia-Pacific [region] for the 21st century.

References

Aaltola, M., Käpylä, J., Mikkola, H. and Behr, T. (2014) *Towards the Geopolitics of Flows: Implications for Finland*, FIIA Report No. 40 (Helsinki: The Finnish Institute of International Affairs). Available at: www.fiia.fi/en/publication/towards-the-geopolitics-of-flows, accessed 31 January 2018.

Baru, S. (2012) 'A New Era of Geo-economics: Assessing the Interplay of Economic and Political Risk', at the *IISS Seminar*, 23–25 March Available at: www.iiss.org/-/media// images/events/conferences%20from%20import/seminars/papers/64319.pdf, accessed 16 October 2016.

Baru, S. and Dogra, S. (eds) (2015) *Power Shifts and New Blocs in the Global Trading System* (London: International Institute for Strategic Studies).

Bergsten, C. F. (2016) 'We Are All Geoeconomists Now', *Foreign Affairs*, May/June 2016 Issue. Available at: www.foreignaffairs.com/articles/2016-04-06/we-are-all-geoeconomists-now, accessed 10 October 2016.

Blackwill, R. D. and Harris, J. M. (2016a) 'The Lost Art of Economic Statecraft: Restoring an American Tradition', *Foreign Affairs*, March/April 2016 Issue. Available at: www.foreignaffairs.com/articles/2016-02-16/lost-art-economic-statecraft, accessed 17 October 2016.

Blackwill, R. D. and Harris, J. M. (2016b) *War by Other Means: Geo-economics and Statecraft* (Cambridge, MA: Harvard University Press).

Blanke, J. and Kaspersen, A. (2015) 'Business, Like Government, Must Master Geo-economics', *World Economic Forum*, 6 February. Available at: www.weforum.org/ agenda/2015/02/business-like-government-must-master-geo-economics, accessed 13 October 2016.

Brands, H. (2014) *What Good Is Grand Strategy? Power and Purpose in American Statecraft from Harry S. Truman to George W. Bush* (Ithaca, NY: Cornell University Press).

Bremmer, I. (2008) 'The Return of State Capitalism', *Survival*, 50, 3, pp. 55–64.

Brzezinski, Z. (1997) *The Grand Chessboard: American Primacy and Its Geostrategic Imperatives* (New York: Basic Books).

Burrows, M. J. and Harris, J. M. (2009) 'Revisiting the Future: Geopolitical Effects of the Financial Crisis', *Washington Quarterly*, 32, 2, pp. 27–38.

Cooper, R. N. (1972) 'Trade Policy is Foreign Policy', *Foreign Policy*, 9, pp. 18–36.

Fairgrieve, J. (1915) *Geography and World Power* (London: London University Press).

Fairgrieve, J. and Young, E. (1921) *The Gateways of Commerce: An Introduction to Economic Geography* (London: George Philip & Son Ltd).

Fukuyama, F. (1989) 'The End of History?', *The National Interest*, 19, pp. 3–18.

Grevi, G. (2011) 'Geo-economics and Global Governance', in Martiningui, A. and Youngs, R. (eds), *Challenges for European Foreign Policy in 2012: What Kind of Geo-economic Europe?* (Madrid: Fundación para las Relaciones Internacionales y el Diálogo Exterior), pp. 27–36.

Hirschman, A. O. (1980) [1945] *National Power and the Structure of Foreign Trade* (Berkeley: University of California Press).

Kaplan, R. D. (2017) 'The Return of Marco Polo's World and the U.S. Military Response', *Center for New American Security*, May. Available at: http://stories.cnas. org/the-return-of-marco-polos-world-and-the-u-s-military-response, accessed 21 November 2017.

Kennedy, P. (1987) *The Rise and Fall of the Great Powers: Economic Change and Military Conflict From 1500 to 2000* (New York: Random House).

Keohane, R. O. and Nye, J. S. (eds) (1971) *Transnational Relations and World Politics* (Cambridge, MA: Harvard University Press).

Keohane, R. O. and Nye, J. S. (1977) *Power and Interdependence* (Boston, MA: Little, Brown).

Khanna, P. (2016) *Connectography: Mapping the Future of Global Civilization* (New York: Random House).

Kirshner, J. (2005) 'Currency and Coercion in the Twenty-First Century', *European University Institute*, EUI Working Paper RSCAS No. 2005/13. Available at: http://cadmus.eui.eu/bitstream/handle/1814/3362/05_13.pdf, accessed 29 September 2016.

Krasner, S. D. (1976) 'State Power and the Structure of International Trade', *World Politics*, 28, 3, pp. 317–347.

Krugman, P. (1994) 'Competitiveness: A Dangerous Obsession', *Foreign Affairs*, March/April 1994 Issue. Available at: www.foreignaffairs.com/articles/1994-03-01/competitiveness-dangerous-obsession, accessed 1 October 2016.

Kundnani, H. (2011) 'Germany as a Geo-economic Power', *Washington Quarterly*, 34, 3, pp. 31–45.

Lacoste, Y. (1997) 'Géopolitique, économie et nation', *Géoéconomie*, 50, pp. 39–44.

Lorot, P. (1997) 'De la géopolitique à la géoéconomie', *Géoéconomie*, 50, pp. 9–19.

Luttwak, E. N. (1990) 'From Geopolitics to Geo-economics: Logic of Conflict, Grammar of Commerce', *The National Interest*, 20, pp. 17–23.

Luttwak, E. N. (2012) *The Rise of China vs. The Logic of Strategy* (Cambridge, MA: Harvard University Press).

Mackinder, H. J. (1904) 'The Geographical Pivot of History', *Geographical Journal*, 23, 4, pp. 421–437.

Mastanduno, M. (2009) 'System Maker and Privilege Taker: U.S. Power and the International Political Economy', *World Politics*, 61, 1, pp. 121–154.

Mearsheimer, J. J. (2001) *The Tragedy of Great Power Politics* (New York: Norton).

Nye, J. S. (2017) 'Xi Jinping's Marco Polo Strategy', *Project Syndicate*, 12 June. Available at: http://prosyn.org/e3IskU2, accessed 21 November 2017.

O'Neill, J. (2011) *The Growth Map: Economic Opportunity in the BRICs and Beyond* (New York: Portfolio).

O'Rourke, K. H. (2009) 'Politics and Trade: Lessons from Past Globalisations', *Bruegel Essay and Lecture Series*. Available at: http://bruegel.org/wp-content/uploads/imported/publications/el_0209_poltrade.pdf, accessed 6 October 2016.

Rosecrance, R. N. (1986) *The Rise of the Trading State: Commerce and Conquest in the Modern World* (New York: Basic Books).

Scholvin, S. (2016) 'Geopolitics: An Overview of Concepts and Empirical Examples from International Relations', *The Finnish Institute of International Affairs*, FIIA Working Paper No. 91. Available at www.fiia.fi/en/publication/geopolitics, accessed 31 January 2018.

Schuman, F. L. (1942) 'Let Us Learn our Geopolitics', *Current History*, 2, 9, pp. 161–165.

Waltz, K. (2000) 'Globalisation and American Power', *The National Interest*, Spring 2000. Available at: http://nationalinterest.org/article/globalization-and-american-power-1225, accessed 6 October 2016.

Wheatley, A. (2013) *The Power of Currencies and Currencies of Power* (London: International Institute for Strategic Studies).

Wigell, M. (2016) 'Conceptualizing Regional Powers' Geo-economic Strategies: Neo-imperialism, Neo-mercantilism, Hegemony, and Liberal-institutionalism', *Asia Europe Journal*, 14, 2, pp. 135–151.

Wigell, M. and Vihma, A. (2016) 'Geopolitics Versus Geoeconomics: the Case of Russia's Geostrategy and Its Effects on the EU', *International Affairs*, 92, 3, pp. 605–627.

Wright, T. (2015) 'The Rise and Fall of the Unipolar Concert', *Washington Quarterly*, 37, 4, pp. 7–24.

Youngs, R. (2011) 'Geo-economic Futures', in Martiningui, A. and Youngs, R. (eds), *Challenges for European Foreign Policy in 2012: What Kind of Geo-economic Europe?* (Madrid: Fundación para las Relaciones Internacionales y el Diálogo Exterior), pp. 13–17.

Zakaria, F. (1999) *From Wealth to Power: The Unusual Origins of America's World Role* (Princeton, NJ: Princeton University Press).

Zhao, M. (2015) 'China's New Silk Road Initiative', *Istituto Affari Internazionali*, Working paper No. 15/37. Available at: www.iai.it/sites/default/files/iaiwp1537.pdf, accessed 11 October 2016.

Zoellick, R. B. (2016) 'Trade Is a National Security Imperative', *The Wall Street Journal*, 16 May. Available at: www.wsj.com/articles/trade-is-a-national-security-imperative-14634 40063, accessed 16 October 2016.

3 Interdependence as dependence

Economic security in the age of global interconnectedness

Christian O. Fjäder

Introduction

This work revolves around two closely related, yet inherently conflicting forces increasingly influential in the contemporary international system. On the one hand, it acknowledges the notion that our contemporary world is increasingly characterised by interdependence between the various international actors, and that this phenomenon is largely beneficial to all parties involved. On the other hand, it argues that interdependence is not always symmetrical and thus is not necessarily evenly distributed among the parties involved. As such, interdependence can manifest itself as dependence of one party on others.

The emergence of more open global markets and increasing freedom of access to the global flows of capital, goods, information, services, and people are creating new opportunities for business, civic organisations, individuals and societies at large. Moreover, in the systemic sense, interdependence can also mean that international actors become more sensitive to each other's interests as the breadth and degrees of interdependence increase. As such, this phenomenon of international interdependence has also been seen to create unprecedented conditions for continuing peace, stability and prosperity. The notion was put forward eloquently in international relations theory by Keohane and Nye (1977, 1998) in their work on the theory of complex interdependencies. The world of complex interdependencies, woven together by series of reciprocal transactions, in multiple policy areas and through multiple channels and between multiple actors, was expected to result in a world where security and force matter less. According to Moravcsik (2009), Keohane and Nye, whilst acknowledging the basic realist assumption about the anarchic nature of the international system, challenged the realist notion of inter-state relations being dominated by a zero-sum game of security interests. They also questioned the effectiveness of military force in an interdependent world, and argued that international regimes and organisations can significantly alleviate the effects of anarchy in international relations (Moravcsik 2009).

Closely connected to the theory of complex interdependencies is the process of globalisation. Resting on similar logic, globalisation has made the world more interdependent, not just in economic terms, but also across multiple issue areas ranging from culture to information technology. The dominant current thinking seems to be that the increasingly global flows of capital, goods, information, and people across borders benefit all countries involved. However, at the same time, these flows become critical to the economy of each country, and severing these connections would incur significant damage (Milner 2009). Consequently, connectivity to these flows is becoming a critical security consideration to nation-states. For instance, a report by the Finnish Institute of International Affairs argued that the increasing dependence of a society's vital functions on transnational networks and flows are exacerbating the perception of dependencies as a source of vulnerability (Aaltola *et al.* 2014). The importance of interconnectedness and interdependence is thus likely to grow from a national security perspective. Realists would thus be tempted to view interdependence as a vulnerability presenting potential sources or avenues for disruptive practices that could be used as means of power politics and, hence, endanger states' security interests. The use of geo-economic means, such as sanctions, would be mostly viewed in this context, and considered secondary to military power. As such, realists could seek to reduce such use of economic power to a manifestation of neo-mercantilism. However, reducing geo-economics to commercial realism overlooks a variety of other goals and uses of geo-economics as geostrategic power, rather a proper understanding of the use of economic measures as an integrated element of geostrategy would require a more eclectic approach, which would be open to both realist and liberal understandings of the strategic use of economic power (Wigell 2016).

Moreover, as pointed out in the introduction of this volume, the geo-economics in the age of connectedness is different from that in the age of traditional geopolitics. Whilst the focus on military security and territorial expansion is arguably lesser in comparison, the recent events in Ukraine and elsewhere would seem to suggest that there is still an unexplored relationship between geo-economic power and territorial conflicts in contemporary international relations (Mattlin and Wigell 2016).

This chapter looks at how the rapidly increasing global economic interconnectivity is emerging as both a national and an international security issue. It discusses the concept of interdependence, its asymmetric aspects and the way this entails sources of power in bargaining relationships between states as well as systemic risks. The risks include disruptions in global supply chains and illicit trade flows, as well as how the asymmetric aspects of contemporary economic interdependence enable novel disruptive practices with far-reaching consequences for national security strategies. As such, it shows how a geo-economic analytical perspective can contribute to shed light on the often-overlooked vulnerabilities inherent to the interdependent character of the early twenty-first-century international system.

Sensitivity versus vulnerability interdependence

The world is increasingly seen as more interconnected and interdependent, but what do we mean by interdependence? Moreover, within the context of this work, what is the difference between dependence and interdependence? Keohane and Nye referred to the distinction between interdependence and dependence in the following manner 'dependence means a state of being determined or significantly affected by external forces. Interdependence most simply defined, means mutual dependence. Interdependence in world politics refers to situations characterised by reciprocal effects among countries or among actors in different countries' (Keohane and Nye 1977, p. 8).

Another way to understand the dimensions of power stemming from interdependent relations is to examine the distinction between sensitivity and vulnerability interdependence. By sensitivity interdependence, Keohane and Nye referred to degrees of responsiveness of one party to carry out costly changes within any particular policy framework in terms of adapting to actions of others. By vulnerability interdependence they referred to opportunity costs from disrupting the particular relationship and the extent to which actors are able to control the sensitivity to the actions of others. Baldwin (1980) argues that the distinction between these two types of interdependence is useful, because they imply differences in degrees and directions of dependence, which determine the dynamics of the interdependent relation. Baldwin, however, suggests a change in labelling from 'sensitivity interdependence' to 'mutual sensitivity' in order to highlight the essence of the interdependence dynamics between parties involved.

Some types and usage of interdependence may be seen as a source of increasing cooperation and decreasing tension, whilst others may have the opposite effect. Keohane and Nye (1977) also pointed out the asymmetric nature of interdependence, and acknowledged that it can lead into polarisation between autonomy and dependence, the latter being potentially antonymic to the concept of interdependence. Moreover, they argued that asymmetric dependence could be a source of power bargaining between actors, favouring the parties that are less dependent on others, potentially enabling the asymmetric relationship to be used as a coercive tool towards other more dependent actors. Hence, the difference between positive and negative types of interdependence is that whereas in the former type, benefits are largely shared and it therefore becomes difficult for one party to turn the interdependent relationship into a tool towards inflicting disproportionate damage on another, the latter type enables the condition to be used as leverage. According to Wright (2013), such a negative type of asymmetric interdependence can potentially create a spiralling crisis cycle if one side attempts to exploit the other's vulnerability by utilising its asymmetric superiority, inviting the other to retaliate in another area where it holds superiority. This would be roughly equivalent to the security dilemma (Herz 1950), a phenomenon more familiar from the sphere of hard security.

Under current circumstances, with rising tensions in the international system, and the visible return of strategic competition between major powers, global interdependence is therefore emerging as a national security issue and potential concern. Herein, interdependence is increasingly perceived as vulnerability interdependence, which has a tendency to become securitised as vulnerability dependence from a national security perspective (Leonard 2016). In the security policy debate, dependence is often perceived as the antonym of independence, and thus as a potential challenge to state sovereignty through the reduced control over resources critical for national security. According to this view, it is still primarily the government's responsibility to guarantee the continuous operation of systems that are considered essential components of the daily life of citizens, ranging from electricity to financial services and telecommunication. Dependence on others in these areas is typically perceived as a vulnerability, which must be mitigated somehow (Fjäder 2016).

The perception of interdependence as a potential vulnerability links interdependence to national security by emphasising its disruptive aspects and loss of sovereign control. At the same time, it can also be seen as a capacity redundancy that goes beyond the scale that an individual state can produce. For instance, small states can now increasingly utilise global infrastructures to gain scale of resources otherwise impossible for them, or utilise them as redundancies that are located outside their sovereign territory, but can be utilised towards improving national security. For instance, Estonia's decision to backup critical data in its overseas embassies would serve as a novel example of such measures. Hence, interdependence can be viewed as a phenomenon that can both support national security goals by providing alternative sources for resources or additional scales of them, whilst also representing potential risks to it because of the disruptive practices it enables. This chapter focuses especially on asymmetric aspects of interdependence that implicate the centrality of the dependence aspect, which arguably leaves space for disruptive practices. By doing so, it aims to contribute to the emerging eclectic discourse in geo-economics and security in contemporary international relations.

As the world becomes both more interconnected and interdependent, the more we will see extra-sovereign and extra-territorial dependencies emerging in areas that traditionally are seen as critical for national security. This is perhaps most evident in the context of critical infrastructures. In advanced economies, most critical infrastructures are not only privately owned and operated, but increasingly under foreign ownership, or at least critically dependent on resources and structures that are extra-sovereign (outside the sovereign territory of the country of services), or even extra-territorial (not tied to any particular location). Albeit such connectivity would seem to neglect the limitations of geography, geo-economics can offer an important analytical aspect towards understanding how geography, economic activity and security will interact in the contemporary international relations in the context of conflicting forces of interdependence and power politics.

An increasingly interdependent world

As the *KOF Index of Globalization* demonstrates, globalisation has advanced significantly since 1970 (Swiss Federal Institute of Technology 2017). But how interdependent are we? In areas such as environmental policies this is becoming acknowledged as rather obvious, as they are nearly impossible to neatly arrange according to sovereign territories. The same applies increasingly to security policies, where they relate to transnational threats, most obviously in regard to issues such as illegal trafficking of arms, narcotics, and people, terrorism, and more recently, cyber security (Milner 2009). In a more generic context, interdependence applies to anything systemic where value is added, or in the context of security, where value is at risk. The most obvious example is of course economics, where creating value has been seen as most dependent on international interdependence (Zürn 2007).

In the economic context, Zürn (2007) suggests measuring the levels of international interconnectedness of societies by the rise of transboundary transactions relative to transactions that take place within a national territory. Such measurements of economic interdependence are applied primarily to financial flows and trade in goods and services, but also to the other flows – information and people. For instance, the *DHL Global Connectedness Index* analyses 12 types of capital, information, people, and trade (goods and services) flows by examining their depth – defined as international flows relative to the size of domestic economy – and breadth, meaning their geographical distribution. The Index also sheds light on the directionality of these flows, comparing outward and inward flows, using data from 140 countries, which account for 99 per cent of the global gross domestic product (GDP) and 95 per cent of the global population. The 2014 Index found that overall, the depth of global connectedness remains in fact relatively limited, despite a recovery from a temporary downturn after the global

Table 3.1 DHL global connectedness index 2005–2014

Rank (2014)	Country	2012	2010	2008	2005
1	Netherlands	1	1	1	1
2	Ireland	3	2	5	2
3	Singapore	2	3	3	4
4	Belgium	5	5	4	5
5	Luxembourg	4	4	2	3
6	Switzerland	6	6	6	6
7	United Kingdom	7	7	8	7
8	Denmark	10	9	9	11
9	Germany	8	10	10	8
10	Sweden	9	8	7	9
11	Hong Kong (China)	11	14	16	13
12	United Arab Emirates	16	18	21	19
13	Korea, Republic (ROK)	12	19	24	31
14	France	15	12	11	10
15	Norway	13	11	12	12
16	Israel	14	16	13	14
17	Hungary	17	13	15	23
18	Taiwan	19	17	19	21
19	Thailand	18	25	28	30
20	Austria	23	21	22	16

Source: Pankaj and Altman (2014).

financial crises in 2008 and 2012. The study concluded that countries that are wealthy and relatively small are also the most connected: Hong Kong, Singapore and Luxembourg. Emerging markets lag behind developed economies, despite having more potential for benefiting from it. It also argued that the proportion of international activities was on average only between 10 and 20 per cent, much lower than most observers would predict. Whilst the level varies between different areas, the study pointed out that value added exported globally was only about 23 per cent of the total. Finally, the study pointed out that a the-world-is-flat scenario of globalisation breaking the barrier of geographic distance may still not have happened, as the weighted average distance of interactions was only 4,904 kilometres. It would appear that some home bias persists, and geographical proximity still matters in international interactions.

Global Flows in a Digital Age report, published by the McKinsey Global Institute (Manyika *et al.* 2014), took a similar approach to global flows by examining the state and future of international inflows and outflows, utilising data from 195 countries. The study found that the total value of global flows of finance, goods, and services was approximately US$26 trillion in 2012, accounting for approximately 36 per cent of the global GDP, 1.5 times more than in 1990. Moreover, it estimated that global flows contribute between US$250 billion and 450 billion annually to global growth, representing 15 to 25 per cent of the total. The share of global flows of finance, goods and services could further increase to US$54 trillion, equalling 36

Table 3.2 MGI global ranking 2014

Rank	Country	Goods	Services	Financial	People (2010)	Data and communication (2013)
1	Germany	3	5	7	5	2
2	Hong Kong, China	1	4	3	14	–
3	United States	8	9	5	1	7
4	Singapore	2	3	4	18	5
5	United Kingdom	13	6	9	7	3
6	Netherlands	6	7	15	29	1
7	France	9	19	36	15	4
8	Canada	16	22	13	9	18
9	Russia	19	30	16	2	21
10	Italy	11	20	31	16	10
11	Belgium	4	8	30	39	11
12	Spain	21	12	35	12	12
13	Switzerland	23	16	11	28	17
14	Ireland	29	1	23	23	24
15	Sweden	28	15	17	45	6
16	Saudi Arabia	20	29	19	8	44
17	Australia	32	34	34	11	30
18	Malaysia	10	23	34	26	32
19	Poland	22	31	28	34	22
20	South Korea	7	14	25	58	34

Source: Manyika *et al.* (2014).

per cent of the total global GDP, according to a conservative scenario or even to US$85 trillion, equalling 49 per cent of global GDP, according to a more optimistic scenario. The report in general argues that an increasing share of global economic activity already involves international transactions. Trade remains the largest flow in terms of its share of the global GDP (24 per cent) but global flows are also significant in finance, where foreign sources of financing constitute one third of the total. In communication and data flows, one quarter are international. The proportional share of cross-border flows in people and services flows, on the other hand, remains markedly low, constituting only 3 per cent and 7 per cent of the total respectively.

The report also highlights the benefits of international connectivity to states, arguing that countries that are highly connected benefit approximately 40 per cent more from the global flows than those that are less connected. Moreover, it argues that there is still substantial potential to be realised from increasing global connectedness, especially for the emerging economies. Although emerging markets are growing their share fast, developed economies are still much more connected to global flows. The flows from emerging economies are also markedly directed to other emerging economies, the so-called South–South trade accounting for 60 per cent of the total. The McKinsey report, much like the DHL report, also points to evidence of a geographical bias in flows, culminating in the steadily large share of intra-regional flows, albeit the levels vary from flow to flow and between regions. Intra-regional flows are most dominant in data, people, and services flows, whilst trade in goods and financial flows are increasingly global.

In sum, both reports underline benefits from the globalisation of flows, and leveraging further benefits from the still unutilised potential with increasing participation in the flows. As such, the underlining assumption appears to be that higher connectivity fosters increased (sensitivity) interdependence, creating a positive cycle that benefits parties involved proportionally to their participation in the process. At the same time, both reports point to the shortcomings of interdependence, in particular in relation to the still substantial geographic bias, suggesting that deterritorialisation is still not the dominant reality. Moreover, such optimistic accounts pay very little attention to the old and new disruptive practices that can break the positive cycle and turn sensitivity interdependence into vulnerability interdependence. The failure of both – the traditional liberal and realist – paradigms to explain this duality becomes apparent in this context. Liberal and institutional accounts have often overlooked the potential for disruptive practices, whilst emphasising the stability-enhancing aspects of interdependence. On the other hand, realist accounts tend to focus on military power and conflict in an anarchic world, whilst underestimating the stability-enhancing aspects of interdependence (Wigell 2016).

Disruptive practices in the interdependent world

Economic sanctions

Russia's illegal annexation of the Crimean Peninsula, and the ensuing conflict with Ukraine in Donbass has once again elevated geopolitics as an issue in international relations (Mead 2014). Yet, an exclusive focus on geopolitics and military means obscures the fact that much power politics is conducted by economic means. In our interdependent world, the use of military means to pursue strategic goals has become increasingly ineffective. In a world of global flows and interconnectivity, strategic competition revolves less around the control of territory than around the functional control of these flows penetrating state space (Khanna 2016). For instance, the efforts by Western powers to isolate Russia from the international community from spring 2014 onwards have centred on economic sanctions, including import bans, travel bans, and the freezing of assets of individuals.

Indeed, states advance strategic goals through a variety of economic means, ranging from trade policy, investment policy, economic and financial sanctions, aid policy and programmes, financial and monetary policy to energy policy and commodities. For instance, the utilisation of trade as a weapon in conflict has a long history, stretching back to at least the Peloponnesian War. In modern age, such practices played a prominent part during the First World War. As an analytical framework, geo-economics points towards the substantially increased trade interdependence between the conflicting parties, and the way it provided an avenue for pursuing strategic aims by economic means. For instance, the *Trading with the Enemy Act*, signed by President Woodrow Wilson in 1917, gave the president of the United States power to oversee or restrict any and all trade with countries deemed hostile. During the Second World War, the United States established the Office of Economic Warfare (1943) in order to direct economic efforts towards war goals. After the war, the United States established the Marshall Plan to help European states recover from the war, but also to curb Soviet expansionism. Countries such as Italy and Greece, with influential communist parties and thus running the risk of gliding into the Soviet sphere, were tied into the US-led liberal order by the economic means inherent in the Marshall Plan. The Bretton Woods Conference in 1944, a watershed event to establish economic security in the post-war years, created the international economic institutions – the World Bank in 1944 and the International Monetary Fund in 1945 – that have formed a major pillar of the liberal international order, and on which the United States has based its grand strategy (see Chapter 7 in this volume). The emergence of the Cold War also witnessed the emergence of export control mechanisms to exclude the Soviet Union and its allies from critical resources and technology (Blackwill and Harris 2016).

Since the end of the Cold War, this geo-economic tool box has become larger and more sophisticated, encompassing an ever-increasing selection of instruments, including full and partial embargoes, sanctions against companies and individuals, such as bans on financial transactions and travel, and also the intentional manipulation of refugee flows, as recently demonstrated in the case of Turkey's use of Syrian refugees as political leverage against the European Union (Greenhill 2016). Moreover, new disruptive practices have emerged to address the weaknesses presented by the increasing connectedness, particularly cyber and hybrid warfare. These practices somewhat merge the projection of economic and military power, indicating that a clear distinction between geopolitics and geo-economics, as proposed in Chapter 1 of this volume, is not always feasible. All of the previously mentioned ways of power projection are policy instruments beyond diplomacy, but short of war with hybrid warfare currently testing this distinction. They aim at altering, cutting or disrupting the target's connections to international flows, in order to coerce it to change its policy to match the demands of the entity that applies these instruments. In some cases, such measures have also been used as paving the way for armed conflict by weakening the target's ability to amass economic or societal resources for defence (or offence when used with pre-emptive intentions).

Governments and international organisations have imposed economic sanctions in an effort to coerce their targets to adjust their behaviour to correspond with the interests of the imposing states or international norms. The motives for applying sanctions are consequently diverse, and may include rather specific foreign policy goals. Traditionally, sanctions have been comprehensive in scope, and indiscriminate in effect, albeit targeted to disrupt customary economic and financial flows as a punishment for non-compliance. Since 9/11, however, the trend has been to focus on the utilisation of smart sanctions, targeting specified businesses or individuals, whilst attempting to minimise the collateral impact on the population of the target country and possibly third parties (Zarate 2013; see also Chapter 8 in this volume). The selection of different forms of sanctions has at the same time broadened, and now includes such measures as capital restraints, freezing of assets, travel bans on individuals, and a variety of trade restrictions.

The popularity of sanctions is connected to the perception that they incur lower cost than the use of military force, being less risky and confrontational, but that they nonetheless provide a coercive means that goes beyond diplomacy. As such they are often justified with a motivation to avoid direct military confrontation, whilst still representing a sufficiently efficient tool for coercing the target to adjust its behaviour. The increased interconnectedness, and the complexity it brings, has made economic sanctions a key policy tool that sometimes can provide a more effective coercive tool than outright military force.

However, the historical track record of economic sanctions is mixed. With regard to their effectiveness, it seems that it may vary a lot according to both domestic context in the target country as well as international context. In any case, in an interconnected world, the utility of sanctions is ambiguous. On the one hand, new connectivity, such as the dependency of electronic banking payment transactions on the SWIFT (the Society for Worldwide Interbank Financial Telecommunications) network, provides effective new avenues for sanctions (Blackwill and Harris 2016). In case of the current sanctions policy of the United States, excluding Russia from the SWIFT has been described as the 'nuclear option' that would effectively inflict great damage on the Russian economy, and isolate it from vital global flows (Tett 2015). On the other hand, there is a flipside to this interconnectivity and the opportunities for sanctions that it provides. Major powers that the United States may want to target with economic sanctions now own vast amounts of financial assets in the United States, making the use of counter-sanctions and retaliation a potent counter-balancing instrument, as they may be able to incur significant damage to the US economy. For instance, China can potentially use its US dollar reserves as polit-ical leverage. Saudi Arabia has threatened to sell US government bonds worth hundreds of billions of dollars if secret sections of the 9/11 report are released (Mazzetti 2016). Table 3.3 ranks major foreign holders of US treasury securities, providing a rough estimate of such counter-sanctioning potential.

Critical infrastructures

The dichotomy between openness and market-orientation to secure economic competitiveness, on the one side, and national security, on the other, is perhaps most evident in critical infrastructure protection (CIP). It is a policy field dedic-ated to protecting national critical infrastructure, so delivering, enabling and sup-porting the provision of critical services to the citizens, communities and the economy. Whereas the definitions vary from country to country, in most cases 'critical' refers to infrastructure that provides essential and life sustaining ser-vices required for the economic and social wellbeing of citizens, national and public security, and key government functions (OECD 2008). The sectors typically considered as critical infrastructure are: banking and finance,

Table 3.3 Major foreign holders of US treasury securities as of June 2015 (in billions of dollars)

Rank	Country	Holdings
1	China, PRC	1,240.8
2	Japan	1,147.7
3	Ireland	270.6
4	Cayman Islands	269.4
5	Brazil	251.6
6	Switzerland	237.7
7	United Kingdom	231.3
8	Luxembourg	225.0
9	Taiwan, ROC	187.9
10	Hong Kong, SAR	184.7
11	Belgium	156.3
12	India	117.2
13	Singapore	106.9
14	Germany	99.4
15	Saudi Arabia	98.3
16	Russia	90.9
17	Canada	85.3
18	Korea, ROK	82.1
19	Bermuda	68.9
20	United Arab Emirates	66.2

Source: US Department of the Treasury (n.d.).

communications, energy, food supply chains, health, national security and defence-related assets, transport, and water services. Moreover, whilst the definitions of infrastructure in most cases refer to physical infrastructures, some countries now also include intangible assets, such as supply chains that enable the functioning of physical infrastructure and/or deliver critical services. For instance, the Australian government's *Critical Infrastructure Resilience Strategy* defines critical infrastructure as:

> those physical facilities, supply chains, information technologies and communication networks which, if destroyed, degraded or rendered unavailable for an extended period, would significantly impact on the social or economic wellbeing of the nation or affect Australia's ability to conduct national defence and ensure national security.
>
> (Australian Government 2010, p. 1)

Whilst the physical structures are mostly local in a sense that they reside in a given territory, the resources enabling and supporting them are not necessary local, but can originate on the other side of the world. Moreover, these dependencies are not only related to resources and materials, but increasingly include data (remote) technical support and maintenance processes and services that are globally spread in order to maximise cost efficiencies provided by the global value chain. In many cases, the physical connection between systems extends beyond borders, for instance electricity transmission networks or the international submarine cables that carry the majority of global telecommunications traffic.

This type of transnational dynamic has been addressed in security policy only in few instances thus far. One such exception is the European Union Council's *Directive on European Critical Infrastructures* and the *European Programme for Critical Infrastructure Protection* (EPCIP), which sets an EU-wide framework for activities aimed at improving the protection of critical infrastructure in Europe across all member states of the European Union, and in all relevant sectors of economic activity. The Directive acknowledges an increase in transnational, and indeed, global dependencies in critical infrastructures, and proposes five types of interdependencies: physical, information, geospatial, policy and process, and societal (European Union 2008).

The other transnational exception is Canada's plan to address risks related to the shared critical infrastructure with the United States, which includes a pilot project that would produce a joint regional resilience assessment and risk analysis for the Maine–New Brunswick region (Government of Canada 2015).

The issue of transnational dependencies has also been raised as a preoccupation in national security strategies. For instance, Britain's national security strategy – *A Strong Britain in the Age of Uncertainty* – states that Britain is more vulnerable to global threats 'because we are one the most open societies, in a word that is more networked than ever before' (Government UK – Cabinet Office 2008, p. 3). It also refers to a multitude of new threats, including those posed by non-state actors, including food and water supply, energy security, and the impact of climate change. Following a similar logic, Canada's national security policy – *Securing an Open Society* – states that: 'there can be no greater role, no more important obligation for a government, than the protection and safety of its citizens. But as all Canadians know, we live in an increasingly interconnected, complex and often dangerous world' (Government of Canada 2015). The Netherlands has also adopted an overarching international security strategy in order to respond to large-scale and rapid changes in the global system, whether they are economic, political or security related in nature. The strategy underlines uncertainty and the difficulty to distinguish between internal and external security in this new reality. The emerging trend that critical infrastructures increasingly require access to resources and systems outside the sovereign territory of the state suggests that economic security increasingly depends on the continuous connections to the nodes that facilitate such flows. As such, this development elevates economic security on the scale of strategic priority for a growing number of states. Where geo-economic analysis can prove particularly useful is in improving our understanding on where these nodes are located and why, as well as which locations are seen as acceptable and unacceptable, thus shedding light on the nature of interdependence. This is particularly critical considering that interdependence can be argued to denote either sensitivity or vulnerability aspects, depending on the context. After all, economic policy instruments can be used for both as tools for exerting political influence, as well as for purely economic ends (Wigell 2016).

Conclusion

As a variety of indices of globalisation and international connectedness would appear to suggest, our contemporary world is arguably more interconnected and probably more interdependent than ever before. As such, one could assume that international actors' sensitivity to each other's interest would be growing and that this in turn would be beneficial to the stability of the system, much as predicted by Keohane and Nye. When different international actors – in this case primarily states – are increasingly interdependent in multiple policy areas, they are unlikely to consider the use of force or coercion to advance their independent interests because of the fear that such actions are increasingly likely to 'bite back'.

At the same time, however, notions of vulnerability interdependence, emphasising the dependence aspect of interdependence, are also (perhaps ironically) emerging as stronger the further interdependence advances. The fear of others taking advantage of the asymmetric nature of interdependence and using it as a bargaining tool to advance their own goals at the cost of the weaker parties can be a powerful deterrent for smaller and weaker states against entering such relationships, as well as for the bigger and stronger states to utilise disruptive practices to advance political goals. Moreover, the use of disruptive practices, such as economic sanctions, obviously further feeds these fears. The disruptive practices, old and new, are likely to be emphasised in situations of conflict and crisis, as well as experimented in times of peace, particularly in the context of heightened tensions. As such, the use of disruptive practices and the sentiments of vulnerability interdependence they stimulate may have the potential to lead into a situation resembling the security dilemma, as predicted by realism. However, the risks of disruptive practices to international interdependence should not be exaggerated. The costs of utilising disruptive practices are unpredictable, as are the gains. Consequently, the emerging reality is more likely to be a balancing act between the potentially significant benefits to be reaped from increasing interdependence and the vulnerabilities and potentially costly risks it brings with it. Some of these risks are systemic, and cannot be governed by individual nation-states. Yet some are too sensitive to share responsibilities over them with others.

Moreover, although it is rather easy to argue that geography is no longer destiny, it still clearly matters. At the same time, connectivity is perhaps not destiny yet, but it is certainly important to both competitiveness and security. As a consequence, it would appear that, at least for now, two words are in existence simultaneously; one of territorially bound sovereign states, and another dictated by extra-sovereign (and increasingly extra-territorial) flows. How states operate their security in such a dichotomy is something traditional liberal and realist approaches have trouble in explaining. Geo-economics offers one useful analytical tool for exploring this dichotomy, but in order to fulfil its potential we must adopt an eclectic approach to the study of geo-economics and power (Wigell 2016).

References

Aaltola, M., Käpylä, J., Mikkola, H. and Behr, T. (2014) *Towards the Geopolitics of Flows: Implications for Finland*, FIIA Report No. 40 (Helsinki: The Finnish Institute of International Affairs). Available at: www.fiia.fi/en/publication/towards-the-geopolitics-of-flows, accessed 4 December 2017.

Australian Government. (2010) 'Critical Infrastructure Resilience Strategy'. *Australian Government*. Available at: www.tisn.gov.au/Documents/Australian+Government+s+Critical+Infrastructure+Resilience+Strategy.pdf, accessed 29 April 2018.

Baldwin, D. A. (1980) 'Interdependence and Power: A Conceptual Analysis', *International Organization*, 34, 4, pp. 471–506.

Blackwill, R. and Harris, J. (2016) *War by Other Means: Geoeconomics and Statecraft* (Cambridge, MA: Harvard University Press).

European Union. (2008) 'Council Directive 2008//114/EC', *European Union*. Available at: http://eur-lex.europa.eu/LexUriServ/LexUriServ.do?uri=OJ:L:2008:345:0075:0082:EN:PDF, accessed 30 May 2016.

Fjäder, C. (2016) 'National Security in a Hyper-connected World: Global Interdependence and National Security', in Masys, A. J. (ed.), *Exploring the Security Landscape: Non-Traditional Security Challenges* (Cham: Springer), pp. 31–58.

Government of Canada. (2015) 'Securing an Open Society: Canada's National Security Policy', *Government of Canada*. Available at: www.publicsafety.gc.ca/cnt/ntnl-scrt/scrng-eng.aspx, accessed 31 August 2016.

Government UK – Cabinet Office. (2008) 'The National Security Strategy of the United Kingdom. Security in an Interdependent World', *Government UK*. Available at: www. gov.uk/government/uploads/system/uploads/attachment_data/file/228539/7291.pdf, accessed 10 November 2017.

Greenhill, K. M. (2016) 'The Weaponisation of Migration', in Leonard, M. (ed.), *Connectivity Wars: Why Migration, Finance and Trade Are the Geo-economic Battlegrounds of the Future* (London: European Council on Foreign Relations), pp. 76–80.

Herz, J. H. (1950) 'Idealist Internationalism and the Security Dilemma', *World Politics*, 2, 2, pp. 157–180.

Keohane, R. O. and Nye, J. S. (1977) *Power and Interdependence: World Politics in Transition* (Boston, MA: Little, Brown).

Keohane, R. and Nye, J. S. (1998) 'Power and Interdependence in the Information Age', *Foreign Affairs*, 20, 5, pp. 81–94.

Khanna, P. (2016) *Connectography: Mapping the Future of Global Civilization* (New York: Random House).

Leonard, M. (2016) 'Introduction: Connectivity Wars', in Leonard, M. (ed.), *Connectivity Wars: Why Migration, Finance and Trade Are the Geo-economic Battlegrounds of the Future* (London: European Council on Foreign Relations), pp. 13–27.

Manyika, J., Bughin, J., Lund, S., Nottebohm, O., Poulter, D., Jauch, S. and Ramaswamy, S. (2014) 'Global Flows in a Digital Age', *McKinsey Global Institute*, April. Available at: www.mckinsey.com/business-functions/strategy-and-corporate-finance/our-insights/global-flows-in-a-digital-age, accessed 22 November 2017.

Mattlin, M. and Wigell, M. (2016) 'Geoeconomics in the Context of Restive Regional Powers', *Asia Europe Journal*, 14, 2, pp. 125–134.

Mazzetti, M. (2016) 'Saudi Arabia Warns of Economic Fallout if Congress Passes 9/11 Bill', *New York Times*, 15 April. Available at: www.nytimes.com/2016/04/16/world/middleeast/saudi-arabia-warns-ofeconomic-fallout-if-congress-passes-9-11-bill.html?, accessed 9 November 2017.

Mead, W. R. (2014) 'The Return of Geopolitics: The Revenge of the Revisionist Powers', *Foreign Affairs*, 93, 3, pp. 69–79.

Milner, H. (2009) 'Power, Interdependence, and Nonstate Actors in World Politics: Research Frontiers', in Milner, H. V. and Moravcsik, A. (eds), *Power, Interdependence, and Nonstate Actors in World Politics* (Princeton, NJ and Oxford: Princeton University Press), pp. 3–28.

Moravcsik, A. (2009) 'Robert Keohane: Political Theorist', in Milner, H. V. and Moravcsik, A. (eds), *Power, Interdependence, and Nonstate Actors in World Politics* (Princeton, NJ and Oxford: Princeton University Press), pp. 243–263.

OECD. (2008) 'Protection of "Critical Infrastructure" and the Role of Investment Policies Relating to National Security', *OECD*, May 2008. Available at: www.oecd.org/daf/inv/investment-policy/40700392.pdf, accessed 8 May 2013.

Pankaj, G. and Altman, S. A. (2014) 'DHL Global Connectedness Index 2014', *Deutsche Post DHL*, November. Available at: www.dhl.com/en/about_us/logistics_insights/studies_research/global_connectedness_index/global_connectedness_index.html#.VFff5MkpXuM, accessed 28 May 2015.

Swiss Federal Institute of Technology Zurich. (2017) 'KOF Index of Globalization', *Swiss Federal Institute of Technology Zurich*. Available at: http://globalization.kof.ethz.ch/, accessed 22 November 2017.

Tett, G. (2015) 'Russian Banker Warns West over SWIFT', *Financial Times*, 23 January. Available at: www.ft.com/content/7020c50c-a30a-11e4-9c06-00144feab7de, accessed 22 November 2017.

US Department of Treasury. (n.d.) 'Treasury International Capital (TIC) system', *U.S. Department of Treasury*. Available at: www.treasury.gov/resource-center/data-chart-center/tic/Pages/index.aspx, accessed 22 November 2017.

Wigell, M. (2016) '"Conceptualizing Regional Powers" Geoeconomic Strategies: Neo-imperialism, Neo-mercantilism, Hegemony, and Liberal Institutionalism', *Asia Europe Journal*, 14, 2, pp. 135–151.

Wright, T. (2013) 'Shifting through Interdependence', *The Washington Quarterly*, 36, 4, pp. 7–23.

Zarate, J. (2013) *Treasury's War: The Unleashing of a New Era of Financial Warfare* (New York: Public Affairs).

Zürn, M. (2007) 'From Interdependence to Globalization', in Carlsnaes, W., Risse, T. and Simmons, B. A. (eds), *Handbook of International Relations* (London: Sage Publications), pp. 235–254.

4 Critical infrastructure in geostrategic competition

Comparing the US and Chinese Silk Road projects

Juha Käpylä and Mika Aaltola[1]

Introduction

Any geostrategic analysis is likely to be affected by the historical context specific to the region in question. Herein, the adoption of a geopolitical lens helps to specify the focus on certain geostrategically important features. The territorial distribution of resources and other geographical topographies can provide clarity to a complex scenario and help to zoom in on the struggle between major powers and the way geography affects that struggle. Geopolitics, with its focus on the topographical chessboard, offers useful insights into the strategic games played by the major powers. At the same time, geopolitical approaches have historically been criticised for being ideological, reductionist and determinist (e.g. Starr 2013). More recently, they have been said to suffer from shortages in their ability to describe, prescribe and predict events (e.g. Fettweis 2015).

Geo-economic approaches broaden this often too reductive approach by introducing wider patterns relating to economic connectivities, asymmetries and dependencies that states attempt to use to their strategic benefit. As highlighted in the introduction to this volume, the central idea of geo-economic analysis is to broaden the relationship between security, power and territory by emphasising the ability to leverage and manipulate 'the economic binds that tie states together'.

This chapter is interested in the role of key logistical flows and, in particular, how two major powers – the United States and China – attempt to use control over critical infrastructures to their power-political benefit. The functional control over man-made environments, such as critical infrastructures, provides concrete means of asymmetric power exertion. It also amounts to a novel kind of territorial control that actors – empowered by their position in the overall dynamism of these key logistical flows and infrastructures – can utilise. The way in which cities and regions, for instance, are linked through the global flows of resources, goods, people and data, is starting to play an increasingly important part in geostrategic scenarios. These engineered linkages and networks – the hub-and-spoke systems of roads, sea-lines, data cables, airports, etc. – can be rerouted and rewired with major power-political consequences.

Territory can be seen as a function of its uses. When the uses of a particular territory increase, the strategic weight of the area increases. Conversely, when the territory's uses decrease, its strategic weight diminishes. This functional understanding of space changes the geostrategic paradigms that inform power-political games based on scarce resources on a finite territory. Not only does it change the importance given to particular territories in relative terms, but also how resources as such are viewed; not necessarily as finite, but as constantly innovated and mobile through technological means.

With these general ideas in mind, the chapter investigates the two competing Silk Road initiatives that were launched by the United States and China, respectively, in the Greater Central Asia region in the 2010s in order to shed light on this geo-economic form of power politics. In this new 'Great Game', the focus is less on territorial control and key strategic resources, as was the case in the old geopolitical Great Game, waged between the British Empire and Russia during the nineteenth century. While territory and natural resources certainly remain a part of the equation, the focus is increasingly on establishing and controlling the key logistical flows and interconnectivities of the region.

US geo-economics in Greater Central Asia: the new Silk Road initiative

A nexus between technology, connectivity and territory is central to US strategic thinking. Mahanian ideas concerning the importance of maritime lifelines and corridors have always been a central focus in US geostrategy, both to enable international trade flows and secure projection of military power. The country's past also shows the importance of engineered terrestrial connectivity, for instance, when the United States built railways across North America in the late 1800s. The rise of aviation enabled new forms of airborne connectivity and power. Reinforced by subsequent attempts at developing space and cyber connectivity, the United States can, indeed, be considered a nation with a strong focus on connectivity and mobility (Aaltola, Käpylä and Vuorisalo 2014).

Given the landlocked nature of Central Asia, US strategic thinking concerning the region has already for some time revolved around the development of logistical infrastructure, and through this, the creation of the sort of new connections that would favour regional development and Washington's interests. In the early post-Cold War era, the idea was to link the region westwards (to the Caucasus and, by extension, Europe). More recently, the idea has been to link it southwards (to Pakistan and India), thereby limiting its north- and eastbound connectivity (to Russia and China). In the US view, the region and its rich natural resources should neither be monopolised by Russia, nor should they help catalyse China's geostrategic ambitions. Regional roads, railways and pipelines have thus become to be seen from the perspective of a new Great Game. Deriving from its global grand-strategic vision that does not favour the emergence of a global peer competitor, a long-term goal for the United States in Central Asia has arguably been to create a friendly buffer zone between China and Russia by leveraging Western technological know-how and foreign direct investment in the region (Kucera 2013a; 2013b; Mankoff 2013).

With regard to Afghanistan in the post-9/11 era, the United States has also had to find logistical networks for its military supplies, although this calculus began to change with Barack Obama, who was elected president with a commitment to end costly foreign wars. Herein, the idea of improving regional connectivity and infrastructure in Central Asia took on a new importance, so as to help develop stable societies with interconnected and self-sustaining economies, enabling the United States to reduce (and ultimately withdraw) its direct military presence from the region.

These ideas became embodied in the notion of a new Silk Road. Informed by debates in Washington's think tanks and drawing from lessons learned in creating military logistics networks and supply flows into Afghanistan, the Obama administration decided to develop its own regional Silk Road plan. In particular, the plan drew conceptual inspiration from the northern distribution network, a successful network of logistical routes to Afghanistan set up by the US military along three key vectors: the northern route passing through Tajikistan and Kyrgyzstan, the north-western route passing through Uzbekistan, Kazakhstan, Russia and Latvia, and the western route passing through Uzbekistan, Kazakhstan, Azerbaijan and Georgia (Kuchins, Sanderson and Gordon 2009, 2010; Lee 2012).

Then Secretary of State Hillary Clinton (2011a; 2011b) laid out the political outlines for the post-withdrawal Silk Road strategy in the summer of 2011. Although the strategy centred on Afghanistan and its political and economic viability after the eventual withdrawal of US military forces, it also included a strong regional element, as Afghanistan could not be thought of as economically viable, without enhancing its regional interconnectivities. The landlocked Central Asian states were considered key participants in a win-win scenario. From the US perspective, they needed infrastructure development, harmonisation and liberalisation of trade policies, as well as promotion of good governance – especially reduction in corruption and rent-seeking by elites – in order to fully benefit from their natural resources and other potential sources of socio-economic development. In the process, Afghanistan would be able to take advantage of the emerging markets in the wider Central Asia. In short, the Silk Road plan sought to integrate Greater Central Asia in order to improve Afghanistan's uncertain political situation and lessen its dependency on Western aid. The US leadership thus appeared to have drawn the conclusion that it could better achieve its goals for Afghanistan and the region more broadly through infrastructure development and investment than through (mere) military presence and economic aid.

Yet, this idea was not altogether new, as the US engagement in Afghanistan had already relied on the counter-insurgency doctrine (US Government 2009), which emphasised the creation of local and national capabilities and 'winning the hearts and minds' of target populations, for example through 'short-term stabilization projects' (Clinton 2011b). From this perspective, the Silk Road initiative complemented, and built upon, the more localised multi-billion-dollar nation-building effort by the United States in Afghanistan. These efforts consisted of, for instance, the construction or repair of roads and bridges to facilitate trade, transport and people-to-people connectivity in Afghanistan and beyond. Key projects included the Afghan Ring Road that connects major Afghan cities, and the Tajikistan-Afghanistan bridge across the Panji River (BBC 2007; Special Inspector General for Afghanistan Reconstruction 2016). The United States also provided financial support for the construction of energy transmission lines, hydropower plants and related reforms across the country. To improve cyber connectivity, the United States provided technical assistance to the establishment of a network of fibre optic cables in the country (Tracy 2013). At the same time, the Silk Road framework also complemented and supported existing infrastructure initiatives in the region – such as transport corridors advanced by the Central Asia Regional Economic Cooperation Programme, which is coordinated by the Asian Development Bank (Blake 2013).[2]

As noted, the hope was that the integration of the whole region into a primarily north-south network of trade, transit and communication would produce a stable and increasingly prosperous Afghanistan as a hub of regional links and value chains (Fedorenko 2013). Afghanistan was envisioned as the new 'heart of Asia'. A key component of the plan consisted of the growing economies of Pakistan and India that were in need of the abundant natural resources from Central Asia. To respond to this need, the Silk Road initiative envisioned the construction and extension of infrastructure to connect the Central Asian states to Pakistan and India via Afghanistan.

In concrete terms, the US State Department identified up to 40 infrastructure projects to pursue in the region (Mankoff 2013; Kucera 2011). These included initiatives to develop energy transmission networks, energy pipelines, transport connections and information networks. The two key projects of regional connectivity that the US strategy set forth were (1) the Turkmenistan-Afghanistan-Pakistan-India (TAPI) gas pipeline, which is to transport Turkmen natural gas to the growing and resource-hungry markets in India; and (2) the CASA-1000 energy transmission network[3] to transport surplus hydropower from Kyrgyzstan and Tajikistan to Afghanistan and Pakistan (Tracy 2013; Blake 2013).

Yet, in hindsight, the plan contained a key paradox. The United States was using infrastructure as a way of supplementing its military toolbox and to eventually wind down the costly operation in Afghanistan. At the same time, it was marketing its infrastructure ideas as apolitical, functional policy options for the region's countries and for other self-interested great powers. Irrespective of the flaws of the plan, it illustrates the geostrategic nature of advancing trans-regional connectivity and economic activity.

The transformation of the Silk Road strategy

The US plan for the new Silk Road had various drivers. As mentioned, a concrete roadmap for the period after troop reduction in Afghanistan was necessary. The Obama administration needed to show that it had an exit strategy based on a comprehensive vision for Afghanistan that included the whole region. The absence of a concrete plan could have contributed to the destabilisation of the security situation in Afghanistan, if the United States and its partners would have appeared to have lost interest in the country and the region. A failure to accomplish the broader goal of a self-sustaining Afghanistan might have further undermined the willingness of allies and partners to join US-led missions in the future. The lack of a vision could also have further alienated the Afghan population, creating conditions for disorder and radicalisation. The United States needed to signal that it was not in Afghanistan only for the sake of its own security (Starr and Kuchins 2010).

Furthermore, while it was assumed that a self-sustaining future for the Afghan society required close regional cooperation, it was also clear that non-Western powers in the region would present the United States with a strategic challenge. It was assumed that China and Russia would increase their regional engagement, if the United States was seen as decreasing its attention to and involvement in the region. As discussed below, China's footprint and influence in Central Asia has grown significantly already for some time. During the Obama years, this created pressure to find possible win-win scenarios with the People's Republic in Central Asia. The Obama administration ultimately concluded that China's ventures could contribute to its efforts towards regional economic growth and integration. While Obama's United States still considered itself an important regional partner and believed that US firms would have a role to play, China was explicitly recognised as the future 'leader [in Central Asia] in trade and investments' (Tracy 2013).[4]

The willingness to entertain the idea of possible win-win scenarios with China in Central Asia has now changed, as the Trump administration has taken over the lead of US foreign policy. The Obama mode of active multilateral engagement has been replaced by a more competitive vision that builds on transactional politics (preferably though not necessarily on bilateral terms) and a tendency to harness harder forms of power for relative advantage (Sinkkonen 2018). President Trump's National Security Advisor H. R. McMaster together with Director of the National Economic Council Gary D. Cohn summed up the current view of the administration:

> [...] the world is not a 'global community' but an arena where nations, nongovernmental actors and businesses engage and compete for advantage. We bring to this forum unmatched military, political, economic, cultural and moral strength. Rather than deny this elemental nature of international affairs, we embrace it.
>
> (McMaster and Cohn 2017)

This emergence of a more competitive vision has meant, for example, that the 'shared spaces' of Obama's geostrategic vision – the high seas, space, cyber domain, and airspace, which were a key feature of the 2015 *National Security Strategy* (NSS) – have changed into mere 'domains' in the 2017 document prepared by the Trump administration. It has also meant that the win-win type of inclusiveness, which came to characterise the Silk Road initiative during the Obama years, has been replaced by more adversarial rhetoric, especially with regard to China.

In this regard, the latest NSS argues that

> China and Russia want to shape a world antithetical to US values and interests. China seeks to displace the United States in the Indo-Pacific region, expand the reaches of its state-driven economic model, and reorder the region in its favour.
>
> (White House 2017, p. 25)

Without directly referring to the Belt and Road project, the document also maintains that 'China is investing billions of dollars in infrastructure' and targeting the developing world in order 'to expand influence' and to diminish 'the sovereignty of many states in the Indo-Pacific' (White House 2017, pp. 38, 46). Furthermore, Afghanistan is still recognised as an important piece of the puzzle in Central Asia, and the preferred direction of regional connectivity has been reaffirmed to be strictly from north to south. As the document puts it:

> We will continue to partner with Afghanistan to promote peace and security in the region. […] We will help South Asian nations maintain their sovereign as China increases its influence in the region. […] We will encourage the economic integration of Central and South Asia to promote prosperity and economic linkages that will bolster connectivity and trade. And we will encourage India to increase its economic assistance in the region. In Pakistan, we will build trade and investment ties as security improves and as Pakistan demonstrates that it will assist the United States in our counterterrorism goals.
>
> (White House 2017, p. 50)

In short, contemporary US geostrategy locates Chinese infrastructure projects in the realm of zero-sum competition among great powers. This is not surprising, as Washington's geostrategic thinking has a strong legacy of seeing commercial infrastructures as part of the toolbox aimed at advancing US interests around the world (Kurečić 2010, p. 21).

However, while more inclusive, it can be argued that the Obama administration's Silk Road initiative already embodied some of these more competitive geostrategic elements. Especially important was the growing strategic partnership between the United States and India, and the latter's role in the strategic balancing act between the United States and China. During the Obama era, India was defined as the 'indispensable partner' for the twenty-first century, based on converging strategic interests, shared democratic values and a shared vision for the region (Sherman 2012; see also Burns 2014). From this perspective, it is no wonder that the US vision for the region favoured primarily north-to-south connections seeking to link Central Asia, including Afghanistan, to India instead of China.

Sensing China's growing power and influence in the region, the Herculean task for the Trump administration now appears to be the development of a competing regional platform with a sufficiently powerful hub. Instead of the more limited Silk Road concept, the United States appears to be approaching the task from the point of view of (advancing) a free, open and connected Indo-Pacific area (Tillerson 2017; see also Panda 2017). This could give further weight to India as the regional balancer of China, and contain the Chinese geo-economic expansion towards the west.

However, countering China's growing economic influence will be a difficult and costly endeavour, and presents the United States with a conundrum in Central Asia. If the stabilisation of Afghanistan is premised on its economic growth and if this is to a large degree a function of Afghanistan's integration to the region as well as the area's integration to broader global markets, then China is geographically well placed and its gravitational pull is hard to resist (Mankoff 2013). Under President Trump's leadership, the United States appears more inwardly focused. Infrastructure investments by the Trump administration are thus likely to be primarily domestic in nature, even if the more competitive geo-strategic vision of this administration would demand significant international investments. In the long run, it seems likely that China will be more capable of funding critical infrastructure projects and reap related strategic gains in Central Asia.

From the point of view of geostrategic competition, it is also noteworthy that – although designed with a clear north-to-south axis – the Obama administration's Silk Road strategy excluded both Iran (with whom President Obama sought an agreement on that country's nuclear programme, as analysed in Chapter 8 of this volume) and Russia (with whom he wanted to 'reset' relations). This was the case even though Russia facilitated the flow of critical US military supplies via the northern distribution network throughout the war in Afghanistan.

Looking into the future, it is unlikely that Washington's economic cooperation in Central Asia with either Iran or Russia will flourish any time soon. Reflecting its competitive worldview, Trump's United States is clearly seeking (at least in rhetoric, see e.g. Ross 2018) to counter Iran and perhaps even undo the nuclear agreement, whereas relations with Russia are at a post-Cold War low and will most likely remain so for the time being (Katz 2018).

China's geo-economic challenge: the Belt and Road initiative

China's vision for its modern Silk Road imitates but also goes beyond the US strategy. What is today known as the Belt and Road initiative envisions the development of transport infrastructure to facilitate connectivity, trade and resource flows, and ultimately also Chinese economic and political influence. The People's Republic has been engaged in financing and building up a vast network of land-based connections – highways, railways, oil and gas pipelines – as well as oil and gas fields, mineral mines, sites of industrial production and logistics, special economic zones, ports and airports. Such forays have taken place in western China, across Central Asia and beyond, all the way to Africa and Europe. These efforts have been supported by other components of the initiative, such as strategic communication with key partners, the leveraging of financial investments, policy harmonisation and cultural communication (Szczudlik-Tatar 2013).

The motivation behind China's infrastructure projects is the relatively constrained access it has to the high seas. China's Silk Road initiative includes maritime dimensions, most notably in the southern maritime route through which the '21st-century maritime Silk Road' passes (Xinhuanet 2013). More recently, China has officially confirmed a vision of a 'polar Silk Road' in the Arctic (Reuters 2018). However, these directions present China with significant strategic challenges. Although Beijing is trying to secure its maritime access by investing in port infrastructure along the southern route – and presumably also in the Arctic in the future (Kynge 2017) – as well as by building up island-based infrastructure in the South China Sea, its terrestrial plans for Eurasia have so far appeared more feasible. On land, China's explicit objective is to reconnect the mainland not only to Central Asia, but to Europe, the Middle East and even Africa in a way that supports the Chinese view of integration and development.

The vision for the terrestrial component (the belt) was initially presented by President Xi Jinping in a speech while on tour in Central Asia in September 2013. Xi proposed the building of an 'economic belt along the Silk Road' that would span the Eurasian continent from the Pacific to the Baltic Sea. According to Xi, this massive economic area, inhabited by close to 3 billion people, 'represents the biggest market in the world with unparalleled potential' (Wu and Zhang 2013).

According to initially circulated plans available in the public domain, the terrestrial route goes through Central Asia, the Middle East and Turkey towards Germany and ending up in the Dutch port of Rotterdam. From Rotterdam, there is also a connection southwards, to Venice, Italy, where the route links with the maritime leg of the Silk Road. The maritime road begins on the Chinese east coast and passes through the Strait of Malacca to Kolkata in India. It then continues to Nairobi on the west coast of Africa. From there it heads northwards, all the way to the Mediterranean, ending in Venice (Tiezzi 2014).

Subsequently, Chinese plans have evolved. To illustrate, the vision for terrestrial connectivity is sometimes summarised by the idea of 'five fingers', each finger being a corridor of mobility from China outwards and vice versa (e.g. Khanna 2012; Ng 2017). In 2015, the Chinese government released an official policy paper entitled *Visions and Actions on Jointly Building Silk Road Economic Belt and 21st Century Maritime Silk Road*, which further outlined China's growing aspirations and made it clear that the initial visualisations of the Silk Road are far from representative of the scope of China's plan (National Development and Reform Commission 2015).

In fact, given the emerging nature of the project, the exact objects of development are not set in stone. The creation of new funding mechanisms, such as the

Silk Road Fund and the multilateral Asian Infrastructure Investment Bank, together with the massive amount of investments available, virtually guarantee the (growing) multiplicity of potential development projects. Simultaneously, this is likely to provide China with flexible geo-economic leverage. Many cities and countries are eager to build relations with China in order to become part of the emerging networks of economic connectivity. Yet, how many of these infrastructure projects will be implemented remains an open question. Given the estimated costs that could surpass US$1 trillion (Perlez and Huang 2017), there is also no guarantee that adequate funding will eventually be available for each and every project or that host nations will ultimately be able to manage sustainably their increasingly high debts levels (He 2018). At the same time, the very existence of enticing plans already changes economic thinking and potentially also political calculations, for example by improving responsiveness to China's interests in their target audiences, thereby producing geo-economic effects.

China's idea to revive the Silk Road and launch the comprehensive Belt and Road initiative can be read as part of the broader and on-going Chinese westward expansion that began with a strong focus on domestic modernisation (Panda 2013; Wang 2012). The strategic attention of modern China – both economically and politically – has been primarily on its coastal areas. This pattern has benefited coastal cities and their industrial development. The establishment of special economic zones in southeast China further accentuated this process. At the same time, the western regions have remained less developed and short on interaction with the wider world (Szczudlik-Tatar 2013; Wang 2012).

Spearheaded by the *Great Western Development Strategy*, the government began taking the development of the western regions seriously in the early 2000s (Cooley 2012; Wang 2012). The strategy has started to produce some results, for example by increasing economic activity and reducing migration flows to the more industrialised coastal areas (Chen 2014). At the same time, this process has resulted in increased demand for energy, available in the near vicinity of Central Asia.

Moreover, domestic infrastructure projects also seek to improve domestic political cohesion, which is arguably a key interest for the current political leadership. In particular, the development strategy is related to securing territorial integrity and maintaining political stability in China's western regions, most notably in the multi-ethnic Xinjiang region that remains the home of the politically active Uyghur population. From Beijing's perspective, modernisation and urbanisation are ways to decrease the popularity of local ethnic and cultural identifications. Through development, the dangers of domestic political instability and outright separatism are expected to decline. At the same time, China has no serious reservations about using coercive means to maintain domestic security and stability (Brugier 2014; Clarke 2017). Indeed, the People's Republic has also advanced regional security cooperation through the Shanghai Cooperation Organisation to combat what it considers the 'three evils' – namely religious extremism, separatism, and terrorism – in its western provinces and, beyond its own borders, in Central Asia (Cooley 2012; Roney 2013).

China's pivot to the west has also less explicit strategic objectives beyond its borders. On the one hand, the government fears potential domino effects, whereby instability in neighbouring states would spill over to western China. From this perspective, the People's Republic has an interest in stabilising Central Asia through a combination of improved political relations, economic development and security cooperation. Thus, it aims for strategic partnerships and growing regional economic investments, and also pursues the improvement of regional capabilities to fight the 'three evils' (Brugier 2014; Szczudlik-Tatar 2013).

On the other hand, China's expansion towards the west has an important global geostrategic aspect. To counter the rise of China in general and in the Asia-Pacific in particular, the United States has sought to rebalance its strategic attention to that region (Gaens 2018; for a political formulation see Clinton 2011c). This has led to fears of containment in China, and to a sense that Washington is trying to undermine China's relationships and standing in the (Asia-Pacific) region. As fears have accentuated, especially now during the Trump administration and its more competitive worldview, China has recognised the danger of an open confrontation with the United States, wherefore it pursues a policy that combines military build-up at home with politico-economic diplomacy abroad (Wang 2012, 2015; Sun 2013). The win-win facade of infrastructure development and regional connectivity hides zero-sum-oriented objectives that focus on countering US policies of containment, particularly by changing regional patterns of dependencies and asymmetries in ways that further favour Chinese efforts and increase China's influence.

In comparison to the conflict-prone seas close to Chinese territory – particularly the South China Sea – Central Asia and the Middle East present the leadership in Beijing with more favourable options. For example, the substantial reduction of US forces in Afghanistan has opened up geopolitical and geo-economic space in Central Asia into which China can advance and from which it can reap economic, political, and security benefits with almost no risk of a direct military confrontation between the two great powers. This is clearly something that is much more difficult to achieve in the Asia-Pacific.

To a significant degree, China's Silk Road initiative has rivalled the US economic strategy and geostrategic vision. Yet, China and the United States also have some common interests that could serve as a basis to jointly advance regional prosperity and stability. In Afghanistan, Washington even signalled that the People's Republic could contribute more to the stabilisation of Afghanistan in the wake of the US withdrawal (Wang 2012; Sun 2013). Recent reporting suggests that China has upped its game in this respect, for example by conducting joint patrolling with Afghan soldiers. China is reportedly even considering supporting the establishment of a military base in the Wakhan Corridor, a narrow strip of territory in north-eastern Afghanistan that extends to China and separates Tajikistan from Pakistan (Jackson and Abbas 2018).

The geo-economic reconnection of the Greater Central Asia region has the potential to further alter geostrategic dynamics. China has become an increasingly important investment and trading partner for the Central Asian states. Beijing's

Belt and Road vision challenges Moscow's attempt to expand the Eurasian Economic Union to Central Asia. This is not favourable to that union, which already has other challenges to tackle (Roberts *et al.* 2014). While China and Russia share strategic interests to counter US hegemony and promote a multipolar world order, Russia is not likely to appreciate a significant expansion of Chinese economic influence through energy and transport links to Central Asia. They will weaken Russia's economic influence there and reinforce China politically in a sphere of influence that Moscow has traditionally considered its own. Already today, Russia is easily viewed as a mere junior partner of the People's Republic in Central Asia (Brill Olcott 2013; Cooley 2012) – a fact that Moscow arguably does not appreciate.

Despite these fears, and probably driven by sheer necessity in the increasingly inflamed post-2014 international situation, Russia has been seeking new energy deals and investments from China – particularly for expensive and technologically challenging hydrocarbon extraction projects in East Siberia and the Arctic – with terms that are likely to favour Beijing. For example, the China National Petroleum Corporation (CNPC) and the Silk Road Fund have helped finance Novatek's Yamal liquefied natural gas (LNG) project in a difficult international situation. They now possess significant minority holdings (and related influence) in the venture and can benefit from a new source of LNG (Reuters 2016a; 2016b). The role of a junior partner may turn out to be the best available role for Russia vis-à-vis China, at least in the near future. This dilemma was apparently something that the Trump administration had planned to use as leverage to reset the deteriorated US-Russia relations. However, a confluence of events has led to an increasingly cold era between Washington and Moscow (Katz 2018).

The Chinese western pivot also aims at securing a sustainable supply of energy for its growing economy. This requires the diversification of production sites and routes through which energy is imported. Greater Central Asia provides a key resource base for realising these objectives. Within the framework of the Belt and Road initiative, China has agreed on investment, trade and loan agreements to secure the needed political support as well as concrete extraction facilities and pipelines in the region. For example, in the context of launching the Silk Road project in 2013 in Kazakhstan, CNPC announced a multi-billion US$ investment in the Kasghan offshore oil field (located in the Caspian Sea), from which oil is transported to China via existing pipelines. Other notable agreements were subsequently unveiled with Uzbekistan (in terms of oil, gas, and uranium supplies), as well as in Turkmenistan, where China has committed to developing natural gas infrastructure, including pipelines, for the massive Galkynysh gas field (Feng 2014; Szczudlik-Tatar 2013).

China has also become one of the top importers of Middle Eastern oil. However, the imports from the Middle East present China with a vexing strategic challenge. Although very unlikely, the United States could cut the supply route by blocking the Strait of Malacca. This increases the importance of alternative transport routes. The risk of supply cuts in mind, the People's Republic has invested in the deep-sea port of Gwadar in Pakistan and the related multimodal overland transport corridor between Kashgar in western China and Gwadar, a strategy addressed in Chapter 14 of this volume. The focus on the Polar Silk Road in the Arctic can also ease China's security of supply *problematique*, given Russia's presence and influence in the region.

Comparing US and Chinese geo-economics

There are both significant differences and similarities between the geo-economic approaches adopted by the United States and China in Greater Central Asia. They can be compared and contrasted in terms of critical connections and their characteristics.

Geographical scope: the US Silk Road initiative and its infrastructure development efforts have been geographically limited, focused on connecting Afghanistan to the regional flows of energy and trade in order to reduce the country's costly dependency on the United States and its allies as security providers. China's Belt and Road initiative – and its focus on infrastructure development – is, already by design, geographically much wider than the US approach, spanning multiple continents and numerous cities. Furthermore, China's initiative also has a clear domestic aspect, as Beijing has sought to advance economic growth as well as political stability and cohesion internally, especially in the less developed western parts of the country.

Strategic intent: whereas the broad geostrategic intent of the US Silk Road initiative has been more containment-oriented, China's global approach aims to secure its own economic growth and political stability, and through them, growing global political aspirations. The US plan has also been more reactive, particularly with regard to the situation in Afghanistan, whereas the Chinese one is more proactive in establishing facts on the ground to facilitate China's expanding economic and political reach.

Win-win vs. zero-sum approach: while China was not initially a part of the equation, US plans evolved towards a win-win situation that could also include a Chinese component. This was mostly due to the recognition of China's growing economic and political presence in Central Asia. However, the situation has arguably transformed under the Trump administration, which seems to adhere to a zero-sum approach in order to contain regional rivals and especially China's growing influence. Instead of a resuscitated Silk Road initiative in Central Asia, initial signs point towards a broader Indo-Pacific approach with a competitive edge. Although Chinese ventures are typically branded as apolitical and mutually beneficial economic and investment projects, it is clear that they are going to change the way in which the regional states and their respective elites are connected or, alternatively, by-passed. They are also likely to affect the way Chinese interests are either respected or, occasionally, criticised.

Key domains: US geostrategy typically concentrates on the maritime domain, where key shipping flows transport circa 90 per cent of global trade by volume and where the United States can project its military power freely. In Central Asia, the US adopted a strategic approach, which sought to advance regional security and connectivity on land. Subsequently, the US has put forth an idea of a broader Indo-Pacific approach that is likely to rely on the maritime domain. Although Chinese geostrategic plans encompass maritime routes, they also include serious efforts at establishing continental logistical corridors. In fact, the land component of the Belt and Road initiative was unveiled by the Chinese leadership before the maritime dimension. The Chinese (terrestrial) plans are less efficient when it comes to high volumes of transported cargo, but more efficient when it comes to speed. Transportation of energy resources over pipelines is a notable exception to this general rule, as it increases both the volume and speed of transported resources. China's security of supply is also improved as a function of the new connections.

Risks: The development of critical infrastructure on land carries significant political risks as the routes cross multiple polities and jurisdictions. China's ability to secure these routes would involve keeping key states and localities along the route from engaging in exceedingly high rent-seeking on development activities and investments. The gradual demand for security provision, especially with regard to the situation in Afghanistan, presents the People's Republic with additional challenges. The overall US maritime focus, meanwhile, allows the superpower to use its considerable military resources to secure shipping activity. However, this approach easily leaves the United States less interested in the more direct geo-economic control of and involvement in the localities and states along terrestrial routes. This is especially the case now that the 'war on terror' and Western interests in Afghanistan have transformed.

Conclusion

Both the United States and China have emphasised the establishment of resource and logistical connectivity in their respective Silk Road strategies – albeit the suggested direction, scope and means of establishment are unique in each. Especially the Chinese strategy focuses on infrastructure development that integrates the regional countries in a selected way to the overall logistical network, whose intensity and access-points can potentially be controlled by China. This form of control over the key resource flows in the Greater Central Asia region affects the ways in which economic dependencies and asymmetries will develop in the future.

By seeking to establish energy and logistics infrastructure, the US Silk Road strategy amounted to a regional and multilateral economic strategy along the north-to-south axis, seeking to connect resource-rich Central Asian countries to emerging and energy-hungry markets in Pakistan and India. Afghanistan, given its geographic location, stood as the critical gateway and potential benefactor in-between. Subsequently, the US has started to emphasise broader Indo-Pacific integration. The Chinese strategy, on the other hand, leverages primarily bilateral relations and state funding to establish east-to-west infrastructure connectivity not only with the Chinese neighbourhood, but also further afield, with Europe and Africa. So far, Afghanistan has been a relatively minor part of Chinese investments, but the continuously fragile security situation in this centrally located country is likely to demand increased attention from the People's Republic, too. This is especially the case if (and when) the United States and its allies withdraw from Afghanistan altogether.

All this suggests that the contemporary geostrategic environment in Greater Central Asia is increasingly organised and defined by the development of infrastructure and the emerging and strengthening force of regional and global flows through them. This implies a strategic shift of balance away from strict traditional geopolitics focused on relatively isolated and self-reliant territorial sovereign states towards taking into account interconnections – and with them new dependencies and asymmetries – within and across existing politico-juridical boundaries. All states involved in Central Asian affairs are reliant on various strategic flows to a growing, even if differing, degree. The ability to establish, maintain and ultimately secure related networks is central to today's power politics.

Notes

1 We have previously discussed the thematic in a chapter published in Rytövuori-Apunen, Helena ed. (2016) *The Regional Security Puzzle around Afghanistan: Bordering Practices in Central Asia and Beyond*. Opladen: Barbara Budrich Publishers. The authors would like to thank Mikael Wigell and Sören Scholvin for comments on an initial draft of this chapter.
2 For additional information, see www.carecprogram.org.
3 See e.g. projects homepage at: www.casa-1000.org/; and World Bank's project description at: http://projects.worldbank.org/P145054?lang=en.
4 Arguably, after John Kerry assumed leadership of the State Department from Clinton, interest to advance regional connectivity explicitly under the rubric of the Silk Road initiative has waned in Washington.

References

Aaltola, A., Käpylä, J. and Vuorisalo, V. (2014) *The Challenge of Global Commons and Flows for US Power: The Perils of Missing the Human Domain* (New York: Ashgate).
BBC. (2007) 'US-made Tajik-Afghan Bridge Opens', *BBC*, 26 August. Available at: http://news.bbc.co.uk/2/hi/asia-pacific/6964429.stm, accessed 8 February 2018.
Blake, R. O. (2013) 'The New Silk Road and Regional Economic Integration', *U.S. Department of State Remarks*, 13 March. Available at: https://2009-2017.state.gov/p/sca/rls/rmks/2013/206167.htm, accessed 8 February 2018.
Brill Olcott, M. (2013) 'China's Unmatched Influence in Central Asia', *Carnegie Endowment for International Peace*, 18 September. Available at: http://carnegieendowment.org/2013/09/18/china-s-unmatched-influence-in-central-asia/gzw2, accessed 31 January 2018.
Brugier, C. (2014) 'China's Way: The New Silk Road', *European Union Institute for Security Studies*, EUISS Brief No. 14. Available at: www.iss.europa.eu/uploads/media/Brief_14_New_Silk_Road.pdf, accessed 8 February 2018.
Burns, N. (2014) 'Passage to India: What Washington Can Do to Revive Relations with New Delhi', *Foreign Affairs*, 93, 5, pp. 132–141.
Chen, Y. (2014) 'China's Westward Strategy', *The Diplomat*, 15 January. Available at: http://thediplomat.com/2014/01/chinas-westward-strategy/, accessed 8 February 2018.

Clarke, M. (2017) 'China's "Three Warfares" in Xinjiang', *East Asia Forum*, 27 November. Available at: www.eastasiaforum.org/2017/11/27/chinas-three-warfares-in-xinjiang/, accessed 8 February 2018.

Clinton, H. (2011a) 'Remarks on India and the United States: A Vision for the 21st Century', *U.S. Department of State*, 20 July. Available at: https://2009-2017.state.gov/secretary/20092013clinton/rm/2011/07/168840.htm, accessed 8 February 2018.

Clinton, H. (2011b) 'Remarks at the New Silk Road Ministerial Meeting', *U.S. Department of State*, 22 September. Available at: https://2009-2017.state.gov/secretary/20092013 clinton/rm/2011/09/173807.htm, accessed 8 February 2018.

Clinton, H. (2011c) 'America's Pacific Century', *Foreign Policy*, November, 189, pp. 56–63.

Cooley, A. (2012) *Great Games, Local Rules: The New Great Power Contest in Central Asia* (Oxford: Oxford University Press).

Fedorenko, F. (2013) 'The New Silk Road Initiatives in Central Asia', *Rethink Institute Washington DC*, Rethink Paper No. 1. Available at: www.rethinkinstitute.org/wp-content/uploads/2013/11/Fedorenko-The-New-Silk-Road.pdf, accessed 8 February 2018.

Feng, E. (2014) 'Marching West: Regional Integration in Central Asia', *The Huffington Post*, 11 January. Available at: www.huffingtonpost.com/china-hands/marching-west-regional-integration_b_4581020.html, accessed 8 February 2018.

Fettweis, C. J. (2015) 'On Heartlands and Chessboards: Classical Geopolitics, Then and Now', *Orbis*, 59, 2, pp. 233–248.

Gaens, B. (2018) 'The United States and the Transforming Security Environment in Asia', in Aaltola, A., Salonius-Pasternak, C., Käpylä, J. and Sinkkonen, V. (eds), *Between Change and Continuity: Making Sense of America's Evolving Global Engagement*, Government's Analysis, Assessment and Research Activities (Helsinki: Prime Minister's Office), pp. 90–98. Available at: www.fiia.fi/en/publication/between-change-and-continuity, accessed 8 February 2018.

He, H. (2018) 'Is China's Belt and Road Infrastructure Development Plan about to Run Out of Money?', *South China Morning Post*, 14 April. Available at: www.scmp.com/news/china/economy/article/2141739/chinas-belt-and-road-infrastructure-development-plan-about-run, accessed 23 April 2018.

Jackson, A. and Abbas, G. (2018) 'China in Talks over Military Base in Remote Afghanistan: Officials', *Yahoo News*, 2 February. Available at: https://sg.news.yahoo.com/china-talks-over-military-remote-afghanistan-officials-030210755.html, accessed 8 February 2018.

Katz, M. N. (2018) 'The US-Russia Relationship', in Aaltola, A., Salonius-Pasternak, C., Käpylä, J. and Sinkkonen, V. (eds), *Between Change and Continuity: Making Sense of America's Evolving Global Engagement*, Government's Analysis, Assessment and Research Activities (Helsinki: Prime Minister's Office), pp. 81–89. Available at: www.fiia.fi/en/publication/between-change-and-continuity, accessed 8 February 2018.

Khanna, P. (2012) 'The New Silk Road is Made of Iron – and Stretches from Scotland to Singapore', *Quartz*, 30 September. Available at: https://qz.com/6140/the-new-silk-road-is-made-of-iron-and-stretches-from-scotland-to-singapore/, accessed 8 February 2018.

Kucera, J. (2011) 'The New Silk Road?', *The Diplomat*, 11 November. Available at: http://thediplomat.com/2011/11/the-new-silk-road/, accessed 8 February 2018.

Kucera, J. (2013a) 'Great Game in Central Asia after Afghanistan', *The Diplomat*, 27 March. Available at: http://thediplomat.com/2013/03/the-great-game-in-central-asia-after-afghanis tan/, accessed 8 February 2018.

Kucera, J. (2013b) 'U.S. Checked in Central Asia', *New York Times*, 4 November. Available at: www.nytimes.com/2013/11/05/opinion/us-checked-in-central-asia.html?_r=0, accessed 9 February 2018.

Kuchins, A. C., Sanderson, T. M. and Gordon, D. A. (2009) 'The Northern Distribution Network and the Modern Silk Road: Planning for Afghanistan's Future', *Center for Strategic & International Studies*, December. Available at: http://csis.org/files/public ation/091217_Kuchins_NorthernDistNet_Web.pdf, accessed 8 February 2018.

Kuchins, A. C., Sanderson, T. M. and Gordon, D. A. (2010) 'Afghanistan: Building the Missing Link in the Modern Silk Road', *The Washington Quarterly*, 33, 2, pp. 33–47.

Kurečić, P. (2010) 'The New Great Game: Rivalry of Geostrategies and Geoeconomies in Central Asia', *Croatian Geographical Bulletin*, 72, 1, pp. 21–48.

Kynge, J. (2017) 'Chinese Purchase of Overseas Ports Top $20bn in Past Year', *Financial Times*, 16 July. Available at: www.ft.com/content/e00fcfd4-6883-11e7-8526-7b38dcaef614, accessed 8 February 2018.

Lee, G. (2012) 'The New Silk Road and the Northern Distribution Network: A Golden Road to Central Asian Trade Reform?', *Open Society Foundation*, Occasional Paper Series No. 8. Available at: www.opensocietyfoundations.org/sites/default/files/OPS-No-8-20121019.pdf, accessed 8 February 2018.

McMaster, H. R. and Cohn, G. D. (2017) 'America First Doesn't Mean America Alone', *The Wall Street Journal*, 30 May. Available at: www.wsj.com/articles/america-first-doesnt-mean-america-alone-1496187426, accessed 4 September 2017.

Mankoff, J. (2013) 'The United States and Central Asia after 2014', *Center for Strategic & International Studies*, January. Available at: http://csis.org/files/publication/130122_Mankoff_USCentralAsia_Web.pdf, accessed 8 February 2018.

National Development and Reform Commission. (2015) 'Vision and Actions on Jointly Building Silk Road Economic Belt and 21st-Century Maritime Silk Road', *National Development and Reform Commission (NDRC) of People's Republic of China*, 28 March. Available at: http://en.ndrc.gov.cn/newsrelease/201503/t20150330_669367.html, accessed 8 February 2018.

Ng, E. (2017) 'Chinese Firms' Planned Investments of US$350b in Projects along New Silk Road Exposed to Risk', *South China Morning Post*, 24 October. Available at: www.scmp.com/business/companies/article/2116784/chinese-firms-planned-investments-us350b-projects-along-new-silk, accessed 8 February 2018.

Panda, A. (2013) 'China's Pivot West', *The Diplomat*, 29 October. Available at: https://thediplomat.com/2013/10/chinas-pivot-west/, accessed 8 February 2018.

Panda, A. (2017) 'Is the Trump Administration About to Take on China's Belt and Road Initiative', *The Diplomat*, 19 October. Available at: https://thediplomat.com/2017/10/is-the-trump-administration-about-to-take-on-chinas-belt-and-road-initiative/, accessed 9 February 2018.

Perlez, J. and Huang, Y. (2017) 'Behind China's $1 Trillion Plan to Shake Up the Economic Order', *New York Times*, 13 May. Available at: www.nytimes.com/2017/05/13/business/china-railway-one-belt-one-road-1-trillion-plan.html, accessed 8 February 2018.

Reuters. (2016a) 'Russia's Novatek Completes Deal to Sell Yamal LNG Stake to China's Silk Road', *Reuters*, 15 March. Available at: https://af.reuters.com/article/commodities News/idAFR4N0ZC01H, accessed 8 February 2018.

Reuters. (2016b) 'China's CNPC: Russia's Yamal LNG to Get Loans of around $10 Billion', *Reuters*, 21 April. Available at: www.reuters.com/article/russia-yamal-china-loans/chinas-cnpc-russias-yamal-lng-to-get-loans-of-around-10-billion-idUSR4N17L02O, accessed 8 February 2018.

Reuters. (2018) 'China Unveils Vision for "Polar Silk Road" across Arctic', *Reuters*, 26 January. Available at: www.reuters.com/article/us-china-arctic/china-unveils-vision-for-polar-silk-road-across-arctic-idUSKBN1FF0J8, accessed 8 February 2018.

Roberts, S., Anaïs, M., Moshes, A. and Pynnöniemi, K. (2014) 'The Eurasian Economic Union: Breaking the Pattern of Post-Soviet Integration?', *The Finnish Institute of International Affairs*, FIIA Analysis No. 3. Available at: www.fiia.fi/en/publication/the-eurasian-economic-union, accessed 8 February 2018.

Roney, T. (2013) 'The Shanghai Cooperation Organization: China's NATO?', *The Diplomat*, 11 September. Available at: http://thediplomat.com/2013/09/the-shanghai-cooperation-organization-chinas-nato-2/, accessed 8 February 2018.

Ross, D. (2018) 'Trump Is All Talk on Iran', *Foreign Policy*, 8 February. Available at: https://foreignpolicy.com/2018/02/08/trump-is-all-talk-on-iran/, accessed 9 February 2018.

Sherman, W. (2012) 'The United States and India: An Indispensable Partnership for the 21st Century', *U.S. Department of State*, 2 April. Available at: https://2009-2017.state.gov/p/us/rm/2012/187401.htm, accessed 31 January 2018.

Sinkkonen, V. (2018) 'US Foreign Policy: the "Trump Doctrine"', in Aaltola, A., Salonius-Pasternak, C., Käpylä, J. and Sinkkonen, V. (eds), *Between Change and Continuity: Making Sense of America's Evolving Global Engagement*, Government's Analysis, Assessment and Research Activities (Helsinki: Prime Minister's Office), pp. 36–44. Available at: www.fiia.fi/en/publication/between-change-and-continuity, accessed 8 February 2018.

Special Inspector General for Afghanistan Reconstruction. (2016) 'Afghanistan's Road Infrastructure: Sustainment Challenges and Lack of Repairs Put U.S. Investment at Risk', *Special Inspector General for Afghanistan Reconstruction*, SIGAR 17–11 Audit Report. Available at: www.sigar.mil/pdf/audits/SIGAR-17-11-AR.pdf, accessed 9 February 2018.

Starr, S. F. and Kuchins, A. C. (2010) 'The Key to Success in Afghanistan: A Modern Silk Road Strategy', *Central Asia-Caucasus Institute and Silk Road Studies Program*, May. Available at: http://csis.org/files/publication/100610_key_to_success_in_afghanistan.pdf, accessed 8 February 2018.

Sun, Y. (2013) 'March West: China's Response to the U.S. Rebalancing', *Brookings Institution*, 31 January. Available at: www.brookings.edu/blogs/up-front/posts/2013/01/31-china-us-sun, accessed 8 February 2018.

Szczudlik-Tatar, J. (2013) 'China's New Silk Road Diplomacy', *The Polish Institute of International Affairs*, PISM Policy Paper No. 34 (82). Available at: www.pism.pl/files/?id_plik=15818, accessed 8 February 2018.

Tiezzi, S. (2014) '"China's New Silk Road" Vision Revealed', *The Diplomat*, 9 May. Available at: http://thediplomat.com/2014/05/chinas-new-silk-road-vision-revealed/, accessed 8 February 2018.

Tillerson, R. (2017) 'Remarks on "Defining Our Relationship with India for the Next Century"', U.S. Department of State, 18 October. Available at: www.state.gov/secretary/remarks/2017/10/274913.htm, accessed 9 February 2018.

Tracy, L. M. (2013) 'The United States and the New Silk Road', *U.S. Department of State*, 25 October. Available at: https://2009-2017.state.gov/p/sca/rls/rmks/2013/215906.htm, accessed 8 February 2018.

US Government. (2009) 'Counterinsurgency Guide', *U.S. Government*, January. Available at: www.state.gov/documents/organization/119629.pdf, accessed 8 February 2018.

Wang, J. (2012) '"Marching Westwards": The Rebalancing of China's Geostrategy', *International and Strategic Studies Report*, 73.

Wang, Z. (2015) 'China's Alternative Diplomacy', *The Diplomat*, 30 January. Available at: http://thediplomat.com/2015/01/chinas-alternative-diplomacy/, accessed 31 January.

White House. (2017) 'National Security Strategy of the United States of America', *The White House*, December. Available at: www.whitehouse.gov/wp-content/uploads/2017/12/NSS-Final-12-18-2017-0905-2.pdf, accessed 8 February 2018.

Wu, J. and Zhang, Y. (2013) 'Xi Proposes a "New Silk Road" with Central Asia', *China Daily*, 8 September. Available at: http://usa.chinadaily.com.cn/china/2013-09/08/content_16952304.htm, accessed 8 February 2018.

Xinhuanet. (2013) 'China to Pave Way for Maritime Silk Road', *Xinhuanet*, 11 October. Available at: http://news.xinhuanet.com/english/china/2013-10/11/c_132790018.htm, accessed 25 June 2016.

5 Germany's liberal geo-economics

Using markets for strategic objectives

Hans Kundnani[1]

Introduction

When Edward Luttwak first wrote about a shift from geopolitics to geo-economics, his argument was essentially that economic power was displacing military power in international politics. Unlike others who saw cooperation replacing competition in the post-Cold War world, he believed that international relations would continue to follow the 'logic of conflict', which he called 'adversarial, zero-sum, and paradoxical' (1990, p. 17). Luttwak suggested that states would increasingly use 'disposable capital in lieu of firepower, civilian innovation in lieu of military-technical advancement, and market penetration in lieu of garrisons and bases' (1990, p. 17). Thus, for Luttwak, geo-economics primarily referred to the use of economic means for strategic objectives in a highly conflictive way – what he called 'the logic of war in the grammar of commerce' (1990, p. 19).

Since roughly the 2008 financial crisis, there has been a second wave of thinking about geo-economics (Baru 2012).[2] But the term is now often used in a confusing way. When contemporary writers refer to geo-economics, they often mean something different from, and 'softer' than what Luttwak had in mind. In particular, they use the term not to describe a foreign policy that uses economic means to pursue strategic objectives, but rather a foreign policy in pursuit of economic objectives – an approach that is sometimes also, confusingly, referred to as mercantilism (e.g. Martiningui and Youngs 2012). In other words, there are what might be called hard and soft definitions of geo-economics. Part of the confusion goes back to Luttwak himself. Although he concentrated on means rather than objectives, he did also suggest that a shift in means would lead to a recalibration of objectives: 'as the relevance of military threats and military alliances wanes, geo-economic priorities and modalities are becoming dominant in state action' (1990, p. 20).

The use of the soft definition of geo-economics – the pursuit of economic objectives – has led to a tendency to associate geo-economics exclusively with economic nationalism and to see it as incompatible with economic liberalism. On the basis of this tendency, much discussion of geo-economics has focussed on a perceived threat to, or even end of, the current form globalisation (e.g.

Leonard 2015). However, as Blackwill and Harris have recently shown, this opposition of geo-economics and economic liberalism is a false one. They argue that 'to the extent that leaders pursue prescriptions of economic liberalism (minimal state intervention, free trade, etc.) in the belief that these policies serve geopolitical interests, liberalism, too, falls comfortably among the many shades of geo-economics' (2016, p. 32). The reference to geopolitical objectives in the context of a geo-economic approach here is somewhat confusing. For consistency, I will use the term strategic objectives and use the term geopolitics to refer only to the use of political and military tools in the pursuit of such strategic objectives.

More importantly, I think that it is possible to imagine a version of geo-economics that is liberal in the economic sense – what might be called 'liberal geo-economics'. In the remainder of this chapter, I will use the term liberalism to refer specifically to economic liberalism. The relationship of geo-economics to the different concept of liberalism in international relations theory is another question that is outside the scope of my analysis. Wigell (2016) provides clear answers to this question, identifying Germany as an example of what he calls a 'liberal institutionalist' geo-economic power.

I (Kundnani 2011) have elsewhere argued that Germany should be understood as a 'geo-economic power'. This chapter argues that Germany's approach to the use of economic tools for strategic objectives within the European Union should be understood as an example of such a liberal, or perhaps even neoliberal, geo-economics. In particular, the chapter examines German policy in the context of the Eurozone and argues that, within it, Germany primarily uses markets to achieve its strategic objectives. While Germany is sometimes described as mercantilist, particularly because of its persistent current account surplus, its policy towards the Eurozone should in a different sense be seen as broadly liberal. In fact, German policy in the Eurozone can be seen as comparable to that of the United States in developing countries – often seen as the paradigmatic case of neoliberalism in an international context.

In the first section of this chapter, I elaborate on liberal geo-economics as a foreign policy strategy, and discuss the differences between geo-economic approaches by Western democracies on the one hand and authoritarian states on the other. In the second and third sections, I analyse how Germany has applied liberal geo-economics beyond the European Union and within it. In particular, I concentrate on Germany's recent confrontation with Russia and the Eurozone crisis. The fourth section puts Germany's liberal geo-economics in the context of the history of neoliberalism, and argues that Germany has used economic means to impose its preferences within the Eurozone in an analogous way to US policy in developing countries in the 1980s.

Liberal geo-economics

Much of the second wave of geo-economics has focussed specifically on the way authoritarian states, in particular China, Russia and the Arab Gulf states, use economic tools for strategic purposes (e.g. Baru 2012; Luttwak 2012; Thirlwell 2010; Wigell and Vihma 2016). In the last few years, particular attention has been given to Chinese infrastructure initiatives like the Belt and Road Initiative and the creation of new institutions like the Asian Infrastructure Investment Bank (e.g. Hilpert and Wacker 2015; see also Chapters 10 and 11 in this volume). As Blackwill and Harris write, the second wave of geo-economics 'is largely a story of the modern return of state capitalism' (2016, p. 9). States now own some of the world's biggest companies. They are among the world's largest investors and the biggest players in bond markets. These states are able to use state-owned enterprises (SOEs), state-owned banks (SOBs), sovereign wealth funds (SWFs) and national oil corporations (NOCs) as instruments of foreign policy. Hillary Clinton accordingly pointed out in a speech in 2011 that some 'governments are entering markets directly through their cash reserves, natural resources, and businesses they own and control'. They are shaping markets 'not just for profit, but to build and exercise power on behalf of the state'.[3]

According to this story of the return of state capitalism, Western democracies with open economies are at a distinct disadvantage because they do not control economic resources in the same way as authoritarian states do. Of course, China also faces difficulties of its own in using state resources for strategic objectives (Kärkkäinen 2016). Still, Western democracies appear to be limited in geo-economic power politics because they cannot use SOEs, SOBs, SWFs, and NOCs as instruments in the same way as China, Russia, and the Gulf states do. Admittedly, some Western democracies do have SOEs and SOBs – especially since the de facto nationalisation of some European banks following the financial crisis. France and Norway even possess SWFs, but these are exceptions rather than the rule. Since the neoliberal turn in the 1980s, Western democracies have sought to reduce their involvement in the economy to regulation and taxation and some limited subsidies. As such, they are relatively limited in the way they can use economic tools.

Critics of the idea of geo-economics are aware of these limits to the possibilities for democratic market states to use economic power for strategic purposes. Maull (1991) argued already during the first wave of geo-economics that the fear about German and Japanese economic domination 'fails to take adequately into account the nature of technological and economic power [, which] differs profoundly from traditional state power'. In particular, 'the resources of these forms of power are in the hands of economic actors such as firms or banks, which pursue their own objectives and strategies. Economic "power" thus cannot be easily manipulated and targeted by governments'.

Thus, at least in terms of trade and investment and energy policy, democracies do not seem to have the same options that authoritarian states do. Nor is it just that they do not possess the same resources – what Blackwill and Harris (2016) call 'geo-economic endowments'. It is also that democracies are to some extent constrained by the ideology of economic liberalism. After all, they have in the past deployed state-owned resources, for example at the time of the Marshall Plan, and could in theory once again do so. They could even once again nationalise companies, and deploy them to coerce other states in the way authoritarian states do. What prevents them is to a large extent the prevalence of the belief that this would be 'bad economics'. In other words, it is not so much that Western states are unable to deploy economic resources in the way that authoritarian states do but that they are unwilling to do so.

This suggests that the crucial difference between Western democracies and authoritarian states is not so much regime type as economic ideology. There is a tendency, based on the experience of the evolution of Western societies, to assume that economic and political liberalism always go together. But it is possible to imagine a democracy with state-capitalist economic ideology – Brazil under Lula da Silva and Dilma Rousseff may come closest – that would be able to deploy economic resources in a similar way as authoritarian states do. The reason the Arab Gulf states, China, and Russia seem to be at an advantage in geo-economics is not so much because they are authoritarian states but because, as Blackwill and Harris write, they are 'content to use the modern tools of economics and finance without regard for the liberal and neoliberal economic handling instructions and understandings that have traditionally accompanied their use' (2016, p. 13).

However, though European Union member states and the United States do not own the same economic resources as authoritarian states, they are nevertheless able to use, and have used economic means – albeit in a different way from authoritarian states. In particular, they can use markets to coerce or encourage other states to do what they want them to – what might be called 'liberal geo-economics'. For example, in what Blackwill and Harris call 'one of the most brazen geo-economic actions in the past century' (2016, p. 3), the United States forced the United Kingdom to end its invasion of Egypt and withdraw from the Suez Canal in 1956 by threatening to instigate a collapse of the pound. The United Kingdom was already experiencing a run on its currency and the prospect of an embargo by Arab oil exporters. President Eisenhower blocked the British request for an emergency loan from the International Monetary Fund (IMF), and threatened to dump part of the holdings of UK debt owned by the United States (Wheatley 2013, p. 20).

The smart sanctions that the United States has developed since 9/11, and used against non-state actors such as al-Qaeda, and countries such as Iran and Russia, are another, more contemporary example of the use of economic tools within a liberal context. What makes them different from traditional trade sanctions is that they seek to leverage the role of private sector actors, in particular banks and other financial institutions – the arteries of the international financial system (Zarate 2013; see also Chapter 8 in this volume). Rather than banning private sector actors from engaging with sanctioned entities or states, they simply seek to impose costs on them for doing so and thus change their calculus of interests. These sanctions can be seen as a twenty-first-century version of the naval blockade. They are effective above all because of the predominant role of the US dollar in the international financial system, and the size of the US market (Wheatley 2013).

US-led trade agreements, such as the Transatlantic Trade and Investment Partnership (TTIP), and the Trans-Pacific Partnership (TPP), are also liberal geo-economic tools (see Chapter 7 in this volume). The argument for these trade agreements, which were proposed by the Obama administration and have now been dropped by the Trump administration, was sometimes made in win-win liberal economic terms and sometimes in zero-sum strategic terms (Froman 2014; Rodrik 2015). The TTIP, it was argued, would help 'set rules and standards for trade in the 21st century' and thus support the liberal international order (Pritzker 2016). Some even referred to it as an 'economic NATO' (e.g. Ignatius 2012; Rasmussen 2013). Meanwhile, the TPP, it was argued, would help strengthen links between the United States and Asian countries. It was thus seen by some as a form of geo-economic containment of China (e.g. Tellis 2015). Whether the TPP and the TTIP would have been successful in achieving these objectives is beside the point. The point here is simply that these two economic initiatives were believed by their proponents to help achieve strategic objectives that go beyond economics.

These examples illustrate that it is perfectly possible to conceive a liberal version of geo-economics in the hard sense, with the term liberal being understood in the economic sense. Economic liberals can seek to use economic tools for strategic purposes as much as economic nationalists or mercantilists. Where they differ is in how exactly these tools should be deployed, and what role the state should play in the deployment of these tools. Whereas mercantilists view extensive state intervention in the economy to be the in the national interest, liberals see 'laissez-faire as merely a better means of advancing the interests of the state' (Blackwill and Harris 2016, p. 31). In particular, where they differ is on the question of whether the state should itself deploy economic resources to coerce other states or alternatively seek to leverage the market to coerce other states – in other words, whether states should use economic tools directly or indirectly.

Germany as a geo-economic power beyond the European Union

In an essay published in summer 2011, I argued that Germany was a 'geo-economic power' (Kundnani 2011). Before German reunification in 1990, and even in the first decade after it, the Federal Republic had come closer than any other state (apart, perhaps, from Japan) to the ideal typical role of a 'civilian power' that Maull (1991) had described – in other words, a power that seeks above all to 'civilise' international relations. But by 2010, this concept no longer seemed to capture Germany as an actor in international politics. In the 2000s, Germany's commitment to multilateralism seemed to have weakened somewhat – it became more Eurosceptic and more willing to break with its allies and partners – and its foreign policy seemed to have become more realist as its economy became more export-dependent. In particular, with the euro crisis that began in 2010, it seemed willing to use its economic power to impose its preferences on others in the Eurozone.

At the same time, however, Germany was a long way from again becoming a classical great power with a 'normal' attitude to the use of military force, as realist theorists such as John Mearsheimer (1990) had feared after the end of the Cold War. Rather, Germany's foreign policy seemed to be characterised by an unusual mixture of economic assertiveness within the European Union, and military abstinence beyond the European Union. This contrast was particularly striking after Germany's abstention in the UN Security Council Resolution on the introduction of a no-fly zone over Libya in 2011. Seeing these developments, I had the impression that Luttwak's concept of geo-economics was a useful way of understanding German foreign policy. I even went so far as to suggest that the combination of Germany's willingness to use economic tools and its reluctance to use military tools made it 'the purest example of a geo-economic power in the world today' (2011, p. 42).

Most of the discussion that has taken place about whether Germany is a geo-economic power, as I had argued, has focussed on German foreign policy beyond the European Union (e.g. Szabo 2015). In particular, since the Ukraine crisis, many observers have perceived a dramatic change in German foreign policy. According to some observers, Germany has even rediscovered geopolitics. These observers suggest that even if there had been a 'primacy of economics' in German foreign policy before the Ukraine crisis, it had been only a temporary aberration, and that the 'primacy of politics' had now been restored (author's own conversations with European and US analysts and policymakers). That in turn showed that Germany was no longer a geo-economic power, as I had argued. I had 'improperly extrapolated from the foreign policy of the "black-yellow" government between 2009 and 2013', as Maull put it at a discussion at the German Council on Foreign Relations in Berlin in February 2015.

German policy towards Russia has certainly changed since the Ukraine crisis began. Going back to Gerhard Schröder's time in office, Russia had been the paradigmatic case of a tendency in German foreign policy to pursue economic objectives beyond the European Union. After the annexation of Crimea, however, Chancellor Angela Merkel was prepared to overrule large sections of the German business community, and impose tough sanctions against Russia. Thus, Germany subordinated its extensive economic interests in Russia to the strategic interest of protecting the European security order that was now threatened by Russian revisionism. In other words, Germany's response to the Ukraine crisis seemed to suggest it was reprioritising strategic objectives over economic ones, though it remains unclear whether Germany will remain committed to this new approach in the medium term.

However, even if it lasts, Germany's tough new approach to Russia is based largely on economic rather than military means. While Chancellor Merkel has supported sanctions against Russia, she has blocked various other attempts to use military means as part of a new strategy of containment against Russia. For example, ahead of the NATO summit in Wales in 2014, Germany opposed plans to create a permanent military presence in Central and Eastern Europe. In February 2015, when a debate started in the United States about providing direct military assistance to Ukraine, and reports suggested that the Obama administration was taking a 'fresh look' at the issue (Gordon and Schmitt 2015), Merkel immediately and publicly opposed it (Gordon, Smale and Erlanger 2015). The point here is not whether German policy was right or wrong, but that even after the Ukraine crisis Germany continued to be very reluctant to use military means. As a result, the approach of the European Union towards Russia, led by Germany, was largely geo-economic (Moravcsik 2016).

Though the strategic shock of the Ukraine crisis did lead to a new focus on defence policy, it is not yet clear what its outcome will be. Germany has taken steps to increase defence spending, but it remains uncertain whether Germany's defence spending will significantly increase as a proportion of its gross domestic product, let alone reach the 2 per cent target. During the last years, Germany has also made a significant military contribution to the fight against the so-called Islamic State. For example, in 2014 it supplied machine guns, anti-tank rockets and five armoured personnel carriers to the Kurdish Peshmerga in northern Iraq, and sent 150 soldiers to train Kurdish security forces. After the terror attacks in Paris in November 2015, Germany provided six reconnaissance Tornados and sent a frigate to the Mediterranean in order to support the military operations led by France. Germany also expanded the deployment of its army as part of the UN mission in Mali. However, there is nothing new about these steps, apart perhaps from the supply of weapons to a conflict region. After all, the German army has taken part in peacekeeping operations since the 1990s, and has even been involved in combat operations in Afghanistan and Kosovo.

Therefore, it seems misleading to argue that Germany has rediscovered geopolitics. Rather, it seems to have discovered the hard version of geo-economics. Though it may now be reprioritising strategic objectives over economic ones, and hence become a 'harder' kind of geo-economic power beyond the European Union, it remains deeply sceptical about the use of military means. Moreover, even this shift from economic to strategic objectives seems for the moment to be limited to Germany's Russia policy – and recent developments such as the Nord Stream II gas pipeline project shows that the old tendency in German Russia policy still exists. Meanwhile, elsewhere in the world, Germany is still to a large extent acting as a geo-economic power in the soft sense – in other words, as a power that primarily pursues economic objectives.

German geo-economics within the European Union

Regardless of how one should understand the changes taking place in German policy towards the rest of the world beyond the European Union, there also remains a question about whether Germany is acting as a geo-economic power within the European Union – and if so, in what sense. Germany has acted as a geo-economic power in the hard sense within the European Union, because it has been willing to use its economic power to impose its preferences on other Eurozone countries, particularly since the Eurozone crisis began in 2010. When I wrote about Germany's 'economic assertiveness' in my 2011 article, it was primarily this role of Germany within the Eurozone that I had in mind. Indeed, such was Germany's assertiveness in this context that there was much discussion about Germany as a European hegemon and even about a German empire (Kundnani 2012a; 2012b).

The reason why it has been difficult to recognise Germany as a geo-economic power within the European Union may be the complexity of its intentions – as in the case of US-led trade initiatives such as TTIP and TPP. Both critics and supporters of Germany's policy in the Eurozone have been reluctant, for different reasons, to describe it as pursuing strategic objectives. Critics tend to see Germany as pursuing merely commercial or economic objectives, and accuse it of mercantilism – particularly because Germany refuses to take measures to reduce its persistent current account surplus (e.g. Wolf 2012). Those who are more sympathetic to German policy see it as a normative power that seeks to establish and maintain rules (e.g. Rachman 2017).

In reality, Germany's strategic objective has been to prevent a break-up of the European single currency, and with it a collapse of the European Union itself. It would be too simplistic to reduce Germany's commitment to the euro and the European Union to economic benefits. Generations of German policymakers have internalised the idea that European integration is in the national interest in a much broader sense. In particular, it is seen as having been central to the security and rehabilitation of the Federal Republic. Blackwill and Harris write that Germany's push to create the single currency itself should be seen as a geo-economic initiative that aimed to 'preempt Western fears over Germany's increasing strength' (2016, p. 28).

This is not to say that Germany's objectives during the Eurozone crisis have been exclusively strategic. It clearly has also pursued economic objectives. In particular, it has sought to prevent the emergence of a 'transfer union' – in other words, an European Union in which fiscally responsible member states would pay for fiscally irresponsible ones. This is the reason Germany has persistently opposed a mutualisation of European debt in the form of Eurobonds. It has also sought to maintain price stability – a longstanding German preference. In other words, although Germany has pursued a mixture of economic and strategic objectives during the Eurozone crisis, it still makes sense to think of it as a geo-economic power: 'states can and often do design geoeconomic policies that simultaneously advance multiple interests – geopolitical, economic, and otherwise' (Blackwill and Harris 2016, p. 27).

Since the crisis began, Germany has attempted to reconcile its economic and strategic objectives by offering crisis countries loans (bailouts), while making them conditional on fiscal consolidation and structural reform. This began with the first bailout for Greece in 2010, which required it to reduce its deficit through a combination of cutting government spending, raising revenue through privatising state assets, and reforming the labour market. As the crisis spread to other countries over the next few years, Germany also pushed through the Fiscal Compact, which commits EU member states to introduce something similar to the balanced-budget amendment – the so-called *Schuldenbremse* – that Germany had introduced in 2009. A series of other measures pushed by Germany, such as the European Semester, step up the coordination and monitoring of fiscal deficits, targeted debt and deficits, and introduce sanctions against non-compliant states – in particular the European Commission's Excessive Deficit Procedure.

This means that Germany has sought to constitutionalise economic decision-making in the Eurozone – establishing and enforcing rules – and in doing so to institutionalise its own preferences. There has been much discussion about whether these preferences primarily reflected ideas or interests. Some have argued that the German approach has been informed by norms derived from German economics (in particular, the theory of ordoliberalism) and from German history (in particular, the collective memory of hyperinflation) (e.g. Bofinger 2016; Dullien and Guérot 2012). Others argue that Germany's preferences simply reflect its national interests as a creditor country (e.g. Burda 2015). But the source of Germany's preferences is beside the point here. Since it has sought to use its economic power as the largest creditor country in the Eurozone to export its preferences to the rest of the continent, it seems appropriate to refer to it as a geo-economic power in the hard sense.

Unlike in the case of its policy towards Russia, there has not been a significant shift in Germany's approach to the Eurozone in the last few years. If anything, Germany has gone even further than it had earlier in the crisis in the use of its economic power. Perhaps the most dramatic and extreme illustration of Germany's hard geo-economics in the Eurozone is the emergency summit held in Brussels in July 2015. At the summit, Finance Minister Wolfgang Schäuble proposed to place € 50 billion of Greek assets in a trust fund in Luxembourg, and temporarily eject Greece from the Eurozone if it did not agree to the creditors' terms. Greece eventually agreed to the creditors' terms, which laid the basis for a third bailout shortly afterwards. Nevertheless, the summit may come to be seen as a turning point in the crisis. For example, the Belgian economist Paul de Grauwe, a widely recognised expert on the euro, said a new template for Eurozone governance had been created: 'submit to German rule or leave'.[4]

German neoliberalism

Although Germany's economic policy in the context of the Eurozone has been described, with some justification, as mercantilist, it is rather liberal in another sense, or as I show in this section, neoliberal. In fact, German economists and policymakers reject the accusation of mercantilism precisely because they do not see it as the role of the state to reduce Germany's current account surplus. They argue that the surplus is an outcome variable rather than a policy variable. According to them, it reflects the relative competitiveness of the German economy. It is the product of market forces and not a deliberate strategy by the German government. In particular, they argue it would be inappropriate for the government to intervene in the economy to raise wages or take other measures so as to increase aggregate demand (author's own conversations). In short, Germany's economic policy is anti-Keynesian.

Germany's approach to the Eurozone crisis should be seen as liberal because of the way Germany has sought to use market forces to discipline other Eurozone countries. It used fluctuations in interest rates to force Eurozone countries such as Italy and Spain to implement structural reforms that it regarded as necessary to make the Eurozone more competitive (Woodruff 2016). 'Market interest rates do play a role in pushing governments towards reforms', Jens Weidmann, president of the German Bundesbank, said in an interview with the *Financial Times* in 2011.[5] It has even been suggested that German officials asked China to stop buying debt of distressed Eurozone states in order to maintain pressure to carry out structural reform (Otero-Iglesias 2014). Germany has also sought to use this kind of market pressure to push Eurozone countries to agree to the further steps of integration.

Specifically, Germany's approach to the Eurozone should be seen as neoliberal. The concept of neoliberalism has been used in multiple different ways (Venugopal 2015). But according to a recent, much-discussed paper by three IMF officials, the so-called neoliberal agenda has two elements: first, increased competition through the opening up of domestic markets, including financial markets, to foreign competition; and second, a smaller role for the state, achieved through austerity and privatisation (Ostry, Loungani and Furceri 2016). Germany has pursued both of these elements in its Eurozone policy. In particular, since the creation of the euro, it has focussed on reducing the role of the state. The Maastricht criteria and the Stability and Growth Pact, which were both driven by Germany, have set limits on the ability of governments to run fiscal deficits and accumulate debt. In contrast to many German policymakers, the aforementioned IMF officials identify austerity as a problematic feature of the neoliberal agenda that should now be re-assessed.

That Germany's approach to the Eurozone is a neoliberal one becomes even clearer when one compares it with the approach of the United States towards developing countries in the 1980s, which is often seen as a paradigmatic case of neoliberalism in an international context. Neoliberalism is generally seen as having been 'exported internationally via multilateral institutions and economic experts' (Davies 2014, p. 314) – in particular, through the IMF. It was Germany that insisted, despite opposition from other EU member states and the European Commission, on involving the IMF in the first bailout of Greece (Art 2015). With the IMF on board, the response to the crisis followed the same basic approach that the IMF had taken in developing countries in the 1980s: structural adjustment in exchange for loans.

Thus, Germany can be seen as applying methods that had previously been applied only to developing countries within the European Union itself. As Blyth has put it: 'It was the Global South where the policies unleashed upon the periphery of Europe [...] were road tested' (2013, p. 160). This helps to explain the outrage of some Europeans to German proposals in the euro crisis such as the involvement of the IMF. Greece's Finance Minister Giorgos Papaconstantinou claimed that French President Nicolas Sarkozy was 'apoplectic' at the decision to involve the IMF. 'The IMF is not for Europe', Sarkozy said, according to Papaconstantinou. 'It's for Burkina Faso' (2016, location 1465–1470).

The idea that German policy in the Eurozone resembles US policy towards developing countries in the 1980s – a version of neoliberalism that Venugopal has called 'a project of neo-colonial domination' (2015, pp. 175–176) – is in itself shocking. After all, Germany has quite different legal and moral obligations to its Eurozone partners than the United States had to developing countries. Many pro-Europeans, including Schäuble, think of the European Union as a *Schicksalsgemeinschaft*, or community of fate, based on solidarity. The smaller group of 19 EU member states that joined the single currency made an even deeper political and economic commitment to each other. One might expect that countries that share a single currency would have an obligation to undertake adjustment in a more symmetrical way than in other debt crises. However, the burden of adjustment has been on the debtor countries in the Eurozone much like in other debt crises. In that sense, Germany has acted as a normal creditor country.

However, in some ways, Germany's approach to the euro crisis has been even more extreme than US policy towards developing countries. The creation of the single currency has deprived Eurozone countries of the option of devaluing their currency, which is one of the few options that debtor countries usually have. Hence, adjustment in the Eurozone was not just asymmetric but had to be based entirely on internal devaluation – in other words, cuts in wages and other costs. Several economists, most prominently Joseph Stiglitz (2016), argue that this harsh internal devaluation led to extremely high levels of unemployment in Greece and Spain. As explained above, the institutional framework of the European Union has also allowed Germany to be more intrusive, and go further in transforming societies in the name of competitiveness than the United States was able to in developing countries.

Conclusion

In the second wave of discussion around geo-economics, which has focussed on the use of economic power by authoritarian states such China, Russia and the Arab Gulf states, there has been a tendency to equate the concept with economic nationalism as opposed to economic liberalism. However, this approach is too simple. The equation of geo-economics and economic nationalism underplays the way that Western democracies, including Germany and the United States, have sought to use economic means for strategic objectives. Whereas authoritarian states deploy economic power directly, it appears that Western democracies use economic power indirectly, relying on market forces to coerce other states. This approach might be called liberal geo-economics.

In this chapter, I have taken up the main argument from my 2011 article that Germany is a geo-economic power. The way Germany has reacted to the crisis in Ukraine – imposing sanctions on Russia but opposing the use of military power – confirms the geo-economic paradigm of German foreign policy. Rather than discovering geopolitics, Germany shifted to a hard version of geo-economics, meaning the pursuit of strategic objectives. It appears to have replaced soft geo-economics, which aims at economic objectives and was more characteristic of Germany's approach towards Russia before the crisis. I have shown that Germany's reaction to the Eurozone crisis is an example of liberal geo-economics. Germany's liberal – or rather neoliberal – approach might somewhat obscure that what we are witnessing is geo-economics: the use of economic power, in particular loans, to achieve strategic objectives. It is liberal geo-economics, because of the way Germany has used market pressure, in particular interest rate fluctuations, to coerce other Eurozone countries to agree to measures that institutionalise its own preferences and constitutionalise economic decision-making within the framework of the European single currency.

Notes

1 The author is grateful to Mikael Wigell and Sören Scholvin for the suggestions that they made on an earlier draft of this chapter.
2 In his contribution to this volume, Braz Baracuhy identifies four generations of thinking about geo-economics. The first and second generations, at the beginning of the twentieth century and in the 1970s and 1980s, pre-date the term itself. The third and fourth generations correspond to what Baru (2012) calls the two waves of geo-economics. Thus Baracuhy's categorisation amplifies rather than contradicts Baru's.
3 Speech given on 14 October 2011. Available at www.state.gov/secretary/20092013clinton/rm/2011/10/175552.htm.
4 Tweet from 12 July 2015. Available at twitter.com/pdegrauwe/status/620348860481 806336.
5 Interview published on 13 November 2011. Available at www.ft.com/content/b3a2d19e-0de4-11e1-9d40-00144feabdc0.

References

Art, D. (2015) 'The German Rescue of the Eurozone: How Germany Is Getting the Eurozone it Always Wanted', *Political Science Quarterly*, 130, 2, pp. 181–212.

Baru, S. (2012) 'Geo-economics and Strategy', *Survival*, 54, 3, pp. 47–58.

Blackwill, R. D. and Harris, J. M. (2016) *War by Other Means: Geoeconomics and Statecraft* (Cambridge, MA: Harvard University Press).

Blyth, M. (2013) *Austerity. The History of a Dangerous Idea* (New York: Oxford University Press).

Bofinger, P. (2016) 'German Macroeconomics: The Long Shadow of Walter Eucken', in Bratsiotis, G. and Cobham, D. (eds), *German Macro: How It's Different and Why That Matters*, European Policy Centre, pp. 8–19. Available at: www.epc.eu/documents/uploads/pub_6497_german_macro_how_it_s_different_and_why_that_matters.pdf, accessed 21 November 2017.

Burda, M. (2015) 'Dispelling Three Myths on Economics in Germany', *VoxEU.org*. Available at: http://voxeu.org/article/dispelling-three-myths-economics-germany, accessed 18 November 2016.

Davies, W. (2014) 'Neoliberalism: A Bibliographic Review', *Theory, Culture and Society*, 31, 7/8, pp. 309–317.

Dullien, S. and Guérot, U. (2012) 'The Long Shadow of Ordoliberalism: Germany's Approach to the Euro Crisis', *European Council on Foreign Relations*, Policy Briefing. Available at: www.ecfr.eu/page/-/ECFR49_GERMANY_BRIEF.pdf, accessed 21 November 2017.

Froman, M. B. (2014) 'The Strategic Logic of Trade', *Foreign Affairs*, November/December 2014 Issue. Available at: www.foreignaffairs.com/articles/americas/strategic-logic-trade, accessed 18 November 2016.

Gordon, M. R. and Schmitt, E. (2015) 'U.S. Considers Supplying Arms to Ukraine Forces, Officials Say', *New York Times*, 1 February.

Gordon, M. R., Smale, A. and Erlanger, S. (2015) 'Western Nations Split on Arming Kiev Forces', *New York Times*, 7 February.

Hilpert, H. G. and Wacker. G. (2015) 'Geoeconomics Meets Geopolitics: China's New Economic and Foreign Policy Initiatives', *German Institute for International and Security Affairs*, SWP Comments. Available at: www.swp-berlin.org/fileadmin/contents/products/comments/2015C33_hlp_wkr.pdf, accessed 18 November 2016.

Ignatius, D. (2012) 'A Free-trade Agreement with Europe?', *Washington Post*, 5 December. Available at: www.washingtonpost.com/opinions/david-ignatius-a-free-trade-agreement-with-europe/2012/12/05/7880b6b2-3f02-11e2-bca3-aadc9b7e29c5_story.html?utm_term=.76e9414ca4b3, accessed 29 September 2017.

Kärkkäinen, A. (2016) 'Does China Have a Geoeconomic Strategy towards Zimbabwe? The Case of the Zimbabwean Natural Resource Sector', *Asia Europe Journal*, 14, 2, pp. 185–202.

Kundnani, H. (2011) 'Germany as a Geo-economic Power', *Washington Quarterly*, 34, 3, pp. 31–45.

Kundnani, H. (2012a) 'Was für ein Hegemon? Berlins Politik Führt zu keinem Deutschen, sondern einem Chaotischen Europa', *Deutsche Gesellschaft für Auswärtige Politik e.V.* Available at: https://zeitschrift-ip.dgap.org/de/ip-die-zeitschrift/archiv/jahrgang-2012/mai-juni/was-f%C3%BCr-ein-hegemon, accessed 18 November 2016.

Kundnani, H. (2012b) 'A German Empire?', *Project Syndicate*, 21 June. Available at: www.project-syndicate.org/blog/a-german-empire?barrier=true, accessed 18 November 2016.

Leonard, M. (2015) 'Geo-economics: Seven Challenges to Globalization', *World Economic Forum*. Available at: www3.weforum.org/docs/WEF_Geo-economics_7_Challenges_Globalization_2015_report.pdf, accessed 18 November 2016.

Luttwak, E. N. (1990) 'From Geopolitics to Geo-economics: Logic of Conflict, Grammar of Commerce', *The National Interest*, 20, pp. 17–23.

Luttwak, E. N. (2012) *The Rise of China vs. The Logic of Strategy* (Cambridge, MA: Harvard University Press).

Martiningui, A. and Youngs, R. (2012) *Challenges for European Foreign Policy in 2012: What kind of Geo-economic Europe?* (Madrid: Fundación para las Relaciones Internacionales y el Diálogo Exterior).

Maull, H. W. (1991) 'Germany and Japan: The New Civilian Powers', *Foreign Affairs*, Winter 1990/91 Issue. Available at: www.foreignaffairs.com/articles/46262/hanns-w-maull/germany-and-japan-the-new-civilian-powers, accessed 18 November 2016.

Mearsheimer, J. J. (1990) 'Back to the Future: Instability in Europe after the Cold War', *International Security*, 15, 1, pp. 5–56.

Moravcsik, A. (2016) 'Lessons from Ukraine: Why a Europe-Led Geo-economic Strategy is Succeeding', *Transatlantic Academy*, 2015–2016 Paper Series No. 10. Available at: www.gmfus.org/file/8807/download, accessed 18 November 2016.

Ostry, J. D., Loungani, P. and Furceri, D. (2016) 'Neoliberalism: Oversold?', *Finance and Development*, 53, 2, pp. 38–41.

Otero-Iglesias, M. (2014) 'The Euro for China: Too Important to Fail and Too Difficult to Rescue', *Pacific Review*, 27, 5, pp. 703–728.

Papaconstantinou, G. (2016) *Game Over. The Inside Story of the Greek Crisis* [Kindle edition].

Pritzker, P. (2016) 'Why U.S. Leadership on Trade and Investment is a Linchpin of the International Liberal Order', *Brookings*, 8 June. Available at: www.brookings.edu/blog/order-from-chaos/2016/06/08/why-u-s-leadership-on-trade-and-investment-is-a-linchpin-of-the-international-liberal-order/, accessed 29 September 2017.

Rachman, G. (2017) 'The Isolation of Angela Merkel's Germany', *Financial Times*, 6 March 2017. Available at: www.ft.com/content/19e7bc4e-0010-11e7-8d8e-a5e3738f9ae4?mhq5j=e7, accessed 29 September 2017.

Rasmussen, A. F. (2013) 'Speech at the Confederation of Danish Industry conference', 7 October. Available at: www.nato.int/cps/en/natolive/opinions_103863.htm, accessed 29 September 2017.

Rodrik, D. (2015) 'The Muddled Case for Trade Agreements', *Project Syndicate*, 11 July. Available at: www.project-syndicate.org/commentary/regional-trade-agreement-corporate-capture-by-dani-rodrik-2015-06, accessed 21 November 2017.

Stiglitz, J. E. (2016) *The Euro: How a Common Currency Threatens the Future* (New York: Norton).

Szabo, S. F. (2015) *Germany, Russia, and the Rise of Geo-economics* (London: Bloomsbury).

Tellis, A. J. (2015) 'The Geopolitics of the TTIP and the TPP', in Baru, S. and Dogra, S. (eds), *Power Shifts and New Blocs in the Global Trading System* (London: International Institute for Strategic Studies), pp. 93–119.

Thirlwell, M. P. (2010) 'The Return of Geo-economics: Globalisation and National Security', *Lowy Institute*, Perspectives. Available at: www.lowyinstitute.org/sites/default/files/pubfiles/Thirlwell%2C_The_return_of_geo-economics_web_and_print_1.pdf, accessed 18 November 2016.

Venugopal, R. (2015) 'Neoliberalism as Concept', *Economy and Society*, 44, 2, pp. 165–187.

Wheatley, A. (2013) 'The Origins and Use of Currency Power', in Wheatley, A. (ed.), *The Power of Currencies and the Currencies of Power* (London: International Institute for Strategic Studies), pp. 17–43.

Wigell, M. (2016) 'Conceptualizing Regional Powers' Geoeconomic Strategies: Neo-imperialism, Neo-mercantilism, Hegemony, and Liberal Institutionalism', *Asia Europe Journal*, 14, 2, pp. 135–151.

Wigell, M. and Vihma, A. (2016) 'Geopolitics versus Geoeconomics: the Case of Russia's Geostrategy and its Effects on the EU', *International Affairs*, 92, 3, pp. 605–627.

Wolf, M. (2012) 'Why Exit is an Option for Germany', *Financial Times*, 25 September. Available at: www.ft.com/content/1e2f2cd0-064e-11e2-bd29-00144feabdc0, accessed 24 October 2017.

Woodruff, D. M. (2016) 'Governing by Panic: The Politics of the Eurozone Crisis', *Politics and Society*, 44, 1, pp. 81–116.

Zarate, J. (2013) *Treasury's War: The Unleashing of a New Era of Financial Warfare* (New York: Public Affairs).

6 The Russian 'pivot' to Asia-Pacific

Geo-economic expectations and disappointments

Pavel K. Baev[1]

Introduction

The spectacularly dynamic Asia-Pacific region is the part of the world where geo-economics, understood as the use of economic tools by states for achieving strategic aims, has a unique and fast-evolving prominence. In much of current security analyses and media commentary, it is the escalation of tensions around tiny islets, in the South China Sea in particular, which gets the prime attention. In fact, the most important dynamic here is in conflict resolution, so that the region, which for more than a century saw a succession of devastating wars, is now the home of the phenomenon known as the East Asian peace.[2] It goes beyond the scope of this analysis to provide an explanation of this phenomenon, but it is essential to point out that the main driving force in its evolution is of geo-economic nature, as state actors seek to advance their strategic interests primarily by economic means. In one state after another, including China since the beginning of 1980s, political leadership made a conscious choice for economic modernisation and growth, and against scoring victories in external and domestic conflicts (Tønnesson 2017). This sustained priority has determined the diminished importance of military force as an instrument of policy and the pivotal importance of economic levers for securing the most advantageous position in the highly competitive environment.

Russia was late in recognising the power of economic dynamics in Asia-Pacific, and has started to undertake political efforts towards connecting with this growth area only since the beginning of the 2000s, when the resonance of the 1997–1999 crisis subsided. President Dmitry Medvedev's proposition for modernisation energised those efforts, and the 2012 summit of the Asia-Pacific Economic Cooperation (APEC) forum in Vladivostok provided a useful focal point for them. The new pivot of US policy, announced by President Barack Obama at the start of this decade, also convinced Russian leadership of the urgent need to pay more attention to the interplay of strategic and economic developments in Asia-Pacific, and to expand ties with eastern neighbours. This need has become overwhelming since 2014, with the onset of a new confrontation between Russia and the West, caused by the annexation of Crimea and the aggression into eastern Ukraine. However, the results of Russian attempts to gain new strength and status from turning to Asia, and above all from upgrading the strategic partnership with China, are not only disappointing for Moscow but also alarming for its counterparts in both Europe and Asia.

This chapter aims to combine an evaluation of Russia's application of economic instruments towards its strategic aims in Asia-Pacific, and an assessment of possible consequences of disappointment in the Russian leadership about the lack of success in this geo-economics Russian-style. It starts with examining the trajectory of Russian efforts at connecting with the success story of sustained economic growth in East Asia and gaining a position of strength in the complex geo-economic interactions in Asia-Pacific. The analysis then proceeds to examine the process and the context of making a natural gas mega-deal with China in May 2014, and to uncovering how Russia has found itself on the receiving end of Asian geo-economics. Finally, Russian efforts at producing a better blend of geo-economics and geopolitics are evaluated.

The trajectory of Russian geo-economic manoeuvring

The Russian leadership's understanding of globalisation may not be particularly sophisticated in its rather underdeveloped vision of a multipolar world, but one remarkable feature is the proposition that the need to control the production of natural resources, particularly hydrocarbons, is what drives the increasing competition between major centres of power. This proposition comes out as clearly in the National Security Strategy, approved by Vladimir Putin on the last day of 2015, as it did in the series of previous fundamental state documents (Oliker 2016). The 2016 *Foreign Policy Concept* also identifies the escalation of a 'struggle for resources' as a driver of increasing global tensions, and points to global power potential shifting to the Asia-Pacific region (Frolov 2016). Expanding state control over the development of natural resources and, in particular, over the energy sector is a natural corollary from this assumption. This fixation on control makes such state-owned super corporations as Gazprom and Rosneft Russia's instruments of choice for engaging in the strategic competition between major powers.

In Western analyses, galvanised by the 'gas skirmish' of 2006 and 'gas war' of 2009 (in which Ukraine was the immediate target of Russian supply cuts, but the European Union was the main addressee), the prime attention has been on Russia's 'weaponisation' of its oil-and-gas exports to Europe (e.g. Hedlund 2014). Yet, in the ongoing crisis between Russia and Ukraine, the 'gas weapon' has turned out to be of little use for Moscow. It can hardly be wielded because this would undermine Gazprom's struggles to defend its share of the fast-changing European market. However, Russian proactive geo-economics has not been limited to the European theatre, but it has also been utilised in Asia-Pacific. Here as well, Moscow's choice of failproof instrument has been oil-and-gas exports.

In the late 1980s, Mikhail Gorbachev's 'new political thinking' generated many ideas congenial to the East Asian peace, but they were propagated in vain, as the Soviet economic crisis acquired catastrophic proportions. The newly born

Russian state inherited very low level of engagement with and respect in Asia-Pacific. The post-Soviet economic crisis of the 1990s affected the Russian Far East even worse than its other regions, which effectively cut Russia out of the evolving economic dynamics in East Asia (Treisman 2010).

On the path of recovery from the 1998 economic crisis, Russian energy companies, such as TNK-BP and Yukos, which were looking for new markets for their productive assets in Eastern Siberia, began exploring opportunities for reconnecting with Asia. However, the Putin administration saw a powerful geo-economic means in these assets and decided to take them away from maverick oligarchs. By unleashing a series of forceful actions aimed at capturing control over key projects, the Kremlin sought to acquire the means by which to carry out its geo-economic plans for the Asia-Pacific region. In 2007, Russian and British owners of TNK-BP had to sell the controlling stake in the Kovykta gas field to Gazprom (Kramer 2007). In 2006, the international consortium led by Shell was forced to sell 50 per cent of the shares in the well-developed Sakhalin-2 project to Gazprom (Bradshaw 2014). The most dramatic move was the destruction of Yukos and the imprisonment of its owner Mikhail Khodorkovsky. The downside of these manoeuvrings was the severe delay of development of these assets. The development of the Kovykta gas field was put on hold until 2014. Plans for expanding production in the Sakhalin-2 project were cancelled. The destruction of Yukos had huge repercussions for the whole Russian energy sector and delayed the construction of an oil pipeline to China by a decade (Sixsmith 2010).

Overall, in the 2000s, the policy of establishing state control over major energy projects in Eastern Siberia and the Far East resulted in their serious disorganisation and mismanagement. It was not until the 2010s that it opened up opportunities for Kremlin to execute geo-economic plans.

The making of the gas mega-deal

The sharp but short crisis in Russian relations with the West following the 2008 Georgian war prompted Moscow to attempt a half-turn to the East (Karaganov 2011). Suddenly, many business channels towards the East that for years had been covered by bureaucratic red tape were unblocked, and the slow-moving construction of the Eastern Siberia–Pacific Ocean (ESPO) oil pipeline accelerated to a Stakhanovite rush (Baev 2008). Having temporarily stepped down to the position of prime minister, Putin made sure that this project received all necessary support and engaged in playing two potential customers for the East Siberian crude – China and Japan – against one another. As one attentive observer argued, 'Moscow's wishful thinking led its geopolitical calculation of the trilateral game way off target' (Itoh 2011, p. 22). In order to stimulate this competition, Putin insisted on moving on with constructing the 2,100-kilometre long second stage of ESPO to the Kozmino oil terminal immediately after the first stage to Skovorodino (2,750 kilometres) was laid by the end of 2009, with the spur to Daqing (about 1,000 kilometres, opened at the end of 2010). The whole project was finished in December 2012, nearly in time for the APEC summit in Vladivostok.

Moscow's geo-economic plan was based on the premise that this new flow of oil would create such an attraction for Asian investors that Russian authorities would be able not only to get the best bargain but could also trade energy contracts for political influence (Saneev and Sokolov 2014). Yet, as the plan did not envisage any opening of the Russian energy sector to Asian or Western oil companies, the proposition never yielded tangible fruit. The lure of Russian oil was not strong enough to attract savvy Asian investors into the projects, which were seen as based on an uncertain economic rationale and affected by harsh investment climate.

As the Russian leadership understood that their plan had not yielded much success, it took a pause in its geo-economic pivot to Asia for one and a half years. As the explosion of the Ukrainian crisis produced a rupture in Russia's economic ties with Europe, urgent measures for breaking Russia's isolation and compensating for the losses became necessary. The only way to achieve these results in the shortest possible time was to upgrade the strategic partnership with China, which had been strengthening, but still fitted the uncomplimentary description of an 'axis of convenience', as Lo (2008) called it. In order to achieve an upgrade, Putin instructed Gazprom to make all necessary concessions needed for concluding the long-negotiated contract on constructing a gas pipeline to China from the underdeveloped Kovykta and Chayanda gas fields. In real terms, the scale of these concessions turned out to be less than the desperate situation dictated, because Beijing chose to refrain from playing hardball, perhaps in order to support the partner in need (Baev 2014).

The agreement between Gazprom and the China National Petroleum Corporation was signed with great fanfares during Putin's visit to Shanghai in May 2014, and the political resonance of this 'epochal event' (Putin's words) was amplified by a media spin on the 'US\$ 400 billion deal' (Perlez 2014). Some Russian experts described it as a 'window to Asia', conveniently leaving out the fact that Turkmenistan already exported natural gas to China, twice as much as Gazprom was optimistically promising by the end of the decade (e.g. Grivach 2014). However, by the end of 2014, some sceptical voices started to argue that in this contract, the linkage between the price of gas and the market oil price, which was Gazprom's obstinate bargaining position that the Chinese had accepted just on the eve of Putin's visit, was not necessarily a great idea because it contained no protection against the volatility of the global oil market (Krutihin 2014).

The collapse of oil prices at the beginning of 2015 undermined the foundation of the mega-deal, which suddenly became twice smaller in terms of projected revenues but twice heavier in terms of the necessary investments into developing the gas fields and constructing the 3,200-kilometre pipeline grandiloquently called Sila Sibiri (Power of Siberia) (Chow 2015). Putin persisted on selling the proposition of the second pipeline connecting the operational gas fields on the Yamal peninsula with Xinjian, but Beijing agreed only on a non-binding memorandum of understanding, assuming that Moscow's dream of achieving the flexibility of switching the gas flows from Europe to China was a recipe for supply insecurity (O'Sullivan 2014). China is even exploring the proposition for adding imports of liquefied natural gas (LNG) from the United States to its diversified energy sources (Clemente 2017). The window that Moscow sought to open into the Asian markets was turning into a self-made trap.

Russia at the receiving end of Chinese geo-economics

Russian proactive geo-economic policy in Asia-Pacific suffered a series of setbacks in 2015, 2016 and since early 2017, Putin has found himself in the uncomfortable position of becoming a target for geo-economic pressure from China, as well as from Japan and other Asian players in the game. The underlying Russian weakness was caused by the drop in oil prices, which turned out to be not only a temporary spasm, as in early 2009, but at least a midterm trend establishing a plateau of US$40 to US$60 per barrel. This buyers-ruled market has effectively denied Russian state-owned companies opportunities to deal with their customers from their habitual position of power. The Russian leadership still finds it difficult to internalise this new reality of glut on the global energy market, with serious repercussions for their foreign and security policy-making in general, particularly in the Asia-Pacific (Henderson and Mitrova 2016). Instead of setting feasible strategic goals in this region, Putin keeps aiming at a status boost. While deniable, his misapplication of economic levers has resulted in accumulating damage to Russia's reputation and net status loss.

As Putin's third presidential term was coming to an end, the Russian authorities had to acknowledge three major unforeseen consequences of their efforts at energising the pivot to Asia-Pacific. The first was the narrowing of Russia's envisaged diverse connections with the East Asian economies, as a consequence of its upgraded strategic partnership with China, about which some Moscow experts had warned already in 2014 (e.g. Inozemtsev 2014). For instance, Russia's traditional ties with Vietnam started to deteriorate as the Vietnamese government grew suspicious of the trajectory of the Russia–China partnership and opted for a greater opening up to the United States (Baev and Tønnesson 2015). As a result, instead of gaining status, Russia has become seriously dependent upon China, which finds good value in this pro forma equal partnership (Flikke 2016). Building useful ties with the Trump administration, Beijing tends to take Russia for granted and gives greater priority to establishing a new type of great power relations with the United States, a priority that emerged already in mid-2016 (Zeng and Breslin 2016).

The second consequence was the failure to build a solid economic foundation for upgrading the strategic partnership with China. Against the ambitious political promises, the volume of bilateral trade decreased by about a third in 2015 and remained stagnant in 2016 and 2017, not only because of low Russian oil export prices, but also because of the shrinking of the Russian consumer market for Chinese goods (Gabuev 2016a). The agreement to connect the Russia-led Eurasian Economic Union with the Chinese One Belt–One Road initiative made political sense but has yielded few if any economic fruits (Bashkatova 2017). Moscow had to give up the proposition of a western gas corridor to China from Yamal, and to beg for rescheduling the implementation of the Kovykta–Chayanda gas contract, because Beijing remains stingy with prepayments. China is in a position of considerable strength, since it has no difficulties in covering its gas demand, and expects no shortages in the near future. By contrast, Russia will have to sustain huge investments in order to deliver its contractual commitments, despite not yielding meaningful profits from them. In spring 2016, Gazprom secured a €2 billion loan from the Bank of China, which makes it possible to keep promising first deliveries of gas via the Sila Sibiri by early 2020 (Foy 2017).

The third undesirable consequence has been Russia's lack of success in its attempts to increase arms exports to East Asia. Russian leadership tends to see the capacity of selling reasonably modern weapons as a major geo-economic asset, complementing its oil-and-gas instruments and making it possible to reach the states that are competitors on the energy market. Many Western analysts have predicted that arms export would become a key component of Russia's pivot to Asia, which both adds a crucial component to the partnership with China and helps to diversify ties across the region (e.g. Blank and Kim 2014). However, Moscow's efforts to expand markets in Southeast Asia have brought unimpressive results, despite it having tried to negotiate barter deals for fruit (Moscow Times 2015). Vietnam has traditionally been the main customer of Russian arms exports, and while existing contracts signed at the start of the decade come into force on schedule, no new contracts have been signed. It is not clear whether the reason for this is Moscow's reluctance to irritate Beijing, or Hanoi's desire to achieve greater diversity of supply by turning to Washington (Defence Industry Daily 2016). Seeking to add material content to the upgraded strategic partnership with China, the Russian leadership had overcome its previous reservations against supplying China with state-of-the-art modern weapons by mid-2015, and agreed to sell S-400 surface-to-air missiles and Su-35 fighters (Clover 2016). Again, this has made China one of the main importers of Russian weapons, but only four (out of 24) Su-35 fighters and four batteries of S-400 were confirmed as delivered by the end of 2017 (Nikolski 2016). It is clear that Beijing puts emphasis on domestically produced armaments in the fast-moving reforms of the People's Liberation Army.

These deficiencies in executing the laborious pivot are aggravated by the depression/stagnation in the Russian economy, and as a result, Moscow not only faces a shortage of geo-economic means, but also finds itself a target of geo-economic manoeuvres of its Asian neighbours. China is certainly the protagonist, and the pronounced reluctance to invest, particularly in the Far East, is combined with some special cases, where generosity is suddenly demonstrated (Kashin 2017). For instance, demonstrative neglect by Chinese investors of such high-profile events as the St. Petersburg Economic Forum in June 2016 and June 2017 (at which Indian Prime Minister Narendra Modi was the guest of honour) or the Eastern Economic Forum in Vladivostok in September 2016 and September 2017 (at which Japanese Prime Minister Shinzo Abe was the guest of honour), are testimony of China's subtle deployment of geo-economic instruments.

This blatant lack of interest stands in sharp contrast to the decision of investing as much as US$12 billion in the troubled Yamal-LNG project, despite the very questionable cost-efficiency (Marson 2016). The motivation behind this decision had little to do with obtaining a new source of natural gas. Instead, it had everything to do with a particular sort of chequebook diplomacy, which involved doing Putin the favour of rescuing Gennady Timchenko, the owner of Novatek (the company that manages the Yamal-LNG project) from a financial trap. This oligarch is a known member of Putin's inner circle of courtiers (duly sanctioned by the United States and the European Union), who also serves as the chair of Russian–Chinese Business Council. Granting Timchenko's project a new lease on life, China expected some sort of political reciprocity (Gabuev 2016b). Indeed, Putin felt obliged to return the favour, so a political service of some kind was to be provided. The occasion arrived already in July 2016, when the Permanent Court of Arbitration in The Hague issued a verdict on the case brought by the Philippines regarding the South China Sea dispute. Beijing was upset by the tribunal's firm rejection of its claims, and Moscow's first reaction was rather neutral, but after visiting China for the G20 summit, Putin expressed full support for Xi Jinping's assertive stance (Thayer 2016).

Overall, it might be envisaged that as Russia continues to sink deeper into economic stagnation while seeking to sustain confrontation with the West, China will be able to exploit new opportunities for converting its partner's economic dependency into political concessions. Other Asia-Pacific nations, first of all Japan, are attempting or may shortly follow suit.

Russian recipes for mixing geo-economics with geopolitics

Geopolitics remains a prevalent strain in Russian political thinking, so every geo-economic design produced in Moscow has geopolitical undercurrents, and this mix has many particular elements in the policy aimed at Asia-Pacific. The US pivot to this region is seen primarily in military power terms, and Russia seeks to show commitment to maintaining a balance. For instance, when preparing a major (but failed) economic breakthrough with the 2012 APEC summit, President Medvedev opted for visiting Kunashir (one of the disputed South Kuril islands), and then ordered a deployment of S-300 surface-to-air missile systems to the island. Having become Russia's prime minister, Medvedev reiterated the assertive message visiting Iturup in August 2015 (Blagov 2015). Japan issued angry protestations against that unprecedented 'rudeness', but the Russian leadership apparently considered it necessary to establish that it was prepared to engage with Asia-Pacific according to the perceived rules of the game in this region. These rules are interpreted in Moscow not as underpinning the evolution of the East Asian peace, but as sustaining fierce quarrels about tiny islets and bitter disagreements about historical grievances. Accordingly, Russia combines the emphasis on cultivating economic ties with a firm political stance on territorial and maritime disputes.

This combination required a convincing reinforcement of hard-power means in the Far East, which during Soviet times had been a heavily militarised bastion, but the 1990s demilitarisation left it degraded and depopulated. Russia's key military advantage is the possession of nuclear capabilities, and Putin took personal credit for the decision to modernise the base for strategic submarines at Vilyuchinsk, Kamchatka, dismissing sound strategic reasons to concentrate the much reduced fleet of these submarines on the Kola peninsula bases (Koleshnikov 2006; Kristensen 2015). A key part of that decision was to deploy up to four strategic submarines of the new Borei class to the Pacific fleet, despite the difficulties in their maintenance far away from the main production plant in Severodvinsk (Simha 2016).

Another part of the plan for restoring Russian geopolitical might was the increase of power projection capabilities of the Pacific fleet, and the quickest way to achieve it was the agreement to purchase two Mistral-class amphibious assault ships from France (with the licence to construct two more). The Russian navy command was initially suspicious about that political deal, but the admirals soon discovered that there was no other option for adding major surface combatants to the combat order of their fleets, and so they started to prepare for operating the unfamiliar Mistrals (Kennedy and Pant 2016; RIA-Novosti 2011). While the ships were under construction in Saint-Nazaire, Russia sought to demonstrate the fast progress in modernising its air power, not shying away from occasional violations of Japanese airspace.

A particular component of the ambition for boosting the security profile of the Far East was the mega-project for constructing a new cosmodrome (spaceport) in the Amur oblast, which would make it possible to reduce the dependency of the Russian space programme on launches from Baikonur, Kazakhstan. The master plan involved developing a cluster of scientific labs and high-tech enterprises around Vostochny, which should have been attractive to Asian partners. No expenses were spared in building the infrastructure which became one of Putin's pet projects.

However, the execution of all these ambitious propositions varied from poor to disastrous. The first space launch was successfully performed at the Vostochny cosmodrome in April 2016, but the scale of waste and misappropriation of this hugely expensive construction reached such a spectacular level that it became a symbol of corruption, failure of the second launch in late November 2017 illuminated that symbolism (Burskaya 2015). Attempts to demonstrate air power resulted in the crashes of two Tu-95MS strategic bombers at the Ukrainka air base in summer 2015, unprecedented for these aircraft, which had been the main asset of the Soviet Union's long-range air force in the 1970s and 1980s (Huard 2015). The bitterest disappointment was France cancelling the contract to deliver the newly constructed Mistral-class helicopter carriers due to sanctions imposed on Russia during its aggression in Ukraine. The navy command had to pretend that there was no real need for this type of ship, but their requests for large amphibious ships and aircraft carriers have a slim chance to be funded in any foreseeable future (Gorenburg 2017). A less visible but still significant setback affected the deterrence capabilities of the squadron of strategic submarines when the new Bulava missile proved to be unreliable (Litovkin 2016). As of the end of 2017, two Borei-class submarines are based at Vilyuchinsk, but they have not been able to perform a single missile test from the patrol area of the Sea of Okhotsk.

Russia has not been successful in modernising its military might in the Pacific theatre, but Moscow still sees the need to compensate for the erosion of its geo-economic strength with an increase in geopolitical power projection. Putin tried in vain to lure Asian investors to Vladivostok, declaring the city to be business-friendly and open for tourists, who might presumably find its casinos more attractive than its foggy climate (Meyer and Rudnitsky 2016). Nevertheless, he has felt the need to reinforce his position in the talks with Japan, which deployed a set of geo-economic means, including a hard-to-refuse proposition for a gas pipeline from Sakhalin to Hokkaido, by the deployment of anti-ship missile batteries on Iturup and Kunashir (Ryall, Dominguez and Gibson 2016). Even greater resonance was generated by the weeklong joint naval exercises with China in the South China Sea in September 2016 (Feng 2016). However, the problem with this experiment in showing naval might is that it was not performed in support of some Russian proactive geo-economic move. To the contrary – it was performed in return for China's successful geo-economic advance with the targeted investment into the Yamal-LNG project, which accentuated Moscow's economic and political dependency on Beijing's generosity and goodwill.

Russia tries to impress its Asian neighbours, including the member states of the Association of Southeast Asian Nations, with its determination to counter US attempts of asserting military dominance. Indeed, the region has grave concerns about the reliability of US security guarantees, and the propensity of the Trump administration to manipulate military instruments. However, Russian demonstrations are only aggravating these concerns – and they certainly do not generate any new respect towards Russia. The securitised behaviour of the Russian leadership is seen as a product of economic feebleness, which itself is a result of bad governance. The combination of geopolitical posturing and geo-economic manoeuvring that Moscow is developing for Asia-Pacific is different from its more complex designs in Europe (Wigell and Vihma 2016). However, at the end of Putin's third presidency, the provisional results are similar: The application of military instruments is clearly counterproductive for achieving economic goals, even in the particular direction of upgrading partnership with China, and certainly unhelpful for the key task of attracting investment.

Conclusion

Since the advent of its current confrontation with the West, Russia has undertaken resolute and even desperate efforts to connect with the dynamic Asia-Pacific region, and to increase its role in managing its conflicts. However, as of the end of 2017, it has few reasons to be satisfied with the fruits of these efforts. Despite the preoccupation with power politics, there is an understanding in Moscow that political processes in this vast region are driven by economic modernisation and growth, so the main content of its pivot should be geo-economic in nature. The working assumption in the Kremlin has been that the capacity for and firm control over exporting valuable natural resources, above all hydrocarbons, grants Russian leadership a position of geo-economic advantage. That assumption has proven to be wrong: The devalued resources pay scant if any political dividends, and the reality has turned out to be a position of geo-economic dependence and weakness. This is above all a result of Russia's economic decline and therefore its diminishing geo-economic power. As shown above, China has been quick to take advantage of the Kremlin's diminishing capabilities, driving its own geo-economic interests at the expense of Russia. The East Asian states understand that Russia's confrontation with the West will demand a concentration of Moscow's attention and prioritisation in resource allocation to the Western theatre, whatever the rhetoric of pivoting to the East.

The apparent weakness of Russian geo-economic posture has exposed it to economic manipulations and pressure from its Asian neighbours, mainly China, but also Japan. President Putin refused to be swayed by Japanese economic incentives towards making a deal on the disputed islands, but has left the door open for further application of financial and business levers. With China, it is far more difficult to resist the subtle but effective geo-economic pressure, and Putin's shift from neutral to a more China-supportive stance on the legal dispute over the South China Sea indicates that more concessions will be demanded and extracted for the economic lifelines that Beijing throws to Moscow.

In the Kremlin's confrontation-centred worldview, the only way for Russia to escape the position of geo-economic weakness and to deter geo-economic operations by its Asian neighbours is to increase the reliance on geopolitical, and particularly, military instruments. Here again, the ambitious plans for modernisation of these hard-power means have been curtailed by various setbacks, so that even the intention to expand arms export to Southeast Asia remains unfulfilled. This shortage of military might, caused not least by the strategic need to concentrate resources and assets on the Western front, can be compensated by the greater readiness to use it. The Russian leadership refuses to acknowledge the counter-productiveness of combining geo-economic and geopolitical means in its Asian neighbourhood. Having gained unique experience in projecting power and harvesting political dividends from it, Russia may be tempted to experiment with direct application of military instruments, expecting that immediate economic losses would be insignificant and greater benefits would come from the newly gained position of power.

Notes

1 Support for my research on Russia–China relations by the Norwegian Defence Ministry is greatly appreciated. The author would also like to thank Sören Scholvin and Mikael Wigell for comments on earlier drafts.
2 This phenomenon was in the focus of the East Asian peace programme led by Stein Tønnesson at the Uppsala University in 2013–2017. For the very impressive list of publications, visit www.pcr.uu.se/research/eap.

References

Baev, P. (2008) 'Asia-Pacific and the LNG: The Lure of New Markets', in Baryschm, K. (ed.), *Pipelines, Politics and Power – The Future of EU-Russia Energy Relations* (London: CER), pp. 83–92. Available at: www.cer.org.uk/sites/default/files/public ations/attachments/pdf/2011/rp_851-271.pdf, accessed 23 November 2017.

Baev, P. (2014) 'Upgrading Russia's Quasi-strategic Pseudo-partnership with China', *PONARS Eurasia*, Ponars Euroasia Policy Memo No. 337, August. Available at: www. ponarseurasia.org/memo/upgrading-russia%E2%80%99s-quasi-strategic-pseudo-partnership-china, accessed 23 November 2017.

Baev, P. K. and Tønnesson, S. (2015) 'Can Russia Keep Its Special Ties with Vietnam while Moving Closer and Closer to China?', *International Area Studies Review*, 18, 3, pp. 312–325.

Bashkatova, A. (2017) 'Евразийский союз становится китайским', [Eurasian Union Becomes Chinese], *Независимая газета*, 14 July. Available at: www.ng.ru/ economics/2017-07-14/1_7029_china.html, accessed 23 November 2017.

Blagov, S. (2015) 'Russia Takes Hard-line Stance on Territorial Dispute with Japan', *Asia Times*, 23 August. Available at: www.atimes.com/article/russia-takes-hard-line-stance-on-territorial-dispute-with-japan/, accessed 23 November 2017.

Blank, S. and Kim, Y. (2014) 'Arms Sales and Russia's Future as an Asian Power', *Asian Politics & Policy*, 6, 2, pp. 267–284.

Bradshaw, M. (2014) 'The Second Battle for Sakhalin', *Oil & Gas Monitor*, 8 October. Available at: www.oilgasmonitor.com/second-battle-sakhalin/, accessed 23 November 2017.

Burskaya, Z. (2015) 'Вам оказана великая честь – строить космодром', [You Have Great Honour to Build the Cosmodrome], *Новая газета*, 10 July. Available at: www. novayagazeta.ru/articles/2015/07/10/64858-171-vam-okazana-velikaya-chest-8212-stroit-kosmodrom-187, accessed 23 November 2017.

Chow, E. C. (2015) 'Russia-China Gas Deal and Redeal', *Center for Strategic & International Studies*, 11 May. Available at: www.csis.org/analysis/russia-china-gas-deal-and-redeal, accessed 23 November 2017.

Clemente, J. (2017) 'US Liquefied Natural Gas to China is a Game-Changer', *Forbes*, 25 May. Available at: www.forbes.com/sites/judeclemente/2017/05/25/u-s-liquefied-natural-gas-to-china-is-a-game-changer/#adbd11a671a0, accessed 23 November 2017.

Clover, C. (2016) 'Russia Resumes Advanced Weapons Sales to China', *Financial Times*, 3 November. Available at: www.ft.com/content/90b1ada2-a18e-11e6-86d5-4e36b35c 3550, accessed 23 November 2017.

Defense Industry Daily. (2016) 'Vietnam's Restocking: Subs, Ships, Sukhois, and Now Perhaps F-16s and P-3s?', *Defetnse Industry Daily*, 28 June. Available at: www. defenseindustrydaily.com/vietnams-russian-restocking-subs-ships-sukhois-and-more-05396/, accessed 23 November 2017.

Feng, H. (2016) 'The Great Russia-China South China Sea Naval Hook Up (and Why It Matters)', *National Interest*, 7 October. Available at: http://nationalinterest.org/blog/ the-buzz/the-great-russia-china-south-china-sea-naval-hook-why-it-17966, accessed 23 November 2017.

Flikke, G. (2016) 'Sino-Russian Relations: Status Exchange or Imbalanced Relationship?', *Problems of Post-Communism*, 63, 3, pp. 159–170.

Foy, H. (2017) 'Gazprom Confident of $400bn Chinese Gas Supply', *Financial Times*, 6 July. Available at: www.ft.com/content/623c7396-60cc-11e7-91a7-502f7ee26895, accessed 23 November 2017.

Frolov, V. (2016) 'Russia's New Foreign Policy – A Show of Force and Power Projection', *Moscow Times*, 6 December. Available at: https://themoscowtimes.com/articles/russias-new-foreign-policy-based-on-force-and-power-projection-56431, accessed 23 November 2017.

Gabuev, A. (2016a) 'A Pivot to Nowhere: The Realities of Russia's Asia Policy', *Carnegie Moscow Center*, 22 April. Available at: http://carnegie.ru/commentary/?fa=63408, accessed 23 November 2017.

Gabuev, A. (2016b) 'China's Pivot to Putin's Friends', *Foreign Policy*, 25 June. Available at: http://foreignpolicy.com/2016/06/25/chinas-pivot-to-putin-friends-xi-russia-gazprom-timchenko-sinopec/, accessed 23 November 2017.

Gorenburg, D. (2017) 'Russia's New and Unrealistic Naval Doctrine', *War-on-the-Rocks*, 26 July. Available at: https://warontherocks.com/2017/07/russias-new-and-unrealistic-naval-doctrine/, accessed 23 November 2017.

Grivach, A. (2014) 'A Window to Asia', *Russia in Global Affairs*, 23 September. Available at: http://eng.globalaffairs.ru/number/A-Window-to-Asia-16999, accessed 23 November 2017.

Hedlund, S. (2014) *Putin's Energy Agenda: The Contradictions of Russia's Resource Wealth* (Boulder, CO: Lynne Rienner).

Henderson, J. and Mitrova, T. (2016) 'Energy Relations between Russia and China: Playing Chess with the Dragon', *The Oxford Institute for Energy Studies*, OIES Paper, August. Available at: www.oxfordenergy.org/wpcms/wp-content/uploads/2016/08/Energy-Relations-between-Russia-and-China-Playing-Chess-with-the-Dragon-WPM-67.pdf, accessed 23 November 2017.

Huard, P. R. (2015) 'Russia's Blast from the Past: Beware the Tu-95 Bear Strategic Bomber', *National Interest*, 22 August. Available at: http://nationalinterest.org/blog/the-buzz/russias-blast-the-past-beware-the-tu-95-bear-strategic-13669, accessed 23 November 2017.

Inozemtsev, V. (2014) 'Мы уже давно подсели на китайскую иглу', [We Have Developed Dependency upon the Chinese Needle], interview with *Новая газета*, 17 October. Available at: www.novayagazeta.ru/articles/2014/10/17/61602-171-my-uzhe-davno-podseli-na-kitayskuyu-iglu-187, accessed 23 November 2017.

Itoh, S. (2011) 'Russia Looks East: Energy Markets and Geopolitics in North-East Asia', *Center for Strategic & International Studies*, July. Available at: https://csis-prod.s3.amazonaws.com/s3fs-public/legacy_files/files/publication/110721_Itoh_Russia LooksEast_Web.pdf, accessed 23 November 2017.

Karaganov, S. (2011) 'Азиатская стратегия', [The Asian Strategy], *Russia in Global Affairs*, 17 June. Available at: www.globalaffairs.ru/pubcol/Aziatskaya-strategiya-15234, accessed 23 November 2017.

Kashin, V. (2017) 'Много ли Китай инвестирует в Россию?', [How Much is China Investing in Russia?], Валдай Международный дискуссионный клуб, 9 June. Available at: http://ru.valdaiclub.com/a/highlights/mnogo-li-kitay-investiruet-v-rossiyu/, accessed 23 November 2017.

Kennedy, G. and Pant, H. V. (2016) 'Introduction', in Kennedy, G. and Pant, H. V. (eds), *Assessing Maritime Power in in Asia-Pacific, The Impact of American Strategic Re-Balance* (London: Routledge), pp. 1–7.

Kolesnikov, A. (2006) 'Commander-in-Chief Visits Kamchatka', *Kommersant*, 6 September. Available at: www.kommersant.com/p801780/r_1/Russian_presidents_visit_to_Kamchatka_unnerved_some_federal_officials/, accessed 5 May 2016.

Kramer, A. E. (2007) 'Moscow Presses BP to Sell a Big Gas Field to Gazprom', *New York Times*, 23 June. Available at: www.nytimes.com/2007/06/23/business/worldbusiness/23gazprom.html, accessed 23 November 2017.

Kristensen, H. M. (2015) 'Russian Pacific Fleet Prepares for Arrival of New Missile Submarines', *Federation of American Scientists*, 14 September. Available at: https://fas.org/blogs/security/2015/09/pacificfleet/, accessed 23 November 2017.

Krutihin, M. (2014) 'Михаил Крутихин: Как Китай переигрывает «Роснефть» и «Газпром»', [How China Outplays Rosneft and Gazprom], *Ведомост*, 18 September. Available at: www.vedomosti.ru/opinion/articles/2014/09/18/poddavki-skitaem, accessed 23 November 2017.

Litovkin, N. (2016) 'What's Wrong with Russia's New Bulava Missile?', *Russia Beyond the Headlines*, 3 October. Available at: www.rbth.com/defence/2016/10/03/whats-wrong-with-russias-new-bulava-missile_635311, accessed 25 April 2018.

Lo, B. (2008) *Axis of Convenience: Moscow, Beijing and the New Geopolitics* (Washington DC: Brookings Institution Press).

Marson, J. (2016) 'Russian Natural Gas Project Gets Funding from China', *Wall Street Journal*, 29 April. Available at: www.wsj.com/articles/russian-natural-gas-project-gets-funding-from-china-1461934776, accessed 23 November 2017.

Meyer, R. and Rudnitsky, J. (2016) 'Putin's Making a Big Bet on Building Vegas in Vladivostok', *Bloomberg*, 31 August. Available at: www.bloomberg.com/news/articles/2016-08-31/putin-s-gamble-on-far-east-las-vegas-stirs-fears-of-china-influx, accessed 23 November 2017.

Moscow Times. (2015) 'Russia is Ready to Give Thailand Weapons in Exchange for Fruit, Rubber', *Moscow Times*, 15 June. Available at: https://themoscowtimes.com/articles/russia-ready-to-give-thailand-weapons-in-exchange-for-fruit-rubber-48186, accessed 23 November 2017.

Nikolski, A. (2016) 'Китай вернулся в пятерку крупнейших импортеров российского оружия', [China Returned to the List of Five Top Importers of Russian Arms], *Ведомост*, 1 November. Available at: www.vedomosti.ru/politics/articles/2016/11/02/663309-kitai-krupneishih-importerov, accessed 23 November 2017.

Oliker, O. (2016) 'Unpacking Russia's New National Security Strategy', *Center for Strategic & International Studies*, 7 January. Available at: www.csis.org/analysis/unpacking-russias-new-national-security-strategy, accessed 23 November 2017.

O'Sullivan, M. L. (2014) 'New China-Russia Gas Pact is No Big Deal', *Bloomberg View*, 14 November. Available at: www.bloomberg.com/view/articles/2014-11-14/new-chinarussia-gas-pact-is-no-big-deal, accessed 23 November 2017.

Perlez, J. (2014) 'China and Russia Reach 30-Year Gas Deal', *New York Times*, 21 May. Available at: www.nytimes.com/2014/05/22/world/asia/china-russia-gas-deal.html?_r=0, accessed 23 November 2017.

RIA-Novosti. (2011) 'Первые два "Мистраля" планируется направить на Тихоокеанский флот', [The First Two Mistrals Will Join the Pacific Fleet], 9 February. Available at: https://ria.ru/defense_safety/20110209/332397885.html, accessed 23 November 2017.

Ryall, J., Dominguez, G. and Gibson, N. (2016) 'Russia Deploys Bal and Bastion-P Missile System to Disputed Kuril Islands', *Jane's 360*, 23 November. Available at: www.janes.com/article/65714/russia-deploys-bal-and-bastion-p-missile-systems-to-disputed-kuril-islands-says-report, accessed 23 November 2017.

Saneev, B. and Sokolov, D. (2014) 'Russia's Energy Development in Eastern Siberia and the Far East and Relations with East Asian Countries in the Energy Sector', in Akaha,

T. and Vassilieva, A. (eds), *Russia and East Asia: Informal and Gradual Integration* (London and New York: Routledge), pp. 188–199.

Simha, R. K. (2016) 'Why Russian Subs Will Once Again Dominate the Pacific', *Russia Beyond the Headlines*, 21 July. Available at: http://rbth.com/blogs/continental_drift/2016/07/21/why-russian-subs-will-once-again-dominate-the-pacific_613635, accessed 23 November 2017.

Sixsmith, M. (2010) *Putin's Oil: The Yukos Affair and the Struggle for Russia* (New York and London: Continuum).

Thayer, C. A. (2016) 'Does Russia Have a South China Sea Problem?', *National Interest*, 27 September. Available at: http://nationalinterest.org/blog/the-buzz/does-russia-have-south-china-sea-problem-17853, accessed 23 November 2017.

Treisman, D. (2010) 'Russian Politics in a Time of Economic Turmoil', in Åslund, A., Guriev, S. and Kuchin, A. C. (eds), *Russia After the Global Economic Crisis* (Washington D.C.: Peterson Institute for International Economics), pp. 39–57.

Tønnesson, S. (2017) *Explaining the East Asian Peace* (Copenhagen: NIAS Press).

Wigell, M. and Vihma, A. (2016) 'Geopolitics versus Geoeconomics: The Case of Russia's Geostrategy and Its Effects on the EU', *International Affairs*, 92, 3, pp. 605–627.

Zeng, J. and Breslin, S. (2016) 'China's "New Type of Great Power relations": A G2 with Chinese characteristics?', *International Affairs*, 92, 4, pp. 773–794.

7 US grand strategy in flux

Geo-economics, geopolitics and the liberal international order

Kari Möttölä[1]

Introduction

The post-World War II primacy of the United States has been maintained by an internationalist foreign policy conducted interchangeably under various forms of activist liberalism and pragmatic realism. While conditioned by domestic politics and limits of material power, the grand strategy of deep engagement for sustaining a liberal international order has dominated vis-à-vis alternative approaches of retrenchment from global commitments such as offshore balancing and restraint, including isolationism (e.g. Ikenberry 2011; Mearsheimer and Walt 2016; Posen 2014). Based on the hegemonic leadership of the United States, the liberal international order – being an open system of alliances and partnerships, multilateral institutions and common rules – has come under pressure with the rise of China and Russia as illiberal regional and global powers. Consequently, the US grand strategy needs to be adapted to global change where interdependence is not necessarily an engine for cooperation but can as well be a tool for great-power competition (Wright 2017).

The transition to an adapted national strategy is complicated by an apparent discontinuity between the political philosophies of the Obama and Trump presidencies, and made uncertain by the gap between rhetoric and action within the Trump administration (Möttölä 2017). While Barack Obama sought to sustain a liberal international order despite the rise of geo-economic strategies and the return of geopolitics, Donald Trump's economic nationalism seems to question its value for US interests in general, and in global and trade issues in particular.

The Obama administration drew a hybrid model of grand strategy from an understanding of the combined effects of geo-economics and geopolitics for world order. According to this vision, geopolitics fragments the international system, creating distinct regions that follow a logic of their own, contradicting liberal ideals. Geo-economics may also create macro-regions that differ from each other, but the strategy of the United States must aim at maintaining and expanding a uniform economic and trading order based on liberal rules.

In this chapter, I first elaborate on the concepts of geo-economics, geopolitics, geostrategy and grand strategy, and explain how they matter today, and what they look like in the case of the United States and its challengers. Afterwards, I

shed light on US efforts to establish macro-regional trade initiatives, the Trans-
Pacific Partnership (TPP) and the Transatlantic Trade and Investment Partnership (TTIP), and their mixed prospects under Trump. I finally analyse the rivalry
between China and the United States, concluding that instead of the People's
Republic trying to fundamentally change the international order, mutual hedging
predominates between the two genuinely global powers.

Geo-economics, geopolitics, geostrategy and grand strategy

Geo-economics and geopolitics can be seen as manifestations of power. They
are, being combined or standing on their own, part of the toolbox of geostrategy (see Chapter 2 in this volume). Being part of a grand strategy, they have a
spatial dimension, referring to a sphere of influence. As shown by Wigell and
Vihma (2016), there are major differences between geo-economics and
geopolitics with regard to the use of power, suggesting that whereas geo-
economics is an accommodating and covert use of economic power with
long-term strategic contingency and flexibility, geopolitics is confrontational,
overt and military-based, often connected to particular cases and events. A key
reason for the rise of geo-economics is the outstanding relevance of economics
for present-day power shifts in international politics (see Chapter 3 in this
volume). The United States is not only the undisputed military hegemon, but,
concerning economic power, it also enjoys a strong demographic base, benefits from increasing energy self-sufficiency, and remains at the top of higher
education and innovative technology. However, the relative decline of Western
liberal democracies in terms of economic power constitutes a challenge for the
United States and its European partners.

My key argument is that the juxtaposition and the resulting uneven effects of
geo-economics and geopolitics as core elements of foreign policy have caused a
potentially fundamental change in the grand strategy of the United States. US
leadership in world affairs might turn from what was a matter of choice under
unchallenged primacy into adjustment under contested leadership and relative
decline. This change occurs in geo-economics and geopolitics. Although we are
moving towards globalism with expanding zones of common practice and inclusive rules, producing win-win-situations, the long-term and inevitable process of
increasing foreign direct investment, deepening regional integration and expanding world trade seems to be stalling. As a consequence, competition and rivalry
have been thriving; with economic assets being used for political purposes, as in
the case of Russia's use of energy resources as a political leverage vis-à-vis its
Western neighbours and the European Union (Wigell and Vihma 2016). What is
more, there are models of regional economic integration that compete with
Western-dominated liberalism: China's commercial power play – launched by
the Belt and Road initiative (BRI) on infrastructure investments – extends from
Western Europe to East Asia; Russia promotes economic integration in the area
that once constituted the Soviet Union. The United States, in response, has
focussed its geo-economic agenda on revitalising the transatlantic community as

a driver of global rule making, while simultaneously concerting established liberal democracies and new partners within the trans-Pacific community (more on this below).

In geopolitics, we are moving towards regionalisms with diverging rules: Russia has been pushing for re-arranging and renegotiating the post-Cold War order in Europe, using a hybrid strategy of military and other tools; China has expanded its influence over territorial control in the Asia-Pacific region, also with the help of overt and covert military power; in the wider Middle East a mix of great-power collaboration and competition tends to boost rather than calm down chaos and violence with military interference apparently being essential. The Obama administration developed geopolitical strategies in the form of regionally specific military partnerships: enhanced solidarity in the transatlantic community in order to balance against Russia's offensive geopolitics; increased military commitment in East and Southeast Asia, balancing against China; and deepened international partnerships, especially with European states, so as to be able to share the burden of security responsibility in the Middle East.

As said, geopolitics is at present about emerging powers carving out and consolidating their zones of influence. The United States remains the globally leading military power, but Obama's cautious strategy of avoiding direct and large-scale military interventions allowed emerging powers to shape regional security complexes to an increasing extent. Nevertheless, its alliances and partnerships, together with its global military reach, continue to enable the United States to significantly influence all parts of the world. It would be too early to maintain that we are entering a decentralised, regionalised security order (Buzan 2011). The ongoing relevance of the United States for geopolitics all around the world has been demonstrated by its reaction to the crisis in Ukraine, with continuity prevailing from the Obama to the Trump administrations, whereby the superpower has increased its funding of the European Deterrence Initiative, and aimed at reinforcing the readiness of the North Atlantic Treaty Organisation (NATO) vis-à-vis the Russian military advances. Moreover, the United States has taken a leading role in the deployment of multinational forces within Central and East European member states of NATO, including increased exercise activity. The US has also reassured the allies over its commitments to ballistic missile defence and nuclear deterrence policies. The negotiations and the follow-up of the Minsk agreement concerning the simmering conflict in eastern Ukraine have meanwhile been the purview of France and Germany with US backing.

In the domain of geo-economics, the United States together with the European Union have coordinated a response to the Russian military power plays, imposing economic sanctions against Russia. Although the Russian economy has proven resilient and there are no signs of the sanctions affecting Russia's position on Ukraine, they might have been decisive in deterring Russia from further military incursions, and contributing to the stalling of the fighting in eastern Ukraine. On the other hand, the sanctions appear to have reached their limits, as their widening or tightening are not likely to find sufficient support among EU members. Consequently, economic sanctions can only continue to work effectively as a part of a broader policy, meaning that there is a need to combine geo-economics and geopolitics (Moret *et al.* 2016; Weiss and Nephew 2016).

The predominance of geo-economics and its complementation by geopolitics in the US grand strategy becomes apparent in the case of trade policies which will be discussed in the following section. At the same time, in the use of geo-economics, the uncertainty brought about by the Trump transition is at its greatest.

Obama's grand strategy and beyond

A key question is how the United States will retain a leadership position in a liberal world order while geo-economics and geopolitics call for diverging responses to today's challenges. In such a composite geostrategic context, the United States pursues a strategy of hedging with regard to geopolitics: by positioning itself as an effective but flexible player, the superpower tailors its policy towards rising rivals in a patchwork of dynamic regional orders. At the same time, it favours a strategy of wedging in geo-economics: by leading groups of like-minded countries, the United States aims to progress towards uniformity in global economic governance based on liberal market norms and principles.

Foreign policy debates in the United States – shaped by scholars such as Blackwill and Harris (2016a; 2016b), Goldman and Rosenberg (2015), as well as former policymakers like Robert Zoellick (2015) – are increasingly marked by a recognition of the need to use geo-economic instruments, including coercive measures, to accomplish geostrategic objectives, separately or in support of geopolitics. A key question in this regard is whether the United States will be able to repeat the way of global ordering that characterised the immediate post-Second World War years: shaping the international order, and creating a sustainable hegemonic trajectory. In these debates, the United States was in an undisputed position of economic hegemony in the 1950s, being able and willing to build the Bretton Woods institutions and finance the Marshall Plan – the latter serving its strategic objectives in Europe. The recent frustrating experience with a series of military adventures, difficult new security challenges, and the use of geo-economics by China and Russia are other factors that have stressed the necessity of taking a closer look at trade-offs between politico-military and economic components of the grand strategy of the United States.

In practical foreign policy, the Obama administration followed the logic of adapted liberal internationalism with large-scale trade policy initiatives. The geostrategic purpose of the TPP and TTIP arrangements was to serve as geo-economic drivers of a rules-based liberal order shaped by global shifts in economic growth, productivity, modernisation, and development. In response to the unabated effect of globalisation, and using the opportunity left by the stagnant Doha Round, the United States aimed to introduce the interregional trade and investment arrangements to shape the underlying rules and institutions of world order, irrespective of whether the global economic governance remains a patchwork structure for a longer term or returns to the trajectory of global unification.

As envisaged by the Obama administration, the TPP would contribute to rebalancing the situation in East and Southeast Asia as a response to China's increasingly offensive geo-economic strategies, spearheaded by the creation of the Asian Infrastructure Bank (AIIB), the proposal for a Regional Comprehensive Economic Partnership (RCEP) and the BRI. The idea was to bring the United States closer to established and emerging democracies in East and Southeast Asia, all of them united behind the common objective of modernisation and development through rules-based economic governance. From the geopolitical perspective, the TPP would serve to confirm and strengthen the security assurances of the United States towards its regional partners, which find themselves increasingly challenged by China in military terms (Pereira and Cronin 2016). By abandoning the TPP, President Trump might have taken a major strategic risk, unless he is able to come up with an alternative position more beneficial for his country.

The TTIP, on its part, has been designed to generate economic dynamism for the transatlantic economies, and to position the West in the driving seat for future norm building in global economic governance. In the area of geopolitical implications, the TTIP aims to consolidate the transatlantic partnership, which is crucial for European security, by renewing the common purpose of the West, viewed in public discourse to be in decline (Hamilton and Blockmans 2015). With the TPP renounced and the TTIP shelved, pending future negotiations by mutual agreement, the Trump administration will have to make alternative choices beyond war on tariffs in order to shape geo-economics and geopolitics for the early twenty-first century.

Historically, a power shift between the two most powerful states has been a transformative and also a precarious phase in the international system. While the distribution of material capabilities is seen to erode the hegemony of the United States and provide China with increasing power to exercise coercion as part of its foreign policy, legitimate questions have been raised with regard to the relevance and sustainability of liberal internationalism. Beyond that, uncertainty concerning the foreign policy of the United States has been caused by growing populism – often calling for a withdrawal from international commitments – which brought Trump to power (Fukuyama 2016; Overhaus and Brozus 2016).

It is critical to what extent and how the Trump administration will recognise the limitation and transformation of US power, and adapt its grand strategy accordingly in continuation or reversal of the Obama legacy. The path taken by the Obama administration was to become the first step in a long game of strategic patience (Chollet 2016), aimed at securing fundamental objectives of global leadership without having to choose between recasting or replacing liberal internationalism (Indyk, Lieberthal and O'Hanlon 2012; Möttölä 2016). The issue at hand boils down to recognising how and to what extent China – arguably the only other state that can shape the international system decisively – acts not merely as an imposing challenger but as a partner in transforming the international order. With China and the United States as twin powers capable of driving grand strategies of global ordering, US leadership in international affairs will, in the long run, depend on the cunning application of geo-economics, and increasingly also being complemented by geopolitics. The ways in which the United States – and, for that matter, China as well – employs the two components of geostrategy will shape the trajectory of global order (Ikenberry 2015; Wang and Zhu 2015).

China, the United States and the liberal international order

So, what would an unravelling of the US-led liberal order look like against the background of ongoing shifts in grand strategy? There might be a change by default, meaning a power shift, in case China successfully challenges the United States, rising to an equal or higher status in terms of economic and political power. Alternatively, we might witness a change by design – that is, a policy change in the sense of the United States replacing its liberal internationalism by nationalist retrenchment from world affairs. In spite of China's impressive economic and political rise, the first scenario appears unlikely. A recent study focussed on material power, especially military and technological capabilities, concludes that the United States will remain the only superpower in the foreseeable future (Brooks and Wohlforth 2015). The authors suggest that China has risen to an upper category of its own, behind the United States but ahead of the rest, mainly because of its economic ascent. It has moved beyond being a regional great power such as Germany, Japan or Russia, but it is nowhere near to becoming an equal peer of the United States. This means that the international system, measured by the distribution of capabilities among major powers, has changed from a 1+X into a 1+1+X structure. Herein, despite the preponderance of the United States, it would be misleading to speak of unipolarity as China's rise has far-reaching implications.

While the United States today is much more dominant than hegemons in other eras that were marked by power shifts, the usability of military power has been reduced in the early twenty-first century. This change is not only due to the structural changes that Luttwak (1990) addressed in his seminal article. It also results from China posing an increasing military challenge to the United States in East and Southeast Asia (Mearsheimer and Walt 2016; Wright 2017). In view of the president's high-profile economic nationalism, it remains to be seen whether the Trump administration will follow the predecessor's approach or engage in a more fierce geo-economic competition vis-à-vis China, which would make the picture even more complex.

China is, without a doubt, challenging the West, mostly in Eurasia, but also in Africa and Latin America. This challenge is mainly economic: the People's Republic develops industrial capacity and seeks to create demand for Chinese products and services abroad. Its model of economic development is marked by massive state-led investments in infrastructure, neglecting issues that matter to the West, also with regard to the international order: anti-corruption, civil society, public health, and women's rights among others. The liberal world order is already under pressure insofar as the Chinese model of economic development constitutes an alternative for developing countries, making authoritarian regimes attractive as drivers of modernisation. The Chinese leadership also increasingly portrays the People's Republic as an ideational challenger to the West, referring to the historical conception of China as a singularly sovereign power at the centre of world order (Bader 2016; Kallio 2016).

If China were to further advance an alternative to the liberal international order, the stakes for US engagement with China would become higher (Ikenberry 2015). However, key interests of China and the United States have converged, as demonstrated by China's step-by-step integration in the liberal international order, most importantly its membership in the World Trade Organisation. Although China is not following the Western model of openness and transparency, which creates uncertainty for the United States with regard to the prospects of cooperation with China, the People's Republic does aim at pragmatic relations, incorporating the West and other partners at large. It appears that China is not interested in fundamentally changing the international system but is somewhat sceptical regarding regime change. Wang and Zhu (2015) hence conclude that there is no Sino-American clash but rather a mutual hedging in world ordering. Nonetheless, as shown above, there is significant geo-economic and geopolitical friction between China and the United States. The evolution of the post-Cold War international order will be largely determined by the success of the United States to accommodate China's rise in economic, financial, military and political terms.

The second aforementioned scenario, a form of US isolationism, had been considered more unlikely than a fundamental change of the international order, until Trump cast ambiguity over sustained commitments by the United States to its international partnerships, both economically and militarily. Hence liberal internationalism as a grand strategy would be questioned, to the extent Trump would follow through his opposition to, or call for renegotiation of, free trade agreements starting with the North American Free Trade Area and take on the bilateral route by rejecting multilateral solutions of the types of the renounced TPP and the pending TTIP. Alliance solidarity subject to conditionality and economic governance driven by mercantilism in US grand strategy could precipitate a world-wide crisis in what has been known as a liberal international order (Wright 2016).

Conclusion

This chapter has put US grand strategy, which has aimed to maintain the liberal international order, in the context of geo-economics and geopolitics. Geopolitics marks the foreign policies of challengers to the liberal order, and is structurally regionalised. China refers to military power to extend its influence in East and Southeast Asia, particularly over maritime areas. Russia seeks to restructure eastern Europe and Eurasia by resorting to geopolitics, too. While China and Russia engage in geo-economics as well, this component of geostrategy marks the United States and the West at large: projects such as the TPP and the TTIP would aim at shaping macro-regions according to liberal values, while also being directed to those powers that challenge the liberal international order.

At the same time, the United States has engaged in geopolitics, as demonstrated by its military commitment to partners in Europe and the Far East. Through a rebalanced grand strategy, mixing geo-economics and geopolitics, the United States aims to consolidate and extend the liberal international order, which has served its interests for an exceptionally long period of history. As a side note, not only the United States but also other states merge geo-economics and geopolitics in their grand strategies. China's global involvement in trade requires the deployment of naval forces in strategically important parts of the Pacific and Indian Oceans so as to safeguard key sea-lines of communication.

The geo-economic and geopolitical components of the grand strategy of the United States as driven during the Obama era were to have different implications for the international system. With regard to geo-economics, the United States would pursue a wedging strategy aimed at stepwise progress towards a uniform global order. The TPP and the TTIP would eventually serve as rule-makers for a regenerated global economic governance. US geopolitics, conversely, resembles a hedging strategy in which the United States aligns itself to a patchwork of partners, and competes with rival powers in separately evolving regions around the world. Given the president's improvisational and situational approach to policy and publicity, it remains unpredictable to what extent the Trump administration will continue along the path set by its predecessor, ascribing priority to its conception of geo-economics in managing the international order.

Note

1 This text was discussed in workshops on geo-economics, held at the Finnish Institute of International Affairs in October 2015 and February 2016. The author also presented it at the Annual Convention of the International Studies Association in Atlanta in March 2016. He would also like to thank Sören Scholvin and Mikael Wigell for their comments on the drafts of this chapter.

References

Bader, J. A. (2016) 'How Xi Jinping Sees the World … and Why', *Brookings*, Asia Working Group Paper 2, February. Available at: www.brookings.edu/wp-content/uploads/2016/07/xi_jinping_worldview_bader-1.pdf, accessed 3 November 2016.

Blackwill, R. D. and Harris, J. M. (2016a) 'The Lost Art of Economic Statecraft: Restoring an American Tradition', *Foreign Affairs*, 95, 2, pp. 99–110.

Blackwill, R. D. and Harris, J. M. (2016b) *War by Other Means: Geo-economics and Statecraft* (Cambridge, MA: Harvard University Press).

Brooks, S. C. and Wohlforth, W. C. (2015) 'The Rise and Fall of the Great Powers in the Twenty-first Century: China's Rise and the Fate of America's Global Position', *International Security*, 40, 3, pp. 7–53.

Buzan, B. (2011) 'A World without Superpowers: Decentred Globalism', *International Relations*, 25, 1, pp. 3–25.

Chollet, D. (2016) *The Long Game: How Obama Defied Washington and Redefined America's Role in the World* (New York: Public Affairs).

Fukuyama, F. (2016) 'American Political Decay or Renewal?', *Foreign Affairs*, 95, 4, pp. 58–68.

Goldman, Z. K. and Rosenberg, E. (2015) 'American Economic Power and the New Face of Financial Warfare', *Center for a New American Security*, June. Available at: www.cnas.org/publications/reports/economic-statecraft-american-economic-power-and-the-new-face-of-financial-warfare, accessed 21 November 2017.

Hamilton, D. S. and Blockmans, S. (2015) 'TTIP's Broader Geostrategic Implications', in Hamilton, D. S. and Pelkmans, J. (eds), *Rule-Makers or Rule-Takers? Exploring the Transatlantic Trade and Investment Partnership* (London: Rowman & Littlefield), pp. 237–256.

Ikenberry, G. J. (2011) *Liberal Leviathan: The Origins, Crisis, and Transformation of the American World Order* (Princeton, NJ: Princeton University Press).

Ikenberry, G. J. (2015) 'Introduction: The United States, China, and Global Order', in Ikenberry, G. J., Wang, J. and Zhu, F. (eds), *America, China, and the Struggle for World Order: Ideas, Traditions, Historical Legacies, and Global Visions* (New York: Palgrave), pp. 1–18.

Indyk, M. S., Lieberthal, K. G. and O'Hanlon, M. E. (2012) *Bending History: Barack Obama's Foreign Policy* (Washington, DC: Brookings Institution Press).

Kallio, J. (2016) 'China's New Foreign Politics: Xi Jinping's Universal Rule by Virtue?', *The Finnish Institute of International Affairs*, FIIA Briefing Paper No. 189. Available at: www.fiia.fi/en/publication/chinas-new-foreign-politics-2, accessed 9 February 2018.

Luttwak, E. N. (1990) 'From Geopolitics to Geo-economics: Logic of Conflict, Grammar of Commerce', *The National Interest*, 20, pp. 17–23.

Mearsheimer, J. J. and Walt, S. M. (2016) 'The Case for Offshore Balancing: A Superior U.S. Grand Strategy', *Foreign Affairs*, 95, 4, pp. 70–83.

Moret, E., Biersteker, T., Giumelli, F., Portela, C., Veber, M., Bastiat-Jarosz, D. and Bobocea, C. (2016) 'The New Deterrent? International Sanctions against Russia over the Ukraine Crisis, Impacts, Costs and Further Action', *Programme for the Study of International Governance at the Graduate Institute of International and Development Studies*. Available at: http://repository.graduateinstitute.ch/record/294704/files/The%20New%20Deterrent%20International%20Sanctions%20Against%20Russia%20Over%20the%20Ukraine%20Crisis%20-%20Impacts,%20Costs%20and%20Further%20Action.pdf, accessed 21 November 2017.

Möttölä, K. (2016) 'Obama's Grand Strategy as Legacy', in Aaltola, M. and Krondlund, A. (2016), *After Rebalance: Visions for the Future of US Foreign Policy and Global Role Beyond 2016*, FIIA Report No. 46 (Helsinki: The Finnish Institute of International Affairs), pp. 39–55. Available at: www.fiia.fi/en/publication/after-rebalance, accessed 9 February 2018.

Möttölä, K. (2017) 'Present at the (Re)creation? Words and Deeds in an Emerging Trump Foreign Policy and the Consequences for European Security', in Aaltola, M. and Gaens, B. (eds), *Managing Unpredictability, Transatlantic Relations in the Trump Era*, FIIA Report No. 51, (Helsinki: the Finnish Institute of International Affairs), pp. 33–54. Available at: www.fiia.fi/en/publication/managing-unpredictability, accessed 9 February 2018.

Overhaus, M. and Brozus, L. (2016) 'US Foreign Policy after the 2016 Elections', *German Institute for International and Security Affairs*, SWP Comments, No. 33, July. Available at: www.swp-berlin.org/fileadmin/contents/products/comments/2016C33_ovs_bzs.pdf, accessed 23 October 2016.

Pereira, D. and Cronin, P. (2016) 'Patrick Cronin and Derwin Pereira – The East Asia Summit and Obama's Asia legacy', *Harvard Kennedy School, Belfer Center for Science and International Affairs*, 15 August. Available at: www.belfercenter.org/publication/patrick-cronin-and-derwin-pereira-east-asia-summit-and-obamas-asia-legacy, accessed 21 November 2017.

Posen, B. R. (2014) *Restraint: A New Foundation for U.S. Grand Strategy* (Ithaca, NY and London: Cornell University Press).

Wang, J. and Zhu, F. (2015) 'Conclusion: The United States, China, and World Order', in Ikenberry, G. J., Wang, J. and Zhu, F. (eds), *America, China, and the Struggle for World Order: Ideas, Traditions, Historical Legacies, and Global Visions* (New York: Palgrave), pp. 359–378.

Weiss, A. S. and Nephew, R. (2016) 'The Role of Sanctions in US–Russian Relations', *Carnegie Endowment for International Peace*, Task Force White Paper, 11 July. Available at: http://carnegieendowment.org/files/6-29-16_Weiss_and_Nephew_Sanctions. pdf, accessed 24 October 2016.

Wigell, M. and Vihma, A. (2016) 'Geopolitics versus Geoeconomics: The Case of Russia's Geostrategy and Its Effects on the EU', *International Affairs*, 92, 3, pp. 605–627.

Wright, T. (2016) 'The 2016 Presidential Campaign and the Crisis of US Foreign Policy' *Lowy Institute*, Analysis, 10 October. Available at: www.lowyinstitute.org/ publications/2016-presidential-campaign-and-crisis-us-foreign-policy, accessed 21 November 2017.

Wright, T. J. (2017) *All Measures Short of War: The Contest for the 21st Century of American Power* (New Haven, CT and London: Yale University Press).

Zoellick, R. B. (2015) 'The Currency of Power: Economics and Security in U.S. Foreign Policy', *Foreign Policy Research Institute*, E-notes, November. Available at: www.fpri. org/wp-content/uploads/2016/01/zoellick_-_dinner_transcript.pdf, accessed 30 October 2016.

8 Leverage of economic sanctions

The case of US sanctions against Iran, 1979–2016

Paul Rivlin[1]

Introduction

The use of sanctions by the United States against Iran since 1979 was a classic example of the use of an economic tool to achieve political objectives (Baru 2012; Luttwak 1990). The sanctions targeted different sectors of the economy and individuals in order to change the political behaviour of the Iranian leadership. They included bans on trade, finance, bans or threats of bans on third parties that traded with Iran, the closing of transportation links, freezes on Iranian funds abroad, and other measures. This chapter examines the evolution and effectiveness of US sanctions against Iran, their scope and design. It places them in the context of US sanctions against other Middle East states and economic developments in Iran.

Between the introduction of sanctions in 1979 and the signing of the Joint Comprehensive Plan of Action (JCPOA) in July 2015,[2] the aim and scope of these sanctions changed. In 1979, US sanctions were designed to secure the release of US hostages held by Iran. In 1984, further US sanctions were imposed on Iran, because it was deemed to be a state sponsor of terrorism. In 2006, the UN Security Council imposed sanctions after Iran refused to suspend its uranium enrichment programme. Initially, US sanctions relating to Iran's nuclear programme targeted investments in oil, gas and petrochemicals, exports of refined petroleum products, as well as business dealings with the Iranian Revolutionary Guard Corps (IRGC), encompassing banking and insurance transactions (including the Central Bank of Iran), shipping, internet and other services. In the first and last cases, deals were made. In the second, no agreement was reached, and US sanctions against Iran remain in force because of its involvement in terrorism. In recent years, the European Union and other countries played a significant role in the sanctions regime on the nuclear issue.

Theories of sanctions

According to Blanchard and Ripsman (2008), the success of economic statecraft (which includes sanctions) depends on whether the economic pain that it inflicts or the gains it engenders result in political costs or opportunities. The political effects of economic statecraft depend on international and domestic political factors, the most important of which is the target state's level of stateness. This has three components: autonomy, capacity, and legitimacy. When economic statecraft motivates key domestic coalitions to push for policy change, high stateness enables target state leaders to resist their calls and defy the sender. Conversely, when economic statecraft convinces target leaders that they ought to comply with the sanctioning party's demands, high stateness enables them to overcome domestic opposition to compromise. In other words, the effectiveness of sanctions will be partly determined by endogenous factors in the state being sanctioned.

Baldwin (1999) criticises much of the literature on sanctions and their effectiveness. The question is whether sanctions will be effective, with respect to the goals and targets set, at what cost, and, in comparison to policy alternatives. The conventional question is whether sanctions can change another state's behaviour without resorting to military force. This is neither sufficient nor primary because the rational policymaker is interested in the expected costs as well as the expected effectiveness of economic sanctions. Even that knowledge, however, is not enough. In addition, policymakers want to know the expected costs and benefits associated with the alternatives.

In an article published in 2011, Drezner evaluated smart sanctions, concluding that the evidence provided moderate support for smart sanctions, those being more humane but less effective than more comprehensive measures. The Libyan case shows the limits of targeted sanctions. A range of policy tools were used to get Libya to alter course, including back-channel negotiations, the Proliferation Security Initiative, and the unspoken threat of military action after the invasion of Iraq in 2003.

> It was the combination of these policy tools – as well as Muhammar Khaddafi's quixotic nature – that led to Libya's acquiescence. [...] The evidence suggests that financial sanctions have hurt both the Iranian and North Korean economies. [...] One former Iranian official admitted in late 2008 that the UN sanctions had increased the price of imports anywhere from 10 to 30 per cent. In neither case, however have the financial sanctions led to concessions at the bargaining table.
>
> (Drezner 2011, pp. 103–104)

This chapter suggests that Drezner's conclusion, at least with regard to Iran, needs modifying.

Sanctions phase 1: from 1979 to 1983

The United States first implemented sanctions against Iran during the hostage crisis that began in November 1979, nine months after the Islamic Revolution. During that month, President Jimmy Carter banned oil imports from Iran, and then froze all Iranian assets worth about US$12 billion, which were subject to the jurisdiction of the United States. In April 1980, the administration imposed an embargo on US trade with and travel to Iran, and also broke off diplomatic relations with Iran (Clawson 2015). These measures came at a time of massive disruption in the Iranian economy following the revolution (Maloney 2016). International oil prices were very low and Iranian oil revenues fell sharply. As a result, its economic growth fell from an average annual rate of 9 per cent in the years from 1960 to 1976 to between minus 3 and minus 5 per cent from 1977 to1980 (Hakimian 2007).

In the same month, President Carter approved a hostage rescue mission by an elite paramilitary unit. It was a dismal failure: several military helicopters broke down in the desert, and eight commandos died when two aircraft collided during a retreat. The failure of the military mission helped to make a deal possible by demonstrating to both sides that there was no military option available to the United States. The United States wanted the hostages freed, and imposed sanctions in order to secure their freedom. The Iranians wanted the sanctions lifted and were prepared to free the hostages in exchange. The deal also defined some of the parameters in which the two sides would operate against each other in the future. Economic measures, especially financial ones, as well as propaganda, were central. There would be no direct military action, although covert military action seems to have been used by both.

On 12 September 1980, Ayatollah Khomeini announced four conditions for the resolution of the crisis. These were the return of the Shah's wealth to Iran; the cancellation of all financial claims against Iran; a pledge by the US of military and political non-interference in Iran, and the release of Iranian assets. This announcement broke the deadlock between the two countries and three days later, Warren Christopher, Deputy Secretary of State, secretly met with Ṣādeq Ṭabāṭabā'i, a close relative of Khomeini. This was the start of final negotiations for the release of the hostages that were held under Algerian auspices. Both countries agreed to end lawsuits. All claims would be referred to international arbitration at an Iran–US Claims Tribunal that was set up in The Hague (Iran Primer 2013; New York Times 1981). On 22 September 1980, Iraq invaded Iran, marking the beginning of a war that lasted eight years. In January 1981, the hostages were released and the US freeze on Iranian funds was cancelled (Encyclopedia Iranica 2004).

The conclusion of this deal suggests that the US response to Iranian hostage-taking was effective because the measures were specific and painful. The US measures presented a major threat to the new regime in Tehran. It desperately needed foreign currency to finance imports and to prove that it could fulfil its pledges to improve the living standards of millions of Iranians who had supported the revolution. According to Maloney

the financial constraints imposed by the assets freeze may not have fully crippled the Iranian economy, which was already reeling as a result of revolutionary chaos, but they magnified the negative consequences of Iran's inept and ideological management and, eventually, the pressures of war.

(2015, p. 431)

The measures taken by the United States were what later became known as smart sanctions, and this is part of the explanation for their success. Such a conclusion should, however, be made with caution, because circumstances in Iran also played a significant role. The regime faced opposition at home both from those who wanted a more radical policy, and those who had supported the occupation of the US embassy and the seizure of the hostages and opponents of the regime. The deal was made after it became apparent to both sides that the United States did not have a military option. This limited US freedom of action might have made it clear to the Iranians that the United States would not budge on sanctions without the release of the hostages.

Sanctions phase 2: from 1984 to 2005

In January 1984, the United States imposed additional sanctions on Iran when the Lebanon-based group Hezbollah was implicated to have played a part in the bombing of the US marine base in Beirut. That year, the United States designated Iran a state sponsor of terrorism. This triggered a range of sanctions, including restrictions on US foreign assistance, a ban on arms transfers, and export controls for dual-use items. As noted, sanctions related to sponsorship of terrorism and human rights abuses were not affected by the nuclear deal and they remain in place today (Goodenough 2016).

Sanctions cover a variety of issues related to the country's internal and external affairs, ranging from weapons proliferation to human rights abuses within Iran to state sponsorship of terrorism and fomenting instability abroad. They target broad sectors as well as specific individuals and entities, both Iranian nationals and foreigners who have dealings with sanctioned Iranians.

Over the years, there have been numerous allegations of terrorism sponsored by Iran. The main incidents include the February 1989 announcement of a fatwa calling for the death of Salman Rushdie, a British author, for his book *The Satanic Verses*, and the suicide bombing of March 1992 at the Israeli Embassy in Buenos Aires that killed 30 and wounded more than 300 people. The Islamic Jihad Organisation, another Shia Islamist militia known for its activities in the 1980s during the Lebanese Civil War, with alleged links to Iran and Hezbollah, claimed responsibility for the attack. The July 1994 bombing of a Jewish community centre in Buenos Aires, which killed 85 and wounded 300, was also blamed on Iran and Hezbollah. Iran is furthermore suspected of organising the June 1996 bombing of the Khobar Towers, a US Air Force housing complex in Saudi Arabia. The United States claimed to have direct evidence of the IRGC's involvement in the attacks. In April 1997, a German court ruled that Iran was responsible for the murders of four Kurdish dissidents in Berlin in 1992. The German government expelled Iranian diplomats and recalled its ambassador from Tehran. The European Union then announced a mass recall of ambassadors from Tehran and joined Germany in suspending the so-called critical dialogue that it was holding with Iran (Goodarzi 2015; Nikou 2016).

In 2002, Israel captured a boat, the Karine A, on its way to Gaza. The ship carried 50 tonnes of advanced weaponry, including Katyusha rockets, rifles, mortar shells, mines, and anti-tank missiles, which had been loaded in Iranian waters (Brandenburg 2016). In 2009, another vessel was stopped with Iranian weapons destined for Hezbollah in Lebanon (Boudreaux 2009). Yet another ship was stopped in 2011 (Weiss 2011). In March 2014, Israel discovered Iranian weapons, including M-302 surface-to-surface missiles on a boat heading for Gaza (BBC 2014). Iran increased its support for President Bashar al-Assad's regime after the Syrian Civil War erupted in 2011. Tehran sent military advisors, equipment, and billions of US dollars in aid, to bolster Iran's interests in Syria. Tehran also created the National Defence Forces – a group of nearly 80,000 Alawites, Shias, and others to assist the Syrian army in combat. High-ranking Iranian officials visited Damascus, and Syrian defence officials have visited Tehran (Goodarzi 2015).

During the 1990s, the United States introduced smart sanctions or selective penalties devised to put pressure on specific groups and avoid the unintended suffering caused by blanket sanctions. They essentially denied access to US markets or financial system to those selling to Iran. Over time, more countries joined the sanctions regime, especially the member states of the European Union, Russia, China, Japan, and South Korea (Fernandez 2012).

The Iran-Iraq Arms Non-Proliferation Act of 1992 subjects any person or entity assisting Tehran in weapons development or acquisition of chemical, biological, nuclear, or destabilising numbers and types of advanced conventional weapons to sanctions. Subsequent non-proliferation legislation and executive actions sanctioned individuals and entities assisting weapons of mass destruction production. Additional bans restrict dual-use exports, a justification for an automobile ban, which was waived under the initial agreement by the five permanent members of the UN Security Council and Germany (the P5+1) with Iran of November 2014, known as the Joint Comprehensive Plan of Action, or JCPOA.

In March 1995, the United States imposed an embargo that banned the participation of US firms in Iranian petroleum development. This occurred after Iran announced a US$1 billion contract with Conoco, an oil company based in the United States, to develop selected oil and gas fields. The Clinton administration then banned all participation of firms from the United States in Iranian petroleum development. In May 1995, this was extended to encompass a total trade and investment embargo on Iran. In 1996, Congress passed the Iran and Libya Sanctions Act, which put pressure on foreign companies not to invest in Iran's oil and gas industry (Clawson 2015).

The move towards smart sanctions was influenced by the humanitarian impact of sanctions that had been imposed on Iraq in the 1990s. They consisted of a near total financial and trade embargo imposed by the United Nations Security Council. The original purposes of these sanctions were to compel Iraq to withdraw from Kuwait, to pay reparations, and to disclose and eliminate any weapons of mass destruction. These sanctions eventually banned all trade and financial resources except for medicine and foodstuffs in humanitarian circumstances, the import of which into Iraq was tightly regulated.

Limitations on Iraqi exports – mainly of oil – made it difficult to fund imports. Following the 1991 Gulf War, a United Nations inter-agency mission assessed that 'the Iraqi people may soon face a further imminent catastrophe, which could include epidemic and famine, if massive life-supporting needs are not rapidly met' (Office of the Iraq Programme Oil-for-Food n.d.). The government of Iraq declined offers contained in UN Security Council resolutions 706 and 712 that would have enabled it to sell limited quantities of oil to finance its people's basic needs. The consequences of the comprehensive embargo on Iraq imposed by the United Nations were catastrophic for the people and the economy. Other factors also played a role: the decision by the Iraqi government to initiate the 1980–1988 war against Iran; the militarisation of the Iraqi economy; Iraq's invasion of Kuwait and the ensuing 1991 Gulf War. While the non-sanctions factors played their different roles, it was the intensity and the open-endedness of the sanctions regime, which bears the major share of the responsibility for the conditions that emerged in Iraq (Abbas 2001).

The effect of the Iraqi episode was to encourage the development of so-called smart sanctions. These were measures that would not have the humanitarian impact of broad trade sanctions but would be more effective by putting direct pressure on individual national policymakers and key organisations in Iran, such as the IRGC. These targeted sanctions included arms embargoes, financial sanctions on the assets of individuals and companies, travel restrictions on the leaders of a sanctioned state, and trade sanctions on particular goods.

In the late 1990s, the United Nations began to develop targeted or smart sanctions by implementing travel bans, asset freezes, and blood-diamond embargoes against the Angolan rebel group UNITA, and by empowering a committee and panel of experts to monitor violations. 'We will propose sanctions [in Angola] with no humanitarian consequences', stated Sergei Lavrov, who then served as Russia's ambassador to the United Nations (Friedman 2012). Following the 9/11 terrorist attacks, President George W. Bush's administration froze the assets of entities supporting international terrorism. This affected dozens of Iranian individuals and institutions, including banks, defence contractors, and the IRGC.

Libya's experiences with international sanctions and subsequent developments including the demise of Muammar Gaddafi may well have influenced Iran's interest in developing nuclear weapons. It is worthwhile examining the Libyan case in order to understand the context within which sanctions against Iran operated.

Sanctions were imposed on Libya from 1978 to 2004 in an effort to persuade Gaddafi to abandon both his unconventional weapons programme and his support for international terrorism. In 2003, he abandoned his support for terrorism abroad and ended the non-conventional weapons programme. In order to understand the development of Libyan policy, it should be remembered that the United States had bombed Libya in April 1986, killing 60 people. This was in retaliation for the April 1986 bombing of a restaurant in West Berlin, where three people had been killed and around 230 injured, among them US soldiers. Two years later, in December 1988, Libya struck again, bombing Pan Am flight

103 in mid-air over Scotland, and then, nine months after that, bringing down a French airliner over Niger – attacks that killed more than 400 people. There were years of damaging sanctions and numerous efforts at diplomatic persuasion before Gaddafi's 2003 announcement and it seems that the decision was his alone. That was the nature of the regime in Libya. Was it reached as a result of threats or promises? There is plenty of documentation suggesting both (Tobey 2014).

The 2003 Libyan policy changes did not guarantee Gaddafi's rule, nor did the agreements he reached with European powers to restrict the movement of migrants from or through Libya northwards. Without nuclear weapons, he did not pose a major threat to Western interests. Western intervention greatly helped to bring about the fall of his regime and his own death, and this may have provided some in Iran with motivation to maintain the nuclear programme.

Sanctions phase 3: from 2006 to 2016

The Iraqi experience suggested that broad, indiscriminate sanctions could create humanitarian crises that undermine their moral justification. The Libyan experience suggested that a combination of specific measures together with an unstated or stated threat to use force might yield better results.

Although the United States had imposed sanctions against Iran that banned most transactions for years, in 2006 it significantly refined those measures. In September 2006, it targeted Bank Saderat – Iran's largest state-owned bank – and the Quds Force of the IRGC for supporting Hezbollah. The United States eliminated a small but significant exception that had existed in the programme, the so-called U-turn authorisation for Bank Saderat. This meant that the bank could no longer process transactions in US dollars through the United States. For a bank with at least 20 per cent of its foreign reserves in US dollars, and for which the oil trade – denominated in the same currency – was its primary livelihood, this was a major threat. Banks in other countries followed, and this encouraged Washington to go further.

In early 2007, the US government used its asset-freezing authority to deny Bank Sepah ongoing access to the US financial system because of its involvement in Iran's nuclear weapons development. Two months after that, the United Nations registered its agreement with the measure and listed Bank Sepah in UN Security Council Resolution 1747, which toughened sanctions against Iran. Later in 2007, measures were announced against other banks: Bank Melli and Bank Mellat (Maloney 2015). In October 2007, the Financial Action Task Force, an inter-governmental body, issued a statement telling member countries to advise their banks about Iran's financial practices. The statement demanded that Iran urgently address its weak anti-money-laundering and anti-terrorist-financing structure. The US Department of the Treasury also engaged in what the under-secretary for terrorism and financial intelligence called an 'unprecedented, high-level outreach to the international private sector', meeting with more than 40 banks worldwide to discuss Iran (Loeffler 2009).

Other sanctions were associated with the aftermath of Iran's 2009 elections, when security forces violently suppressed a budding protest movement, and Iran showed support for US-designated foreign terrorist organisations. In 2007, the Quds Force was sanctioned for destabilising Iraq. In 2011, it was sanctioned for abetting human rights abuses in Syria, as Iran lent its support to the government of Bashar al-Assad, whose security forces were putting down what had begun as a peaceful protest movement. In 2010, US sanctions – including travel restrictions and the freezing of assets – were accompanied by sanctions imposed by the UN Security Council.

The first part of the smart sanctions regime was related to the financial and banking sectors. These were administered by the US Department of the Treasury and sought to isolate Iran from the international financial system. Beyond a prohibition on US-based institutions having financial dealings with Iran, Treasury enforced extra-territorial – or secondary – sanctions: under the 2010 Comprehensive Iran Sanctions, Accountability, and Divestment Act, foreign-based financial institutions or subsidiaries that dealt with sanctioned banks were barred from conducting deals in the United States or in US dollar. The under-secretary of the treasury called these measures a death penalty for any international bank. At the end of 2011, the United States moved to prevent importers of Iranian oil from making payments through Iran's central bank, though it exempted a handful of countries that had made a significant reduction in their purchases. Other measures restricted Iran's access to foreign currencies so that funds from oil importers could only be used for bilateral trade with the purchasing country or to access humanitarian goods. As well as restricting Iran's access to international financial systems, curtailing oil revenue was the principal focus of the Obama administration, as it stepped up pressure on nuclear non-proliferation. Prior to 2012, oil exports provided half the Iranian government's revenue and made up one fifth of the country's gross domestic product. Between 2010 and 2014, the volume of Iranian oil exports fell by 50 per cent (see Table 8.1 further below).

Iran's ability to sell crude oil was particularly affected by the EU ban on Iranian petroleum imports, as well as the imposition of insurance and reinsurance bans by European protection and indemnity clubs, imposed in July 2012. European insurers underwrote most insurance policies for the global tanker fleet. The insurance ban particularly affected Iranian oil exports, as lack of adequate insurance impeded the sales of Iranian crude to all of its customers, including those in Asia. Iranian exports fell as Japanese, Chinese, South Korean, and Indian buyers tried to find alternative insurance policies. Adding to these difficulties was the continued pressure from US sanctions on Iranian oil customers to decrease their purchases (US Energy Information Administration 2015). These measures came on top of sanctions against the oil and gas sectors that denied Iran vital equipment to maintain its fields. Extra-territorial sanctions targeted foreign firms that provided services and investment related to the energy sector, including investment in oil and gas fields, sales of equipment used in refining oil, and participation in activities related to oil export, such as shipbuilding, ports operations, and insurance on transport. Sanctions limited the country's access to foreign technology, capital, and oil-field equipment and services (Vakhshouri 2015). The 1995 embargo that prohibited most US firms from trading with or investing in Iran was relaxed in 2000, and then made nearly total in 2005. The main exception was for the sale of consumer telecommunications equipment and software (European Union External Action 2013). Iran's vulnerability to sanctions was caused by the policies that it followed. This resulted in increased reliance on oil, despite the regime's desire to reduce it (Karshenas and Malik 2011).

The UN Security Council gradually built an international sanctions regime binding on all its member states, following the declaration by the International Atomic Energy Agency from 2005 that Iran was not complying with its safeguards obligations. In a first round of sanctions, in 2006, the UN Security Council unanimously approved measures that included an embargo on materials and technology used in uranium production and enrichment, as well as in the development of ballistic missiles, and blocked financial transactions abetting the nuclear and ballistic-missile programmes. Subsequent UN resolutions in 2007 and 2008 blocked non-humanitarian financial assistance to Iran, and mandated states to inspect cargo suspected of containing prohibited materials, respectively. A fourth binding resolution, approved in June 2010, tightened the international sanctions regime to its current state. It adopted the US approach, linking Iran's oil profits and its banking/financial sector, including its central bank, to proliferation efforts, therefore subjecting them to international sanctioning.

The European Union augmented UN penalties against Iran with sanctions that were, according to the Congressional Research Service, nearly as extensive as those implemented by the United States (Katzman 2017). In 2007, the European Union froze the assets of individuals and entities involved in Iran's nuclear and ballistic-missile programmes, and prohibited the transfer of dual-use items. In 2010, it strengthened its sanctions against Iran, bringing them into line with US measures by preventing European institutions from transacting with Iranian banks, including its central bank, and restricting trade and investment with the country's energy and transport sectors, among others. The EU move to isolate Iran and increase pressure to bring it to negotiations culminated with a 2012 measure banning the import of oil and petrochemical products as well as insurance on shipping, and freezing assets related to Iran's central bank. In 2012, the European Union was the world's largest importer of Iranian oil, averaging 600,000 barrels per day.

Apart from the non-proliferation sanctions, Brussels levied other sanctions – including asset freezes and travel bans for human rights violations, and bans on the export of equipment that could be used for telecommunications surveillance or for internal repression. In March 2012, SWIFT, the Society for Worldwide Interbank Financial Telecommunication, based in Belgium, agreed with the European Union not to forward messages to any Iranian bank or individual that is blacklisted by the European Union. That ban applied to some 30 Iranian banks that Tehran depended on to import and export goods, and sell its oil internationally (Karshenas and Malik 2011; Recknagel 2012).

The effect of sanctions on the Iranian economy

The effect of sanctions on the volume of Iranian oil exports is shown in Table 8.1. The fall in the volume exported resulted in a sharp decline in oil revenues for the economy and for the government. Between 2011 and 2014, the volume of oil exports fell by 56 per cent, while revenues fell by 53 per cent. The fall in prices also contributed to the further dramatic fall in revenues between 2014 and 2015. In recent years, sanctions targeting the oil sector have resulted in the cancellation of projects by foreign companies and affected existing projects (Iran Oil Gas Network n.d.; US Energy Information Administration 2014).

Following the implementation of tighter sanctions in late 2011 and mid-2012, Iranian production dropped dramatically from almost 3.7 million barrels a day in 2011 to 3.1 million in 2014. Although Iran had been subject to four earlier rounds of UN sanctions, the tougher measures imposed by the United States and the European Union severely hampered Iran's ability to export its oil, which also affected oil production (OPEC n.d.; US Energy Information Administration 2015).

Table 8.2 shows that economic growth slowed sharply from an annual average rate of 4.9 per cent between 2006 and 2010 to just under 0.8 per cent from 2011 to 2015. Per capita income growth averaged 3.7 per cent from 2006 to 2010 and minus 1.5 per cent from 2011 to 2015. This slowdown was the result of sanctions and the cumulative effects of the mismanagement of the economy over many years (Maloney 2015).

Since 2012, according to the US Secretary of the Treasury, US sanctions have cost Iran over US$160 billion in lost oil revenues. The JCPOA capped Iran's crude oil exports at about 1.1 million barrels a day but, as of implementation day, Iran was able to export oil without restrictions. Production fell between 2012 and 2015, and Iran avoided an even steeper fall in production by storing about 50 million barrels on tankers in the Persian Gulf or on shore. Not only did Iran's oil exports fall, but Iran was also not paid in hard currency for its oil, other than the US$700 million per month agreed under the JCPOA. Furthermore, Iran was unable to access its hard currency assets held in accounts abroad until

Table 8.1 Iranian oil production and export revenues 2010–2015

	Production (millions of barrels a day)	*Production minus domestic consumption (millions of barrels a day)*	*Revenues ($ billions)*	*Government revenues from oil as percent of GDP*
2010	4.42	2.55	72.2	
2011	4.27	2.57	114.8	10.8
2012	3.81	1.90	101.5	6.6
2013	3.60	1.56	61.9	6.5
2014	3.70	1.68	53.7	5.7
2015	3.90	1.95	18.0	3.9

Sources: BP (2016); Daily Sabah (2015); IMF Country Report: Iran (2011; 2014; 2015). 2011=2011/12, 2012=2012/13, 2013=2013/14, 2014=2014/15, 2015=2015/16 projected.

Table 8.2 GDP growth 2006–2014 (constant prices)

	GDP growth	GDP/capita
2006	5.7	4.5
2007	9.1	7.9
2008	0.9	−0.2
2009	2.3	1.1
2010	6.6	5.3
2011	3.7	2.5
2012	−6.6	−7.8
2013	1.9	−3.2
2014	4.3	3.0
2015 estimate	0.5	−0.8

Source: World Bank (2017a; 2017b).

the JCPOA was implemented. These reserves, held in foreign banks, were estimated at about US$115 billion. Some US$60 billion was owed to creditors such as China or to repay non-performing loans extended to Iranian energy companies working in the Caspian Sea and other areas near Iran.

The International Monetary Fund (IMF 2016) noted that sanctions had affected the exchange rate as well as the inflation rate. The value of the Iranian rial declined about 56 per cent between January 2012 and January 2014 on unofficial markets. The government repeatedly adjusted the official rate. The rate of exchange was between 9,000 and 12,000 to the US dollar between 2007 and September 2013, and in that month it was devalued by 100 per cent to 24,000. In spring 2016, the rate reached just over 30,000. The fall in value of the currency was a major factor causing inflation to accelerate during the period from 2011 to 2013. The decline of the rial, and financial sanctions that complicated obtaining trade credit created difficulties for Iranian manufacturers that are dependent on imported parts. They had to pre-pay for imported parts through time-consuming and circuitous mechanisms. This difficulty was particularly acute in the automotive sector; production of automobiles fell by about 60 per cent between 2011 and 2013 (Central Bank of the Islamic Republic of Iran 2014).

From 2005 until 2012, the nuclear weapons programme increasingly became a political issue in Iran. These were the years in which Mahmoud Ahmadinejad was president. For years, it was a semi-secret programme about which little was said officially. Ahmadinejad changed this and said that the nuclear programme was 'like a train without a brake' that could not be stopped by external pressure. As sanctions intensified, the Iranian public became increasingly aware of the costs of the programme. The unrest following the 2009 elections, and criticisms by conservatives of Ahmadinejad's economic policies created a very divisive political atmosphere within Iran. The 2012 presidential elections were dominated by the nuclear issue, and the election of Hassan Rouhani was a strong indication of the public's preference for a deal with the United States and other powers (Chubin 2015).

Conclusions

What were the objectives of each set of sanctions imposed since 1979 and did they succeed? The aims of US sanctions changed over time. Immediately after the revolution, sanctions were aimed at freeing the hostages taken at the US embassy in Tehran. In the 1980s and 1990s, they were designed to force Iran to cease supporting acts of terrorism and to limit Iran's strategic power in the Middle East more generally. Later, they focussed almost exclusively on the nuclear issue. Did the change in objective determine the degree of success, or the comprehensiveness of the sanctions, or both?

Since the mid-2000s, US sanctions focussed on compelling Iran to limit its nuclear programme to civilian uses and, since 2010, the international community has cooperated with a US-led and UN-authorised sanctions regime in pursuit of that goal. The threat of military action made by the United States differed in intensity over time. The sanctions became more focussed and effective. Financial measures that restricted Iran's access to international capital markets made it very difficult for the country to import. Sanctions on Iranian oil exports made it ever harder to export. The dramatic fall in international oil prices during 2014 meant that oil revenues fell because less was sold and less was earned for each barrel.

Did sanctions work alone, or were there other factors operating in the international environment that brought about the nuclear agreement? One issue was the use of force. The 1981 agreement on the release of US hostages may well have been made possible by the failure of the rescue mission. Did the 2015 nuclear agreement occur for similar reasons? President Obama declared a strong preference for a peaceful solution, but he never ruled out using military force. How did the Iranians understand this? Did they believe him? There is no way of knowing, but the fact that Obama did not rule out the use of force and pledged to end Iran's nuclear threat suggests that, with effective sanctions in place, they took him seriously. The proof is that a deal was made. The sanctions designed to end Iran's non-civilian nuclear programme resulted in an agreement, but they were not stand-alone sanctions. They came on top of other – anti-terrorist – sanctions, and the agreement was signed following the massive squeeze in Iran's oil income resulting from falling international oil prices as well as sanctions.

The internal situation in the country being sanctioned plays a key role in determining the effectiveness of sanctions. This is not a simple matter, as a comparison between the cases of Iraq and Libya shows. Absolute dictators governed both of these states, the leader of one making a deal (or deals) with the West and the other not. Iran is, however, a much larger and more pluralistic society than Iraq and Libya, mainly in terms of interest groups and social classes. It has large groups or forces pulling in different directions. The economics and politics of this balance – between those who favoured President Rouhani and a negotiated solution versus those associated with the IRGC and opposed the negotiations – are perhaps the key issue in Iran. The task for Supreme Leader Khamenei was to stay in power by balancing the views what many perceived as his heart (the IRGC) with those that were his head (Rouhani). The effects of sanctions on those who implement them and those indirectly affected by them are also relevant. The IRGC, operating secretly and on black markets, benefited, while the mass of the population suffered from shortages and rising prices. While the supreme leader was close to the IRGC, he had to consider the social, economic, and ultimately political consequences of its nuclear programme and sanctions.

In Iran, economics played a key role, although it took time. The Iranian leadership was eventually forced to recognise that the opportunity costs of its nuclear military programme were too high. Not only had it invested billions of US dollars that could have gone to more productive uses, but the programme did also result in very damaging sanctions. There was a lot to be gained from a deal with the P5+1, and that was clear from the damage inflicted by sanctions. The Iranian case suggests that sanctions need to be harsh and focussed on specific aims if they are to succeed. Those aims also need to be ones that can be monitored.

Notes

1 The author would like to thank Sören Scholvin and Mikael Wigell for helpful comments on draft versions of this chapter. He is also grateful to the participants of a workshop held at the Finnish Institute of International Affairs in February 2016, where he presented the concepts used in this chapter.
2 The JCPOA required Iran to eliminate its stockpile of medium-enriched uranium, reduce its stockpile of low-enriched uranium by 98 per cent, and reduce the number of gas centrifuges by about two thirds. The agreement provided that in return for verifiably abiding by its commitments, Iran would receive relief from nuclear-related sanctions imposed by the United States, the European Union and the United Nations.

References

Abbas, A. (2001) 'Iraq: Economic Sanctions and Consequences, 1990–2000', *Third World Quarterly*, 22, 2, pp. 205–218.

Baldwin, D. A. (1999) 'The Sanctions Debate and the Logic of Choice', *International Security*, 24, 3, pp. 80–107.

Baru, S. (2012) 'Geo-economics and Strategy', *Survival*, 54, 3, pp. 47–58.

BBC. (2014) 'Israel Halts "Weapons Shipment from Iran"', *BBC*, 5 March. Available at: www.bbc.com/news/world-middle-east-26451421, accessed 24 October 2017.

Blanchard, J-M. F. and Ripsman, N. M. (2008) 'A Political Theory of Economic Statecraft', *Foreign Policy Analysis*, 4, 4, pp. 371–398.

Boudreaux, R. (2009) 'Israel Says Its Navy Intercepted 300 Tons of Weapons Headed for Hezbollah', *Los Angeles Times*, 5 November. Available at: http://articles.latimes.com/2009/nov/05/world/fg-israel-arms-boat5, accessed 24 October 2017.

BP. (2016) 'Statistical Review of World Energy', *BP*. Available at: www.bp.com/content/dam/bp/pdf/energy-economics/statistical-review-2016/bp-statistical-review-of-world-energy-2016-full-report.pdf, accessed 21 November 2017.

Brandenburg, R. (2016) 'Iran and the Palestinians', *Iran Primer*. Available at: http://iranprimer.usip.org/resource/iran-and-palestinians, accessed 24 October 2017.

Central Bank of the Islamic Republic of Iran. (2014) 'Annual Review 1393 (2014/15)', *Central Bank of the Islamic Republic of Iran*. Available at: www.cbi.ir/page/14386.aspx, accessed 24 October 2017.

Chubin, S. (2015) 'The Politics of Iran's Nuclear Program', *Iran Primer*. Available at: http://iranprimer.usip.org/resource/politics-irans-nuclear-program, accessed 24 October 2017.

Clawson, P. (2015) 'US Sanctions', *Iran Primer*. Available at: http://iranprimer.usip.org/resource/us-sanctions, accessed 24 October 2017.

Daily Sabah. (2015) 'Iran's Oil Revenue Falls to $18b in 2015', *Daily Sabah*, 21 October. Available at www.dailysabah.com/energy/2015/10/22/irans-oil-revenue-falls-to-18b-in-2015, accessed November 9, 2017.

Drezner, D. W. (2011) 'Sanctions Sometimes Smart: Targeted Sanctions in Theory and Practice', *International Studies Review*, 13, 1, pp. 98–108.

Encyclopaedia Iranica. (2004) 'Hostage Crisis', *Encyclopaedia Iranica*, last updated 23 March 2012. Available at: www.iranicaonline.org/articles/hostage-crisis, accessed 24 October 2017.

European Union External Action. (2013) 'Joint Plan of Action', *European Union External Action*, 24 November.

Fernandez, J. W. (2012) 'Smart Sanctions: Confronting Security Threats with Economic Statecraft', *U.S. Department of State*, 25 July. Available at: https://2009-2017.state.gov/e/eb/rls/rm/2012/196875.htm, accessed 21 November 2017.

Friedman, U. (2012) 'Smart Sanctions: A Short History', *Foreign Policy*, 23 April. Available at: http://foreignpolicy.com/2012/04/23/smart-sanctions-a-short-history/, accessed 24 October 2017.

Goodarzi, J. M. (2015) 'Iran and Syria: The End of the Road?', *Wilson Center*, Viewpoints No. 79, May. Available at: www.wilsoncenter.org/sites/default/files/iran_syria_end_of_road.pdf, accessed 24 October 2017.

Goodenough, P. (2016) 'Kerry: Terrorists Will Likely Benefit from Some of Iran Sanctions Relief Billions', *CNS News*, 21 January. Available at: www.cnsnews.com/news/article/patrick-goodenough/kerry-terrorists-will-likely-benefit-some-irans-sanction-relief, accessed 24 October 2017.

Hakimian, H. (2007) *Institutional Change, Policy Challenges and Macroeconomic Performance: Case Study of Iran (1979–2004)*. Available at: http://siteresources.worldbank.org/EXTPREMNET/Resources/489960-1338997241035/Growth_Commission_Workshops_Country_Case_Studies_Hakimian_Paper.pdf, accessed 24 October 2017.

IMF. (2011) 'Country Report: Islamic Republic of Iran', *International Monetary Fund*, IMF Country Report No. 11/241. Available at: www.imf.org/external/pubs/ft/scr/2011/cr11241.pdf, accessed 5 December 2017.

IMF. (2014) 'Country Report: Islamic Republic of Iran', *International Monetary Fund*, IMF Country Report No. 14/93. Available at: www.imf.org/external/pubs/ft/scr/2014/cr1493.pdf, accessed 5 December 2017.

IMF. (2015) 'Country Report: Islamic Republic of Iran', *International Monetary Fund*, IMF Country Report No. 15/349. Available at: www.imf.org/external/pubs/ft/scr/2015/cr15349.pdf, accessed 5 December 2017.

IMF. (2016) 'Regional Economic Outlook Update: Middle East and Central Asia', *International Monetary Fund*, World Economic and Financial Surveys, April. Available at: www.imf.org/external/pubs/ft/reo/2016/mcd/eng/pdf/mreo0416.pdf, accessed 24 October 2017.

Iran Oil Gas Network. (n.d.) 'Iran's Oil, Gas and Petrochemical Cancelled Projects', *Iran Oil Gas Network*. Available at: http://iranoilgas.com/projects/?view=canceled, accessed 24 October 2017.

Iran Primer. (2013) 'US-Iran Timeline Since 1979', *Iran Primer*, 17 November. Available at: http://iranprimer.usip.org/blog/2013/nov/17/us-iran-timeline-1979, accessed 24 October 2017.

Karshenas, M. and Malik, A. (2011) 'Oil in the Islamic Republic of Iran', in Collier, P. and Venables, A. J. (eds), *Plundered National? Successes and Failures in National Resource Extraction* (London: Palgrave Macmillan), pp. 114–150.

Katzman, K. (2017) 'Iran Sanctions', *Congressional Research Service*, 13 October. Available at: www.fas.org/sgp/crs/mideast/RS20871.pdf, accessed 24 October 2017.

Loeffler, R. L. (2009) 'Bank Shots – How the Financial System Can Isolate Rogues', *Foreign Affairs*, March/April 2009 Issue. Available at: www.foreignaffairs.com/articles/north-korea/2009-03-01/bank-shots, accessed 24 October 2017.

Luttwak, E. N. (1990) 'From Geo-politics to Geo-economics: Logic of Conflict, Grammar of Commerce', *National Interest*, 20, pp. 17–23.

Maloney, S. (2015) *Iran's Political Economy since the Revolution* (New York and Cambridge: Cambridge University Press).

Maloney, S. (2016) 'The Revolutionary Economy', *Iran Primer*. Available at: http://iranprimer.usip.org/resource/revolutionary-economy, accessed 24 October 2016.

New York Times. (1981) 'Text of Agreement between Iran and the U.S. to Resolve the Hostage Situation', *New York Times*, 20 January. Available at: www.nytimes.com/1981/01/20/world/text-of-agreement-between-iran-and-the-us-to-resolve-the-hostage-situation.html?pagewanted=all, accessed 24 October 2017.

Nikou, S. N. (2016) 'Timeline of Iran's Foreign Relations', *Iran Primer*. Available at: http://iranprimer.usip.org/resource/timeline-irans-foreign-relations, accessed 24 October 2017.

Office of the Iraq Programme Oil-for-Food. (n.d.) *United Nations*. Available at: www.un.org/Depts/oip/background/, accessed 24 October 2017.

OPEC. (n.d.) 'Annual Statistical Bulletin, Various Issues', *OPEC*. Available at: www.opec.org/opec_web/static_files_project/media/downloads/publications/ASB2015_Section3.pdf, accessed 1 September 2016.

Recknagel, C. (2012) 'Explainer: How Does A SWIFT Ban Hurt Iran?', *Radio Free Europe – Radio Liberty*, 16 March. Available at: www.rferl.org/content/explainer_how_does_swift_ban_hurt_iran/24518153.html, accessed 24 October 2017.

Tobey, W. (2014) 'A Message from Tripoli: How Libya Gave Up Its WMD', *Bulletin of the Atomic Scientists*, 3 December. Available at: http://thebulletin.org/message-tripoli-how-libya-gave-its-wmd7834, accessed 24 October 2017.

U.S. Energy Information Administration. (2014) 'Country Analysis Brief: Iran', *U.S. Energy Information Administration*, 21 July. Available at: www.iranwatch.org/sites/default/files/us-doe-irananalysisbrief072114.pdf, accessed 24 October 2017.

U.S. Energy Information Administration. (2015) 'Iran: International Energy Data and Analysis', *U.S. Energy Information Administration*, last updated 19 June 2015. Available at: www.eia.gov/beta/international/analysis_includes/countries_long/Iran/iran.pdf, accessed 24 October 2017.

Vakhshouri, S. (2015) 'Iran Faces Hurdles Hiking Oil Production When Sanctions Lifted', *Oil & Gas Journal*, 1 June. Available at: www.ogj.com/articles/print/volume-113/issue-6/general-interest/iran-faces-hurdles-hiking-oil-production-when-sanctions-lifted.html, accessed 24 October 2017.

Weiss, M. (2011) '50 Tons of Weapons Seized by Israel', *Telegraph*, 16 March. Available at: www.telegraph.co.uk/news/worldnews/middleeast/israel/8385847/50-tons-of-weapons-seized-by-Israel.html, accessed 24 October 2017.

World Bank. (2017a) 'GDP Growth (annual %)', *The World Bank*. Available at: https://data.worldbank.org/indicator/NY.GDP.MKTP.KD.ZG?locations=IR, accessed 5 December 2017.

World Bank. (2017b) 'GDP per Capita Growth (annual %)', *The World Bank*. Available at: https://data.worldbank.org/indicator/NY.GDP.PCAP.KD.ZG?locations=IR, accessed 5 December 2017.

9 Energy and the future of US primacy

The geostrategic consequences of the shale revolution[1]

Niklas Rossbach

Introduction

The United States – the energy superpower, is this what the future holds for the United States? The so-called shale revolution is the result of a new method to produce oil and gas – known as shale gas and tight oil – from resources previously deemed unpractical or uneconomic to extract. The shale revolution began before 2010, but only in the 2010s did decision makers in the United States and elsewhere begin to take notice of the potential strategic impact of the unexpected abundance of gas and oil resources accessible for profitable production in the United States.

How much shale gas and tight oil the United States produces will ultimately depend on how cost-efficient extraction becomes relative to the world oil price, and the pricing of gas in different regions. Because of the shale revolution, the United States was the world's leading producer of natural gas and petroleum hydrocarbons (which includes crude oil), in 2015. However, it is likely to continue to vie with Saudi Arabia for the role of being the world's main oil producer.[2] Of course, shale resources are available globally. Russia has more potentially extractable tight oil than the United States. Algeria, Argentina and China have more shale gas resources (EIA 2013), but it is in the United States that the shale revolution has come about and made a significant impact.

The shale revolution is changing many assumptions about the future of US power and influence in a multipolar world. This chapter analyses the geostrategic consequences of the shale revolution. The following pages demonstrate that the revolution may both help to sustain US primacy, and simultaneously enable the superpower to employ new foreign policy measures – if the US government wishes to do so. The chapter begins with an overview of the rise and supposed decline of the United States as a superpower. It then sheds light on the question of whether the United States is an energy superpower, and whether the United States will become energy independent.

The following pages also discuss two common, but opposed views concerning the impact on foreign policy of the shale revolution. One view holds that the new resources add to US economic power, helping the United States preserve its primacy. In short, the first view holds that the shale revolution is an unexpected but welcome economic windfall that will boost the overall direction of US foreign policy.

The other view argues that shale will help the United States become energy independent, thus freeing the US government from many of its overseas commitments. According to this reasoning, the United States could revert to its original reluctance to make long-term security commitments – what President Thomas Jefferson referred to as having no 'entangling alliances' (LaFeber 2012, p. 44). Such an approach is associated both with the pre-Second World War US isolationism and with statements made by President Donald Trump (e.g. Trump 2015). This analysis shows that both these views are partly erroneous, since the shale revolution works on two levels: the shale revolution has an impact both on the foundation of the US primacy and on what kind of foreign policy tools the United States will have at its disposal.

The rise and potential decline of a superpower

US primacy is often linked to a military perspective, but the United States uses both economic and political means to further its interests. In 2010, at the height of the economic crisis, the chair of the Joint Chiefs of Staff reminded the public that the source of US power is the US economy (CNN Wire Staff 2010).

During the nineteenth century, the United States expanded across the North American continent and rose to become a great power in the 1890s–1910s. At the time, the United States partially tried to copy the European great powers, but not in a race for African territories. Instead, it sought to expand its influence beyond its Pacific shore. The United States even conquered a ready-made colony – the Philippines. However, the United States used more than military means to increase its influence (Beale 1967). When it became a geopolitical factor, its geo-economic power increased too.

Especially important to the economic foundation of the US primacy has been the United States' pre-eminent role in international finance. During the First World War, the US government saw an opportunity for the United States to increase its global influence. The United States began its efforts to try to replace Great Britain as the pre-eminent global financial power. A key part of this political ambition, pursued by the US Secretary of the Treasury, was to replace the British pound sterling with the US dollar as the main global currency. This effort was essential to the ascendance of the United States as a global power (Tooze 2015; also Cassis 2013; Silber 2008). In fact, in the early twentieth-century critics of US imperialism even went so far as to equate US influence with 'dollar diplomacy', pointing to the increased importance of the United States as a result of its financial influence (Nearing and Freeman 1969; Veeser 2007). After the Second World War, the dollar achieved the coveted status of top international reserve currency. In practical terms, this allows the United States to finance itself on credit, while critics argue that it merely enables it to live beyond its means.[3] More importantly, in the energy context, commodities such as oil are often traded in dollars, reducing the currency exchange risk for the United States.

Despite repeated predictions during the twentieth century about US decline, the United States has managed to surprise the world repeatedly. Josef Joffe calls the recurrent narrative of US decline a myth (Joffe 2014). In each instance, every narrative about US decline has been replaced with an equally dramatic story of the United States' return – at least until now. For example, in the 1930s, the United States was in the grips of the Great Depression, following the 1929 Wall Street Crash. Then, the US public tended to favour isolationism, but eventually, at the end of the Second World War, the United States emerged as a new phenomenon, a superpower. In the 1970s, as the Vietnam War ended, US global influence was supposedly waning. Nevertheless, within two decades, the Cold War was over and the United States was the dominant global power.

As major military operations in Afghanistan and Iraq drew a lot of internal criticism and the United States was caught in the midst of the 2008 financial crisis, speculations again started about a US decline. In 2012, even the National Intelligence Council's future analysis report *Global Trends 2030* discussed the possible consequences of US decline (National Intelligence Council 2012). In the last few years, Russian aggression and the difficulty of the United States to steer a decisive course in the Middle East, coupled with severe tensions within the US political system, have contributed to declinists claiming that 'this time it's different' and that the United States will really suffer a decline. Yet, at least since 2014, pundits have been drawing attention to the shale revolution, suggesting that it will help turn things around once more, amounting to the United States' latest comeback (see Kurtzman 2014).

It is not yet clear if a reduced US dependence on energy imports or future US energy exports will have a strategic impact comparable to the establishment of US-led military alliances or dollar diplomacy. Nor is it clear whether or not the US energy revolution will bolster the creditworthiness of the United States and help preserve the dollar's status as the top international reserve currency. After all, unlike in Saudi Arabia and Norway, for example, a national company does not own energy resources in the United States. Nevertheless, the United States is often depicted as being on the cusp of becoming an energy superpower, which suggests that it has found a new way out of the most recent 'decline'-narrative.

The United States – an energy superpower?

In 2012, the United States produced more gas and petroleum hydrocarbons than Russia. In 2013, the United States produced more petroleum hydrocarbons than Saudi Arabia. In 2016, the United States was still the world's leading producer of natural gas and petroleum hydrocarbons.[4] This is an astounding turnaround for the United States. As recently as around 2010, the concern regarding the nation's energy security was its continued energy dependence. In fact, the United States has always been a big energy producer, but during the last decades it has needed much more energy than it has produced on its own (Meyer 2015).

Fracking, the production method for extracting shale gas and tight oil, is increasing the amount of gas and oil the United States is able to produce (Gold

2014; EIA 2016b).[5] The new production of shale energy both is, and is not, an energy revolution. The reason why it is not a revolution is that fracking allows for the increased production of fossil fuels. Hence, the shale energy revolution is not a real energy revolution in the sense of providing the world with a new type of clean energy (see Rossbach 2014). In so far as shale revolution is an energy revolution, it is still mainly a US one.[6] Of course, shale resources are available globally (EIA 2013), but the production of shale might not be so easy in other parts of the world. The US shale revolution came about through private efforts. The breakthrough in fracking happened in the United States because the country has the technological and entrepreneurial skill set, as well as laws that both safeguard investments and are clear about who owns the resources beneath the ground's surface (Gold 2014).

US power is largely a consequence of the US position at the centre of global finance.[7] Like finance, energy is not easily understood from a traditional geopolitical perspective. Analysing energy resources as a basis of national power means more than merely assessing their quantity and accessibility. If more countries turn to shale production, in conjunction with increased trade, the result might also benefit the international order that has existed since 1945, which enabled economic globalisation, and which the United States has led, at least until 2016. In the short term, the shale revolution might primarily benefit the United States relative to other states. This has contributed to speculation about the United States becoming an energy superpower.

Yet, two things make it unlikely for the United States to become an energy superpower. First, while beneficial, the shale energy revolution is unlikely to make the United States a global swing producer of oil. Somewhat simplified, a swing producer means a country that will be able to influence the market price with the help of a significant spare capacity. As a swing producer the United States could, at least in theory, try to make the Organization of Petroleum Exporting Countries obsolete. Tight oil is more expensive to extract than the conventional oil OPEC countries produce, meaning that tight oil requires a higher break-even price to make it profitable to produce. However, the production costs for tight oil have fallen because of improved technology, although concerns remain about the long-term environmental costs of fracking. Nevertheless, the production of tight oil in the United States has proved resilient, despite a lower oil price than when shale production took off. Eventually, as the fracking technology improves, tight oil might also become essential to all the different kinds of oil production that make up conventional oil (Berman 2016; see also Rapier 2016; Yergin 2012, pp. 264–265; Gold 2014, pp. 301–310; Bernell and Simon 2016, p. 113).

Second, the United States does not have state-controlled energy companies, and the government cannot decide when oil should be produced and to whom it should be sold. However, it does have the tools of legislation and permissions of various kinds. The United States took a major step in 2015 when it lifted the ban on exports of crude oil – a ban that had been a national security response to the 1973 international oil crisis.[8] What this suggests is that the United States will pursue a policy attempting to reap the greatest economic benefits from its shale resources, rather than trying to act strategically as a swing producer.

The Trump administration, while less interested in free trade agreements, appears keen on both exports and energy production. It might choose to favour allies, for example gas import dependent countries in the Baltic. However, there might be domestic support for US energy independence and such a policy direction would signal a United States less engaged in the world. Yet, it should be noted how the original purpose of the call for energy independence is often misunderstood.

The myth of energy independence

It was President Richard Nixon, who as a response to the 1973 oil crisis made the term energy independence popular (Yergin 2012, p. 269). The aim was not to isolate the United States from the world, but to return to the level of energy security that the country had enjoyed before the 1970s. With a greater degree of energy security, i.e. fewer energy imports, the United States would not be hamstrung by undue considerations about what effect US policies will have on partners such as Saudi Arabia. The shale revolution holds the promise of returning the United States to the kind of energy security it enjoyed before the 1970s. Furthermore, while the United States banned the export of crude oil in the 1970s, it also pursued multilateral solutions such as establishing the International Energy Agency. Together with other governments, the United States drew up plans to manage disruptions, for example after the use of a so-called energy weapon, such as reduced oil exports (Yergin 2012). Shale production has made the United States less vulnerable to sudden shifts in the global energy market.

By counting all US energy imports together as one (mainly petroleum, gas and coal), a rosy picture emerges indicating that the United States is on its way to ending net imports of energy between 2020 and 2030 (EIA 2015a). However, actual independence is a long way off. While the United States might become a net exporter of natural gas in 2017, it is only likely to become a net exporter of oil under very favourable conditions. Even then, it might take several years and would most likely require a high oil price, and perhaps also reduced US oil consumption, as well as improved production technology (EIA 2015a; 2015b).[9]

The key difference between oil and gas is that oil is the crucial source of energy for the US transport sector (EIA 2015e). While the United States might end its net import of energy, it is not likely to end its import of oil any time soon. Oil and gas are also different stories in terms of security, meaning that the gas the United States imports comes from less problematic parts of the world than some of its oil imports. The United States imports gas from Canada, Norway and Trinidad and Tobago (EIA 2016d). These states are not associated with major security concerns, unlike some oil exporting countries. Hence, oil is more often associated with security concerns, but in fact, the US imports most of its oil from Canada. Mexico is also among the top five exporters to the United States, as is Saudi Arabia, Venezuela and Colombia (EIA 2015f). Out of US petroleum

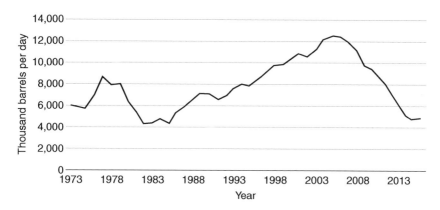

Figure 9.1 US net imports of crude oil and petroleum products (thousand barrels per day).
Source: EIA (2017b).

import, around 16 per cent came from the Persian Gulf in 2015 (EIA 2015g). Accordingly, the US dependency on oil from conflict-ridden parts of the world is less than is often assumed, but stability in the Persian Gulf is important for its indirect impact on the energy markets.

Much more important than from where and how much oil the United States imports is the fact that what it is really importing is the world oil price. Accordingly, isolationism – if it was attempted – could quickly become very uneconomical, since it would be difficult to isolate a national US oil price from the global oil price. The US national security interest concerning oil exports from the Persian Gulf is primarily about safeguarding the flow of oil to the global market, which usually results in a relatively stable oil price at a reasonable level. This benefits the global economy and US energy security, both US interests (see Rossbach 2014; Bernell and Simon 2016; Yergin 2012).

Shale is a win-win for the United States

With the shale revolution, the United States is in a win-win situation when it comes to oil despite not being a net exporter of oil. When the oil price is high, fracking for tight oil makes economic sense. If the United States imports less foreign oil, the trade balance benefits. However, if the oil price falls, the whole US economy benefits from the access to cheap energy.[10] How big the economic benefits are, depends on how cost-efficient fracking becomes, and how well the tight-oil-industry adapts to a shifting oil price by being able to swiftly turn production on and off.

Originally, the high oil price made the production of US tight oil profitable (Economist 2014). With an oil glut and a low oil price, non-tight oil producers such as Saudi Arabia can attempt to make tight oil production unprofitable (Berman

2015). Extracting oil in Saudi Arabia costs perhaps less than US$10 per barrel, whereas the break-even price of tight oil in the United States is much higher, ranging from under US$30 up to nearly US$60 per barrel. However, many energy-exporting countries, such as Saudi Arabia, have a de facto higher break-even price, since their oil exports are the mainstay of their economies. While estimates vary somewhat, Saudi Arabia needs an oil price of around US$90 per barrel to fund all its government services, and Russia might need a price of around US$85 per barrel to meet its budgetary targets (Kennedy 2016; Bentley, Minczeski and Juan 2016). In contrast to these countries, the United States has the advantage of not relying on energy exports to fund its domestic budgetary commitments.

The US shale revolution is already changing global energy relationships. For one, traditional energy exporters of oil and gas need to find new customers to replace the US market. The United States is also likely to contribute to new and changing geostrategic relationships as it develops into an important gas exporter. It is probably the US exports of liquefied natural gas (LNG), effectively gas for overseas export in tankers, which will make the United States a leading energy power.

The United States' desire to export gas is an opportunity for the United States to support a more interconnected global energy market. In fact, there is no global gas price comparable to the world market oil price. There are several regional gas markets around the world, with significant price differences. Sometimes the price of gas is linked to the price of oil. Arguably, this benefits some gas exporters using long-term contracts, such as Russia (Henderson 2016). Companies exporting gas from the United States could carve out a market share in the Asian gas market, which has consumers like South Korea, Japan, China and India. (Note that several of the countries in Southeast Asia are gas producers (EIA 2015h)). This could have the added benefit to the United States of weakening Russia, which is dependent on its energy exports. More importantly, US energy exports are likely to strengthen some existing relationships, for example with energy importers such as Japan – to whom the United States could export gas.

As with oil, a national company does not control gas production in the United States. However, the US government controls export licences for LNG terminals. Under the Obama administration, the government did not try to decide the destination of US energy exports. Following that practice, exports to Asia are likely to be favoured over exports to Europe because of the higher regional price for LNG in Asia (and the revenues are likely to be higher, even taking into account the greater distance to Asia). The recent expansion of the Panama Canal will also make it easier for larger tankers from the US Eastern Seaboard and the Gulf of Mexico to reach the Asian markets (EIA 2016e). However, security concerns could possibly result in government efforts to favour companies exporting to allies in Europe.

The US gas and oil windfall is economically beneficial to the United States. Nevertheless, the amount of new resources combined with the United States role in the world also raises the questions if it is prepared to look beyond economic considerations and use its increased energy security, or indeed its energy resources, as a facet of its foreign policy.

Energy as a foreign policy tool

Like military hardware, energy is a tangible resource. Apart from shale production playing a role in strengthening the economy, the resulting energy resources
can also be used as a foreign policy tool. Either energy can be used as a resource
in its own right, or it can be used to have an indirect impact via the energy price.
Shale is likely to strengthen the overall ties between energy and US foreign
policy. Nevertheless, the United States' improved energy security relative to
other actors, such as China, does not necessarily point towards one specific
policy.

China, which is often presented as the main economic rival of the United
States, saw a less desirable benchmark being reached in 2015 when it surpassed
the United States as the world's biggest oil importer (Sheppard and Meyer
2015).[11] Bruce Jones and David Steven have argued that the United States'
increased energy security opens up new policy opportunities for the United
States with regard to China, as the latter faces increasing energy insecurity. Their
discussion on policy options ranges from marginalising China to merely putting
pressure on Beijing, or even moving towards Sino-US cooperation on energy
security (Jones and Steven 2015).

Until 2016, before the Trump administration took office, the United States
had not attempted to use the US shale revolution for a specific foreign policy
purpose. Nevertheless, influential think tanks have proposed a host of new ways
in which the United States can take advantage of the shale revolution. Some of
the ideas put forward are more fanciful than others, but many proposals are also
in line with furthering the leading global role the United States has had for the
last 70 years. Others point towards a more narrow definition of US interests,
where new energy policies could contribute to some degree of US isolationism.
It is important to keep in mind that while some policy ideas may seem extreme,
it does not mean that they could not be employed in the future. For example, the
Trump administration, which seems less tied to a post-Cold War US foreign
policy consensus, might find merits in ideas that a different and more conventional administration would not consider.

The following ideas and proposals have been compiled from the debate about
the foreign policy potential of the shale revolution. It is by no means exhaustive,
so it can only give an indication about how the shale revolution could be used in
US foreign policy.[12]

- First, the idea of putting the general advantage provided by increased energy
  production to use: the United States could enhance this trend by giving technical aid to states wishing to produce shale gas and tight oil (Blackwill and
  O'Sullivan 2014). The very existence of more oil and gas have already
  helped to dampen the risk of price spikes, especially in the oil market. This
  allows the United States to pursue policies, which could otherwise cause
  economic stress at home and for allies, such as sanctions against oil
  exporters like Iran.[13] As such, a reduced risk of oil spikes makes it easier for

the United States to pursue either its post-Cold War foreign policy or another activist foreign policy.

- Second, the United States could prepare solely for its own security of supply, with a view to an eventual international energy crisis. The United States would thus produce more oil and natural gas for its own domestic needs.[14] This would be a sort of defensive geo-economic policy. It would look solely at national needs, and would probably be the preferred option of a strictly isolationist US.

- Third, by using its Strategic Petroleum Reserve (SPR) or LNG for targeted exports, the US government could help an ally at a time of confrontation with another state. Such a promise of bilateral energy aid would arguably be interpreted as a strategic course of action, similar to strengthening an ally militarily. Originally, the SPR was not intended for such unilateral usage. It was supposed to be used as part of a multilateral effort to strengthen global energy security in times of a crisis (Rosenberg 2014; Victor and Eskreis-Winkler 2008; Rossbach 2014). Using the SPR in pursuit of a specific US foreign policy goal, as suggested here, would appeal to a US government prepared to leverage the United States' new energy security.

The proposals suggest that the US shale revolution has partly upended the underlying logic of the US national security that has helped guide US actions during the last 40 years. Moreover, even though the United States would not become an energy superpower, it could try to use its newfound resources to influence global politics.

Conclusion

This chapter has argued that the United States is not likely to become an energy superpower, nor energy independent. However, the shale revolution makes the United States less dependent on overseas oil exporting partners, which changes the energy security logic that has limited US foreign policy since the 1970s. The shale revolution means that the United States will return to what was originally meant by energy independence – a reduced dependence on imported energy. The United States will thus have a greater degree of energy security and a corresponding greater freedom to shape its foreign policy. The shale revolution also helps change the assumptions about US decline being imminent, and helps generate new ideas about policy options for the United States, for example concerning how the United States can preserve its power and influence. This newfound freedom in foreign policy is a key geostrategic benefit of the shale revolution for the United States.

As stated initially, the shale revolution works on two levels. First, it helps the United States sustain its global primacy, because it benefits the US economy regardless of whether the oil price is high or low. In the coming years, the United States will be in a win-win situation as far as oil is concerned. A low oil price will benefit the US economy as a whole, while a high oil price will increase US oil production. US gas production is likely to remain high and allow US gas exports to become a key factor in the global energy markets.

Second, the shale revolution creates conditions for US governments – such as the Trump administration – to alter the course of US foreign policy. The US shale revolution has already resulted in new producer-consumer relationships globally. States that previously exported gas and oil to the United States have already had to find new markets. Regardless of whether the US government directs energy exports or not, the shale revolution will alter US relations with other countries. Policies concerning US energy, primarily the export of LNG, can also be used as a foreign policy tool. Energy trade is likely to strengthen some existing US relationships in Asia and perhaps in Eastern Europe, and may also result in new relationships. In the future, US governments might try to link energy trade with strategic considerations as a means of shaping specific relationships. In any case, the shale revolution will help sustain US primacy, while at the same time having an impact on what kind of foreign policy the US pursues in the future.

Notes

1 Some aspects of this chapter have also been discussed in Rossbach (2014). The author wishes to thank Sören Scholvin and Mikael Wigell for their helpful comments on earlier drafts.
2 According to the EIA, the United States is today the world's largest producer of petroleum and natural gas hydrocarbons. See EIA (2016a) and Rascouet (2016).
3 In practical terms, this allows the United States to finance itself on credit, while critics argue that it merely enables the United States to live beyond its means (Layne 2012; also Helleiner and Kirshner 2009; Eichengreen 2012).
4 About 60 per cent of the US petroleum hydrocarbons are crude oil and lease condensate. In the case of Saudi Arabia, the percentage of crude oil and lease condensates as part of petroleum hydrocarbons is much higher. According to the EIA, the United States is today the world's largest producer of petroleum and natural gas hydrocarbons (EIA 2017a). For a contrasting view, see Rascouet (2016).
5 Shale gas and tight oil are not strict geological definitions. The term shale oil is usually avoided since it is too similar to oil shale, which is a more specific resource.
6 The shale revolution should not be confused with Canadian unconventional energy production such as oil sands or oil shale (which differs from tight oil and which is a more costly resource to exploit). Canada has neither developed its shale deposits to the same extent as the United States. Until now, Canada has mostly benefited from a rise in shale gas. Tight oil might not be as easily accessible in Canada as in the United States (Topf 2015; Mlada 2016).
7 The US dollar remains the top international reserve currency, although the future of the dollar is debated. For a brief overview of how the American peace, the *Pax Americana*, is dependent on the US role at the heart of the global economy, see Frieden and Lake (2000); see also Eichengreen (2012). For the post-war foundation of American financial power, see Conway (2014).
8 In fact, legislation can be found as far back as the 1920s (see Boersma and Ebinger 2014; BBC 2016).
9 For a general but recent projection, see EIA (2015c). See also EIA (2015d) and EIA (2016c).
10 Precise calculations about the economic benefits requires econometric analysis beyond the scope of this chapter.

11 The United States was until recently the leading global energy consumer. China is said to have surpassed it if measured in oil equivalents, but only in the 2030s will China consume more oil than the United States (IEA 2015; Swartz and Oster 2010).
12 Some of the ideas are also collected in Rossbach (2014).
13 For instance, it was easier for the United States and others to engage in sanctions against Iran when the world oil price did not spike, which was the result of the increased American oil production, as suggested by Blackwill and O'Sullivan (2014).
14 For a contrasting view, see Clayton (2013) and Rossbach (2014).

References

BBC. (2016) 'US Spending Bill Lifts 40-year Ban on Crude Oil Exports', *BBC*, 18 December. Available at: www.bbc.com/news/business-35136831, accessed 7 December 2017.

Beale, H. K. (1967) *Theodore Roosevelt and the Rise of America to World Power* (New York: Collier Books).

Bentley, E., Minczeski, P. and Juan, J. (2016) 'Which Oil Producers Are Breaking Even? Lower Oil Prices Have Made It a Challenge for Some Countries to Balance Their Budgets', *The Wall Street Journal*, 18 January. Available at: http://graphics.wsj.com/oil-producers-break-even-prices/, accessed 7 December 2017.

Berman, A. (2015) 'The Shale Delusion: Why the Party's Over for U.S. Tight Oil', *Oilprice.com*, 14 September. Available at: http://oilprice.com/Energy/Crude-Oil/The-Shale-Delusion-Why-The-Partys-Over-For-US-Tight-Oil.html, accessed 7 December 2017.

Berman, A. (2016) 'Investors Beware: U.S. Tight Oil Is Not the Swing Producer of The World', *Forbes*, 6 January. Available at: www.forbes.com/sites/arthurberman/2016/01/06/investors-beware-u-s-tight-oil-is-not-the-swing-producer-of-the-world/#16491f723fd9, accessed 7 December 2017.

Bernell, D. and Simon, C. A. (2016) *The Energy Security Dilemma: US Policy and Practice* (New York: Routledge).

Blackwill, R. D. and O'Sullivan, M. L. (2014) 'America's Energy Edge: The Geopolitical Consequences of the Shale Revolution', *Foreign Affairs*, 93, 2, pp. 102–114.

Boersma, T. and Ebinger, C. K. (2014) 'Lift the Ban on U.S. Oil Exports', *Brookings*, 23 January. Available at: www.brookings.edu/research/lift-the-ban-on-u-s-oil-exports/, accessed 7 December 2017.

Cassis, Y. (2013) *Crises and Opportunities: The Shaping of Modern Finance* (Oxford: Oxford University Press).

Clayton, B. (2013) 'The Case for Allowing U.S. Crude Oil Exports', *Council on Foreign Relations*, Policy Innovation Memorandum No. 34. Available at: www.cfr.org/sites/default/files/pdf/2013/06/Policy_Innovation_Memo34_Clayton.pdf, accessed 7 December 2017.

CNN Wire Staff. (2010) 'Mullen: Debt is Top National Security Threat' *CNN*, 27 August. Available at: http://edition.cnn.com/2010/US/08/27/debt.security.mullen/, accessed 7 December 2017.

Conway, E. (2014) *The Summit – The Biggest Battle of the Second World War – Fought Behind Closed Doors* (London: Little Brown).

Economist. (2014) 'The Economics of Shale Oil – Saudi America', *The Economist*, 15 February. Available at: www.economist.com/news/united-states/21596553-benefits-shale-oil-are-bigger-many-americans-realise-policy-has-yet-catch, accessed 7 December 2017.

EIA. (2013) 'Shale Oil and Shale Gas Resources Are Globally Abundant', *U.S. Energy Information Administration*, Today in Energy, 10 June. Available at: www.eia.gov/todayinenergy/detail.cfm?id=11611, accessed 7 December 2017.

EIA. (2015a) 'U.S. Energy Imports and Exports to Come Into Balance for First Time Since 1950s', *U.S. Energy Information Administration*, Today in Energy, 15 April. Available at: www.eia.gov/todayinenergy/detail.php?id=20812, accessed 7 December 2017.

EIA. (2015b) 'Projections Show U.S. Becoming a Net Exporter of Natural Gas', *U.S. Energy Information Administration*, Today in Energy, 28 April. Available at: www.eia.gov/todayinenergy/detail.php?id=20992, accessed 7 December 2017.

EIA. (2015c) 'EIA's AEO2017 Projects the United States to Be a Net Energy Exporter in Most Cases', *U.S. Energy Information Administration*, Today in Energy, 5 January. Available at: www.eia.gov/todayinenergy/detail.php?id=29433, accessed 7 December 2017.

EIA. (2015d) 'Increasing Domestic Production of Crude Oil Reduces Net Petroleum Imports', *U.S. Energy Information Administration*, Today in Energy, 21 April. Available at: www.eia.gov/todayinenergy/detail.php?id=20892, accessed 7 December 2017.

EIA. (2015e) 'What Are the Major Sources and Users of Energy in the United States?', *U.S. Energy Information Administration*, Energy in Brief, 29 December. Available at: www.eia.gov/energy_in_brief/article/major_energy_sources_and_users.cfm, accessed 28 September 2015.

EIA. (2015f) 'How Much Petroleum Does the United States Import and Export?', *U.S. Energy Information Administration*, last updated 4 April 2017. Available at: www.eia.gov/tools/faqs/faq.cfm?id=727&t=6, accessed 7 December 2017.

EIA. (2015g) 'Oil: Crude and Petroleum Products Explained', *U.S. Energy Information Administration*. Available at: www.eia.gov/energyexplained/index.cfm?page=oil_imports, accessed 7 December 2017.

EIA. (2015h) 'Natural Gas Prices in Asia Mainly Linked to Crude Oil, but Use of Spot Indexes Increases', *U.S. Energy Information Administration*, Today in Energy, 29 September. Available at: www.eia.gov/todayinenergy/detail.php?id=23132, accessed 7 December 2017.

EIA. (2016a) 'United States Remains Largest Producer of Petroleum and Natural Gas Hydrocarbons', *U.S. Energy Information Administration*, 23 May. Available at: www.eia.gov/todayinenergy/detail.cfm?id=26352, accessed 7 December 2017.

EIA. (2016b) 'Shale in the United States', *U.S. Energy Information Administration*, 15 September. Available at: www.eia.gov/energy_in_brief/article/shale_in_the_united_states.cfm, accessed 15 August 2016.

EIA. (2016c) 'Market Trends: Liquid Fuels, Annual Energy Outlook 2016', *U.S. Energy Information Administration*, 15 September. Available at: www.eia.gov/forecasts/aeo/MT_liquidfuels.cfm, accessed 8 December 2017.

EIA. (2016d) 'U.S. Natural Gas Imports and Exports 2015', *U.S. Energy Information Administration*, 31 May. Available at: www.eia.gov/naturalgas/importsexports/annual/, accessed 15 August 2016.

EIA. (2016e) 'Expanded Panama Canal Reduces Travel Time for Shipments of U.S. LNG to Asian Markets', *U.S. Energy Information Administration*, Today in Energy, 30 June. Available at: www.eia.gov/todayinenergy/detail.php?id=26892, accessed 7 December 2017.

EIA. (2017a) 'United States Remains the World's Top Producer of Petroleum and Natural Gas Hydrocarbons', *U.S. Energy Information Administration*, Today in Energy, 7 June. Available at: www.eia.gov/todayinenergy/detail.php?id=31532, accessed 7 December 2017.

EIA. (2017b) 'U.S. Net Imports of Crude Oil and Petroleum Products', *U.S. Energy Information Administration*. Available at: www.eia.gov/dnav/pet/hist/LeafHandler.ashx?n=pet&s=mttntus2&f=a, accessed 8 December 2017.

Eichengreen, B. (2012) *Exorbitant Privilege: The Rise and Fall of the Dollar and the Future of the International Monetary System* (Oxford: Oxford University Press).

Frieden, J. A. and Lake, D. A. (2000) *International Political Economy – Perspectives on Global Power and Wealth* (London: Routledge).

Gold, R. (2014) *The Boom: How Fracking Ignited the American Energy Revolution and Changed the World* (New York: Simon & Schuster).

Helleiner, E. and Kirshner, J. (eds) (2009) *The Future of the Dollar* (Ithaca, NY and London: Cornell University Press).

Henderson, J. (2016) 'Gazprom – Is 2016 the Year for a Change of Pricing Strategy in Europe?', *The Oxford Institute for Energy Studies*, Oxford Energy Comment, January. Available at: www.oxfordenergy.org/wpcms/wp-content/uploads/2016/02/Gazprom-Is-2016-the-Year-for-a-Change-of-Pricing-Strategy-in-Europe.pdf, accessed 7 December 2017.

IEA. (2015) 'World Energy Outlook 2015 – Executive Summary', *OECD/IEA*. Available at: www.iea.org/Textbase/npsum/WEO2015SUM.pdf, accessed 7 December 2017.

Joffe, J. (2014) *The Myth of America's Decline – Politics, Economics, and a Half Century of False Prophecies* (New York: Liveright Publishing Corporation).

Jones, B. and Steven, D. (2015) *The Risk Pivot – Great Powers, International Security, and the Energy Revolution* (Washington, DC: Brookings Institution Press).

Kennedy, C. (2016) 'Who Will Be Left Standing at The End Of The Oil War', *Oilprice.com*, 22 February. Available at: http://oilprice.com/Energy/Crude-Oil/Who-Will-Be-Left-Standing-At-The-End-Of-The-Oil-War.html, accessed 7 December 2017.

Kurtzman, J. (2014) *Unleashing the Second American Century – Four Forces for Economic Dominance* (New York: Public Affairs).

LaFeber, W. (2012) 'The US Rise to World Power, 1776–1945', in Cox, M. and Stokes, D. (eds), *US Foreign Policy* (second edition) (Oxford: Oxford University Press), pp. 43–58.

Layne, C. (2012) 'US Decline or Primacy? A Debate', in Cox, M. and Stokes, D. (eds), *US Foreign Policy* (second edition) (Oxford: Oxford University Press), pp. 410–418.

Meyer, G. (2015) 'US Close to Ending Era as Net Importer of Energy', *Financial Times*, 14 April. Available at: www.ft.com/content/f6dcbd90-e2bf-11e4-aa1d-00144feab7de, accessed 8 December 2017.

Mlada, S. (2016) 'Canada Shale', *Oil & Gas Financial Journal*. Available at: www.ogfj.com/articles/print/volume-13/issue-4/features/canada-shale.html, accessed 8 December 2017.

National Intelligence Council. (2012) 'Global Trends 2030: Alternative Worlds', *National Intelligence Council*, December. Available at: https://globaltrends2030.files.wordpress.com/2012/11/global-trends-2030-november2012.pdf, accessed 8 December 2017.

Nearing, S. and Freeman, J. (1969) [1925] *Dollar Diplomacy: A Study In American Imperialism* (New York: Modern Reader Paperbacks).

Rapier, R. (2016) 'The Break Even Cost for Shale Oil', *Forbes*, 29 February. Available at: www.forbes.com/sites/rrapier/2016/02/29/the-break-even-cost-for-shale-oil/#2a9b384440d4, accessed 8 December 2017.

Rascouet, A. (2016) 'Saudi Arabia Ousts U.S. as Biggest Oil Producer, IEA Says', *Bloomberg*, 13 September. Available at: www.bloomberg.com/news/articles/2016-09-13/saudi-arabia-overtakes-u-s-as-largest-oil-producer-iea-says, accessed 8 December 2017.

Rosenberg, E. (2014) 'Energy Rush – Shale Production and U.S. National Security', *Center for a New American Security*, 6 February. Available at: www.cnas.org/publications/reports/energy-rush-shale-production-and-u-s-national-security, accessed 8 December 2017.

Rossbach, N. H. (2014) 'Amerikanskt Energioberoende? Säkerhetspolitiska Följder av Okonventionell Energiutvinning av Skiffergas och Skifferolja i USA', *FOI* Report (Stockholm: Totalförsvarets forskninginstitut). Available at: www.foi.se/rapportsamma nfattning?reportNo=FOI-R-3947-SE, accessed 31, January 2018.

Sheppard, D. and Meyer, G. (2015) 'China Oil Imports Surpass Those of US', *Financial Times*, 10 May. Available at: www.ft.com/content/342b3a2e-f5a7-11e4-bc6d-00144feab7de, accessed 8 December 2017.

Silber, W. L. (2008) *When Washington Shut Down Wall Street: The Great Financial Crisis of 1914 and the Origins of America's Monetary Supremacy* (Princeton and Oxford: Princeton University Press).

Swartz, S. and Oster, S. (2010) 'China Tops U.S. in Energy Use', *The Wall Street Journal*, 18 July.

Tooze, A. (2015) *The Deluge: The Great War and the Remaking of Global Order* (New York: Penguin).

Topf, A. (2015) 'Canada Will Find US Shale Oil Revolution Hard Act to Follow', *Energy Post*. Available at: http://energypost.eu/canada-will-find-us-shale-oil-revolution-hard-act-follow/, accessed 8 December 2017.

Trump, D. (2015) *Crippled America: How to Make America Great Again* (New York: Simon and Schuster).

Veeser, C. (2007) *A World Safe for Capitalism: Dollar Diplomacy and America's Rise to Global Power* (New York: Columbia University Press).

Victor, D. G. and Eskreis-Winkler, S. (2008) 'In the Tank – Making the Most of Strategic Oil Reserves', *Foreign Affairs*, 87, 4, pp. 70–83.

Yergin, D. (2012) *The Quest – Energy, Security and the Remaking of the Modern World* (New York: Penguin Books).

10 Learning geo-economics

China's experimental path towards financial and monetary leadership[1]

Mikko Huotari

Introduction

A lot of attention has been paid recently to pathways and consequences of the integration of emerging market powers, particularly the BRICS countries, in the existing global financial and monetary order. Research often focuses on how these countries position themselves individually and as a group regarding their role in multilateral institutions such as the International Monetary Fund (IMF) and the World Bank (Kahler 2013; Heep 2014; Huotari and Hanemann 2014). However, while the necessary institutional adaptation of the international financial institutions (IFI) is stagnating, global financial and monetary order is becoming increasingly fragmented and polycentric (Mittelman 2013). New patterns of capital flows and currency usage, as well as regional and other decentralised patterns of financial and monetary cooperation, are driving this evolving polycentricism.

In this context, China is using its economic leverage to achieve long-term political goals, as it is often not only at the core of these shifting asymmetric interdependences, but also the key driving force of new institutional arrangements that serve to embed its increasing trade, financial and monetary power. With several new initiatives to provide crisis liquidity, long-term (development) financing and a global infrastructure to internationalise its own currency, Beijing is actively promoting institutional innovation across several key domains of global economic order. The stakes seem high, as most observers tend to interpret the (possible) transformation of spheres of authority and solidarity that result from these developments as an unsettling disturbance (Etzioni 2016; Blackwill and Tellis 2015; see also Heilmann *et al.* 2014). This is partly understandable, because after the establishment of the Bretton-Woods institutions, no country has decidedly sought to adapt the international financial and monetary order to its own needs. However, rather than seeing China's new power projection only as a disruptive factor resulting from strategic-instrumental statecraft, this chapter provides a supplementary perspective that stresses policy learning closely aligned with domestic conditions, and offers an explorative approach to Chinese policymakers, which one might call geo-economic engineering.

The very risk-averse strategies that involve the layering and nesting of newly established arrangements are fundamental to China's learning attitude regarding its global financial engagement. China has simultaneously promoted several financial and monetary initiatives that are meant to converge especially in the East Asian region, taking an approach called 'parallel partial-progression' (Fan and Woo 2005) in describing domestic reforms.

The following sections analyse China's geo-economic experiments across three crucial policy fields: (1) crisis liquidity provision through bilateral, regional and minilateral means with the Chiang-Mai Initiative (CMI) and the BRICS Contingent Reserve Arrangement (BRICS CRA) as core initiatives; (2) new China-centred mechanisms for development financing, ranging from relatively small and targeted investment funds to the full-fledged multilateral Asian Infrastructure Investment Bank; (3) domestic and cross-border experimentation related to China's currency internationalisation project.

Providing access to capital during financial crises

China is a newcomer with regard to international cooperation for crisis liquidity provision beyond its curtailed role in the IMF. Owing to the still limited capital account opening and a managed exchange rate, the Chinese economy is still relatively shielded from external financial risks. To date, the Chinese monetary authorities, together with China's currency reserve war chest, would still be capable of dealing with major disruptions from hot money flows and exchange rate fluctuations. Nevertheless, the pressures for China to externalise risk management and engage with or establish new international financial security arrangements have slowly been increasing. As China turns away from its

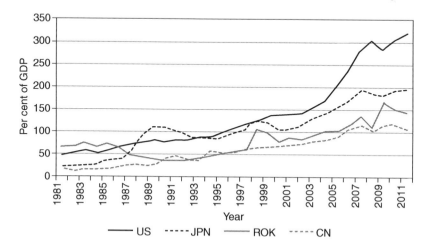

Figure 10.1 Sum of foreign assets and liabilities as per cent of GDP.

Source: updated and extended version of the dataset constructed by Lane and Milesi-Ferreti (2007).

Table 10.1 Schemes for crisis liquidity provision

Arrangement	Date	Size	China's share (%)	Members	Type of engagement
(CMI)	2001	Total: US$95 billion in 2009	17	ASEAN+3	Network of bilateral US$ swap agreements
People's Bank of China (PBoC) Network of Bilateral Local Currency Swap Agreements	2008	More than US$500 billion in 2015	100	More than 32 agreements[1]	Bilateral local currency swap agreements
Chiang-Mai Initiative Multilateralisation (CMIM)	2010	US$240 billion since 2010	32	ASEAN+3	Self-managed reserve pooling arrangement (by earmarking parts of national foreign exchange reserves for regional purposes)
BRICS CRA	2014	US$100 billion since 2014	41	BRICS	Self-managed reserve pooling arrangement

Source: author's research.

Note
1 Agreements have been concluded and extended (indicated by year in brackets) with Indonesia 2009 (2013), Hong Kong 2009 (2013), Korea 2009 (2014), Argentina 2009 (2014), Belarus 2009 (2015), Malaysia 2009 (2015), Iceland 2010 (2013), Singapore 2010 (2013), Pakistan 2011 (2014), Thailand 2011 (2014), Kazakhstan 2011 (2014), Mongolia 2011 (2014), New Zealand 2011 (2014), Uzbekistan 2011, Australia 2012 (2015), Ukraine 2012 (2015), Turkey 2012 (2015), UAE 2012 (2015), UK 2013 (2015), EU/ECB 2013, Albania 2013, Hungary 2013, Brazil 2013, Canada 2014, Qatar 2014, Russia 2014, Sri Lanka 2014, Switzerland 2014, South Africa 2015, Armenia 2015, Suriname 2015, Chile 2015

developmentalist financial insulation, gradually relinquishes capital controls, and rapidly expands its international investment position, Chinese policymakers have increasingly accepted the necessity of engaging more systematically with global, regional or other minilateral attempts to provide liquidity in crisis situations (Wang 2014). With its financial integration ratio growing beyond 100 per cent, and an escalating global presence of Chinese state-affiliated financial institutions and other companies, like Japan earlier, China has developed a greater sense for the need to protect its overseas financial presence.

However, beyond direct creditor interests, motives for China's geo-economic engagement with regard to crisis liquidity provision on the regional scale and among the BRICS stem mainly from fears of indirect contagion and broader considerations regarding political stability and regional order. China's slowly growing capabilities to protect other economies from the potential shocks of rapid reversals of financial flows elevate China's political status and help to shape leadership-followership relations with financial means.

While China continues to call for reforms of the IMF, it has substantially contributed to the increase of available funding through the IMF after the global financial crisis of 2007/2008. Going beyond mere integration in the existing global multilateral system, for instance through direct contributions to the IMF capital base, the Chinese leadership has also made several experimental moves to link-up with existing financial arrangements, improving them or establishing new ones that manage direct and indirect risks emerging from deepening financial ties.

China's relatively new involvement in international schemes for crisis liquidity provision shows strong signs of a very risk-averse and experimental attitude, which provides conditions for effective policy learning. Typical for an experimental policy mode, these moves serve to generate innovative solutions to the question of how to achieve the long-term policy goal of capital account convertibility and deeper financial integration, set forth by the Chinese party elite already in the late 1990s. After a far-reaching proposal by Japan had been blocked back then, China was very eager to engage in rather low-key initiatives to strengthen financial resilience in the region. The initial arrangement of the CMI among the ASEAN+3 countries,[2] a network of bilateral currency swap agreements[3] that gradually expanded between 2001 and 2009, was created to be scalable and to expand along with growing economic needs and political willingness of the involved economies to engage further. Through a period of productive leadership, competition with Japan, China took over the agenda to push for an institutionalisation of regional governance. Eventually, after years of negotiations and with the crisis shock in 2008/2009, the bilateral network was multilateralised in 2010 into a self-managed reserve pool arrangement, becoming the Chiang-Mai Initiative Multilateralisation (Huotari 2015). While this initiative was not particularly costly for China in financial terms, it is still the most visible sign of its pan-East Asian commitment to region-building, and also involves a high degree of careful political balancing of leadership-followership relations.

Another risk-averse gradualist element was built into the framework of CMI – and is still part of the CMIM – with the step-wise decreasing linkage of potential fund-disbursement from IMF programmes. At the outset of the CMI, only 10 per cent of the available sum could have been drawn on without an IMF programme. Over the last 14 years, this de-linked part of CMIM-funding has not been removed but will soon increase to 40 per cent. This nesting of new initiatives with existing arrangements not only helped to avoid political contestation, but also created institutional linkages that allowed for expert deliberations and policy exchange. As another layer of crisis liquidity provision, the People's Bank of China (PBoC) has signed a network of bilateral swap agreements since 2008. These parallel the CMI swaps but involve local currencies, and are currently not very useful as financial insurance instruments. With the likely exception of Pakistan and Argentina, no country has so far drawn on these swap agreements to secure Chinese currency (then converted to US dollars) as a source of crisis liquidity. However, both the language of the PBoC announcements and public debates in potential follower-states during crisis situations (such as in Indonesia and the Philippines in 2009) often assume otherwise, which at least highlights their economic potential and political symbolism as another layer of financial safety arrangements across the globe. The conclusion of these swap agreements, which are expanding from the East Asian region to other economies, again created conditions for extensive policy learning in terms of adequate sizing, negotiation practices, and central bank executive relations.

Compared to more institutionalised arrangements, these bilateral agreements are markedly reversible due to their limited contract durations (usually three years), and they are also open for re-negotiation regarding possible renewing and size. Therefore, they allow the Chinese leadership to minimise potential associated policy risks and adapt arrangements in line with political priorities. However, the CMIM and the BRICS Contingency Reserve Arrangement (CRA) are not full-blown insurance regimes with strong contractual conditions. They involve opt-out clauses and have only very slowly been moving towards deeper institutionalisation and the assumption of legal personality. Ultimate control over the disbursement of earmarked reserves remains in the hands of national central bankers with – so far – relatively limited multilateral institutionalised surveillance.

The tinkering mode of the Chinese geo-economic outreach is well encapsulated in a statement made by a senior PBoC official at an ASEAN+3 meeting in late 2008: 'China's leadership proposed flexible and diversified forms of regional currency and financial cooperation' (PBoC 2008). Chinese policymakers are not only layering and experimenting with several formats (global, regional, bilateral) of crisis liquidity provision, but they have also explicitly used the experiences gained from the institutionalisation process and the governance framework of the CMIM to model the BRICS CRA. Chinese government officials publicly recognise that the BRICS CRA explicitly drew from the successful experiment of the CMIM (Xinhua 2014). While the decision of whether BRICS will also set up a dedicated surveillance unit such as the ASEAN+3 Macroeconomic Research Office[4] has yet to be made, all other basic components will be identical to the CMIM. This includes the general financing mechanism, the IMF-linkage (30 per cent), differentiated multipliers for borrowings, and the distinction of liquidity and precautionary instruments. Crucially, however, compared to the East Asian setting, China has increased its share of contributions from 32 per cent in the ASEAN+3's CMIM to 42 per cent in the BRICS CRA. Chinese leadership, chaired by Chen Yuan, was much more visible throughout the process of institutionalisation. This replication of a governance framework in a completely different contextual setting, with different members and different institutional trajectories, strongly recalls the 'point to surface'-experimental mode in domestic policymaking (Heilmann 2008). Particularly so, because the local initiative – in the CMI case the initiative of Japan – has been taken up by the Chinese leadership and expanded to another context. Seen in this light, we might expect this model to be transferred to other settings, for instance the Shanghai Cooperation Organisation (SCO).

China's risk-averse approach to international crisis liquidity provision allowed for learning not only the technicalities of multilateral financial cooperation and institution-building, but also cautious experimentation with the political externalities of financial relations and the embedded highly sensitive creditor-borrower relations. Eventually, inside CMI(M) Chinese financial foreign policymakers have been learning more than 'how to co-operate' (Sohn 2008). From the global financial crisis and onwards, they have also started 'learning how to lead', often indirectly but effectively (Huotari 2015, p. 327).

According to Chang Junhong, the current Chinese AMRO director, there are intensive internal discussions on ways to strengthen the regional arrangement by further delinking it from the IMF or increasing its size (Chang 2016). At present, the problem seems to be that any further step to strengthen CMIM would mean a consolidation of China's predominance in the East Asian region, and is therefore heavily dependent on leadership-followership negotiations and China-Japan accommodation. It will probably take new crisis shocks or a co-ordinated trilateral push from China, Japan and South Korea to overcome the current barriers.

New outbound financing vehicles

Most Chinese policymakers do not set their policy priorities according to the conventional liberal wisdom that financial intermediation is most effective when integrated on a global scale and when global investors price investment risks to create the right incentives for companies. The dominant motive is to shape the international investment position so that the economy benefits while steering investments in line with overarching industrial policy goals and geo-economic purposes. The maturing of China's position as a creditor has been the declared ambition of Chinese policymakers since the 'going global' policy for outbound direct investment was initiated at the turn of the century. However, it was only after 2007 that the leadership engaged in more concerted efforts to redistribute financial surpluses, to move away from the comparatively unproductive reserve hoarding and to a more active shaping of the creditor position (Chin and Helleiner 2008).

Chinese experts and policymakers had early voiced concerns about the fundamental constraints of the Chinese political economy that forced China into
excessive reserve hoarding, the implied dollar-trap and the costs of reserve accumulation (Yu 2010). While the reserve component of China's asset position is
still over-dominant, the transformation of China's creditor position has now
entered a new stage, symbolised by the recent turn-around in the balance of outbound versus inbound direct investment flows and its rise as a global direct
investor.

As Zhang Ming, a scholar at the Chinese Academy of Social Sciences, argued
in late 2014 with regard to outbound direct investment, the structural adjustment
of the Chinese economy will continue to 'weaken the incentive for FDI, but the
incentive for domestic enterprises to invest abroad would strengthen under the
support of Chinese government, which would reduce the net direct investment
inflow'. Less technically, according to Zhang Yunling, also from the CASS,
these developments signal 'a shift in China's strategic thought, [moving away
from] absorbing foreign investment [to the next step: the] outflow of Chinese
development to its neighbors'. Such a shift would also include other types of
capital flows, Zhang Yunling continued (China Daily 2014).

Beyond direct investment and more in line with the state-led type of development, the Chinese government started to experiment with more risky (and
productive) types of investment in 2007, and for this purpose also established
several new outbound financing vehicles, summarised in Table 10.2. These
new mechanisms will support China's exports of goods and services such as
large-scale infrastructure goods, high speed railway and (nuclear) power
plants, helping the country find outlets for its excess productive capacity in
sectors like cement, steel, construction and equipment-making. Beyond

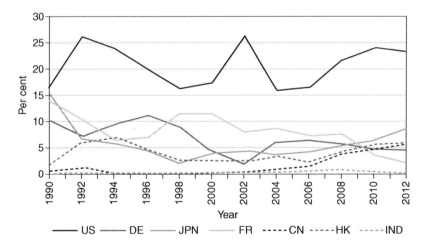

Figure 10.2 China's rise as global direct investor.

Source: author's compilation on the basis of UNCTAD data.

immediate economic motives, these new financial initiatives also blend very well with new foreign policy ambitions and overall strategy, shaping the regional neighbourhood but also enhancing Beijing's global image and influence by investing in a network of diplomatic partners in developing and emerging economies (Zhang 2014; Wang 2014).

Two new multibillion development/infrastructure financing funds create new layers of financial dependencies and complement the Japanese dominated Asian Development Bank as well as the US dominated World Bank. These are the Asian Infrastructure Investment Bank (AIIB), with its governance framework agreed in June 2015 with an initial capital of US$100 billion, and the Silk Road Fund (USS 40 billion), established in spring 2015. Highlighting the precarious balancing act by Chinese financial leaders, the Silk Road Fund is a conflicted financial institution: on the one hand it serves as a strategic policy tool that directs state credits beyond borders, on the other, it tries to establish itself as a profit-oriented market player. However, the CMIM and the AIIB, with the inclusion of the largest European economies – the United Kingdom, France, Italy and Germany – as founding members, are China's most important experiments to actively develop institutionalised multilateral arrangements in global finance.

The flurry of newly established multilateral and semi-public outbound financing vehicles underlines the trial-and-error attitude of the Chinese government, often taking up the initiative of powerful Chinese financial institutions, the China Development Bank (CDB) and the Export and Import Bank of China (EXIM), both of which have a strong international financing profile. In fact, as Zhang Yuzhe (2014) points out, China has been experimenting with 'about a dozen overseas financing mechanisms [that] preceded the recent initiatives'. For a long time, the government mainly mobilised the two state-owned policy banks, the CDB and the EXIM, to facilitate outgoing capital flows. Today, Chinese companies obtain 80 to 90 per cent of their funding from Chinese banks (Zhou and Leung 2015). The CDB and the EXIM have long been among the largest lenders globally (Chin 2014; Huotari and Hanemann 2014). The evolution of the newer investment mechanisms builds on their earlier experience. It often directly involves the CDB, the EXIM and the sovereign wealth fund China Investment Corporation (CIC), but also experiments with new formats including commercial banks and other state-owned funds.

In contrast to crisis liquidity provision, the early financing vehicles promoted by China have often suffered from their limited reversibility, as many of their investment activities have proven less successful than expected, in some cases even creating massive losses for the involved financial institutions. Partly due to inexperience, a lack of risk-management capabilities, but also unforeseen external risks, 'these early funds weathered a variety of challenging situations that managers of the latest initiatives hope to avoid' (Zhang 2014).

Similar to the policy field of crisis liquidity provision, China has also sought to increase its leverage on global patterns of development and infrastructure financing. After it turned into a donor to the World Bank in 2007, China's call for reforms at the global-multilateral level have become more explicit. In

Table 10.2 Selected internationally active outbound financing vehicles

Outbound financing vehicles	Date	Information
China–Africa Development Fund (CAD Fund)	06–2007	CDB, private equity, three stages, first round US$1 billion by CDB, target size US$5 billion
China–ASEAN Fund (CAF)	04–2010	EXIM, CIC, Bank of China, International Finance Corporation (World Bank), private equity, first round US$1 billion, target size US$10 billion
Russia–China Fund (RCF)	10–2011	CIC, Russian Direct Investment Fund, contributing US$1 billion each
Latin America New Equity Investment Platform	03–2012	EXIM, Inter-American Development Bank (IDB), contributing US$150 million each
Latin America/Caribbean Co-Financing Fund	03–2013	PBoC, IDB, co-financing a total of up to US$500 million of IDB public sector loans and up to US$1.5 billion for IDB loans to private sector entities
China–Central and Eastern European Countries Investment Fund I	12–2013	US$500 million, increased to US$1 billion in 2014
New African Development Fund	05–2014	PBoC through African Development Bank; US$2 billion co-financing fund
Maritime Silk Road Fund	05–2014	US$1.6 billion; contributions by Fuzhou Government, CDB Fujian branch and CAD Fund
BRICS New Development Bank (NDB)	07–2014	Borrowing from global capital markets (bond issuance), initial subscribed capital of US$50 billion, authorised capital of US$100 billion
Asian Infrastructure Investment Bank (AIIB)	10–2014	57 founding members, US$100 billion targeted
Qatar Investment Agency-CITIC Fund	11–2014	US$10 billion
China–Mexico Investment Fund	11–2014	US$2.4 billion for infrastructure, mining and energy related projects
Silk Road Fund	11–2014	US$40 billion: 65% reserves, 15% CIC, EXIM 15%, 5% CDB
China–Central and Eastern European Countries (16+1) Investment Fund II	11–2014	US$3 billion, public-private partnerships and leasing
China–Latin America Caribbean Cooperation Fund	01–2015	US$5 billion
SCO Development Bank		Proposed by Li Keqiang in 2013 at SCO summit
China–Central Eastern Europe fund	11–2016	US$11.15 billion, ICBC, Fosun, China Life Insurance
Guotong Fund	12–2016	US$21.79 billion, China Reform Holdings, 10 central State-owned Enterprises, China Postal Savings Bank and others.

Source: author's research.

addition to new capital injections through this global framework, China also contributes directly to the resources of regional development banks such as the African Development Bank (AfDB), the Asian Development Bank (ADB) and the Inter-American Development Bank (IDB). Since 2007, China's financial leaders have also been experimenting with different and competing modes of capital allocation, acquisition, and governance structures of other outbound financing mechanisms. The diversity of tested approaches ranges from EXIM/CDB-supported quasi-sovereign equity funds, a fund of funds type, co-financing funds in which the PBoC partners with regional development banks, to comparatively institutionalised banks with full-fledged multilateral governance frameworks as their basis.

The parallel development and testing of new financing mechanisms allows the Chinese leadership to experiment with governance frameworks that fit to the specific contextual settings of the respective initiatives. As an expression of this experimental mode, an expert at Fudan University argued that the new Chinese-led efforts in international financing 'should adopt more localization by seeking to work with local partners such as national development banks in destination countries' (author interview). Another finance expert, interviewed at the China Centre for International Economic Exchanges, commented that the Silk Road Fund should engage in a 'process of continuous self-correction and improvement', while the more multilateralised banks should continue to seek 'the right balance of participation and governance considerations' (author interview).

As shown in Table 10.2, new funds tend to duplicate the geographic scope of earlier initiatives, but are structured differently, often so because earlier approaches failed to raise the targeted amount of capital or were otherwise subject to criticism. In the case of the AIIB, Chinese debates about the right governance framework were protracted, and included visits to other international institutions dealing with infrastructure investment, such as the European Investment Bank. With major European countries, Australia and South Korea on board, the pressure on China to devise an appropriate governance framework increased substantially, while at the same time wavering between two options: a more commercial and a more developmental direction of the potential financing.

Internationalisation of the renminbi

Similar to Chinese engagement in crisis liquidity provision and outbound financing mechanisms, Beijing's currency initiatives had a very defensive and status quo oriented character for a long time. For instance, given the structural relevance of currency geographies and the powerful authority relations embedded in them, China was consciously avoiding monetary regionalism. During the early 2000s, China chose to superficially welcome Japanese initiatives on monetary coordination in the region. However, being averse to the potential lock-in effects that Japanese advances could have, and knowing well the region-wide lack of willingness to really engage in this arena, the Chinese side became increasingly explicit in their reluctance to play along. After the shock of the 2007/2008 global financial crisis, the leadership eventually moved from rhetorical complaints to very cautious and experimental steps towards currency internationalisation.

After the crisis, the views of Chinese experts who advocated regional initiatives – also in the monetary sphere – were temporarily reinforced. For instance, Zheng Liansheng, a leading expert at the Ministry of Finance's Asia-Pacific Finance and Development Centre, argued that a new push for East Asian monetary cooperation might help to prevent future crises. He advocated for coordination with the IMF and help from ADB and other regional organisations (Sohn 2013). However, the enthusiasm for regionally organised monetary cooperation faded again quickly. Japanese attempts to push for the usage of the 'Asian Currency Unit' or 'Asian Monetary Unit' as a starting point for broader regional monetary cooperation did not take off. In January 2013, an expert involved in the East Asia-wide negotiations on monetary cooperation remarked in a personal conversation with the author that the repeated proposals of Masahiro Kawai, the Japanese Dean of Asian Development Bank Institute during this period, had to be politely rejected.

In China, the preferences and general direction of the debate on regional monetary affairs became more defined. Indicative of a broader line of thinking, in May 2008, Li Yang, director of the Institute of Finance and Banking at the CASS, argued for 'Asian regional currency development' as a crisis prevention mechanism which would leave space for more unilateral measures of what he called 'currency development' to shape the East Asian region (Sohn 2013, p. 17). One of the leading financial experts in China, Xia Bin, explicitly recommended moving forward with the project of renminbi (RMB) internationalisation: 'To enjoy the benefits of globalisation while evading its risks, China has to open the RMB market gradually and in an orderly way, starting with regionalisation.' Regarding the regionalisation-internationalisation tension, he made clear that China was 'not pursuing the optimum target of complete internationalisation of the RMB' but a suboptimal one: 'gradual regionalisation of the currency', as he coined it (China Today 2009).

Today, in a historically unprecedented fashion, the Chinese government seems determined to fully internationalise its currency. It could be argued that since there is no official party document on RMB internationalisation, one cannot speak about a strategy of RMB internationalisation. Indeed, there is no direct mention of RMB internationalisation in the Five-Year Plans. However, there is a broad agreement in the Chinese government concerning the overall goal of RMB internationalisation. Several strategic assessments of this policy circulate inside the Chinese government apparatus, and meticulous planning is being carried out to prepare the necessary steps to grasp what leading experts interviewed by the author have labelled a 'rare historical opportunity'. On closer inspection, the 11th and 12th Five-Year Plans also contained formulations that *imply* the goal of RMB internationalisation.

A SAFE Taskforce report from 2008, with Li Dongrong, the vice-governor of the PBoC as lead author, outlined the rationale, strategic ambitions and instruments for achieving further RMB internationalisation. According to this report, it is 'pressing and would be beneficial to China to promote the renminbi's invoicing and settlement function' (SAFE 2009, p. 1). The authors of the report argue that several aspects of RMB internationalisation, co-ordinated as a top-down approach 'rather than [a] spontaneous effort', have become 'key strategies to deepen the opening-up drive and promote sound and rapid economic development [in China]' (ibid.). The report describes such a pathway as 'conducive to enhancing the strategy of regional cooperation and integration [because China is] now at the epicentre of the economic systems of its neighbouring countries and regions' (ibid.).

In terms of practical steps, around mid-2008, at the height of the global financial crisis, the PBoC made two important decisions: one was to significantly narrow the trading band of the RMB-US dollar exchange rate – de facto fixing the RMB against the US dollar from July 2007 to June 2010 – and the other was to actively promote the international use of the RMB, starting with trade settlement, especially with neighbouring economies (Huang, Wang and Fan 2014). The former step was similar to the PBoC's actions during the Asian financial crisis of 1997/1998. The decision to push more strongly for the internationalisation of the RMB initiated a series of ambitiously experimental but concerted policy measures with far-reaching consequences, leading the international use of the RMB from trade-settlement and investment currency to a currency with a very limited reserve function (Huotari 2015).

In July 2009, when Beijing launched an explorative pilot scheme that allowed the use of the RMB for trade-settlement purposes, the scheme was initially limited to trade with the ASEAN economies as well as Hong Kong and Macau. Only five mainland cities were included: Shanghai, Guangzhou, Shenzhen, Dongguan and Zhuhai. In mid-2010, the coverage of the scheme was expanded to 20 provinces. Since then, the authorisation to settle trade in RMB has been extended nationwide and to other trading partners. The total value of RMB trade settlement virtually exploded after 2010, and ASEAN continues to be one of the regions with the highest share of RMB trade settlement.

While maintaining a high degree of control and constantly adjusting capital account liberalisation to domestic financial conditions, restrictions regarding inward and outward foreign direct and portfolio investment have been relaxed with regard to the use of the RMB. In 2011, approval processes were streamlined with the announcement of the RMB Outward Direct Investment scheme and the creation of the RMB-FDI scheme.

With the relaxation of capital controls, Chinese authorities have further supported the growth of the offshore RMB-denominated bond market in Hong Kong that had already been tested in 2007. Since 2010, this 'Dim-Sum bond market' has attracted much more attention from financial institutions and companies, and despite uncertainties is increasingly recognised as another viable platform for corporate and sovereign financing in East Asia and beyond. Paralleling the expansion in RMB trade settlement and investment, RMB deposits in Hong Kong rose dramatically. Banks in Hong Kong were already allowed to open RMB accounts in 2004, but it was only in mid-2010, when the RMB settlement scheme was introduced, that RMB deposits started being used extensively.

Table 10.3 Emerging global RMB infrastructure: the Hong Kong model goes global

RMB infrastructure	Partner countries, financial centres (as of 2014)
Local currency swap agreements	32 agreements (see Table 10.1, note 1)
Direct trading of currencies	Australia, Eurozone, Kazakhstan, Malaysia, New Zealand, Russia, Singapore, South Korea, United Kingdom
RQFII quota *(99 licenses, total value of >300bn CNY)*	Australia, Canada, Doha, France, Germany, Hong Kong, United Kingdom, Macao, Qatar, Singapore, South Korea, Taiwan
Clearing banks	Bangkok, Doha, Frankfurt, Hong Kong, Kuala Lumpur, London, Luxembourg, Macau, Paris, Seoul, Sydney, Singapore, Taipeh, Toronto

Source: author's compilation.

Together with other forms of bilateral cooperation on financial and monetary issues, the gradually expanding network of currency swap agreements also allows for policy learning with regard to the management of cross-border financial linkages so as to slowly build a global RMB infrastructure, connecting China with other economies and international financial centres. The PBoC cooperation with other offshore centres basically 'copies' the Hong Kong model, with minor adaptations to local conditions and the 'full package' consisting of a swap agreement, clearing bank arrangement and RQFII quota, highlights the experimental nature of China's approach to cross-border financial linkages. In March 2015, the Chinese authorities launched another experiment through which 20 selected financial institutions began testing the China International Payments System (CIPS) that enables and facilitates global RMB payments, adding another layer to the offshore experimentation localised in global financial centres.

A look ahead

Taken together, it appears that China is still experimenting, but has broadly figured out the key components of its roadmap for geo-economic engineering in the financial sphere. The following list comprises the priorities of Chinese foreign economic policy: new ambitious multilateral and semi-public financing vehicles, substantial crisis liquidity provision through regional and minilateral arrangements, and currency internationalisation with a prominent role for the region. The learning that marks China's corresponding policies not only concerns the technicalities of international financial arrangements and regulatory exchanges but, as Wang Hongying puts it, China is also learning 'how to turn its new economic weight into legitimate and effective leadership' (Wang 2014, p. 5).

One of the most interesting aspects that will probably also determine the 'success' of China's geo-economic engagement and experimental financial internationalisation will be the potential mutual support of financial security, development and currency arrangements.

While RMB trade-settlement and bilateral currency swap agreements so far entail no multilateral region-wide 'governance-externalities', attempts to move towards more institutionalised forms of cooperation exist for the BRICS framework (suggested by China in 2011), China and ASEAN, as well as the ASEAN Plus Three (APT). Beijing's decision to push RMB international-isation forward opened the window for China to play a more active role in the process of regional financial and currency cooperation in East Asia. Remark-ably, Premier Li Keqiang endorsed a possible integration of financial and cur-rency cooperation on a regional basis in the framework of APT and CMIM in 2013, a development that would transform regional order in an even more pro-found way, precisely against the backdrop of the time of rapid proceedings in RMB internationalisation.

Following the principles of 'gradual and orderly progress' and 'controlling the risk' (PBoC 2014), Chinese initiatives have already transformed the conduct of regional real and financial transactions in such profound ways that more insti-tutionalised forms of regional monetary cooperation would start from funda-mentally different initial conditions.

In many of the new outbound financing initiatives we already witness attempts to align them with the broader currency internationalisation project, which reinforces their importance for China's new financial diplomacy. A 2015 PBoC announcement which finally formalised the long-standing 'RMB inter-nationalisation' goal as official policy target also mentioned the 'New Silk Eco-nomic Belt' and '21st Century Maritime Silk Road', two projects that strongly build on the new outbound financing vehicles, shall expand the scope for cross-border RMB activity while also deepening currency cooperation (Hong 2015). According to one Xinhua report, Chinese 'experts believe that the Silkroad initi-ative, Asian Infrastructure Investment Bank, Silk Road Fund, BRICS Develop-ment Bank package, not only heavily involve domestic financial institutions, but also helps to promote the internationalization of the RMB' (Xinhua 2015).

The above analysis underlines that Chinese policymakers do not have to choose between full-fledged integration and financial seclusion. The develop-ment of China's geo-economic profile is based on intensive policy learning and risk-averse tinkering with innovative governance solutions that allow for the maintenance of a higher degree of autonomy, and combine the government's strategic guidance with market-driven practices. Self-managed crisis liquidity pools, currency internationalisation taking place within a system of a managed capital account, and the channelling of investment income surplus through out-bound financing vehicles that only slowly pave the way towards a privatisation of foreign assets might be much more than just transitory phenomena. They not only highlight the constraining factor of fragile domestic financial development for China's geo-economic presence, but to some extent also are expressions of an evolving alternative vision for organising foreign economic policy in a regional context.

Notes

1 The author would also like to thank Mikael Wigell and Sören Scholvin for their comments on the earlier drafts of this chapter.
2 This group includes China, South Korea and Japan in addition to the ten ASEAN countries (Singapore, Indonesia, Malaysia, Brunei, the Philippines, Vietnam, Thailand, Cambodia, Laos and Myanmar).
3 Central bank local currency swaps are agreements to exchange domestic currencies to provide central bank with liquidity for different purposes including maintaining financial stability.
4 AMRO is the regional macroeconomic surveillance unit of CMIM. It was set up in Singapore in May 2011 as independent regional surveillance unit to promote objective economic monitoring and was effectively turned into an international organisation in February 2016.

References

Blackwill, R. D. and Tellis, A. J. (2015) 'Revising U.S. Grand Strategy Toward China', *Council on Foreign Relations*, Council Special Report No. 72, March. Available at: http://carnegieendowment.org/files/Tellis_Blackwill.pdf, accessed 1 December 2016.

Chang, J. (2016) 'Keynote Speech at the 6th Asia Research Forum CMIM-Asian Multilateralism and Cooperation', 1 July. Available at: www.amro-asia.org/keynote-speech-by-dr-junhong-chang-amro-director-at-the-6th-asia-research-forum-cmim-asian-multilateralism-and-cooperation/, accessed 1 December 2016.

Chin, G. (2014) 'The BRIC-led Development Bank: Purpose and Politics beyond the G20', *Global Policy*, 5, 3, pp. 366–373.

Chin, G. and Helleiner, E. (2008) 'China as a Creditor: A Rising Financial Power?', *Journal of International Affairs*, 62, 1, pp. 87–102.

China Daily. (2014) 'Policy Banks to Lead Silk Road Infrastructure Fund', *China Daily*, 5 November. Available at: http://usa.chinadaily.com.cn/epaper/2014-11/05/content_1887 3053.htm, accessed 15 March 2015.

China Today. (2009) 'China Tries RMB Regionalization Measure', *China Today*, 19 June. Available at: www.chinatoday.com.cn/ctenglish/se/txt/2009-06/19/content_203295.htm, accessed 15 March 2015.

Etzioni, A. (2016) 'The Asian Infrastructure Investment Bank: A Case Study of Multifaceted Containment', *Asian Perspective*, 40, 2, pp. 173–196.

Fan, G. and Woo, W. T. (2005) ' "Sequencing" or "Parallel Partial Progression": Incoherence Cost and the Optimal Path of Institutional Transformation', *Social Sciences in China*, 27, 1, pp. 87–96.

Heep, S. (2014) *China in Global Finance: Domestic Financial Repression and International Financial Power* (Cham: Springer).

Heilmann, S. (2008) 'Policy Experimentation in China's Economic Rise', *Studies in Comparative International Development*, 43, 1, pp. 1–26.

Heilmann, S., Moritz, R., Huotari, M. and Buckow, J. (2014) 'China's Shadow Foreign Policy: Parallel Structures Challenge the Established International Order', *Mercator Institute for China Studies*, China Monitor No. 18, 28 October. Available at: www. merics.org/fileadmin/user_upload/downloads/China-Monitor/China_Monitor_No_18_en.pdf, accessed 1 December 2016.

Hong, C. (2015) 'It's official! PBoC Wording Formalises "RMB Internationalisation" Target', *Global Capital*, 21 January. Available at: www.globalcapital.com/article/

pymb54c7h0g3/it39s-official-pboc-wording-formalises-39rmb-internationalisation 39-target, accessed 15 March 2015.

Huang, Y., Wang, D. and Fan, G. (2014) 'Paths to a Reserve Currency: Internationalization of the Renminbi and Its Implications', *Asian Development Bank Institute*, Working Paper No. 482, May. Available at: www.adb.org/sites/default/files/public ation/156337/adbi-wp482.pdf, accessed 21 November 2017.

Huotari, M. (2015) 'Finding a New Role in East Asian Financial Order: China's Hesitant Turn towards Leadership', in Gottwald J-C., Harnisch, S. and Bersick, S. (eds), *China's International Roles: Challenging or Supporting International Order?* (London and New York: Routledge), pp. 145–168.

Huotari, M. and Hanemann, T. (2014) 'Emerging Powers and Change in the Global Financial Order', *Global Policy*, 5, 3, pp. 298–310.

Kahler, M. (2013) 'Rising Powers and Global Governance: Negotiating Change in a Resilient Status Quo', *International Affairs*, 89, 3, pp. 711–729.

Lane, P. R. and Milesi-Ferreti, G. M. (2007) 'The External Wealth of Nations Mark II: Revised and Extended Estimates of Foreign Assets and Liabilities, 1970–2004', *Journal of International Economics*, 73, pp. 223–250.

Li, K. (2013) 'Remarks by H. E. Li Keqiang Premier of the State Council of the People's Republic of China at the 16th ASEAN Plus Three Summit', 11 October. Available at: www.fmprc.gov.cn/mfa_eng/topics_665678/lkqzlcxdyldrxlhy_665684/t1089852. shtml, accessed 15 March 2015.

Mittelman, J. (2013) 'Global Bricolage: Emerging Market Powers and Polycentric Governance', *Third World Quarterly*, 34, 1, pp. 23–37.

PBoC. (2008) 'Senior Official of the PBC Interviewed for PBC-BOK Currency Swap Agreement', *People's Bank of China*. Available at: www.pbc.gov.cn/publish/ english/955/2043/20439/20439_.html, accessed 15 March 2015.

PBoC. (2014) 'Treaty for the Establishment of a BRICS Contingency Reserve Arrangement', *People's Bank of China*. Available at: www.pbc.gov.cn/publish/english/955/ 2014/20140717154639176510565/20140717154639176510565.html, accessed 15 March 2015.

SAFE Taskforce. (2009) 'The Use of the Renminbi for Trade and Non-Trade Denomination and Settlement', *China Economist*. Available at: https://s3.amazonaws.com/ ProductionContentBucket/pdf/20100302195533.pdf, accessed 15 March 2015.

Sohn, I. (2008) 'Learning to Co-operate: China's Multilateral Approach to Asian Financial Co-operation', *The China Quarterly*, 194, June, pp. 309–326.

Sohn, I. (2013) 'Between Confrontation and Assimilation: China and the fragmentation of global financial governance', *Journal of Contemporary China*, 22, 82, pp. 630–648.

Wang, H. (2014) '"Taoguang Yanghui" to "Yousuo Zuowei": China's Engagement in Financial Minilateralism', *Centre for International Governance Innovation*, CIGI Papers No. 52, December. Available at: www.cigionline.org/sites/default/files/cigi_ paper_no52.pdf, accessed 15 March 2015.

Xinhua. (2014) '央行：应急储备安排提高金砖国家国际话语权', *Xinhua*, 17 July. Available at: http://rmb.xinhua08.com/a/20140717/1357690.shtml, accessed 15 March 2015.

Xinhua. (2015) '资本净输出趋势下人民币国际化迎最佳窗口期', *Xinhua*, 29 January. Available at: http://rmb.xinhua08.com/a/20150129/1447874.shtml, accessed 15 March 2015.

Yu, Y. (2010) 'The Impact of the Global Financial Crisis on the Chinese Economy and China's Policy Responses', *Third World Network*, TWN Global Economy Series. Available at: www.twn.my/title2/ge/ge25.pdf, accessed 1 December 2016.

Zhang, Y. (2014) 'With New Funds, China Hits a Silk Road Stride', *Caixin*. Available at: http://english.caixin.com/2014-12-03/100758419.html, accessed 15 March 2015.

Zhou, L. and Leung, D. (2015) 'China's Overseas Investments, Explained in 10 Graphics', *World Resources Institute*, 28 January. Available at: www.wri.org/blog/2015/01/china%E2%80%99s-overseas-investments-explained-10-graphics, accessed 15 March 2015.

11 Development lending as financial statecraft?

A comparative exploration of the practices of China and Japan

Mikael Mattlin and Bart Gaens

Introduction[1]

Following the pinnacle of its economic boom in the late 1980s, Japan emerged as the biggest source of overseas development aid. While Japan has since lost this leading position, it is still a formidable power in financing development and a key member of the Development Assistance Committee (DAC) of the Organisation for Economic Cooperation and Development (OECD). Yet, Japan's preferred ways of engaging in development assistance have frequently encountered criticism from within the ranks of the OECD, as well as by scholars of development aid. Japan has been accused of being too focused on its own economic and commercial objectives to the detriment of broader development goals, such as poverty reduction and social development (e.g. Lancaster 2010; Arase 1995).

With China's rapid emergence as a major player on the development assistance scene, some of the criticism that earlier was reserved for Japan has been directed against China (e.g. Bräutigam 2011). These days, China is by far the most important, most talked about and most controversial of the 'emerging donors'. China has become a target for all those who are concerned about lending standards being eroded, insufficient attention being given to social and environmental needs, debt sustainability or transparency and corruption issues – not to mention democracy and good governance (Reilly 2013).

With China's increasing assertiveness, the possible geostrategic objectives of its development assistance have also received increasing attention. Comparisons have been drawn between China's two ambitious projects, the Belt and Road Initiative and the establishment of the Asian Infrastructure Investment Bank (AIIB), and the US Marshall Plan. The Marshall Plan provided aid to rebuild post-war Japan and Europe with a view to expanding and opening up their markets for US products and integrating them into its sphere of influence. Development assistance is, hence, a potential component of geo-economics, which can be broadly understood to revolve around 'the geostrategic use of economic power' (Wigell 2016, p. 137; cf. Youngs' definition 2011, p. 14).

This chapter compares China's practices of providing 'foreign aid' to Japan's Official Development Assistance (ODA) practices.[2] China has traditionally couched its assistance in the rhetoric of non-interference and 'South-South cooperation' between developing countries. As China is not a member of the OECD-DAC, it does not follow their ODA definition when reporting aid, and its foreign aid statistical system is still a work in progress. For historical reasons, China has shunned traditional 'Western' development aid, considering it to be something different from what China does. This implies that there are methodological challenges in directly comparing Japanese ODA to China's development assistance.[3]

Is there credence to the criticism that these two countries pursue mainly their own national objectives with their development assistance? To what extent can the development lending practices of China and Japan be regarded as a form of financial statecraft aimed at promoting the geostrategic aims of these countries? In answering these questions, we adopt a comparative perspective to explore China's and Japan's development lending from three angles: policy thinking, lending forms, and recipient countries. We employ the concept of financial statecraft as a heuristic aid to our analysis.

This chapter is structured as follows. First, we introduce and briefly debate the concept of financial statecraft that forms the key concept of this chapter. We then discuss the historical trajectory of policy thinking on development assistance in Japan and China, followed by a comparative discussion on the lending forms and recipient countries of Japanese and Chinese aid. Before drawing our conclusions, we briefly compare Japan's role in the Asian Development Bank (ADB) and China's founding role in the AIIB.

Financial statecraft

Japan has often been described as an economic giant, but a political dwarf (Lim 2008, p. 200; Söderberg 2005, pp. viii–ix). In its international affairs during the last decades, Japan has relied on the cheque book, not on the gunboat. Similarly, while China's measurable military power is rapidly growing, arguably, what stands out about China's international role is the preference for economic and financial means of influence, not military means. Given this background, it is pertinent to use the term 'financial power' to describe these two countries.

Susan Strange was one of the first researchers who focused on finance as a key component of international power. In her theory on structural power, Strange identified four main channels of power: security, production, knowledge and finance; with finance being the most overlooked aspect (Strange 1997; 2004; Clift and Rosamond 2010). More recently, Juan Zarate (2013) has argued that the United States combats terror threats by targeting the deep sinecures of the international financial infrastructure and channels, utilising precisely what Strange had criticised, namely the (partly hidden) dominance of the USA in the global financial system. However, it took until the 2008 financial crisis until the concept of financial statecraft was coined. With the concept, Steil and Litan (2008) referred to those aspects of economic statecraft that are directed at influencing international capital flows. In as far as development aid is provided with the aims of directing international capital flows in ways that are favourable to the donor, it can be conceptualised as a form of financial statecraft.

Armijo and Katada have recently further refined the concept of financial state-craft by distinguishing between *defensive* ('shield') and *offensive* ('sword') uses of financial statecraft, *bilateral* versus *systemic* targeting and *financial* or *monetary* means (Armijo and Katada 2014, 2015). Bilateral refers to situations where a state seeks to influence or defend against the choices of another state, whereas systemic refers to influencing or defending against world markets. For example, a defensive monetary measure in the bilateral context would be to use capital controls to guard against the currency of a strong neighbour, whereas promoting home markets as a source of global influence is a systemic financial measure (Armijo and Katada 2015). Huotari and Heep (2016), for example, have argued that China has used financial statecraft in a defensive manner. In this chapter, we use Armijo's and Katada's analytical framework to gauge China's and Japan's development aid as a form of financial statecraft.

As Carothers and De Gramont (2013) have shown, any cursory review of the empirical history of ODA would show that ODA is seldom provided purely out of altruistic motivations. Typically, in decisions on providing official development assistance, all sorts of economic, political, and strategic considerations play a role. Thus, it is not surprising that China's first foreign aid was provided to North Korea in the 1950s. The relationship between development aid and political objectives has always been ambivalent and somewhat uneasy. Many sweeping claims have been made that China (or some other country) uses finance as an instrument in pursuit of its geostrategic aims. In some instances, such as the People's Republic of China's diplomatic competition with the Republic of China (Taiwan), there is ample evidence to support the claims (Farnsworth 2011; Wu and Koh 2014; see also Chapter 12 in this volume). Yet when the evidence is taken into closer inspection, the results tend to be equivocal, including in development assistance. If development aid tends to be a mixture of altruistic and self-interested motivations (Gaens and Vogt 2015), then how are we to judge when self-interested motivations dominate?

From the literature (e.g. ActionAid 2005; Orbie and Versluys 2008; Reilly 2013), several potential criteria can be advanced, in particular with regard to assistance that is driven by *economic* interests rather than promoting the rights of the poorest: maintaining a high proportion of aid tied to goods and services from the donor country, preferring loans with relatively non-concessional interest rates to grants or interest-free loans, targeting middle-income countries rather than the low-income and least developed ones, and being excessively focused on tying assistance to resource-extraction that is shipped to the donor country. Claims of political considerations motivating development aid are more difficult to prove. In the following sections, we analyse whether and how China and Japan use development aid strategically to achieve economic or political objectives.

Policy thinking on development assistance

Regarding the historical trajectory of providing development assistance, there are several broad points of similarity between China and Japan. Both were themselves recipients of large-scale international aid before evolving into major global donors. Japan received 34 World Bank loans between 1953–1967, all of which were paid back by 1990 (Watanabe 2005). China has been a major World Bank client. Both countries first provided aid mainly to their near abroad and only later embraced other continents such as Africa. Japan provided assistance through economic cooperation, mainly large official loans for natural resource development projects in developing countries, partly to secure the imports of raw materials to Japan. In the same vein, China has tried to secure its own economic interests through couching its foreign aid as a component of broader economic cooperation. Interestingly, Japan is increasingly trying to compete with China, especially in Africa, by revisiting its former economic cooperation model.

In terms of policy thinking, there are also common elements. Both countries take their own national interest and recipient countries' self-help as starting points for assistance, and focus on building long-term economic and political partnerships. These partnerships are often with middle-income countries (MICs), that target economic development and infrastructure building. There is less emphasis on direct humanitarian and socio-economic goals, such as environmental protection, gender equality, and poverty reduction. For different reasons, both countries have also historically been averse to impressions of interference in the domestic affairs of recipient countries.

In the 1970s and 1980s, Japan's ODA rose along with the country's rapid economic growth. As Japan relocated production to other parts of Asia and imported natural resources from those countries, boosted aid transfers served to compensate for the negative outcomes of Japanese trade – especially their environmental and social impact, and the lack of consideration for basic human needs. Partly as a result of the economic regionalisation process, infrastructure development became a necessary and useful tool for Japanese companies to access local markets (Watanabe 2005). According to the government, the Japanese model of ODA was based on the country's own historical experiences. Just as Japan focused its post-war development on rebuilding its economy, Japanese ODA centres on infrastructure development and capacity building in order to help recipient countries to develop a functioning market economy. For Japan, it has always been imperative that aid recipients become self-reliant and are in charge of their own development, as is clear from Japan's ODA Charter[4] of 2003.

Japan currently dedicates approximately 7 per cent, or US$1.12 billion, of total net ODA to humanitarian aid (MOFA 2016, p. 215 chart IV-17). The introduction of human security to Japan's development philosophy in the Charter of 2003 has added poverty as a dimension to an approach traditionally focused on economic growth. Japan has actively sought to create synergies between aid, economic cooperation, and the promotion of national interests. Under the banner of 'enlightened national interest', it therefore explicitly aims to make the pursuit of Japan's interests and global public interests mutually overlapping. The recent strategic use of ODA as a tool to promote regional security illustrates this: in an effort to balance an increasingly strong Chinese presence in East Asia, Japan has used ODA to increase economic assistance and maritime cooperation with countries in Southeast Asia, especially with Indonesia, the Philippines, and Vietnam.

Despite having emerged as one of the biggest players on the aid scene, China has long been ambivalent about traditional development aid – something that it associates with Western countries. China perceives the OECD/DAC as a 'rich man's club' to which it does not belong. There have even been efforts by Chinese scholars to make a semantic distinction between Western foreign (development) aid (对外援助) and Chinese assistance to foreign countries (援助外国) (Zhang 2009). However, the English version of the most recent Chinese aid White paper is simply entitled *China's Foreign Aid*.

The broad political objectives for China's development assistance stem from the common historical experiences that China shares with many developing countries. These motivations have led Chinese leaders, ever since Premier Zhou Enlai's famous 'eight principles' from 1964, to emphasise that in their dealing with other developing countries, they are neither imposing any conditions, nor asking for any favours. More broadly, the Chinese government often couches its aid in the context of South-South cooperation (Davies *et al.* 2008), where aid is just one component of economic relations and often secondary to and supportive of regular trade and investment. Consequently, China's aid is also often geared towards capacity- and infrastructure-building (Foster *et al.* 2008), and guided by similar self-help ideas as the ones Japan has promoted.

Already as early as 1972, a Chinese representative to the United Nations argued that the aim of bilateral and multilateral aid should be to help recipient countries to act independently on their own initiative and to develop their economy in a self-reliant manner ('其目的都应当是帮助受援国独立自主，自力更生地发展本国经济'; quoted in Xiong 2010). The message is certainly appealing to many developing countries, which for years have told Western donors that they do not wish to be forever dependent on development aid, but instead hope to receive foreign investment in order to develop economic structures and to be able to trade on fair terms.

Lending forms

Japan's ODA philosophy is strongly rooted in a market-oriented strategy. Of Japan's bilateral ODA, 48.9 per cent goes to economic infrastructure (mainly communications, transport and energy), whereas only 17.1 per cent is allocated to social infrastructure (education, sanitation, environment and health) (MOFA 2016, p. 215 chart IV-17). This ODA philosophy has also resulted in an emphasis on low-interest, long-term loans instead of grants. For Japan, this practice has not only ensured that funds are used more efficiently, but it has also enhanced the sustainability of Japan's own development cooperation programme.

Japan's preference for loans over grants is said to be rooted in the country's own experiences. For example, during 1979–2007, the bulk of Japan's ODA to China consisted of loan aid. Japan stopped providing yen loans to China in 2008, but outstanding loans of up to 1.6 trillion yen (US$15.7 billion) are still to be repaid in stages. According to recent figures, Japan provided loans amounting to US$7.4 billion to other countries in 2014 (MOFA 2016, p. 33). In gross terms, Japan was the second biggest provider of ODA in 2013, in net terms the fourth biggest, while China was the sixth biggest on both measures (Kitano and Harada 2014, p. 11; pp. 19–20).

In recent years, China has emerged as a major source of bilateral financing for many developing countries.[5] By some accounts, the lending by the Exim Bank of China and the China Development Bank to developing countries has already surpassed that of the World Bank (e.g. Sanderson and Forsythe 2013). Deborah Bräutigam has argued that concessional loans, or 'financing packages' with a concessional element, only form a small part of *all* of China's bilateral lending (Bräutigam 2011). Much of China's lending is based on commercial terms (Mattlin and Nojonen 2015). However, among items that fall within China's own narrow definition of foreign aid, more than half takes the form of concessional loans. Thus, China's preference for using loans in its foreign assistance exceeds even Japan's (see Figure 11.1).

The Chinese government often does not make a clear distinction between official development assistance and export credits, i.e. a loan facility provided to an exporter by a bank in the same country. Most of what to the external observer may look like Chinese development aid does not conform to generally accepted ODA definitions, but is rather export credits or other forms of official financing with or without some element of concessionality (Bräutigam 2011). Chinese bilateral financing takes numerous forms. Apart from concessional loans, Chinese financial institutions also offer preferential buyers' credits, export sellers' credits, mixed credits, resource-backed loans and credit lines (European Parliament 2011). Much of this is tied to purchases from China.

Tied aid long played an important role in Japan's ODA, too. Tied aid is 'granted on the condition that the beneficiary country will purchase the goods or services involved in a development project from suppliers in the donor country'

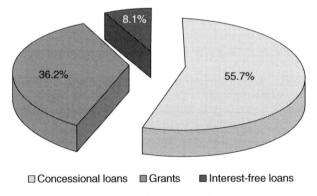

☐ Concessional loans   ▨ Grants   ▮ Interest-free loans

Figure 11.1 China's foreign aid forms 2010–2012.
Source: PRC State Council 2014.

(Orbie and Versluys 2008, p. 80). The tying of aid raises the question of who are the intended beneficiaries of aid. As pointed out by Orbie and Versluys (2008), tied aid increases the development project costs by 20–30 per cent and excludes local production systems. For some, tied aid qualifies as phantom aid, meaning that it is diverted within the aid system for other purposes than the improvement of the most basic and economic rights of people living in the poorest countries.

In global development aid, there has been an overall increase in *untied* aid: from 46 per cent in 2000 to 76 per cent in 2007 (ActionAid 2011). A report from 2009 put the tied aid average figure at 82 per cent (Clay *et al.* 2009). As of the 1980s, Japan has also cut back its reliance on tied loans. In 1987, fully and partially tied aid totalled 48 per cent of Japan's bilateral ODA. Current official figures indicate that only approximately 10 per cent of Japanese bilateral aid is tied (MOFA 2016, p. 256). However, these figures do not tell the whole story, as there are also a plethora of informal tying practices, which help to favour businesses based in the donor countries. According to a 2012 study by the Eurodad (2012), 60 per cent of global aid is still *informally* tied to the use of donor firms. In Chinese aid, there are often also many specific project-related conditions. For example, the Exim Bank of China normally requires that at least 50 per cent of the goods and services in its concessional loans be sourced from Chinese contractors (Mattlin and Nojonen 2015; Nour 2011).

Recipient countries

Japan's focus has typically not been on the least developed countries (LDCs) and poverty reduction, but rather on MICs (OECD 2014, p. 43). In 2012, for example, 72 per cent of Japan's gross ODA disbursements went to MICs, which is significantly higher than the according DAC average of 54 per cent (OECD 2014, p. 95 Table B.3). Furthermore, even though in 2014 Japan disbursed 25 per cent of its total net ODA to LDCs, the top five recipients of gross ODA were Vietnam, India, Indonesia, the Philippines, and Thailand (MOFA 2016, p. 212 chart IV-14) – all countries that are geostrategically important for Japan in its effort to buffer China. Japan's historical tendency to focus on its near abroad remains valid until today, although some diversification has occurred (Figure 11.2).

Japan remains the largest donor in the overall Asian region, providing 47.4 per cent of total aid (MOFA 2016, p. 254 chart IV-27). However, as traditional Asian development partners graduate from eligibility of direct economic assistance, South Asia and Africa are gaining in importance, particularly in terms of net aid. Japan's more proactive policy vis-à-vis those regions reveals an attempt to catch up with China's strong presence there (Sharma 2016).

China, too, directs some of its concessional loans to upper-income MICs, and into commercially viable sectors such as mining and telecommunications (Zhou 2008; Mattlin and Nojonen 2011). This has led to accusations within the OECD that official financing gives Chinese exporters an unfair competitive advantage. According to the guidelines agreed under the auspices of the OECD, countries can only provide concessional loans to commercially non-viable projects.

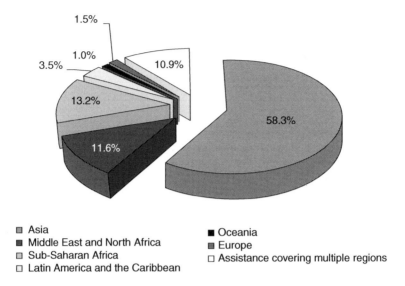

Figure 11.2 Japan's ODA distribution by region 2014.

Source: MOFA 2016, p. 127 chart III-7.

China has no clear prioritisation with regard to which countries it provides aid to. While Chinese policy documents mention helping low-income countries (e.g. PRC State Council 2014), in practice China provides aid and loans to most non-OECD countries, including many countries in Europe (Figure 11.3.). This is very different from many small European countries, which as providers of development aid tend to focus on a narrow set of partner countries such as specific LDCs.

This lack of prioritisation partly stems from China's policy rhetoric emphasising that as long as recipient countries recognise the One China Principle and maintain diplomatic relations with the PRC they are eligible to receive Chinese funding. Providing aid and loans in such an ad hoc manner – typically visiting Chinese leaders will promise large sums of loans and aid – and the lack of proper planning and budgeting procedures for provision of aid has also received criticism within China.[6]

The issue of interference and geostrategic objectives

Japan has been cautious of being perceived as meddling in the internal affairs of smaller ODA recipient countries, not least because Japan's wartime expansionism in East Asia is still a sensitive issue. However, despite Tokyo's sensitivity to allegations of political interference, its ODA is not without political objectives. For one, Japan's ODA charter insists, 'full attention should be paid to efforts for promoting democratization and the introduction of a market-oriented

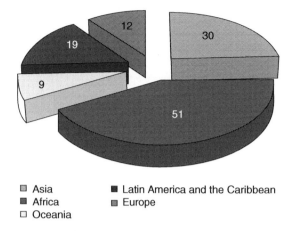

Asia
Africa
Oceania
Latin America and the Caribbean
Europe

Figure 11.3 China's foreign aid by number of recipient countries per region 2010–2012.
Source: PRC State Council 2014.

economy, and the situation regarding the protection of basic human rights and freedoms in the recipient country'. Japan has provided aid as a positive instigator of political change, driving economic reform in order to achieve progress towards democracy, i.e. Japan has applied *positive conditionality*, promising benefits if a state fulfils certain conditions (Smith 2005, p. 75). In Myanmar, for example, Japan has primarily espoused engagement, applying humanitarian assistance and direct aid support as an incentive for democratic change and reward for positive changes. However, Myanmar is one of the rare cases where Japan has also used the stick of negative sanctions (cf. Edström 2009). Japan has generally stuck to the idea that a continuous aid relationship is vital to achieving change.

At least as importantly, development assistance has always been functional in pursuing Japanese geostrategic objectives, and in the creation of spheres of influence through the application of economic power. Here, Myanmar serves as an example, too. Myanmar is one of the key countries in Southeast Asia where Japan is engaging in geostrategic competition with China in an effort to curb Beijing's growing influence in the region. Myanmar's domestic political transition as of 2010–2011 has heightened the country's strategic importance to Japan in terms of economic benefits, natural resources, labour force, and consumption market. Not only did Tokyo make extensive use of the ODA carrot, boosting loan aid, it also took the lead in addressing Myanmar's non-repayable debt by foregoing its own owed amounts in a huge debt relief programme, and by providing additional capital to allow Myanmar to deal with its other debt obligations (Hartley 2017). In light of regional competition with China, connectivity projects play an important role. Japan has actively been seeking to embed cooperation with Myanmar in a regional framework focusing around the Mekong River countries (Reilly 2013). Myanmar forms a key part of the Greater Mekong Subregion East-West Corridor that would increase connectivity between Southeast and South Asia and allow for the bypassing of the Malacca Strait (Hartley 2017).

In order to help accomplish this aim, Japan is investing heavily in Myanmar, utilising what can be seen as financial statecraft. The Japan International Cooperation Agency (JICA) has an important role in the development of the Japan-led Special Economic Zone (SEZ) in Thilawa. This has attracted major Japanese manufacturing companies including Sumitomo, Marubeni and Mitsubishi, which have been engaged in ODA financing projects in Myanmar since the end of the Cold War. In order to expand the SEZ, already housing dozens of Japanese companies, JICA has approved US$340 million in ODA loans for the development of the zone. Japan makes wide use of JICA's Private-Sector Investment Finance tool, which provides loan aid to private corporations engaging in infrastructure development to assist them in local development projects (MOFA 2016, p. 175). Together with large corporate conglomerates, JICA owns 49 per cent of the Thilawa joint venture. Furthermore, Japan disburses aid in order to increase Yangon's electricity generation to supply power to the SEZ. For Japanese manufacturing companies, the nearby Thilawa Port is a vital gateway to the Indian Ocean. Additionally, the new Yangon International Airport will be financed 49 per cent by Tokyo (Strefford 2016). 'Economic cooperation' (経済協力), marked by the use of public funds for investments abroad in close partnership with Japanese companies, is therefore still a core strategy for Japan.

Although China has a different historical background, it has been sensitive about interference in domestic affairs, too. The main underlying reasons are China's historical experiences of quasi-colonisation and partition, fears of external meddling in the issues of Taiwan and Tibet, as well as China's Cold War international position (especially after the break with the Soviet Union) of staying aloof from the two rigid military blocs and identifying with other developing countries as a 'non-aligned' country.

Although Chinese state-owned lenders contend that they do not apply 'political conditionality' (Gao 2007) in their lending decisions, diplomatic relations with the PRC is in practice almost always a condition for receiving, e.g. an Exim Bank concessional loan (Exim Bank 2009). As a rule, Chinese aid and bank credits are given to countries with which China maintains diplomatic ties. For African countries with formal diplomatic ties to the PRC, aid has been semi-automatic (Bräutigam 2007). This has larger trade implications, as the PRC allegedly has asked its trading partners to support the diplomatic isolation of Taiwan (Farnsworth 2011; Mitton 2006). The political condition of adhering to the 'One China Policy' may be enshrined in diplomatic agreements that incorporate the framework agreement for concessional loans (Wu and Koh 2014; Mattlin and Nojonen 2015).

China has become trapped in the origin of its policy. Since Chinese lenders commonly do not have many upfront requirements for their loans (compared to e.g. the World Bank, the IMF or Western bilateral lending agencies), it is also harder for them to *deny* loans to other developing countries with which China maintains diplomatic and political relations. Clearing the 'One China' hurdle is a relatively small barrier compared to the often onerous conditionality and feasibility studies, and reporting requirements imposed by Western or multilateral lenders (Mattlin and Nojonen 2015).

In recent years, China has emerged as a particularly significant alternative source of financing to economically pressed countries that have been squeezed out of international financial markets and financing by international financial institutions – countries such as Angola, Argentina, Zimbabwe, Myanmar, Ecuador and Venezuela. China's interest has often been driven by the prospect of accessing much-needed natural resources, particularly oil, on favourable terms. However, these bilateral relations have tended to be more comprehensive than just loans-for-resources – typically involving a plethora of deals for financing infrastructure and economic development. This is also the case for China-Myanmar relations (see Steinberg and Fan 2012).

Similarly to Japan, China has long provided various forms of economic assistance to Myanmar, e.g. concessional or interest-free loans, although solid data on these are hard to find. Reilly has argued that China has been more 'socialised' into international development assistance norms in Cambodia and Laos, whereas its aid activities have remained opaque and self-interested in Myanmar (Reilly 2012). China's assistance has been provided in the context of strengthening overall bilateral economic and political ties, obviously without the aim of supporting democratic change. As is the case with Chinese development assistance elsewhere, it is difficult to distinguish between 'genuine' development aid and commercially-based projects contracted by Chinese developers. Indeed, prior to political reforms, Myanmar was a major market for China's foreign engineering projects. Hence, most bilateral assistance and cooperation projects are tied to Chinese state-owned enterprises and China's 'go-out' strategy (Steinberg and Fan 2012, pp. 220–228). China has also been concerned with Myanmar's political development, but contrary to Japan, it has suggested reforms with a view to preventing popular unrest and a colour revolution (Ibid. p. 355).

Importantly, even in the countries most dependent on Chinese funding, the ability of the Chinese state to pursue specific political goals has been hampered by *resistant local agency*, as Corkin (2013) has shown in the case of Angola; by *poor coordination* between the involved Chinese corporations and state departments, as Kärkkäinen (2016) has shown in the case of Zimbabwe; by the *client state's rehabilitation of its IFI ties*, as in the case of Ecuador; or by the *disastrous state of local finances*, as in the case of Venezuela.

Japan's role in the ADB compared to China's founding role in the AIIB

Finally, we turn to comparing the roles of Japan and China in two prominent regional multilateral institutions concerned with promoting economic and social development: the ADB and the AIIB. Japan played a driving role in the run-up (1962–1966) to the creation of the ADB. All nine ADB presidents since 1966, when the bank was established, have been Japanese. Japan felt the World Bank did not serve its interests in Asia, hence it set out to create its 'own' bank, as a showcase of its new status in the world and as a tool for leadership in the regional development order (cf. Rathus 2008). By wielding influence in a multilateral development bank, Japan was able to render investments in neighbouring countries – wary of Japan's rise – as politically neutral. A similar motivation can be discerned for China's creation of the AIIB. However, Japan initially let other Asian countries take the initiative, while the US and Europe joined. Japan itself resorted to leading behind the scenes.

Between 1966 and 1972, Japan aimed to build a respectable multilateral bank, to establish Japanese leadership in it, and to make it serve Japanese commercial and economic interests. Manila was chosen as ADB headquarters because of a lingering distrust towards Japanese leadership in the region. Also, Japan had to accept a greater Western share in voting rights than intended. Initially, Japan aimed for the ADB to contribute to opening and developing markets in the Asian region, much in line with Japan's overall development policy. Activities focused on countries with which Japan had strong trading relations (Rathus 2008, p. 89). Half of the ADB's loans during the 1968–1981 period went to Japan's 'backyard garden', particularly to medium-level developing countries in Southeast Asia (Ofreneo 1985). More specifically, over 78 per cent of all of the ADB's loans between 1967 and 1972 went to countries with which Japan had crucial trade links (Indonesia, Thailand, Malaysia, the Philippines and South Korea), and Tokyo received almost 42 per cent of all procurements in 1967–1976 (Wan 1995). From the perspective of geoeconomics, Japan used the multilateral ADB to invest in neighbouring countries highly suspicious of the country's rising influence, as the multilateral institution was seen as a more politically neutral channel, free from special interests and marked by technical professionalism and a long-term perspective (O'Keeffe, Pryke and Wurf 2017).

Between 1972 and 1986, Japan took on a lower profile, aiming to exert silent influence. Tokyo provided more funding but seemingly gained less, while at the same time applying a broader definition of self-interest. This included the objective to show its commitment to the international community. Between 1986 and 1995, after the Plaza Accord, Japan used the ADB to channel Japanese private capital to Asia by improving local infrastructures. Tokyo adopted an increasingly assertive attitude, promoting an 'Asian bank'. The convergence of interests between the ADB and Japan (less focus on immediate gains) became obvious (Lim and Vreeland 2013). As of the 1990s, Japan used its political influence in the ADB to facilitate favourable loans to countries useful for Japan's foreign policy goals at the UNSC. For example, Japan's increased assertiveness coincided with a 30 per cent increase in loans to countries important to Japan's foreign policy objectives (Lim and Vreeland 2013, pp. 64–65).

Especially in light of China's rise, Japan has tried to increase its influence in the organisation, and play a more assertive role. While officially aiming to multilateralise China and socialise the country into the world order, the ADB allowed Japan to bring China into Tokyo's economic sphere, 'in a manner politically acceptable to China' (Rathus 2008, pp. 86–89). Furthermore, Japan recognises that continued ADB loans to China are profitable for the ADB (O'Keeffe, Pryke and Wurf 2017). However, Japan has responded to China's rise by shifting the focus of ADB loans to China. It has scaled back the ADB's operations in China, particularly in areas that might indirectly support military development, and instead moved towards projects related to social infrastructure, for example addressing regional inequality within China (Rathus 2008). Japan can therefore be seen as a textbook case of a government leveraging its influence in international organisations to advance domestic and foreign policy goals.

Japan has been wary of growing Chinese influence in the ADB, contributing to China launching its idea for the AIIB. While the AIIB was preceded by other initiatives, such as the New Development Bank (NDB), it has emerged as China's first serious attempt at establishing a multilateral financial institution where it has the dominant say. China currently holds 30.34 per cent of AIIB vote shares and 26.06 per cent of votes giving it a de facto veto and a position even surpassing the US position in the IMF. Beijing has been keen to stress that it will not exercise its veto and that its votes will be diluted as other countries join. Yet, Beijing will be hard put to convince sceptics that AIIB will not be used to further China's political and strategic objectives. Indeed, China's creation of multilateral development banks, while displaying similar features to the approach taken by Japan in the 1960s, challenges the supposed neutrality of multilateral institutions and has a much more ambitious scope (O'Keeffe, Pryke and Wurf 2017).

The establishment of AIIB, in conjunction with China's strategic Belt and Road Initiative, indicates that, like Japan, China is increasingly putting special emphasis on its own neighbourhood. China's paramount leader Xi Jinping has emphasised 'neighbourhood diplomacy' (周边外交) and building a 'community of shared future' (人类命运共同体) to which the two initiatives explicitly have been linked by Chinese leaders. The BRI covers more than 60 countries, with special emphasis on developing countries in Central and Southern Asia (Fu 2017). Among the 20 country-specific projects approved by the AIIB so far, eight have gone to the South Asian sub-continent, five to ASEAN countries, and four to Central Asia. Furthermore, six out of eight pending projects are destined for South Asia (AIIB 2017).

Although the ADB and the AIIB claim they are partners, an increasing competition can be witnessed between them. After signing a memorandum of understanding (MOU) for cooperation with the AIIB in May 2016, in June the ADB announced it would co-finance a highway project in Pakistan together with the China-led bank (Financial Express 2016). However, at the same time the ADB is responding to China's initiative by expanding its resources for financing infrastructure building, boosting lending capacity and including new measures to attract private investment (Japan Times 2015).

Conclusion: development lending and political objectives

This chapter has explored the various ways in which Japan and China have approached aid provision to other countries. Is there evidence of Japan or China using aid strategically – as tools of financial statecraft – to build economic partnerships that strongly tie recipient countries to the donor country (cf. Lei 2015)? To what extent are the national geostrategic objectives of Japan and China present in policy thinking, lending forms, and ODA targets, and in both countries' roles in regional multilateral institutions? We adopted and adapted the framework of Armijo and Katada as a heuristic tool for analysing various forms of financial statecraft. Table 11.1 outlines different forms of financial statecraft used by either Japan, China or both countries. However, not all of these are directly related to their development lending.

The table is illustrative, but it draws attention to the fact that China and Japan have used comparable forms of financial statecraft. We found broad similarities in historical trajectories, aid philosophy and focus on self-reliance, as well as in lending forms and aid recipients. Both countries have also tried to cement their leading role and thinking on aid provision in regional multilateral institutional settings. We can conclude that China and Japan have been learning from each other and are now increasingly competing in this arena, using similar means.

As for the way this edited volume understands the term geo-economics, it appears that Japan has been more active in trying to shape the East Asian region as its own sphere of influence through financial power, in keeping with Japan's long-standing objective of being the economic leader of Asia. Until recently, China's development lending has been more globally dispersed, and more focused on cultivating a strong relationship with other developing countries,

Table 11.1 Development lending as forms of financial statecraft in Japanese and Chinese lending

	Defensive	*Offensive*
Bilateral	Defending against the currency of a powerful neighbour through capital controls (C)	Sanctions: withholding new loans for political reasons* (J, C) Loans/aid to induce target country to adopt favourable policies or give political support in multilateral settings* (J, C)
Systemic	Promote multilateral banks* (J, C) Promote regional monetary fund (J) Seek greater voice in global financial and monetary governance (J, C) Reserve accumulation (J, C) Promote multiple reserve currencies (C)	Construct institutions of global governance to give oneself disproportionate influence* (J, C) Actively promote own currency as a global reserve and transactions currency* (C) Promote home financial markets as a source of global influence (J, C)

Note
The table is adapted from Armijo and Katada (2015), p. 47. Entries marked with * are those that are directly related to development lending. In the brackets, J stands for Japan and C for China.

especially with commodity exporters and African states. This conforms with China's emphasis on South-South cooperation and self-identification as the leading developing country. However, the establishment of AIIB may portend changes to this approach.

While our discussion points to the importance of promoting broad political objectives, the evidence is more mixed for Japan and China *being successful* in directly using development aid to further specific political goals. Importantly, in the case of both countries, the historical legacy (Japan's war guilt and reluctance to apply negative conditionality; China's policies of non-alignment and non-interference) still weighs heavily and tempers the ability of Tokyo or Beijing to go all out in pursuing national political and economic objectives through development lending. In fact, this can provide considerable leverage to recipient countries in circumstances where Tokyo or Beijing put high emphasis on maintaining good political relations with recipient countries.

In as far as Japan or China have been keen on achieving political aims, this has also provided recipient countries with leverage and negotiating power. For example, China's wide provision of aid to almost all African countries attests to the historical uncertainty over its international status and diplomatic competition with the ROC that has allowed recipients to extract benefits. Similarly, Japan has recently been keen on balancing China's increasing dominance in its backyard, which has allowed smaller neighbours to play the two economic giants against each other to attract a better deal. Myanmar can be seen as a case in point. Based on these observations, we formulate a more general hypothesis: *in bilateral relations, the party for whom good political relations is a more important concern tends to be less sensitive to the associated economic costs, and vice versa.* This assertion can serve as a starting point for future studies.

Notes

1 The authors would like to thank Sören Scholvin and Mikael Wigell for their many helpful comments in the process of writing this chapter.
2 In its policy papers, Japan uses both 'development cooperation' and ODA. China applies the term 'foreign aid' to describe development assistance provided as a non-DAC donor.
3 Kitano and Harada have made a methodical attempt at overcoming these methodological challenges and make Chinese aid more comparable to ODA (Kitano and Harada 2014).
4 The Japanese government issued its first ODA Charter in 1992, and revised it in 2003 to address new development challenges such as peace-building.
5 China's bilateral aid is much larger than its multilateral aid (Kitano and Harada 2014).
6 Discussion in Shanghai with a Chinese economist, 10 September 2016.

References

ActionAid. (2005) 'Real Aid. An Agenda for Making Aid Work', *Action Aid International*. Available at: www.un-ngls.org/orf/cso/cso9/real-aid.pdf, accessed 20 November 2017.

ActionAid. (2011) 'Real Aid. Ending Aid Dependency', *Action Aid International*. Available at: www.actionaid.org/sites/files/actionaid/real_aid_3.pdf, accessed 22 November 2017.

AIIB. (2017) 'Approved Projects', *Asian Infrastructure and Investment Bank*. Available at: www.aiib.org/en/projects/approved/index.html, accessed 20 November 2017.

Arase, D. (1995) *Buying Power: The Political Economy of Japan's Foreign Aid* (London and Boulder, CO: Lynne Rienner Publishers).

Armijo, L. E. and Katada, S. N. (eds) (2014) *The Financial Statecraft of Emerging Powers: Shield and Sword in Asian and Latin America* (Houndmills: Palgrave Macmillan).

Armijo, L. E. and Katada, S. N. (2015) 'Theorizing the Financial Statecraft of Emerging Powers', *New Political Economy*, 20, 1, pp. 42–62.

Bräutigam, D. (2007) 'China, Africa and the International Aid Architecture', *African Development Bank Group*, Working Paper Series No. 107. Available at: www.afdb. org/fileadmin/uploads/afdb/Documents/Publications/WORKING%20107%20%20 PDF%20E33.pdf, accessed 9 February 2018.

Bräutigam, D. (2011) 'Aid "With Chinese Characteristics": Chinese Foreign Aid and Development Finance Meet the OECD–DAC Aid Regime', *Journal of International Development*, 23, pp. 752–764.

Carothers, T. and De Gramont, D. (2013) *Development Aid Confronts Politics: The Almost Revolution* (Washington: Carnegie Endowment for International Peace).

Clay, E. J., Geddes, M. and Natall, L. (2009) 'Untying Aid: Is It Working? Evaluation of the Implementation of the Paris Declaration and of the 2001 DAC Recommendation of Untying ODA to the LDCs', *Danish Institute for International Studies*. Available at: www.oecd.org/dataoecd/51/35/44375975.pdf, accessed 20 November 2017.

Clift, B. and Rosamond, B. (2010) 'Lineages of a British International Political Economy', in Blyth, M. (ed.), *Routledge Handbook of International Political Economy (IPE), IPE as a global conversation* (Abingdon: Routledge), pp. 95–111.

Corkin, L. (2013) *Uncovering African Agency. Angola's Management of China's Credit Lines* (Farnham: Ashgate).

Davies, M., Edinger, H., Tay, N. and Naidu, S. (2008) 'How China Delivers Development Assistance to Africa', *Centre for Chinese Studies, University of Stellenbosch*.

Edström, B. (2009) *Japan and the Myanmar Conundrum* (Stockholm: Institute for Security and Development Policy). Available at: http://isdp.eu/content/uploads/publications/2009_ edstrom_japan-and-the-myanmar-conundrum.pdf, accessed 9 February 2018.

Eurodad. (2012) 'How to Spend It. Smart Procurement for More Effective Aid', *European Network on Debt and Development*. Available at: www.eurodad.org/files/ integration/2012/09/Procurement_report_summary.pdf, accessed 20 November 2017.

European Parliament. (2011) 'Export Finance Activities by the Chinese Government', *European Parliament*, Briefing Paper. Available at: www.europarl.europa.eu/RegData/ etudes/note/join/2011/433862/EXPO-INTA_NT(2011)433862_EN.pdf, accessed 22 November 2017.

Exim Bank. (2009) 'Chinese Government Concessional Loan and Preferential Export Buyers', *The Export-Import Bank of China*.

Farnsworth, E. (2011) 'The New Mercantilism: China's Emerging Role in the Americas', *Current History*, 110, pp. 56–61.

Financial Express. (2016) 'Asian Development Bank Announces First Co-financing with China's AIIB for Pakistan Road', *Financial Express*, 10 June. Available at: www. financialexpress.com/industry/asian-development-bank-announces-first-co-financing-with-chinas-aiib-for-pakistan-road/280483/, accessed 22 November 2017.

Foster, V., Butterfield, W., Chen, C. and Pushak, N. (2008) *Building Bridges: China's Growing Role as Infrastructure Financier for Sub-Saharan Africa* (Washington, DC: The World Bank).

Fu, Y. (2017) 'China's Vision for the World: A Community of Shared Future', *The Diplomat*, 22 June. Available at: https://thediplomat.com/2017/06/chinas-vision-for-the-world-a-community-of-shared-future/, accessed 20 November 2017.

Gaens, B. and Vogt, H. (2015) 'Sympathy or Self-Interest? The Development Agendas of the European Union and Japan in the 2000s', in Bacon, P., Mayer, H. and Nakamura, H. (eds), *The European Union and Japan: A New Chapter in Civilian Power Cooperation?* (Farnham: Ashgate), pp. 151–168.

Gao, Z. (2007) 'Infrastructure Development in Africa Supported by the Export-Import Bank of China', *3rd Annual Meeting of the Infrastructure Consortium in Africa*, 17 January.

Hartley, R. (2017) 'Contemporary Thailand-Japan Economic Relations: What Falling Japanese Investment Reveals about Thailand's Deep, Global Competition, State in the Context of Shifting Regional Orders', *Asia & the Pacific Policy Studies*, 4, 3, pp. 569–585.

Huotari, M. and Heep, S. (2016) 'Learning Geoeconomics: China's Experimental Financial and Monetary Initiatives', *Asia Europe Journal*, 14, 2, pp. 153–171.

Japan Times. (2015) 'Asian Development Bank Pledges to Increase Lending, Cooperate with China-led Bank', *The Japan Times*, 5 May. Available at: www.japantimes.co.jp/news/2015/05/05/national/politics-diplomacy/asian-development-bank-pledges-to-increase-lending-cooperate-with-china-led-bank/, accessed 20 November 2017.

Kärkkäinen, A. (2016) 'Does China Have a Geoeconomic Strategy Towards Zimbabwe? The Case of the Zimbabwean Natural Resource Sector', *Asia Europe Journal*, 14, 2, pp. 185–202.

Kitano, N. and Harada, Y. (2014) 'Estimating China's Foreign Aid 2001–2013', *JICA Research Institute*, JICA-RI Working Paper No. 78. Available at: www.jica.go.jp/jica-ri/publication/workingpaper/jrft3q00000025no-att/JICA-RI_WP_No. 78_2014.pdf, accessed 22 November 2017.

Lancaster, C. (2010) 'Japan's ODA: Naiatsu and Gaiatsu: Domestic Sources and Transnational Influences', in Leheny, D. and Key, W. (eds), *Japanese Aid and The Construction of Global Development. Inescapable Solutions* (London: Routledge), pp. 29–53.

Lei, Y. (2015) 'China's Strategic Partnership with Latin America: A Fulcrum in China's Rise', *International Affairs*, 91, 5, pp. 1047–1068.

Lim, H. S. (2008) *Japan and China in East Asian Integration* (fifth edition) (Singapore: Institute of Southeast Asian Studies).

Lim, D. Y. M. and Vreeland, J. R. (2013) 'Regional Organizations and International Politics. Japanese Influence over the Asian Development Bank and the UN Security Council', *World Politics*, 65, 1, pp. 34–72.

Mattlin, M. and Nojonen, M. (2011) 'Conditionality in Chinese Bilateral Lending', *Bank of Finland*, BOFIT Discussion Papers No. 14. Available at: https://helda.helsinki.fi/bof/handle/123456789/8282, accessed 22 November 2017.

Mattlin, M. and Nojonen, M. (2015) 'Conditionality and Path Dependence in Chinese Lending', *Journal of Contemporary China*, 24, 94, pp. 701–720.

Mitton, R. (2006) 'Beijing Refuses Aid to Hanoi After Rebuff over Taiwan', *Straits Times*, 22 December.

MOFA. (2016) 'Japan's International Cooperation: White Paper on Development Cooperation 2015', *Ministry of Foreign Affairs of Japan*. Available at: www.mofa.go.jp/policy/oda/page23e_000436.html, accessed 29 November 2017.

Nour, S. S. O. M. (2011) 'Assessment of Effectiveness of China Aid in Financing Development in Sudan', *United Nations University*, UNU-MERIT Working Papers No. 2011–005.

OECD. (2014) 'OECD Development Co-operation Peer Reviews: Japan 2014', *OECD*. Available at: www.oecd.org/development/peer-reviews/Japan-peer-review-2014.pdf, accessed 22 November 2017.

Ofreneo, R. E. (1985) 'ADB: Furor over "Privatization"', *World Bulletin*, 56, pp. 56–61.

O'Keeffe, A., Pryke, J., and Wurf, H. (2017) 'Strengthening the Asian Development Bank in 21st Century Asia', *Lowy Institute*. Available at: www.lowyinstitute.org/publications/strengthening-asian-development-bank-21st-century-asia, accessed 22 November 2017.

Orbie, J. and Versluys, H. (2008) 'The European Union's International Development Policy: Leading and Benevolent?' in Orbie, J. (ed.), *Europe's Global Role. External Policies of the European Union* (Farnham: Ashgate), pp. 67–90.

PRC State Council. (2014) 'China's Foreign Aid. Information Office of the State Council', *The State Council of the People's Republic of China*. Available at: http://english.gov.cn/archive/white_paper/2014/08/23/content_281474982986592.htm, accessed 20 November 2017.

Rathus, J. (2008) 'China, Japan and Regional Organisations: The Case of the Asian Development Bank', *Japanese Studies*, 28, 1, pp. 87–99.

Reilly, J. (2012) 'A Norm-Taker or a Norm-Maker? Chinese Aid in Southeast Asia', *Journal of Contemporary China*, 21, 73, pp. 71–91.

Reilly, J. (2013) 'China and Japan in Myanmar: Aid, Natural Resources and Influence', *Asian Studies Review*, 37, 2, pp. 141–157.

Sanderson, H. and Forsythe, M. (2013) *China's Superbank: Debt, Oil and Influence – How China Development Bank is Rewriting the Rules of Finance* (Singapore: John Wiley & Sons).

Sharma, M. (2016) 'Japan's Aid Needs More Imagination', *Bloomberg View*, 7 September. Available at: www.bloomberg.com/view/articles/2016-09-07/why-china-is-beating-japan-in-the-battle-for-mind-share, accessed 20 November 2017.

Smith, K. E. (2005) 'Beyond the Civilian Power Debate?', *Politique Européenne*, 1, 17, pp. 63–82.

Steil, B. and Litan, R. E. (2008) *Financial Statecraft: The Role of Financial Markets in American Foreign Policy* (New Haven, CT: Yale University Press).

Steinberg, D. I. and Fan, H. (2012) *Modern China-Myanmar Relations: Dilemmas of Mutual Dependence* (Copenhagen: NIAS Press).

Strange, S. (1997) *Casino Capitalism* (second edition) (Manchester: Manchester University Press).

Strange, S. (2004) *States and Markets* (second edition) (London: Continuum).

Strefford, P. (2016) 'Japan Set to Reap Returns on Investment in Myanmar', *East Asia Forum*, 31 August. Available at: www.eastasiaforum.org/2016/08/26/japan-set-to-reap-returns-on-investment-in-myanmar/, accessed 29 November 2017.

Söderberg, M. (2005) 'Series Editor's Preface' in Hagström, L. (ed.), *Japan's China Policy: A Relational Power Analysis* (Abingdon: Routledge), pp. viii–ix.

Wan, M. (1995) 'Japan and the Asian Development Bank', *Pacific Affairs*, 68, 4, pp. 509–528.

Watanabe, T. (2005) 'History of Japan's ODA in Brief', in *Fifty Years of Japan ODA – A critical review for ODA reform*, The Reality of Aid, Asia-Pacific 2005 Report. Available at: www.realityofaid.org/wp-content/uploads/2013/02/ROA_Asia_2005_Full_sml1.pdf, accessed 7 December 2017.

Wigell, M. (2016) 'Conceptualizing Regional Powers' Geoeconomic Strategies: Neo-imperialism, Neo-mercantilism, Hegemony, and Liberal Institutionalism', *Asia Europe Journal*, 14, 2, pp. 135–151.

Wu, F. and Koh, D. W. (2014) 'From Financial Assets to Financial Statecraft: The Case of China and Emerging Economies of Africa and Latin America', *Journal of Contemporary China*, 23, 89, pp. 781–803.

Xiong, H. (2010) '中国对外多变援助的理论与实践', 外间评论, 5, pp. 49–61.

Youngs, R. (2011) 'Geo-economic Futures', in Martiningui, A. and Youngs, R. (eds), *Challenges for European Foreign Policy in 2012: What Kind of Geo-economic Europe?* (Madrid: Fundación para las Relaciones Internacionales y el Diálogo Exterior), pp. 13–17.

Zarate, J. C. (2013) *Treasury's War: The Unleashing of a New Era of Financial Warfare* (New York: Public Affairs).

Zhang, H. (2009) '论中国援外不附加政治条件原则的理论基础几现实意义' [China's Non-political Conditionality Aid Principle: Theory and Significance], 当代亚太, 6, pp. 93–105.

Zhou, H. (2008) '中国对外援助与改革开放30年' [China's Foreign Aid and 30 Years of Reform and Opening-up], 世界经济与政治, 11, pp. 33–43.

12 China's economic statecraft in Latin America

Geostrategic implications for the United States[1]

Mikael Wigell and Ana Soliz Landivar

Introduction

The pace of China's expanding presence and influence in Latin America has been astonishing in recent years. Much attention focuses on whether it provides an opportunity or threat to Latin American socio-economic development (Ferchen 2011; Jenkins 2012; Wise 2016). There has been less discussion about the geostrategic dynamics of China's evolving role.[2] In the United States, the prevailing view has been that as long as the Chinese activities are predominantly economic, not military, they pose little threat to the strategic interests of the United States in Latin America (see Ellis 2013; Piccone 2016). By offering new trade opportunities, finance and investments, China is helping to raise the economic potential of the region, which provides opportunities also for US companies (e.g. see Gallagher 2016).

This liberal view overlooks how economic activities may have long-standing strategic consequences. In fact, as this book shows, rising powers commonly use economic statecraft when pursuing strategic objectives on the international stage (see Wigell 2016). Herein, strategic aims are often masked under the guise of commercial, seemingly apolitical activities. Such masking is geo-economics par excellence. The idea is to avoid causing the sort of alarm that more overtly geopolitical actions often generate and which could provoke counter-actions (for a discussion, see Wigell and Vihma 2016). But despite the means being 'soft', the aim may still be 'hard' – to pursue political aims, sometimes even to create a sphere of political influence.

In particular, economic means can be used as a basis for a binding strategy, whereby target states are made increasingly economically dependent on the rising power that gains political leverage. Herein, while the various trade, finance and investment deals offer a host of economic benefits to the targeted countries, at least in the short-term, they may come at the expense of political concessions over the long-term. Such a geo-economic strategy is not only easier to conceal than traditional geopolitics, but it actively creates interest groups with incentives to lobby for it. These interest groups may be local stakeholders or multinational corporations that benefit from the economic incentives and will therefore have an incentive to play down any political threat scenarios that rise from it and portray these threats as merely apolitical and commercial interaction (for a discussion, see Wigell and Vihma 2016). As such, we suggest viewing geo-economics as a strategic practice that assumes foreign policy choices to result from internal political contests, and for an external power to be able to affect the outcome of those internal political struggles through geo-economics. Depending on the reward power of the geo-economic operator, interest groups in target countries may be provided with both the incentives and means to become powerful interlocutors on the external power's behalf.

This chapter analyses China's geo-economics in Latin America, how it is changing the geostrategic environment in the region, and what the strategic implications are for the United States. Having been slow to react to China's geo-economic advance, the United States not only risks being displaced economically, particularly in South America, but also losing important political influence. There can be no doubt that the Trump administration's unilateralism, anti-trade proposals and antagonising rhetoric accelerates this trend, opening up space for the further expansion of China's engagement with the region, especially to countries that hitherto have supported US leadership such as Chile, Colombia, Mexico and Peru.

The chapter is structured as follows. We start by looking at China's economic expansion into Latin America. We underscore how it has been accelerating, how it cannot be explained by purely commercial arguments and how it is making Latin America more dependent on China. We then turn to more specifically analyse China's objectives, how they are geo-economic in nature and therefore strategic. In the penultimate section we analyse how China's geo-economics is shaping the strategic geography in the region and its implications for the United States. We also briefly engage with the Trump administration's regional policies and how they are affecting the strategic scenario. We conclude by highlighting how the United States needs a renewed geo-economic strategy of its own if it is to recover some of its diminished presence and influence in its own 'backyard'.

China's evolving economic role in Latin America

Starting from trade, it should be noted how China has become a central partner for Latin America, while US trade with the region has declined. Between 2000 and 2014, the United States' share of Latin American trade declined from 53.5 per cent to 37.1 per cent (Ortiz Velásquez and Dussel Peters, 2016). Sino-Latin American trade, meanwhile, increased twentyfold from 2001 to 2015, making China the first trading partner for countries such as Brazil, Chile, Peru and Uruguay. In 2015, Latin American exports to China were worth US$103 billion, which equate to around 10 per cent of the region's total exports and making China the second destination for all Latin American exports. Latin American imports from China were worth US$113 billion, so Latin America has a trade deficit with China. However, there are some noteworthy differences between sub-regions. For the region of Central America and the Caribbean, the United States is still by far the most important trading partner, whereas China has become the top trading partner for South America (ECLAC 2017).

An important feature of the evolving Sino-Latin American trade relationship is the heavy concentration of Latin American exports to the primary sectors. Extractives (i.e. oil, gas and minerals) and agriculture account for over 80 per cent of all Latin American exports to China. In contrast, manufacturing accounts for nearly 70 per cent of Latin American imports from China. This skewed Sino-Latin American trade relationship has raised concerns about the 'reprimarisation' of the Latin American economies (OECD/ECLAC/CAF 2015).

Since 2010, China has also emerged as a key source of new investments in Latin America, while US and European financial flows have continued to decline (ECLAC 2015; Financial Times 2016a). In 2016, Chinese companies made a total amount of US$3.3 billion in new (greenfield) foreign direct investment (FDI) in Latin America. They also spent the total amount of US$12.4 billion on mergers and acquisitions in the region (Ray and Gallagher 2017). Chinese FDI flows have been accelerated recently, reaching a total amount of US$11.9 billion in 2015. As with trade, Chinese investments have been concentrated to the extractive sectors.

In recent years, Chinese investments have also increasingly focused on infrastructure. From 2005 until 2016, China invested US$5.5 billion into 91 infrastructure projects in the region (Dussel Peters 2017). Those projects include the region's most ambitious projects such as developing a transcontinental railway linking Brazil's Atlantic coast to Peru's Pacific coast, the construction of the Two-Ocean Tunnel between Argentina and Chile, and the building of three nuclear plants in Argentina. There is also a project to build a transoceanic shipping canal in Nicaragua that, if completed, will rival the Panama Canal and give China a significant presence in Central America. These megaprojects come on top of a long list of projects in Latin American infrastructure proposed by the Chinese in recent years. The Chinese are building or upgrading railways, roads, ports and airports all over the continent.[3]

Table 12.1 Latin American countries estimated FDI flows from China 1990–2015 (in US$ millions)

	1990–2009	2010	2011	2012	2013	2014	2015
Argentina	143	3100	2450	600	120	na	300
Brazil	255	9563	5676	6067	2580	1161	6230
Chile	na	5	0	76	19	na	na
Colombia	1677	6	293	996	776	na	50
Ecuador	1619	45	59	86	88	79	94
Mexico	146	9	2	74	15	70	na
Peru	2262	84	829	1307	4626	9605	2142
Venezuela	240	900	1045	1225	2445	1000	na

Source: Economic Commission for Latin America and the Caribbean (ECLAC), on the basis of official information Pérez Ludeña (2017), Thomson Reuters, FDI Markets, Heritage Foundation and information from the respective companies.

Note
na=not available.

Table 12.2 Top Chinese infrastructure projects in Latin America

Year	No of projects	Amount (US$ million)
2010	14	15080
2011	10	4130
2012	9	5330
2013	9	2750
2014	14	6260
2015	15	16130

Source: Dussel Peters and Armony (2017).

With regard to these infrastructure projects, an important aspect pertains to them usually being implemented by Chinese state-owned enterprises, with minuscular participation by private enterprises. It suggests China views these projects from a geo-economic perspective, not necessarily paying as much attention to their commercial aspects as to their geostrategic value. Indeed, many of the Chinese-driven infrastructure projects have no obvious routes to profitability, at least not in the short-term (e.g. Gustafson 2016). This approach differs from US and European investments, which usually are made by private enterprises that evaluate any investments from a strictly commercial viewpoint. Through its state-led approach, the Chinese can pursue build-own-operate agreements that combine planning, managing, constructing, and financing, in a complete solution that enables China to control the implementation of the project at all stages. These mega-deals offer a range of short-term incentives for local actors, such as providing technology and generous financing plans to cover development costs, and therefore create a range of incentives for local actors to cooperate with China. At the same time, they may create long-term liabilities with China, making host governments de facto dependent on China (for a discussion, see Mattlin and Nojonen 2015). Particularly the loans-for-resources and loans-for-infrastructure deals between China and Latin American countries, which often involve Chinese actors being given operating control long into the future, risk making the latter liable to China for extended periods of time.

In conjunction with these major infrastructure projects and various loans-for-resources agreements, Chinese lending to Latin American governments has been rising dramatically in recent years, reaching US$29 billion in 2015, almost twice as much as the combined total lending by the World Bank and the Inter-American Development Bank. The bulk of this lending has been directed to four countries: Argentina, Brazil, Ecuador and, particularly, Venezuela (see Figure 12.1). In addition, China has offered a further US$35 billion in new regional funds for infrastructure and industrial cooperation. All in all, China has emerged as Latin America's biggest creditor (see Ray, Gallagher and Sarmiento 2016). The prospect of future cash flows with non-conditionality concerning (Western) good governance standards, together with multibillion dollar investment deals, not only provide strong incentives for Latin American governments to cooperate with China, but also allows China to structure these deals, if need be, so as to create rent-seeking opportunities for businessmen and corrupt officials, who will thus develop strong incentives to become vocal advocates of Chinese interests.

Reports of corruption, irregularities in bidding processes, opaque transactions and an overall lack of transparency have already for some time emerged in relation to Chinese investment projects (e.g. Armony 2012). A recent example involves the major loan-for-infrastructure deals agreed between former Argentine president Cristina Fernández de Kirchner and Chinese President Xi Jinping in 2014. They involved the building of two giant hydroelectric dams in the Kirchner family's heartland, in the province of Santa Cruz. The deal was made without following normal bureaucratic procedures and has spurned a myriad of suspicions concerning corruption (e.g. La Nación 2016; Watts 2015). Argentina's new president, Mauricio Macri, questioning the lack of transparency in the agreements, vowed to review and potentially cancel the projects, but soon

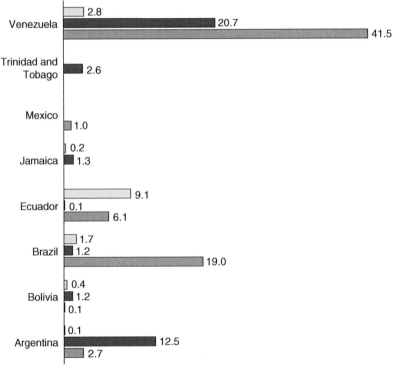

Country loans total in billions US dollars

▢Other   ■For infrastructure projects   ▪For energy projects

Figure 12.1 Chinese loans to Latin America 2005–2015.

Source: authors' own compilation based on data from China-Latin America Finance Database (Inter-American Dialogue, n.d.).

found his hands tied in the process (Patey 2017). It shows the difficulty of escaping these mega-deals, once they have been agreed upon.

Hence, as evidenced by this economic data, China is clearly positioning itself as an increasingly important economic actor in Latin America. The economic slowdown in both China and Latin America observed since 2014 is not about to alter these trends. Under President Xi, China has moved to intensify its relations with Latin America, as demonstrated not only by the accelerating number of summit visits, but also the enhanced institutionalised cooperation. The cooperation plan signed at the first meeting of the China-Community of Latin American and Caribbean States (China-CELAC) forum in January 2015 aims at doubling annual trade and significantly increasing China's investment stock within the next decade (Xi 2015). A survey of infrastructure executives and specialists, conducted by the Financial Times Confidential Research, found the appetite among big Chinese investors to remain high as they are thinking of longer-term strategic goals (Financial Times 2016b).

China's objectives

China has strong motives for its involvement in Latin America, some of which are clearly geo-economic, while others may also include more commercial considerations (see Yu 2015; Ellis 2013; 2016). First, the continent provides an important source of the raw materials that China needs to sustain its rapid industrialisation and increasing demand for foodstuffs. This can be noted in the composition of Chinese imports from Latin America and the way it has been evolving over time. Imports are heavily concentrated on primary products and resource-based manufactures. The importance of securing access to natural resources is also reflected in the financial flows from China to Latin America. Three quarters of Chinese mergers and acquisitions in the region over the last

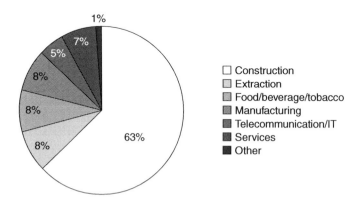

Figure 12.2 Sector distribution of Chinese greenfield foreign direct investment in Latin America and the Caribbean 2010–2014 (total US$70b).

Source: Ray and Gallagher 2015.

five years were in extractive industries (oil, gas and mining). Looking at the composition of Chinese investments, two thirds were in infrastructure and public works, much of which is related to gaining access to raw materials. Much of the remaining investments focused directly on agriculture, energy and minerals (Ray and Gallagher 2015).

Second, access to the Latin American markets allows China to diversify and expand its export base. Chinese policymakers have been concerned about the country's overdependence on markets in North America and Europe, leaving it vulnerable to risks such as rising protectionism and economic slumps in those markets (Holslag 2016). The region also provides a convenient market for Chinese efforts to export industrial capacity and expand its manufacturing base (Jenkins 2012). Herein, China is pursuing a dynamic mercantilism through which it is buying raw materials from the region, adding value to them through domestic production, and then re-exporting this value-added production to Latin America. Part of this mercantilism also involves promoting the international-isation of Chinese corporations through diplomatic and financial assistance. Chinese engineering companies, in particular, are looking for new markets as domestic growth is slowing, and these efforts are effectively nourished through export credits and government-to-government loans. In general terms, the aim is the extension of state capitalism as part of China's 'go-out' policy, which was launched at the turn of the century and functions as a high-level endorsement for the expansion of Chinese enterprises abroad (Holslag 2006; 2016; Wu and De Wei 2014).

Third, engaging in Latin America is viewed by Chinese policymakers as an avenue for bolstering the role of the Chinese currency in international markets (Yu 2015). The Yuan has garnered increasing regional importance with Argentina, Brazil and Chile already having significant bilateral currency swap arrangements. The aforementioned cooperation plan envisages increasing currency swaps in bilateral trade. Worried about the dominant position of the US dollar in global financial markets, which is seen as a potential threat to China's economic security and preventing it from becoming a global financial player, the Chinese government has been pushing for the internationalisation of the Yuan in global trade and investment. With Chile, China has also agreed to set up a Yuan clearing bank (Reuters 2015).

Fourth, Latin America represents a major arena for China in its efforts to diplomatically isolate Taiwan. Half of the 24 countries in the world that recognise the government of Taiwan are in Latin America and the Caribbean. This diplomatic contest has influenced China's economic engagement with the region. China has been using economic incentives, selectively as sticks and carrots, to bid for the non-recognition of Taiwan (Urdinez *et al.* 2016; Wu and De Wei 2014). On the one hand, countries that recognise Taiwan have found their access to the Chinese market restricted. On the other hand, Costa Rica's shift in allegiance from Taiwan to China in 2007 was followed by a major aid package for public works, the Chinese purchase of US$300 million Costa Rican government bonds, a billion-dollar joint venture to upgrade the country's oil refinery, and better access for Costa Rican products to the Chinese markets (Bowley 2008). It served as a powerful demonstration to the other countries in the region of the benefits involved with severing their relations with Taiwan and switching them to China. Indeed, taking note of these economic inducements, Panama followed suit in 2017 (Horton and Myers Lee 2017). China's financial and investment outreach to Latin America and the Caribbean also shows a clear preference to engage with those states that recognise Beijing over Taipei. None of the regional states that recognise Taiwan is part of the list of the top 13 destinations of Chinese lending (Piccone 2016). Chinese investment commitments similarly seem to favour countries with close diplomatic ties to Beijing (Urdinez *et al.* 2016). Piccone (2016) also points out how the Chinese commitment to finance a Honduran hydroelectric project have stalled repeatedly, a likely reason being Honduras' continuous recognition of Taipei.

Finally, Latin America has broader strategic significance for China by way of securing political alliances in support of its rise as an emerging superpower and as a counterweight against US attempts to contain it. It should be noted how China treats the Community of Latin America and Caribbean States (CELAC) as its principal interlocutor in Latin America, and how the Chinese president has emphasised China's support for the growing role of the Bolivarian Alliance for the Americas (ALBA) and the Union of South American Nations (UNASUR) (Piccone 2016). All three are newer regional organisations that purposefully excludes the United States. Chinese policymakers largely see the United States' 'Pivot to Asia' as a containment strategy targeted against China and, as argued by Yu, by deepening economic interdependence and integration between itself and Latin America, China wishes to create a 'sphere of influence' in the traditional 'backyard' of the United States … in retaliation for the US containment and encirclement of China, and as a fulcrum in its rise as a global power capable of challenging US dominance and reshaping the current world system in a fashion more to its liking (Yu 2015, p. 1048). Careful not to be seen as openly challenging the United States, China thus applies geo-economics as a more subtle strategy of balancing against the global superpower and cement its relationship with Latin American countries. Such 'soft balancing', while being conducted by economic means, is calibrated to avoid the sort of counter-reaction than more traditional geopolitics would trigger.[4]

While official Chinese policy documents and high-level public statements obviously do not disclose the country's complete set of strategic intentions for engaging with Latin America, seeking to present them in the most non-threatening manner possible and underlining mutual interests, it is nevertheless remarkable how openly they convey Chinese geo-economic considerations. China has published two official 'white papers' on its policy towards Latin America and the Caribbean. The first one, released in November 2008, explicitly recognised that China views its engagement with Latin America and the Caribbean from a 'strategic plane'. It provided a framework for China's subsequent expansion into the region through trade, investment and finance (Central People's Government of the People's Republic of China 2008). The second one, released in November 2016, not only recognises that China's engagement with Latin America and the Caribbean is strategically important to the development of the Chinese economy, but also explicitly refers to the goal of advancing 'multi-polarization', 'global governance reform' and the promotion of regional multilateralism (People's Daily 2016). As for the last one, it makes references to CELAC, as the primary regional organisation. The new white paper also makes explicit statements to the 'One China Principle' as the foundation for establishing and developing state-to-state relations with the countries of the region.

The new Chinese policy white paper characterises itself as a 'blueprint for the future'. Herein, it refers to the '1+3+6' Chinese engagement framework presented by President Xi during his second trip to the region in 2014 (Ministry of Foreign Affairs of the People's Republic of China 2014), the 2015–2019 'Cooperation Plan' of the China-CELAC Forum, advanced by China in its summit with leaders of the region in January 2015 (China-CELAC Forum 2015), as well as the new 3×3 mode of cooperation presented by Prime Minister Li Keqiang in his key note at the China-Brazil Business Summit in May 2015 (Zhang 2015). The 1+3+6 concept refers to the five-year 'Cooperation Plan' with CELAC as a 'single' roadmap for cooperation ('1'), the three pillars for advancing it: trade, investment, and finance ('3'), and the six focus areas: energy, natural resources, infrastructure, agriculture, manufacturing, scientific innovation, and information technology ('6'). The 3×3 model ties in with the above focus areas by referring to China's desire to focus on building logistics, electricity and data connections, as well as expanding the three financing channels of funds, credit loans and insurance.

Strategic implications for the United States

For the United States, China's rapidly growing economic leverage in Latin America provides a set of geostrategic challenges. The growing Sino-Latin American economic ties have the potential to significantly alter the strategic geography of the continent with major implications for US leverage. As shown by an IMF report, economic links between countries in Latin America are weak and instead have tended to cluster around the United States (Beaton *et al.* 2017). Latin American countries have been linked to the United States, through a hub-and-spoke structure, with many of the most important transport corridors, trade and financial arrangements favouring economic interaction with the United States on a bilateral basis (e.g. Biegon 2017; Scheinin 1999).

Part of the explanation for Latin America's lack of integration stems from geography. In South America, the Andes mountain range, the Amazon basin with its dense, almost insurmountable rain forest, as well as the sheer connecting distance, have constituted major natural geographic barriers to intra-regional trade and the development of regional production chains. As a result, the sort of natural economic ties that would cause pressure for deeper integration have simply not been there (e.g. Scholvin and Malamud 2014). As Malamud and Rodriguez (2014, p. 119) explain:

Regional initiatives are limited by low levels of trade interdependence and interconnectivity (due to large distances and poor infrastructure), and by the attraction of extra-regional poles. All the South American economies are predominantly commodity-exporting, and their populations and resources – which are spread along the Atlantic, Caribbean and Pacific shorelines but are very sparse in the hinterlands – are oriented outward rather than in a neighborly direction.

However, particularly in South America, and to a lesser extent in Central America, this economic geography looks set to alter as a result of the major Chinese-driven infrastructure projects. These new infrastructure projects, many of which focus on building bi-oceanic corridors, may now start to unleash stronger regional policies and commitment by helping to connect the different sub-regions of South America. To the extent that such regional momentum would be channelled into the relatively new regional organisations such as UNASUR, which excludes the United States, it would undermine US leadership in the region. Already, the new infrastructure is redirecting the commercial flows of South America towards the Pacific, as evidenced by comparing the evolution of trade volumes between South America and China with those between South America and the United States (Ortiz Velásquez and Dussel Peters 2016). Japan, South Korea and India have also become increasingly important trade partners for the region (see Mesquita Moreira and Estevadeordal 2015; Myers and Kuwayama 2016; Roett and Paz 2017).

In general, China's economic engagement with the region gives Latin American countries the opportunity to pursue greater autonomy from the United States and Western institutions (Chávez 2015). The most obvious example is the way Chinese investments, loans and export revenues to the countries of the ALBA have helped them forge a path independent of US efforts to pursue its policy agenda in the region (see also Chapter 13 in this volume). Venezuela is the most obvious example, but also countries such as Bolivia and Ecuador, traditionally large recipients of US aid, could not be persuaded by the United States to accept its conditions for aid continuation. As a result, Bolivia moved to expel the US Agency for International Development (USAID) in 2013, having already expelled the US Ambassador and the US Drug Enforcement Agency in 2008 (Santamaria 2013a). Having failed to reach a consensus in its negotiations with Ecuador, USAID decided to cancel its aid programme there in 2013 (Santamaria 2013b). In addition, Chinese economic backing has also indirectly enabled these countries to help set up regional institutions such as UNASUR and the CELAC that excludes the United States (Ellis 2013).

Comparing Chinese lending to Latin American countries with US foreign aid from 2000 to 2015 (Figure 12.3), we can see how Chinese loans increasingly have been targeting countries where US foreign aid has been decreasing. Chinese lending has thus increasingly been replacing US conditional aid. It is hardly far-fetched to assume it to have consequences for the US policy agenda in the region, and even at the global level. Analyses have found a positive correlation

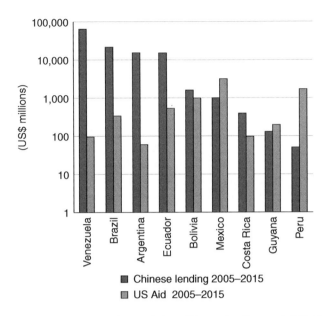

Figure 12.3 Comparison of the Chinese lending and US foreign aid in Latin
America 2005–2015.

Source: authors' own compilation, based on data from Inter-American Dialogue, and the
United States Agency for International Development (USAID).

between China's growing economic ties to the region and voting behaviour on
human rights issues at the United Nations (Flores-Macías and Kreps 2013). The
trend is particular for countries such as Bolivia, Ecuador and Venezuela that
have been showing growing consistency with Chinese views on international
issues, while Mexico and Central America continue to trend towards US posi-
tions (see Piccone 2016).

In the strategically important sector of space technology, countries such as
Bolivia, Ecuador, Nicaragua and Venezuela have all recently launched their own
programmes with support from China. This important aspect has been relatively
neglected in the scholarly debate on China-Latin America relations (for exceptions,
see Ellis 2010; Delgado-López 2012; Noesselt and Soliz Landivar 2013). Until
2008, Argentina and Brazil were the only states in Latin America with their own
satellite agencies, relying heavily on technological cooperation with the United
States (in the case of Argentina) or European countries like France (in the case of
Brazil). Now, also these two countries have moved to establish close partnerships
with China, in order to decrease their dependence on the United States and Europe.
China's support for Latin America's space technology includes investment in satellite construction, the launching of satellites from Chinese launching sites, and
professional training of satellite operators. With Chinese financial and technological support, these countries have also initiated joint space programs in a direct

effort to decrease their dependence on the United States in this sector, an initiative that can be traced back to a meeting of UNASUR member states' defence ministers in 2011 (Noesselt and Soliz Landivar 2013).

The rhetoric and politics of the Trump administration is helping to accelerate these tendencies. President Trump's anti-trade rhetoric has increased interest for more trade with China among the Latin American countries. The announcement by the incoming Trump administration that the United States was abandoning the Trans-Pacific Partnership (TPP) was immediately followed by signals from Chile, Mexico and Peru to seek closer trade relations with China (Reuters 2016; Santiago Times 2016). Chinese President Xi Jinping also immediately grabbed the opportunity to invite them to join the regional economic grouping that he is promoting – the Regional Comprehensive Economic Partnership (RCEP) and the Free Trade Area of the Asia-Pacific (FTAAP) – an invitation that was apparently well-received (América Economía 2016). China has also positioned itself to gain from president Trump's threat to withdraw from the North American Free Trade Agreement (NAFTA). Following the decision by General Motors to cancel plans to build a factory in Mexico, China's state-owned JAC Motors announced plans to invest US$2.2 billion in a car factory in the country. Indeed, as shown by the analysis of Urdinez *et al.* (2016), China is filling the void left by diminishing economic links between the United States and Latin America.

Thus, in the economic realm, China clearly offers an alternative to the United States, and as Eric Farnsworth has noted: 'In a post-Cold War world, where global competition is as much economic as military, the inability or unwillingness to contend for markets abroad has strategic implications' (Farnsworth 2012, p. 84). With much of the United States' influence having traditionally been built around its geo-economic nodality – i.e. by being the core of economic networks in the hemisphere – the economic protectionism currently under display with the Trump administration is bound to have serious consequences for not only the commercial but also the strategic position of the United States in Latin America. Dumping NAFTA and other free-trade agreements, or unilaterally curtailing market access, will weaken precisely those actors that are the United States' strongest supporters in the region. Herein, this effect will be compounded by the fact that many countries in the region currently trade under preferential trade agreements with the United States. As pointed out by Long and Friedman (2017, p. 3), 'These have the effect of aligning certain economic sectors' interests with the United States.' In some cases, the United States has also tied these agreements to specific policy goals, such as anti-drug cooperation under the 1991 Andean Trade Preferences Act (Long and Friedman 2017). If repealed, the United States will lose important political levers that come from these agreements.

Conclusions

Geo-economics is designed to drive political objectives by economic means and ideally it wants to shape the way target states define their national interests. It assumes that how target states define their national interests will result from internal political contests, and that the economic statecraft of an external power can affect the outcome of those internal political struggles (Abdelal and Kirshner 1999; also Vihma and Wigell 2016). US economic 'reward power', working through financial and trade inducements such as the preferential trade agreements referred to above, has had the effect of empowering pro-US constituencies in Latin America, paving the way for the 'Washington Consensus', the 'War on Drugs', and other US-led initiatives in the region. Yet, as things stand now, it is China that most enthusiastically is vying for influence in Latin America through the use of economic means. The United States, under the Trump administration, seems content on giving up on these economic instruments.

By not engaging in the geo-economic competition with China in Latin America, the United States not only risk being displaced economically but losing important political influence that may have repercussions for the future of the liberal world order. China's economic statecraft has already weakened the United States' 'structural power' (see May 1996) in the region, i.e. its ability to control important regional organisations and power structures, as evidenced by the growing importance of CELAC that excludes the United States. As such, China's economic expansion into Latin America not only provides it with the potential means to wield political influence over issues such as the Taiwan question, but by binding the region more tightly to itself through longer-term financial and investment deals, it sets the stage for a more far-reaching pivot among Latin American countries towards China. The major Chinese-led infrastructure projects currently under way in Latin America also have the potential, as analysed above, to start shifting particularly South America's economic geography. With the new economic links tying the region more closely together in an east-west direction, instead of the north-south links following the traditional US-centric hub-and-spoke pattern, a prominent basis of the United States' hemispheric leadership will start to erode.

Yet, China also faces its own difficulties in Latin America. There are growing concerns in the region about possible neo-dependency structures and many countries are involved in trade disputes with China, as they worry over the mercantilist nature of the Chinese trading patterns (Jenkins 2012). China's ambitious infrastructure projects are also facing some resistance, particularly from environmental groups. In addition, the Chinese have sometimes found it difficult to navigate the bureaucratic systems of Latin American states (Romero 2015). In general, there seems to be a growing wariness towards these projects, as initial expectations with regard to their job generating effect have seldom been met, not least because of the workers often having been brought from China instead of hiring locally (Ray *et al.* 2015). As a result, many projects have been suspended or even cancelled. The political and economic upheavals underway in many countries in the region also makes it difficult for the infrastructure projects to get the necessary attention and backing from political leaders. The change of guard to more pro-Western leadership in key countries such as Argentina, Brazil, and Peru, adds to the growing uncertainty surrounding big infrastructure projects such as the Twin-Ocean Rail and Two-Ocean Tunnel.

At some point, the United States may wish to revive its own geo-economic strategy towards Latin America, so as to be able to re-engage more deeply with the countries in the region. Depending on the depth of the structural shifts currently taking place in Latin America's strategic environment, the United States may not be able to just revive the old hub-and-spoke system and conditioned-based cooperation. With the new east-west links and China offering trade, loans and investment without any conditions tied to human rights and 'good governance', the United States will have to find new ways to approach Latin America. This may involve offering economic incentives to Latin America that does not make immediate commercial sense, but helps build longer-term strategic partnerships and cooperation. The United States will probably also need to engage with Latin America on a more equal footing by offering actual multilateralism, in contrast to China's more bilateral approach to engage with the countries in the region. Should it want to, this bilateralism allows China to use its preponderant resources to cement a hierarchical relationship in which Latin American states are made more dependent on China. Inherent to such a bilateral approach is also the tendency to focus on reaping national benefits at the expense of mutual benefits. Instead, using a more multilateral framework, the United States could offer its own economic incentives to the countries in the region and make a new push for inter-regional trade integration, paving the way for more mutually beneficial cooperation and long-term, collective gains. From the perspective of Latin America, this more multilateral approach would help Latin American states band together and base the relationship on reciprocity, instead of being exposed to the severe power asymmetries inherit to the current relationship with China.

Notes

1 The authors would like to thank Sören Scholvin for his helpful comments on an earlier draft of this chapter.
2 Exceptions include Ellis (2013, 2017) and Piccone (2016).
3 For information, see China Global Investment Tracker (2016), www.aei.org/china-global-investment-tracker/.
4 On the strategic differences between traditional geopolitics and geo-economics, see Wigell and Vihma (2016).

References

Abdelal, R. and Kirshner, J. (1999) 'Strategy, Economic Relations, and the Definition of National Interests', *Security Studies*, 9, 1–2, pp. 119–156.
América Economía. (2016) 'No todo es TPP: mega TLC con China seduce a México, Perú y Chile', *América Economía*, 23 November. Available at: www.americaeconomia.com/economia-mercados/comercio/no-todo-es-ttp-mega-tlc-con-china-seduce-mexico-peru-y-chile, accessed 23 January 2018.
Armony, A. C. (2012) 'Exporting Corruption', *Americas Quarterly*, 6, 1, pp. 104–107.
Beaton, K., Cebotari, A., Komaromi, A. and Ding, X. (2017) 'Trade Integration in Latin America: A Network Perspective', *International Monetary Fund* (IMF), Working Paper WP/17/148. Available at: www.imf.org/en/Publications/WP/Issues/2017/06/29/Trade-Integration-in-Latin-America-44971, accessed 23 January 2018.

Biegon, R. (2017) *US Power in Latin America: Renewing Hegemony* (London: Routledge).

Bowley, G. (2008) 'Cash Helped China Win Costa Rica's Recognition', *New York Times*, 12 September. Available at: www.nytimes.com/2008/09/13/world/asia/13costa.html?m trref=undefined&gwh=E3553E0895E303EC4401899B64C94CE1&gwt=pay, accessed 23 January 2018.

Central People's Government of the People's Republic of China. (2008) 'China's Policy Paper on Latin America and the Caribbean', *The Central People's Government of the People's Republic of China*. Available at: www.gov.cn/english/official/2008-11/05/ content_1140347.htm, accessed 23 January 2018.

Chávez, N. (2015) 'Latin America, United States and China: Strategic Continental Relations', in Bonilla Soria, A. and Milet García, P. (eds.), *Latin America, the Caribbean and China: Sub-regional Strategic Scenarios* (San José: FLACSO), pp. 74–103.

China-CELAC Forum. (2015) 'Cooperation Plan (2015–2019)', *China-CELAC Forum*, 23 January. Available at: www.chinacelacforum.org/eng/zywj_3/t1230944.htm, accessed 23 January 2018.

Delgado-López, L. M. (2012) 'Sino-Latin American Space Cooperation: A Smart Move', *Space Policy*, 28, 1, pp. 7–14.

Dussel Peters, E. (2017) 'Evolución estratégica de la relación entre América Latina y el Caribe y China (2000–2016): La relevancia de los proyectos de infraestructura de China', in Dussel Peters, E. (ed.), *América Latina y el Caribe y China: Economía, Comercio e Inversión 2017*. Available at: www.redalc-china.org/v21/images/docs/ RedALCChina-2017-economia.pdf, accessed 28 January 2018.

ECLAC. (2015) *The European Union and Latin America and the Caribbean in the New Economic and Social Context* (Santiago de Chile: United Nations Publication). Available at: http://repositorio.cepal.org/handle/11362/38230, accessed 9 February 2018.

ECLAC. (2017) *International Trade Outlook for Latin America and the Caribbean: Recovery in an Uncertain Context* (Santiago de Chile: United Nations Publication). Available at: http://repositorio.cepal.org/handle/11362/42316, accessed 9 February 2018.

Ellis, R. E. (2010) 'Advances in China-Latin America Space Cooperation', *China Brief*, 10, 14, pp. 5–6.

Ellis, R. E. (2013) 'The Strategic Dimension of Chinese Engagement with Latin America', *William J. Perry Center for Hemispheric Defense Studies*, Perry Paper Series, No. 1. Available at: http://chds.dodlive.mil/files/2013/12/pub-PP-ellis.pdf, accessed 23 January 2018.

Ellis, R. E. (2016) 'China's Geo-economic role in Latin America', in *Geo-economics with Chinese Characteristics: How China's Economic Might is Reshaping World Politics*, World Economic Forum, pp. 23–25. Available at: www3.weforum.org/docs/WEF_ Geoeconomics_with_Chinese_Characteristics.pdf, accessed 23 January 2018.

Ellis, R. (2017) 'The Strategic Context of China's Advance in Latin America: An Update', Note d'actualité 17/24, Observatoire Chine. Available at: www.centreasia.eu/ sites/default/files/publications_pdf/17-ellis-amerique_latine_180417.pdf, accessed 28 January 2018.

Farnsworth, E. (2012) 'Memo to Washington: China's Growing Presence in Latin America', *Americas Quarterly*, 6, 1, pp. 80–87.

Ferchen, M. (2011) 'China-Latin America Relations: Long-term Boon or Short-term Boom?', *The Chinese Journal of International Politics*, 4, 1, pp. 55–86.

Financial Times. (2016a) 'US Investment in Its Backyard in Decline', *Financial Times*, 15 September.

Financial Times. (2016b) 'China Takes Long View on Latin American Infrastructure Investment', *Financial Times*, 26 May.

Flores-Macías, G. A. and Kreps, S. E. (2013) 'The Foreign Policy Consequences of Trade: China's Commercial Relations with Africa and Latin America, 1992–2006', *Journal of Politics*, 75, 2, pp. 357–371.

Gallagher, K. P. (2016) *The China Triangle: Latin America's China Boom and the Fate of the Washington Consensus* (New York: Oxford University Press).

Gustafson, I. (2016) 'The Dubious Impact of Chinese Investment in Latin America', *Council on Hemispheric Affairs*. Available at: www.coha.org/the-dubious-impact-of-chinese-investment-in-latin-america/, accessed 10 October 2017.

Holslag, J. (2006) 'China's New Mercantilism in Central Africa', *African and Asian Studies*, 5, 2, pp. 133–169.

Holslag, J. (2016) 'Geoeconomics in a Globalized World: The Case of China's Export Policy', *Asia Europe Journal*, 14, 2, pp. 173–184.

Horton, C. and Myers, S. L. (2017) 'Panama Establishes Ties with China, Further Isolating Taiwan', *New York Times*, 13 June. Available at: www.nytimes.com/2017/06/13/world/asia/taiwan-panama-china-diplomatic-recognition.html?mtrref=undefined&gwh=2D36C3D28CBE97992C2F85E60D90C1A9&gwt=pay, accessed 23 January 2018.

Jenkins, R. (2012) 'Latin America and China – A New Dependency?', *Third World Quarterly*, 33, 7, pp. 1337–1358.

La Nación. (2016) 'Dos vergonzosas represas', *La Nación*, 2 January. Available at: www.lanacion.com.ar/1858776-dos-vergonzosas-represas, accessed 22 January 2018.

Long, T. and Friedman, M. P. (2017) 'Policy Series: Trump and Latin America: Asymmetry and the Problem of Influence', *The International Security Studies Forum (ISSF)*, 17 May. Available at: https://issforum.org/roundtables/policy/1-5aj-latin-america, accessed 23 January 2018.

Malamud, A. and Rodriguez, J. C. C. (2014) 'Straddling the Region and the World: Brazil's Dual Foreign Policy Comes of Age', in Herzog, M. and Robins, P. (eds.), *The Role, Position and Agency of Cusp States in International Relations* (London: Routledge), pp. 111–128.

Mattlin, M. and Nojonen, M. (2015) 'Conditionality and Path Dependence in Chinese Lending', *Journal of Contemporary China*, 24, 94, pp. 701–720.

May, C. (1996) 'Strange Fruit: Susan Strange's Theory of Structural Power in the International Political Economy', *Global Society*, 10, 2, pp. 167–189.

Mesquita Moreira, M. and Estevadeordal, A. (2015) *Korea and Latin America and the Caribbean: Striving for a Diverse and Dynamic Relationship* (Washington, DC: Inter-American Development Bank).

Ministry of Foreign Affairs of the People's Republic of China. (2014) 'Xi Jinping Attends China-Latin America and the Caribbean Summit and Delivers Keynote Speech, Comprehensively Expounding China's Policies and Propositions Toward Latin America, Announcing Establishment of China-Latin America Comprehensive Cooperative Partnership of Equality, Mutual Benefit and Common Development, and Establishment of China-CELAC Forum', *Ministry of Foreign Affairs of the People's Republic of China*, 18 July. Available at: www.fmprc.gov.cn/mfa_eng/topics_665678/xjpzxcxjzgjldrdlch wdbxagtwnrlgbjxgsfwbcxzlldrhw/t1176650.shtml, accessed 23 January 2018.

Myers, M. and Kuwayama, M. (2016) 'A New Phase in Japan-Latin America and the Caribbean Relations', *The Dialogue*, Japan-Latin America Report February 2016. Available at: www.thedialogue.org/wp-content/uploads/2016/02/Dialogue-Japan-LAC-Relations-WEB.pdf, accessed 23 January 2018.

Noesselt, N. and Soliz Landivar, A. (2013) 'China in Latin America: Competition in the United States "Strategic Backyard"', *German Institute of Global and Area Studies (GIGA)*, GIGA Focus No. 7. Available at: www.giga-hamburg.de/de/system/files/publications/gf_international_1307.pdf, accessed 23 January 2018.

OECD/ECLAC/CAF. (2015) *Latin American Economic Outlook 2016: Towards a New Partnerships with China* (Paris: OECD Publishing).

Ortiz Velásquez, S. and Dussel Peters, E. (2016) 'La nueva relación entre América Latina y el Caribe y China: ¿Promueve la integración o Desintegración Comercial?' in Dussel Peters, E. (ed.), *La nueva relación comercial de América Latina y el Caribe con China: ¿integración o desintegración regional?* (Mexico: Unión de Universidades de América Latina y el Caribe), pp. 13–58. Available at: www3.eco.unicamp.br/neit/images/destaque/2016_La_nueva_relacion_comercial_ALC_China.pdf#page=15, accessed 23 January 2018.

Patey, L. (2017) 'China Made Mauricio Macri a Deal He Couldn't Refuse', *Foreign Policy*, 24 January. Available at: http://foreignpolicy.com/2017/01/24/china-made-mauricio-macri-a-deal-he-couldnt-refuse/, accessed 10 September 2017.

People's Daily. (2016) 'Full text of China's Policy Paper on Latin America and the Caribbean', *People's Daily*, 24 November. Available at: http://en.people.cn/n3/2016/1124/c90000-9146474.html, accessed 23 January 2018.

Piccone, T. (2016) 'The Geopolitics of China's Rise in Latin America', *Brookings*, Geoeconomics and Global Issues No. 2. Available at: www.chinhnghia.com/the-geopolitics-of-chinas-rise-in-latin-america_ted-piccone.pdf, accessed 23 January 2018.

Ray, R., and Gallagher, K. (2015) 'China-Latin America Economic Bulletin 2015 Edition', *Boston University*, Global Economic Governance Initiative, Discussion Paper 2015–9. Available at: www.bu.edu/pardeeschool/files/2015/02/Economic-Bulletin-2015.pdf, accessed 23 January 2018.

Ray, R., Gallagher, K. P., Lopez, A. and Sanborn, C. (2015) 'China in Latin America: Lessons for South-South Cooperation and Sustainable Development', *Boston University*, Global Economic Governance Initiative. Available at: www.bu.edu/pardeeschool/files/2014/12/Working-Group-Final-Report.pdf, accessed 23 January 2018.

Ray, R., Gallagher, K. and Sarmiento, R. (2016) 'China-Latin America Economic Bulletin 2016 Edition', *Boston University*, Global Economic Governance Initiative, Discussion Paper 2016–3. Available at: www.bu.edu/pardeeschool/files/2016/04/China-LAC.Bulletin_2016.pdf, accessed 22 January 2018.

Ray, R. and Gallagher, K. (2017) 'China-Latin America Economic Bulletin 2017 Edition', *Boston University, Global Economic Governance Initiative*, Discussion Paper 2017–1. Available at: www.bu.edu/pardeeschool/files/2014/11/Economic-Bulletin.16-17-Bulletin.Draft_.pdf, accessed 28 January 2018.

Reuters. (2015) 'China Looks to Boost the Use of Yuan in Latin America', *Reuters*, 26 May. Available at: www.reuters.com/article/us-chile-china/china-looks-to-boost-use-of-yuan-in-latin-america-idUSKBN0OA19E20150526, accessed 23 January 2018.

Reuters. (2016) 'Peru Says TPP Can Be Replaced with New Trade Deal, Sans U.S.', *Reuters*, 11 November. Available at: www.reuters.com/article/us-trade-tpp-peru/peru-says-tpp-can-be-replaced-with-new-trade-deal-sans-u-s-idUSKBN13626H, accessed 23 January 2018.

Roett, R. and Paz, G. (2017) 'Latin America and the Asian Giants: Evolving Ties with China and India', *Brookings*, 27 September. Available at: www.brookings.edu/book/latin-america-and-the-asian-giants/, accessed 23 January 2018.

Romero, S. (2015) 'China's Ambitious Rail Projects Crash Into Harsh Realities in Latin America', *New York Times*, 3 October. Available at: www.nytimes.com/2015/10/04/

world/americas/chinas-ambitious-rail-projects-crash-into-harsh-realities-in-latin-america.html, accessed 23 January 2018.

Santamaria, C. (2013a) 'USAID Out of Bolivia: What Happens Now?', *Devex*, 2 May. Available at: www.devex.com/news/usaid-out-of-bolivia-what-happens-now-80847, accessed 23 January 2018.

Santamaria, C. (2013b) 'After Bolivia, USAID Now Out of Ecuador Too', *Devex*, 16 December, available at: www.devex.com/news/after-bolivia-usaid-now-out-of-ecuador-too-82511, accessed 23 January 2018.

Santiago Times. (2016) 'Chile Committed to Integration Despite Trump's Rejection of TPP', *The Santiago Times*, 23 November. Available at: http://santiagotimes. cl/2016/11/23/chile-committed-to-integration-despite-trumps-rejection-of-tpp/, accessed 9 February 2018.

Scheinin, D. (1999) 'The New Dollar Diplomacy in Latin America', *American Studies International*, 37, 3, pp. 81–99.

Scholvin, S. and Malamud, A. (2014) 'Is There a Geoeconomic Node in South America? Geography, Politics and Brazil's Role in Regional Economic Integration', *Instituto de Ciências Sociais da Universidade de Lisboa*, ICS Working Paper, N 2/2014. Available at: www.ics.ul.pt/publicacoes/workingpapers/wp2014/wp2014_2. pdf, accessed 9 February 2018.

Urdinez, F., Mouron, F., Schenoni, L. L. and De Oliveira, A. (2016) 'Chinese Economic Statecraft and U.S. Hegemony in Latin America: An Empirical Analysis, 2003–2014', *Latin American Politics and Society*, 58, 4, pp. 3–30.

Vihma, A. and Wigell, M. (2016) 'Unclear and Present Danger: Russia's Geoeconomics and the Nord Stream II pipeline', *Global Affairs*, 2, 4, pp. 377–388.

Watts, J. (2015) 'Argentina Leader Leaves Controversial Legacy with Patagonia Dams Project', *Guardian*, 1 December. Available at: www.theguardian.com/world/2015/dec/01/argentina-president-cristina-fernandez-de-kirchner-patagonia-hydroelectric-dam-project, accessed 22 January 2018.

Wise, C. (2016) 'China and Latin America's Emerging Economies: New Realities Amid Old Challenges', *Latin American Policy*, 7, 1, pp. 26–51.

Wigell, M. (2016) '"Conceptualizing Regional Powers" Geoeconomic Strategies: Neo-Imperialism, Neo-Mercantilism, Hegemony, and Liberal Institutionalism', *Asia Europe Journal*, 14, 2, pp. 135–151.

Wigell, M. and Vihma, A. (2016) 'Geopolitics versus Geoeconomics: The Case of Russia's Geostrategy and Its Effects on the EU', *International Affairs*, 92, 3, pp. 605–627.

Wu, F. and De Wei, K. (2014) 'From Financial Assets to Financial Statecraft: The Case of China and Emerging Economies of Africa and Latin America', *Journal of Contemporary China*, 23, 89, pp. 781–803.

Xi, J. (2015) 'Jointly Writing a New Chapter of the China-CELAC Comprehensive Cooperative Partnership', keynote speech by President Xi Jinping at First Ministerial Meeting of China-CELAC Forum, 8 January. Available at: www.fmprc.gov.cn/mfa_eng/zxxx_662805/t1227318.shtml, accessed 31 January 2018.

Yu, L. (2015) 'China's Strategic Partnership with Latin America: A Fulcrum in China's Rise', *International Affairs*, 91 5, pp. 1047–1068.

Zhang, D. (2015) '3 ×3 Mode Can Connect China and Latin American Industries', *CCTV. com*, 21 May. Available at: http://english.cntv.cn/2015/05/21/ARTI1432193490919535. shtml, accessed 23 January 2018.

13 Oil as a strategic means in Venezuela's foreign policy

The cases of ALBA and Petrocaribe, 1998–2013

Martha Lucía Márquez Restrepo[1]

Introduction

Oil has been a driver of Venezuela's domestic and foreign policies since 1922, when major findings began providing the state with a stream of oil rent. This rent allowed Venezuela's nation-building to start in earnest, with the creation of the national army and infrastructure projects that have connected different parts of the country ever since. Furthermore, the distribution of oil rents helped forge the political pact that formed the basis for Venezuela's transition to democracy in 1958.[2] From then onwards oil rents have defined the traits that today characterise the Venezuelan state: paternalism and hyper-activism. In other words, Venezuela has devoted much of its resource income to subsidies for decades. Some authors have also referred to it as a populist state of conciliated interests (e.g. Caballero 1999).

Oil has also been decisive in upholding the image that the Venezuelan people have regarding their state. The anthropologist Fernando Coronil (2002) explains that the Venezuelan people understand themselves as a community on the basis of a common property, which is the nation's subsoil. According to this image, resource abundance couples with the misleading idea that the country is rich and that the state is capable of acting as a sort of magician that can turn the fantasies of the people into reality (Romero 1999).

This chapter finds itself in the same line of reasoning, focussing on the importance of oil in Venezuela's foreign policy during the presidency of Hugo Chávez (1998–2013), particularly on his two most important foreign policy initiatives: the Bolivarian Alliance for the Peoples of Our America (Alianza Bolivariana para los Pueblos de Nuestra América, ALBA) and Petrocaribe. The chapter highlights how important oil has been for Venezuela to achieve its strategic goals in the Caribbean and in Central America. The strategic goals can be listed as follows: to position Venezuela as a regional power, while balancing against Brazil and the United States; to exert influence in the Caribbean, something which has been considered vital for Venezuela since the 1960s; to promote the so-called Socialism of the Twenty-first Century (Socialismo del Siglo XXI); to obtain the political support of states in the Caribbean and in Central America in international fora such as the Organisation of American States (OAS).

The chapter is organised as follows: it begins with a characterisation of Venezuela's foreign policy during the Chávez era, focussing on how the above strategic goals were pursued by using oil as a strategic means. Then, it specifically assesses ALBA and Petrocaribe; the basic ideas that guide ALBA, and the concrete projects carried out under the Petrocaribe agreement. The chapter concludes with an analysis of the costs and benefits of Venezuela's oil-based geo-economic strategy.

Venezuela's foreign policy during the Chávez era

In the course of the 1980s, several Latin American governments approached the United States, seeking advice on macro-economic policies and favourable conditions to renegotiate their foreign debt. Except for a very few states, Latin America adopted policies based on the Washington Consensus – a set of neoliberal economic paradigms strongly supported by the United States and major international organisations such as the World Bank. From the late 1990s onwards, left-wing parties gained power in many Latin American countries, producing a major foreign policy shift and a rupture with the Washington Consensus. Under these left-wing governments, many Latin American states began seeking more autonomy from the United States and promoting an alternative, multipolar global and regional order.

Venezuela assumed this new course and became a driver of it during the Chávez presidency. During that time, Chávez tapped into the general rejection of neoliberalism, and what was perceived as the aggressive foreign policy of the George W. Bush administration. In Venezuela, as in most Latin American states, foreign policy is a presidential prerogative. Hence, the political creed and personal worldview of President Chávez are critical to understanding Venezuela's foreign policy in the era studied in this chapter. For Chávez, the world divides sharply into states that adhere to neoliberalism and states that pursue other models. Venezuela's efforts to forge a path independent from the United States manifested itself for the first time in 1999, when Chávez denied humanitarian aid offered by the United States intended to alleviate the emergency caused by floods in the Venezuelan state of Vargas. He also forbade the US Air Force the use of Venezuelan airspace to combat drug trafficking (Ellner 2009).

Consistent with this anti-imperialist position and soft balancing strategy against the United States,[3] Venezuela began promoting a multipolar order, exemplified by its proposition to reform the UN Security Council. Hugo Chávez proposed to enlarge it by including countries from the Third World as permanent members. On the regional level, Venezuela made efforts to undermine organisations seen as being dominated by the United States – most importantly the OAS – and US-led initiatives such as the Free Trade Area of the Americas. It supported new organisations such as the Community of Latin American and Caribbean States, and the Union of South American Nations (Sanahuja 2014; Serbín 2010).

The government plan, presented by Chávez during the 2012 election campaign, explicitly stated that Venezuela aimed to balance against the United States and become a regional power of its own (Comando Campaña Carabobo 2012). The so-called post-neoliberal models of regional integration were to grant privilege to political and social goals over commercial ones (more on this below). Positioning Venezuela as a regional power has not only been directed against the United States, but also against Brazil, which has been pursuing a course of regional hegemony of its own. In order to compete with Brazil without directly antagonising it, Venezuela has sought to tie the Caribbean and Central America to itself, regions traditionally of little relevance to Brazil. What is more, gaining support of the plentiful small Caribbean and Central American states has proven extremely helpful to boost Venezuela's position in international organisations, particularly in the OAS (Arriagada Herrera 2006).

Chávez's project of regional leadership also benefited from the economic and political rise of states like China and Russia. Traditionally, neither China nor Russia has been an important partner for Venezuela. Yet today the People's Republic of China is Venezuela's main creditor. Russia is its most important provider of military equipment, including weapons. These close relations also manifest themselves in numerous joint ventures formed between the state-owned oil company Petroleum of Venezuela (Petróleos de Venezuela, PDVSA) and Chinese and Russian state-owned companies.

The abundance of oil reserves has provided Venezuela with a powerful economic means that can be used to pursue strategic aims. This is particularly so because these reserves are state-controlled. The Venezuelan oil industry was nationalised in the 1970s. As part of liberalisation policies of the 1980s, contracts were signed with foreign companies that amounted to a large-scale privatisation. During the Chávez presidency, those agreements were repealed,

Table 13.1 PDVSA's joint ventures with Chinese and Russian partners

Name	Partner	Foundation	Share held by PDVSA
Petrolera Paria	China (Sinopec)	2007	60
Petrolera Sino-Venezolana	China (China National Petroleum Corporation)	2006	75
Petrozamora	Russia (Gazprombank)	2006	60
PetroMiranda	Russia (Rosneft)	2010	60
PetroUrica	China (China National Petroleum Corporation)	2010	60
PetroSinovensa	China (China National Petroleum Corporation)	2008	60
PetroMonagas	Russia (Rosneft)	2008	83,33
PetroVictoria	Russia (Rosneft)	2013	60
Petrozumano	China (China National Petroleum Corporation)	2007	60
Petrolera Sino-Venezolana (caracoles)	China (China National Petroleum Corporation)	2006	75

Source: author's own compilation.

and PDVSA regained a privileged position in the Venezuelan oil sector. Owing to the exploration carried out by PDVSA and its partners, Venezuela's own domestic oil reserves increased from 66 million barrels in 1995 to 300 million barrels in 2015, making Venezuela the country with the most proven oil reserves in the world (almost 18 per cent of the global proven reserves) (BP 2016). Furthermore, the General Hydrocarbon Law of 2001 (Ley General de Hidrocarburos) allowed the government to raise royalties on oil rents from 20 to 80 per cent of the average export price, providing the state with an enormous oil windfall when the oil price was booming throughout the 2000s. This windfall has formed the basis of Venezuela's petro-diplomacy, whereby it has offered energy-related carrots to Caribbean and Central American states, inducing them to cooperate with Venezuela. Here, unlike conventional geo-economics – which puts emphasis on wielding economic leverage as a stick to pressure other countries, for instance threatening price increases or cut-offs – Venezuela's inducement-oriented energy geo-economics have included price cuts for oil exports and investments, loans and side payments, so as to build patron-client relationships with more minor powers in the neighbourhood.[4] The most important instruments for this petro-diplomacy have been ALBA and Petrocaribe.

ALBA and Petrocaribe

ALBA was launched in 2004 as the Bolivarian Alternative; basically an agreement between Cuba and Venezuela on academic exchange programmes, tariff cuts, tax exemptions for state investments and mixed enterprises, and the equal treatment of airplanes and ships in the territory of the other country. Two years later, Bolivia joined and its proposal to complement ALBA with the People's Trade Treaty (Tratado de Comercio de los Pueblos) was adopted. This treaty led to agreements on the exchange of goods and services meant to satisfy the basic needs of the people of the ALBA countries, arguably on the basis of reciprocity, solidarity and the transfer of technology.[5] Nicaragua joined the organisation in 2007. Dominica and Honduras followed in 2008; although the latter left in 2010. Antigua and Barbuda, Ecuador, and St Vincent and the Grenadines became members in 2009.

ALBA has been characterised as 'post-neoliberal regionalism' and 'strategic regionalism'. It emerged as a counterweight to open regionalism, which, being heavily focussed on trade issues, dominated regional integration dynamics in the 1980s and 1990s (Aponte García 2014). Meanwhile, ALBA was designed to pursue multi-dimensional integration: to harmonise commercial integration with political and social aspects of cooperation. ALBA's official documents emphasise the objective to improve the quality of life in all member countries and ensure their political solidarity. A major focus is put on South-South relations. Regarding economic issues, there is a focus on infrastructure development. State-led and state-owned companies are presented as a critical strategic means of development (Menzi and Zapata 2013).

In order to advance these objectives, several institutions have been set up. In 2007, the Bank of ALBA was created, with Venezuela using its petro-dollars to finance the bank, paying for socio-economic development projects in the member countries. The similarly operating ALBA-Caribe Fund opened in 2006 with a US$50 million contribution from Venezuela. The fund and its projects are administrated by PDVSA.

However, Venezuela's most important means to exert international influence during the Chávez era was Petrocaribe. In 2003, President Chávez presented an initiative called Petroamerica. His idea was to balance against the energy integration project promoted by the United States through the North American Free Trade Agreement (NAFTA), the Puebla-Panama Plan. This plan, also known as the Meso-America Integration and Development Project, first announced in 2001 by Mexico's president Vicente Fox, is a regional mechanism aimed at implementing projects that deliver regional public goods for inclusive development and integration of Belize, Colombia, Costa Rica, the Dominican Republic, El Salvador, Guatemala, Honduras, Mexico, Nicaragua and Panama. Arguably, the plan also creates benefits for companies from the United States. Additionally, Chávez sought to prevent the signing of agreements to permit private investment in Latin American state-owned energy companies. A year later, Chávez's initiative was renamed Petrocaribe (Vargas 2005).

The most important feature of Petrocaribe is that member states of can purchase Venezuelan oil at advantageous prices. Under this scheme, Venezuela effectively decreases the price by up to 50 per cent if the cost of a barrel is more than US$100 on the global market. The agreement sets quotas for each member state. Initiatives to refine oil and carry out joint energy infrastructure projects were also included in the Petrocaribe's agenad. A total of US$360 million has been invested in the construction of refineries in the Petrocaribe countries. In particular, investments have been made to build fuel storage facilities. One of the first of these joint ventures was Cuvenpetrol. Venezuela contributed 49 per cent to Cuvenpetrol's capital so as to reactivate an oil refinery in the Cuban city of Cienfuegos. About 65,000 barrels of oil can now be refined there every day. Petrojam was created by Jamaica and Venezuela, and the company increased the production of a refinery in Kingston, which today reaches an output of 35,000 barrels a day. Other projects financed under the Petrocaribe agreement include power plants in Antigua and Barbuda, Haiti, and Nicaragua, a fuel distribution facility in Granada, and storage facilities for oil and gas in the island states of St Kitts and Nevis, and St Vincent and the Grenadines (Aponte García 2014).

Petrocaribe has offered considerable benefits for Venezuela's partners in terms of energy security. By 2014, it covered 32 per cent of their oil demand and financed nearly half of their oil expenditure, equivalent to US$28 billion. Cuba benefited most, receiving 98 million barrels of subsidised oil a day in 2014. Electrification programmes have had a major impact in Haiti, where only 28 per cent of the population enjoy those services, and Nicaragua, where only 66 per cent do. The members of Petrocaribe have also benefited from technology transfers, especially through the joint ventures with PDVSA that affect the entire oil and gas value chain.

Table 13.2 Mixed companies created under the Petrocaribe agreement

Country	Company	Ownership
Antigua and Barbuda	West Indies Company	PDV Caribe 25%,[1] Antigua and Barbuda (state) 51%; other partner 24%
Belize	ALBA Petrocaribe Belize Energy	PDV Caribe 55% Belize Petroleum and Energy 45%
Dominica	PDV Caribe Dominica	PDV Caribe 55% Dominica National Petroleum 45%
Dominican Republic	Refidomsa	PDV Caribe 49% Dominican Republic (state) 51%
Granada	PDV Grenada	PDV Caribe 55% Petrocaribe Grenada[2] 45%
Haiti	Société d'Investissement Pétion Bolivar	PDV Caribe 51% Haiti (state) 49%
Jamaica	Petrojam	PDV Caribe 49% Petroleum Corporation of Jamaica 51%
Nicaragua	ALBA de Nicaragua	PDV Caribe 51% Petronic[3] 49%
St Kitts and Nevis	PDV St Kitts Nevis	PDV Caribe 55% St Kitts Nevis Energy Company 45%
St Vincent and the Grenadines	PDV St Vincent and Grenadines	PDV Caribe 55% St Vincent and the Grenadines (state) 45%
El Salvador	ALBA Petróleos de El Salvador	PDV Caribe 60% ENEPASA[4] 40%
Suriname	PDV Suriname	PDV Caribe 50% Surfuel[5] 50%

Source: PDVSA 2015.

Notes
1 PDV Caribe provides planning, organisation and development of sources to transport, receive, store, distribute and commercialise hydrocarbons. The company was incorporated in 2005. It is based in Antigua and Barbuda and operates as a subsidiary of PDVSA.
2 Petrocaribe Grenada Limited is a state-owned company.
3 Petronic is a state-owned company.
4 ENEPASA (Asociación Intermunicipal de Energía para El Salvador) is an association founded by mayoralities.
5 Surfuel is a state-owned company.

Costs and benefits for Venezuela

Owning the largest oil reserves in the world and having consolidated state control over them, Venezuela during the Chávez era practiced a foreign policy strategy of what one may call oil geo-economics, most prominently through ALBA and Petrocaribe. This allowed Venezuela to achieve some of its foreign policy goals temporarily, albeit at a great economic cost. With ALBA and Petrocaribe, Venezuela managed to considerably strengthen its influence in the Caribbean and Central America, and to soft balance against the United States. For example, cheap oil imports from Venezuela have helped Cuba resist US economic coercion. ALBA, questioning the North American hegemony, promotes different values practiced in the free market circles (such as NAFTA) in which Venezuela participates.

States such as Antigua and Barbuda, Jamaica and Suriname – ideologically distant from the Socialism of the Twenty-first Century – have cooperated with Venezuela for practical reasons. This guaranteed Venezuela political support in fora such as the OAS, where the ALBA states have blocked resolutions to condemn Venezuela because of its human rights abuses and disregard of democratic principles. For instance, in 2016 there were not enough votes for the Permanent Council of the OAS to apply the Democratic Charter due to Venezuela's violation of democracy. In June 2017, an insufficient number of votes resulted in an inability to pass a resolution to request Nicolás Maduro's government to suspend the elections for the National Constituent Assembly. The countries that voted against the resolution were Nicaragua, St Kitts and Nevis; St Vincent and the Grenadines, Bolivia, and Dominica. Ecuador, El Salvador, Grenada, Haiti, the Dominican Republic, Suriname, Trinidad and Tobago, and Antigua and Barbuda abstained from voting.

However, the economic costs of Venezuela's strategy have been high. Although there is no exact figure, it is estimated that until 2014 Venezuela spent more than US$100 billion on subsidies and social programmes through ALBA and Petrocaribe, amounting to more than its entire foreign debt to China. It is also estimated that Venezuela has destined between 25 and 30 per cent of its oil exporting potential to sustaining the two organisations (Hernández and Chaudry 2015). The member states of Petrocaribe owe Venezuela nearly US$23 billion (La Razón 2016) – a debt

Table 13.3 Debt of Petrocaribe states to Venezuela

Country	Debt in US$ million
Antigua and Barbuda	355
Belize	291
Dominica	70
Dominican Republic	200
Granada	102
Haiti	1,500
Jamaica	99
Nicaragua	2,700
St Kitts and Nevis	83
Guyana	580
St Vincent and the Grenadines	67
El Salvador	943
Cuba	14,000[1]

Source: de Alba 2016.

Note
1 LATAM PM (2016).

they have not serviced in a timely manner. Venezuela, now in need of repayments, has had to grant discounts on these repayments. For instance, the Dominican Republic ended up paying US$1.9 billion for a debt of US$4.1 billion; Jamaica paid US$1.5 billion for a debt that was twice as much (Canuto 2015; de Alba 2016).

It should also be noted that, despite ALBA and Petrocaribe, Venezuela has failed to end its dependence on the United States. Refineries in the United States still process much of Venezuela's heavy crude oil, and Chávez' arch-enemy remains the biggest market for Venezuela's exports (BP 2016). Beyond that, ALBA and Petro-caribe have failed to guarantee food supply in Venezuela. Some member countries pay their oil debts with overpriced agricultural products, but these imports do not add up to the severe shortage of food supplies currently affecting Venezuela.

The ongoing economic crisis in Venezuela, largely caused by the collapse of the global oil price, and domestic corruption and mismanagement, raises questions about the sustainability of ALBA and Petrocaribe. In 2015, the would-be regional power did not manage to fully uphold its exportation quota under the Petrocaribe agreement. This is partly due to its obligation to favour oil exports to China, which service Venezuela's debt and guarantee continuing lending from the People's Republic. Moreover, the current domestic political situation is not promising. The future of the Socialism of the Twenty-First Century, now led by Maduro, looks uncertain. Should the Venezuelan opposition take over, it would almost certainly suspend ALBA and Petrocaribe, having been outspoken about Venezuela giving away its oil for years.

Notes

1 The author is indebted to Mikael Wigell and Sören Scholvin for their support in writing this chapter.
2 In that year, Venezuela's main political parties agreed to respect the outcomes of future elections so as to prevent another military dictatorship. Although this pact excluded the communist party, it ensured social inclusion – or rather compensation through measures such as agrarian reform and the introduction of a system of social security – paid for with the oil rent.
3 The concept of soft balancing was developed by Pape (2005) in order to capture the reaction of major powers to the unilateral foreign policy of the last Bush administration. Contrary to hard balancing, which refers to military powers, soft balancing is a non-military and often indirect approach directed against a hegemon. Flemes and Wehner (2013, 2015) apply the concept to secondary powers in South America, including Venezuela, vis-à-vis Brazil.
4 For a discussion of different forms of geo-economics beyond Chapter 1 of this volume, see Wigell (2016), and Wigell and Vihma (2016).
5 Key treaties and various other documents on ALBA are available at www.alba-tcp.org.

References

Aponte García, M. (2014) *El nuevo regionalismo estratégico* (Buenos Aires: CLACSO).
Arriagada Herrera, G. (2006) *Petróleo y gas en América Latina. Un análisis político y de relaciones internacionales a partir de la política venezolana* (Madrid: Real Instituto Elcano).

BP. (2016) 'BP Statistical Review of World Energy June 2016', *BP*. Available at: www.bp.com/content/dam/bp/pdf/energy-economics/statistical-review-2016/bp-statistical-review-of-world-energy-2016-full-report.pdf, accessed 13 August 2017.

Caballero, M. (1999) *Las crisis de la Venezuela contemporánea* (Caracas: Monte Ávila).

Canuto, O. (2015) 'Los precios del petróleo y el futuro de petrocaribe', *Huffington Post*, 19 October. Available at: www.huffingtonpost.com/otaviano-canuto/precios-de-petroleo-y-el_b_8333136.html, accessed 13 August 2017.

Comando Campaña Carabobo. (2012) 'Propuesta del candidato de la patria, Comandante Hugo Chávez, para la gestión bolivariana socialista 2013–2019', *Comando Campaña Carabobo*. Available at: www.mppeuct.gob.ve/sites/default/files/descargables/programa-patria-2013-2019.pdf, accessed 13 August 2017.

Coronil, F. (2002) *El estado mágico. Naturaleza, dinero y modernidad en Venezuela* (Caracas: Nueva Sociedad).

de Alba, M. (2016) 'Petrocaribe: ¿el comienzo del fin?; por Mariano de Alba', *Pro Davinci*, 1 July. Available at: http://prodavinci.com/2016/07/01/actualidad/petrocaribe-el-comienzo-del-fin-por-mariano-de-alba, accessed 13 August 2017.

Ellner, S. (2009) 'La política exterior del gobierno de Chávez: la retórica chavista y los asuntos sustanciales', *Revista Venezolana de Economía y Ciencias Sociales*, 15, 1, pp. 115–132.

Flemes, D. and Wehner, L. (2013) 'Reacciones estratégicas en Sudamérica ante el ascenso de Brasil', *Foreign Affairs Latinoamérica*, 13, 4, pp. 107–114.

Flemes, D. and Wehner, L. (2015) 'Drivers of Strategic Contestation: The Case of South America', *International Politics*, 52, 2, pp. 163–177.

Hernández, D. and Chaudry, Y. (2015) *La alianza bolivariana para los pueblos de nuestra América – Tratado de comercio de los Pueblos (ALBA-TCP): vigencia y viabilidad en el actual contexto venezolano y regional*. (Caracas: Friedrich Ebert Stiftung).

La Razón. (2016) 'Venezuela mantiene acuerdos de Petrocaribe a pesar de la deuda de 23 mil millones de dólares', *La Razón*. Available at: www.larazon.net/2016/08/venezuela-mantiene-acuerdos-de-petrocaribe-a-pesar-de-la-deuda-de-23-mil-millones-de-dolares/, accessed 7 December 2017.

LATAMPM. (2016) 'Venezuelan Collapse Poses a Threat to 17 Nation' *LATAMPM, Policy and Markets in Latin America*. Available at: https://latampm.com/2016/02/29/venezuelan-collapse-poses-a-threat-to-17-nations/, accessed 7 December 2017.

Menzi, D. and Zapata. (2013) 'Geopolítica, economía y solidaridad internacional en la nueva cooperación sur-sur. El caso de la Venezuela de bolivariana y Petrocaribe', *América Latina Hoy*, 63, pp. 65–89.

Pape, R. A. (2005) 'Soft Balancing against the United States', *International Security*, 30, 1, pp. 7–45.

PDVSA. (2015) 'Informe de gestión anual 2015: Líder mundial en reservas probadas de crudo', *PDVSA*. Available at: www.pdvsa.com/images/pdf/RELACION%20CON%20INVERSIONISTAS/Informes%20Anuales/informe%20de%20gestion/2015/Informe%20Gestio%CC%81n%20Anual%20%202015.pdf, accessed 13 August 2017.

Romero, A. (1999) *Decadencia y crisis de la democracia ¿A dónde va la democracia venezolana?* (Caracas: Panapo).

Sanahuja, J. A. (2014) 'Enfoques diferenciados y marcos comunes en el regionalismo Latinoamericano: alcance y Perspectivas de UNASUR y CELAC', *Pensamiento propio*, 19, pp. 75–99.

Serbín, A. (2010) *Chávez, Venezuela y la reconfiguración política de América Latina y el Caribe* (Buenos Aires: Siglo XXI).

Vargas, M. D. (2005) 'La integración Energética en América del Sur: la iniciativa de Petroamérica', *Revista de Estudios Latinoamericanos*, 40, pp. 265–288.

Wigell, M. (2016) 'Conceptualizing Regional Powers' Geoeconomics Strategies: Neo-imperialism, Neo-mercantilism, Hegemony, and Liberal Institutionalism', *Asia Europe Journal*, 14, 2, pp. 135–151.

Wigell, M. and Vihma, A. (2016) 'Geopolitics versus Geoeconomics: The Case of Russia's Geostrategy and Its Effects on the EU', *International Affairs*, 92, 3, pp. 605–627.

14 India, Pakistan and the contest for regional hegemony

The role of geo-economics

Smruti S. Pattanaik[1]

Introduction

Unlike in Europe or elsewhere in the world, contestation to exert geo-economic influence remains nascent in South Asia. Yet, geo-economics clearly plays an important role in relations between India and Pakistan, which have been highly conflictive since the partition of British India. Pakistan, geographically smaller and weaker in terms of gross national power, has strived to attain parity with India by all means, especially by disproportionately investing in national defence. As a consequence, the army has assumed a pre-eminent position in the Pakistani society and state. Security considerations have become the dominant feature of domestic and foreign policies.

Following their nuclearisation in 1998, the rivalry between India and Pakistan has attained a new dimension. One might expect that due to nuclear parity – that is, neither India nor Pakistan can win a confrontation in which all available military means are used – the geopolitical dimension of the Indian–Pakistani relationship would become less salient, and the logic of geo-economics would gain some relevance with investment and trade becoming the new currency of power. Indeed, both India and Pakistan have been using various geo-economic instruments to expand their influence in Central and South Asia, and the relationship between the two antagonists has clearly started to take a geo-economic character, being 'a continuation of war by other means' (Bell 1990, p. 466).

This chapter applies Luttwak's arguments on geo-economics, examining how India and Pakistan have injected the grammar of commerce into the logic of conflict in their bilateral relationship. Luttwak argued that 'as territorial entities [...] states cannot follow a commercial logic that ignores their state boundaries' (1990, p. 18). According to him,

> in the new geo-economic era, not only the causes but also the instruments of conflict must be economic[:] the more or less disguised restrictions of imports, the more or less concealed subsidization of exports, the funding of competitive technology projects [and] the provision of competitive infrastructures and more.
>
> (1990, p. 21)

Hence, the key question this chapter focuses on is: how does India apply geo-economic instruments to expand its influence in Central and South Asia and how does Pakistan react?

This chapter consist of three main sections. First, the respective national power of India and Pakistan is assessed. The fundaments of their geo-economic strategies are compared. Second, transport infrastructure projects in Central Asia – the key geo-economic instrument applied by the two states – and regional trade are analysed. Third, regional integration and bilateral cooperation in South Asia, facilitated by business organisations and companies, are examined from the perspective of geo-economics.

National power and determinants of geo-economic policies

India and Pakistan differ a lot in economic and military parameters. India is much larger, has a greater population and a much higher gross domestic product (GDP). The *Global Competitiveness Index* (2018) puts India clearly ahead of Pakistan. This index measures the competitiveness of countries, referring to essential features such as efficiency of the labour market, higher education and innovativeness, institutional quality and sophistication of infrastructure. These differences are reflected by the comparative potential of India and Pakistan to use geo-economics as an instrument of foreign policy. Pakistan lags behind even in conventional military terms. Only the possession of a nuclear weapon has enabled Pakistan to maintain some sort of strategic parity with India.

Before delving into the logic of their behaviour, it is necessary to discuss several factors that influence geo-economic policies in India and Pakistan. In Pakistan, the army continues to play a dominant role in strategic decision-making. Pakistan's policy on India is piloted by the army, which is distrustful of India and sees India as the perennial enemy, always conspiring to destroy Pakistan. In Pakistan, it is a general perception that India does not accept the

Table 14.1 Comparative national power of India and Pakistan

	India	*Pakistan*
Land area	3,287,240 sq.km #	796,096 sq km ##
Population	1.3 billion	202 million
GDP	US$2,263.8 billion*	US$278.9 billion*
GDP per capita	US$1,709.6**	US$1,443.6**
Global Competitiveness Index ranking	40***	115***
Military expenditure in per cent of GDP	2.5****	3.4****

Sources #=http://censusindia.gov.in/Census_And_You/area_and_population.aspx; ##=www.pbscensus.gov.pk/sites/default/files/Files/PAKISTAN.pdf; *=https://databank.worldbank.org/data/download/GDP.pdf; **=http://reports.weforum.org/global-competitiveness-index-2017-2018/competitiveness-rankings/; ***=https://data.worldbank.org/indicator/NY.GDP.PCAP.CD; ****=Military expenditure by country as percentage of gross domestic product, 1988–2002 © SIPRI 2017, www.sipri.org/sites/default/files/Milex-share-of-GDP.pdf.

very existence of Pakistan and would undo partition if the army were weaker. Therefore the 'main features and contours [of the Pakistani army] ha[ve] owed their prominence to perpetual confrontation with India', as Siddiqui notes (1978, p. 6).

Conversely, the civilian government is open to the idea of close economic relations with India. It believes that economic engagement would normalise the bilateral relationship and diminish the salience of the military in politics. A comparison of political party manifestos from the 1990s, 2008 and 2013 demonstrates that all major parties are willing to improve relations with India. Business lobbies are keen on trade with India, with the exception of the agricultural sector. They fear that large agricultural subsidies provided in India would make their products unable to compete (Hussain 2013). Similar concerns mark the automotive, pharmaceuticals and textiles sectors (Ahmed and Batool 2015). In India, the government and civil society organisations think that closer economic relations would transform the conflict dynamics (Ali, Mujahid and Rehman 2015; Ministry of Commerce 2011). The Indian military is not averse to trade with Pakistan and largely confines itself to military affairs. In both India and in Pakistan, state bureaucracies are strong and nurture the zero-sum-mentality.

The respective geographical locations of the two states influence the ways in which India and Pakistan use geo-economic policies against each other. India shares common borders with all South Asian countries. Given India's pre-eminence and its strategic location, the prospects of regional economic integration in South Asia depend on the choices that India makes. Pakistan also benefits from locational factors: it controls India's access to Afghanistan and Central Asia, which hold considerable prospects as trading partners for India. Pakistan is keen to emerge itself as a major player in Afghanistan and Central Asia, and it is determined to use its locational advantage to stymie India's economic expansion into the region: it is unwilling to serve as a transit country for India–Afghanistan and India–Central Asian trade. Meanwhile, India is the dominant player in South Asia. Pakistan cannot challenge India's dominance there. In this context, given the perception of insecurity held by Pakistan military vis-à-vis India, India's interest in regional economic integration is likely to be misinterpreted as a measure to enhance India's regional economic strength at the expense of Pakistan.

Another key factor explains India's preference for using geo-economic instruments in the regional context. Having undertaken measures to liberalise its economy since the early 1990s, India has witnessed unprecedented economic growth and has come into possession of significant amounts of available capital. This capital could be invested in transport infrastructure to help India expand its regional trade and access energy resources beyond its borders. Being successful in this regard would obviously further stimulate domestic economic growth, reinforcing the very fundament of India's geo-economic power. Accordingly, the next section sheds light on how India has pursued infrastructural and other development projects in Afghanistan, Central Asia and Iran.

Transport corridors and trade

As noted, India's influence in South Asia is a foregone conclusion and Pakistan does not have the capacity to contest against its long-term rival in this particular region. However, Pakistan wants to trump India, in terms of influence, in Afghanistan and Central Asia. While India has global power ambitions, Pakistan's objective is merely to limit India's rise (Fair 2014). Thus, Pakistan has sought to find partners with whom it could balance against India. For example, to compensate for its lack of economic power, Islamabad has eagerly joined the China–Pakistan Economic Corridor (CPEC). The CPEC aims at making Pakistan, in particular the port of Gwadar, a trade hub that interlinks Afghanistan and Central Asia globally.

India, on its part, has invested in Iran's Chabahar Port to connect to Afghanistan and Central Asia, and to provide an alternative route for Afghanistan's overseas trade to wean it off from Pakistan's overbearing influence. In terms of distance, the two ports are similarly attractive to Afghanistan and the Central Asian countries. In general, India's geo-economic approach to Afghanistan and Iran appears to benefit from the fact that these two countries welcome Indian investment, particularly in infrastructure projects. Afghanistan and Iran signed a transit agreement with India in 2015 that will help India to increase its trade with Central Asia.[2]

The Indian–Pakistani competition over access to Afghanistan and Central Asia dates back to the disintegration of Soviet Union, which led to the independence of resource-rich republics in Central Asia. Pakistan's relevance with regard to the Central Asian theatre resulted (and still results) from the fact that it has been able to influence events in Afghanistan; and stabilising Afghanistan – destabilised by civil wars, foreign occupations and oppressive rule since the 1970s – is a necessary condition for integrating Central Asia and its plentiful resources into the global economy or, at least, into a Central Asian–South Asian regional economy. For Pakistan, the early 1990s provided a historic opportunity to install a friendly regime in Kabul, which would neither question the legitimacy of the Durand Line nor advance Pashtunisation.[3] An Islamabad-brokered government in Afghanistan was also expected to be more amenable to facilitate opportunities for investment and trade for Pakistani companies as well as their access to Central Asian resources. Furthermore, a friendly government in Kabul would keep India out of the contest for influence in Afghanistan and Central Asia. At that time, the Pakistani government considered the Taliban their best bet.

Table 14.2 Distances between Central Asian cities and regional ports (in kilometres)

	Ashgabat	*Astana*	*Bishkek*	*Dushanbe*	*Kabul*	*Tashkent*
Gwadar	2,400	4,500	3,300	2,200	1,600	2,700
Chahbahar	1,900	4,700	3,500	2,600	2,500	2,900

Source: compiled from USAID Trade Project, p. 5. http://pdf.usaid.gov/pdf_docs/PA00K244.pdf.

Soon after the fall of Taliban regime in 2001, Indian diplomats returned to Afghanistan. India's engagement with Afghanistan is geared towards denying Pakistan a monopolistic influence in Afghanistan and Central Asia – as noted, by providing alternative transport corridors to the world market. India announced US$2 billion in aid for education, community-based development projects, humanitarian assistance and infrastructure projects. The projects were mostly carried out in the Pashtun-dominated southern part of Afghanistan, a region over which Pakistan exercises strong influence. During the visit to India of Afghanistan's president Ashraf Ghani in September 2016, India announced another US$1 billion credit line. As noted, the transport infrastructure projects financed by these credit lines are not only meant to provide Afghanistan with access to non-Pakistani ports, they also facilitate India's trade links with Central Asia. For this purpose, India has pushed forward its Connect Central Asia Policy. This policy aims at proactive economic and political contact with Central Asia. It is concentrated on the Turkmenistan–Afghanistan–Pakistan–India (TAPI) pipeline and reactivating the International North–South Transport Corridor. The Connect Central Asia Policy also seeks to embed Afghanistan into the evolving regional institutional framework.

India advanced its goals in Afghanistan and Central Asia due to the acrimonious relations between Afghanistan and Pakistan, and Afghanistan's own interest to unlock itself from its trade dependency on Pakistan. Pakistan's relations with Afghanistan are fraught with deep mistrust and suspicion. Successive governments in Kabul have often held Islamabad responsible for violence that threatens domestic political stability in Afghanistan, as President Ghani demonstrated in his speech at the Heart of Asia Ministerial Conference in December 2016. Kabul's close relationship with India is discomforting for Pakistan. The Afghanistan–Pakistan Trade and Transit Treaty (APTTA) – a treaty that was brokered by the United States – aimed at facilitating Afghanistan's international trade through Pakistan, thus disincentivising Afghanistan's close relationship with India. Pakistan refused to extend the APTTA to include India, even though the Indian government had expressed its interest in joining the treaty. The minutes of the APTTA, which were signed by the commerce ministers of Afghanistan and Pakistan, explicitly state that 'no Indian export to Afghanistan will be allowed through Wagah', as the newspaper *Dawn* reported on 19 July 2010 (Kiani 2010).[4]

While strategic considerations appear to have guided Pakistan's position with regard to India's membership in the APTTA, as suggested by a report by the *Business Recorder* on 29 April 2016, economic motivations also explain why Pakistan has tried to prevent India from accessing Afghanistan and Central Asia. In 2014, for example, India's request to export wheat through Pakistan to Afghanistan was objected to by Pakistani business people who feared that their strong position in the Afghan market would suffer if subsidised wheat from India reached the country, as reported in *Dawn* on 27 October 2014 (Khan 2014). Pakistan has also used violent means to obstruct India's expansion into Afghanistan and Central Asia: Indian investments in Afghanistan – especially transport infrastructure projects, including people working on them, but also the embassy in Kabul and the consulate in Kandahar – have come under frequent attacks by armed groups that have safe havens in Pakistan.

Afghanistan rejected Pakistan's US$500 million of investments in infrastructure, arguing that Pakistan should rather spend the money on containing terrorism emanating from its own territory. Meanwhile, India's total credit line of US$3 billion (since 2001), including the recently announced US$1 billion, has been welcomed. Given this strategic focus and the aforementioned considerable gap between India and Pakistan in terms of economic power, it is not surprising that Pakistan's exports to Central Asia are nothing but a fraction of India's exports to the region. With the fall of the Taliban regime in 2001, Afghanistan, reached via Iran, emerged as a major route for India's trade with Central Asia. The growth of Pakistan's trade with Central Asia in this decade is due to the APTTA and bilateral infrastructure projects with Afghanistan and the aforementioned cooperation between Pakistan and China.

Trade relations look somewhat different for Afghanistan: 33 per cent of Afghanistan's exports went to India in 2015, 40 per cent to Pakistan; Pakistan dominates Afghanistan's imports with a share of 17.4 per cent, whereas India's share is only 1.7 per cent, according to data retrieved from the ITC Trade Map (2016).

To counter India's influence, Pakistan has formed the Committee for Reconstruction and Rehabilitation of Afghanistan to oversee various projects. It has pledged US$500 million worth of projects for Afghanistan's education, health and infrastructure sectors and is providing 3,000 scholarships to Afghan students. In addition to the CEPC, Pakistan has joined the Central Asia Regional Economic Cooperation (CAREC), whose other member states are Afghanistan, Azerbaijan, China, Kazakhstan, Kyrgyzstan, Mongolia, Tajikistan, Turkmenistan and Uzbekistan. CAREC promotes transport connectivity so as to better exploit energy resources and facilitate trade. Transport corridors advanced by CAREC are to link the landlocked member countries and China's western provinces to ports in Pakistan. From a geostrategic perspective, it is crucial that all these corridors depend on Afghanistan as the key transit country – apparently in addition to Pakistan. This is one of the reasons why Pakistan is highly suspicious of any close relationship between Afghanistan and India. Indeed, the government of Afghanistan refused to sign an agreement with Pakistan in 2016 that would have eased Pakistan's trade with Central Asia through Afghanistan. Afghanistan insisted (and continues to insist) that Pakistan grant similar transit rights to India in return.

Table 14.3 India's and Pakistan's exports to Central Asia (in US$ million)

	2003	2005	2007	2009	2011	2013	2015
India	118.8	173.9	211.8	261.7	414.1	543.4	417.9
Pakistan	18.0	16.8	11.9	9.1	11.9	22.4	27.8

Source: data extrapolated from the International Trade Centre, Trade Map (2016). www.trademap.org/Index.aspx.

Regional integration and bilateral cooperation

After initial suspicion on the objectives of the South Asian Association for Regional Co-operation (SAARC), India now appears to be willing to advance regional integration, which would further its own economic interests. Particularly after 2005 it has been trying to use the SAARC as a means to enhance regional trade and the physical connectivity between the regional states. The decision to accept Afghanistan as a member of the SAARC in 2007 was at least partly motivated by India's interest in physically connecting with Central Asia via Afghanistan and Pakistan. It appears likely that the Indian government thought that advancing this national goal through a multilateral organisation would receive a favourable response from the regional states, especially from Pakistan.

Meanwhile, Pakistan has been trying to stall regional integration. As noted, it does not see the Indian-driven transport corridors as a mutually beneficial initiative and fears that they will strengthen India's economic footprint in Afghanistan and Central Asia. Out of fear of boosting India's role in the region, Pakistan has also refused to sign the SAARC Motor Vehicle Agreement (or SAARC MVA), which could have facilitated physical movement of cargo and passengers within the region. By blocking an agreement on free physical movement, Pakistan has apparently hampered regional trade. As a result, India has opted for subregional integration through an initiative with Bangladesh, Bhutan and Nepal – the BBIN MVA. This initiative allows for the efficient movement of people and goods across the borders of the four states. Earlier, while ratifying the South Asia Free Trade Agreement, Pakistan stressed that its trade with India would continue to be governed by a positive list – that is, a list of specified items that may be traded bilaterally. The common practice in international trade relations is negative lists, which tend to be less restrictive because of the simple fact that allowing and forbidding the trade of specific goods is a time-consuming administrative and political process.

Table 14.4 shows that India's trade with SAARC countries stands at US$20.2 billion, compared to Pakistan's US$5.2 billion in 2015. Ninety per cent of Pakistan's regional trade is in fact trade with Afghanistan and India, showing

Table 14.4 India's and Pakistan's intra-SAARC trade (in US$ billion)

		2003	2005	2007	2009	2011	2013	2015
India	Exports	3.875	5.400	7.848	7.374	12.936	16.900	17.258
	Imports	0.634	1.380	1.713	1.516	2.501	2.156	2.952
	Total	4.510	6.780	9.561	8.889	15.439	19.056	20.210
Pakistan	Exports	0.749	1.798	1.622	2.198	4.235	3.446	3.010
	Imports	0.346	0.765	1.479	1.335	1.953	2.303	2.198
	Total	1.095	2.562	3.102	3.533	6.188	5.748	5.203

Source: table prepared by author based on data obtained from ITC Trade Map, www.trademap.org/Index.aspx (2016).

that Pakistan hardly trades with the remaining SAARC countries. India has increased its trade with Afghanistan in particular in the second half of the 2000s due to Afghanistan joining the SAARC. Moreover, an additional bilateral trade agreement was signed between Afghanistan and India. As noted, Pakistan still remains the most important trading partner for Afghanistan. What is more, India has a massive trade surplus vis-à-vis its neighbouring countries. This is because the SAARC countries mostly import primary sector goods from India that feed into their export-oriented industries. Bilateral agreements have helped to boost India's regional trade: Bangladesh benefits from duty-free access to the Indian market for some textile products, and a Bangladeshi–Indian treaty on investment promotion was ratified in 2009. Nepal and India have also signed agreements on investment promotion and free trade. A free trade agreement has been signed by India and Sri Lanka, and an agreement on economic and technological cooperation is being negotiated. As explained below, there have even been agreements between India and Pakistan to ease economic interaction.

To undermine India's regional dominance, Pakistan has been pushing to make China, which currently has the status of observer, a full member of the SAARC. As a full member and partner to Pakistan, China would help Pakistan to become a true geo-economic rival for India in Central Asia and Afghanistan, mostly because of the aforementioned transport corridors.

Lately there have been signs of rapprochement between India and Pakistan: for example, the two countries have signed an agreement on a natural gas pipeline that is to be built in collaboration with Afghanistan and Turkmenistan, the aforementioned TAPI Pipeline. Concrete steps to ease economic interaction have been taken. They concern the number of cities that businesspersons are allowed to visit and the duration of business visas. Indian and Pakistani business communities have been the main driver for these changes. The efforts by the business communities to push their respective governments into making economic engagements resembles 'the instrumentalization of the state by economic interest groups that seek to manipulate its activities on the international scene for their own purposes', discussed by Luttwak (1990, p. 19).

Such efforts date back more than 20 years. In 1996, the Karachi Chamber of Commerce and Industry wrote that 'the pattern of US–China economic relations should be adopted as a model while delineating a policy towards India' (1996, p. 1). In 2012, the ministers of commerce of India and Pakistan set up the Pakistan–India Joint Business Forum, comprising of 15 leading businesspersons from both countries. The forum allows business representatives to talk about critical issues and make recommendations to their governments, for instance on trade facilitation.

Individual companies have also been actively trying to persuade politicians to lift restrictions on Indian–Pakistani trade. Most importantly, the Jindal Group, an international manufacturing giant with interests in cement, petroleum and steel amongst other sectors, has facilitated a bilateral political dialogue. The group's director, Sajjan Jindal, has developed personal relationships with both the Indian and the Pakistan prime ministers. He has supposedly used these personal relationships to bring both sides together. The business interests that the Jindal Group has in an Indian–Pakistan rapprochement are apparent: the company is part of the Afghan Iron Steel Consortium, which has won the bid to invest in major mines in Afghanistan. Access to Afghanistan through Pakistan – the shortest land route from India – being denied would mean exporting the minerals from Afghanistan through ports in Iran, making transport rather expensive.

Conclusion

As explained in the introduction of this book, military power appears to have become less important in international relations. States strive for economic advantage over others, focussing on attractiveness for foreign investments, industrial development, market expansion and similar issues. This chapter has shown that India pursues a geo-economic approach to Central and South Asia, seeking to expand its trade relationship and thereby gaining influence, mainly through building transport corridors. Pakistan, conversely, tries to block India's economic expansion by delaying tactics with regard to regional integration. Pakistan also exploits its crucial location as a transit country between India and Central Asia. Efforts to advance a constructive geo-economic strategy of its own – for example by building transport corridors that link its landlocked neighbouring countries globally – exist but have so far been of rather limited success. However, Pakistan's potential partnership with China may change this.

Furthermore, the chapter has demonstrated that various interest groups play a crucial role in influencing the geo-economic policies of India and Pakistan. The business sectors in both countries push, with some exceptions, for economic engagement, whereas the army in Pakistan continues to sustain a paradigm of hostility. As a general conclusion, the India–Pakistan case appears to imply that geo-economics works better for states that possess a great economic potential than for states that do not. As noted, India has a higher GDP than Pakistan. The *Global Competitiveness Index* puts India clearly ahead, too. Using its superior economic power, India has made considerable inroads into Afghanistan and Central Asia despite the denial of transit rights by Pakistan.

Nevertheless, the two rivals have taken tentative steps towards bilateral economic cooperation, despite reservations from Pakistan's army and even some sectors of the Pakistani economy. With regard to global dynamics, greater economic cooperation would serve India's interests, whereas a military confrontation would derail its aspirations to become a global power. This is likely to incentivise Pakistan to work against the normalisation of bilateral relations and reinforce its strategy to frustrate India's ambitions in Afghanistan and Central Asia.

Notes

1 First ideas of a geo-economic analysis of the Indian–Pakistani relationship were presented by the author at a workshop held at the Finnish Institute of International Affairs in February 2016. The author would like to thank Sören Scholvin and Mikael Wigell for their comments on the drafts of this chapter.

2 These convictions have been expressed in a speech held by Afghanistan's president at the Institute for Defence Studies and Analysis in 2016 (available at www.youtube.com/watch?v=Dg_va6Uyuf4) and in the 2003 Delhi Declaration by India and Iran (available at the website of India's Ministry of External Affairs).

3 The Durand Line has separated Afghanistan and Pakistan since the colonial era. Afghanistan has contested this border, arguing that it has been imposed by the British and divides the Pashtuns who live in the border region.

Pashtunisation aims at creating a homeland for the Pashtuns, who are the largest ethnic group in Afghanistan and the second largest in Pakistan.

4 Wagah is a border stop on the route from Amritsar (Punjab, India) to Lahore (Punjab, Pakistan).

References

Ahmed, V. and Batool, A., (2015) 'India-Pakistan Trade: Perspectives from the Automobile Sector in Pakistan', *Indian Council for Research on International Economic Relations*, Working Paper No. 293, January. Available at: http://icrier.org/pdf/Working_Paper_293.pdf, accessed 5 December 2016.

Ali, M., Muhajid, N. and Rehman, A. (2015) 'Pakistan–India Relations: Peace through Bilateral Trade', *Developing Country Studies*, 5, 2, pp. 81–88.

Bell, D. (1990) 'Germany: The Enduring Fear. A New Nationalism or a New Europe', *Dissent*, 37, 4, pp. 461–468.

Fair, C. (2014) *Fighting to the End: The Pakistan Army's Way of War* (Oxford: Oxford University Press).

Hussain, S. T. (2013) 'Trade in Agriculture with India: View from Pakistan', *India-Pakistan Trade Newsletter*. Available at: http://indiapakistantrade.org/pdf/India-Pakistan-newsletter_Issue_4.pdf, accessed 12 December 2016.

International Trade Centre. (2016) 'ITC Trade Map', *International Trade Centre*. Available at: www.trademap.org/Index.aspx, accessed 4 December 2016.

Karachi Chamber of Commerce and Industries. (1996) *Freer Trade with India: Its Raison d'être and Impact* (Karachi: Karachi Chamber of Commerce and Industries).

Khan, A. F. (2014) 'India Seeks Transit Facility for Wheat Export to Afghanistan', *Dawn*, 27 October. Available at: www.dawn.com/news/1140643, accessed 12 February 2018.

Kiani, K. (2010) 'Afghanistan Allowed to Use Wagah for Export to India: Pakistan-Afghan Accord on Transit Trade', *Dawn*, 19 July. Available at: www.dawn.com/news/548084, accessed 12 February 2018.

Luttwak, E. N. (1990) 'From Geopolitics to Geo-economics: Logic of Conflict, Grammar of Commerce', *The National Interest*, 20, pp. 17–23.

Ministry of Commerce [of India]. (2011) 'Joint Statement of the 5th Round of Talks on Commercial and Economic Co-operation between Commerce Secretaries of India and Pakistan', *Ministry of Commerce*. Available at: http://commerce.nic.in/trade/JPS 27-28Apr2011.pdf, accessed 4 December 2016.

Siddiqui, A. R. (1978) 'Armed Forces: Tasks and Missions', *Defence Journal*, 4, 1–2, n.p.

World Economic Forum. (2016) *The Global Competitiveness Report 2017–2018*. Available at www.weforum.org/reports/the-global-competitiveness-report-2017-2018, accessed 25 April 2018.

World Economic Forum. (2016) 'The World Competitiveness Report 2016–2017', *World Economic Forum*, Insight Report. Available at: www3.weforum.org/docs/GCR2016-2017/05FullReport/TheGlobalCompetitivenessReport2016-2017_FINAL.pdf, accessed 22 January 2017.

15 Geo-economics and geopolitics in sub-Saharan African power politics[1]

Sören Scholvin

Introduction

Over the last two decades, economists, geographers and political scientists have engaged in intense debate about emerging powers. In addition to being featured in numerous publications that deal with global issues, emerging powers, including South Africa, have often been conceptualised as regional hegemons that advance projects of regional leadership (e.g. Adekeye, Adebayo and Landsberg 2007; Flemes 2009; Schoeman 2003; Schoeman and Alden 2003; Scholvin 2013; Simon 1998). In spite of frequent claims that not only leaders but also potential followers are the subject of scrutiny (e.g. Cooper, Higgott and Nossal 1991), research on how other states react to the leadership projects of emerging powers remains thin. For sub-Saharan Africa, even general studies of the foreign policies of what Ebert, Flemes and Strüver (2014) call 'secondary powers' – that is, the second-most powerful states in regional hierarchies – are scarce.[2]

In this chapter, I bring the empirical gap of research on secondary powers together with a key question regarding the concept of geo-economics. Scholars who coined the term in the early 1990s, in particular Huntington (1993) and Luttwak (1990), were convinced that military means of power had become redundant and were being replaced by economic means that states now apply in pursuit of their foreign policy objectives. However an increasing number of researchers to whom I refer below argue that geo-economics and geopolitics co-occur. The two types of geostrategy hardly ever stand on their own. It appears that whilst some states put more emphasis on military might and occasionally refer to economic power (e.g. Wigell and Vihma 2016), others simply back-up their geo-economic practices with brute force as an ultima ratio (e.g. Chapter 8 in this volume).

With regard to emerging powers and from the perspective of the realist school of international relations (or IR realism), secondary powers can be expected to pursue competitive or even confrontational policies vis-à-vis the hegemons in their respective regions. The concept of contestation, originally advanced by Ebert, Flemes and Strüver (2014), captures this interaction between hegemons, on the one side, and secondary powers, on the other. Elsewhere, I (2017a) have adapted the initial definition of contestation, suggesting that there is intended and unintended contestation. The former constitutes a set of 'counterpolicies of secondary states that seek to achieve the goal of maintaining external security vis-à-vis the primary power' (Ebert, Flemes and Strüver 2014, p. 222). Unintended contestation, conversely, constitutes a set of policies that boost the self-determination of secondary powers vis-à-vis the primary power, even though this is not their purpose.

This chapter does not focus on the distinction of intended and unintended contestation. It provides an analysis of contestation against South Africa so as to learn about the geo-economic and geopolitical strategies of secondary powers. I first elaborate on the concept of contestation, bringing it together with geo-economics and geopolitics. Afterwards I analyse the foreign policies of secondary powers, identified as such in earlier publications (Scholvin 2017a; 2017b). In this part of the chapter, I determine to what extent they contest against South Africa and what relevance geo-economics and geopolitics play in their contestation.

Contestation, geo-economics and geopolitics

'No state considers itself a pure follower of another state', Flemes and Castro argue (2016, p. 78). Hence one should expect second-most powerful states – actually all states – to somehow contest against hegemons so as to preserve their autonomy and self-determination. From the perspective of IR realism, contestation is an almost self-suggesting strategy because a hegemon poses a potentially deadly threat in an international arena characterised by the principle of anarchy. Contestation is similar but not identical to balancing, as I (2017a; 2017b) argue in other publications on this issue. As a concept, contestation helps to capture the diversity of foreign policy strategies and the practically limitless means used to apply them in practice.

To analyse the policies pursued by secondary powers, it is important to address an analytical hurdle that accompanies the concept: secondary powers may cooperate with extra-regional partners on security and trade or promote a regional integration project that constitutes an alternative to organisations dominated by the regional hegemon. Yet are these policies necessarily driven by an intention to contest against the hegemon? Might they not, in fact, be serving interests that have little or nothing to do with the hegemon? Linked to this, do single incidents of friction between a hegemon and secondary powers or even a series of such incidents prove the existence of a strategy of contestation? To use more academic terminology, the mere co-occurrence of two factors does not mean that these factors are causally related.

It would be incorrect to argue that any alternative explanation and contestation are 'complementary and synergic', as Flemes and Castro do (2016, p. 77). For example, Kenya's military intervention in Somalia is due to security concerns over Islamist militancy (Anderson and McKnight 2012; International Crisis Group 2012; Miyandazi 2012). This explanation does not exclude the possibility that Kenya intervened in Somalia so as to contest against South

Africa; but merely pointing out that this possibility exists is not a way to prove causality. The answer to this conundrum is that contestation exists and matters, even if secondary powers do not contest intentionally. As long as one is interested in the consequences of foreign policy, recognising unintended contestation makes sense because intended contestation and unintended contestation have the same effect on regional relations: they cause friction between the hegemon and the secondary powers, diminishing the prospects of cooperation and increasing the risk of more intense contestation.

So how does contestation relate to geo-economics and geopolitics? In the introduction to this edited volume, my co-editor and I argued that geo-economics (and geopolitics alike) should be defined by its means, not by its ends. Contestation, meanwhile, is defined by its end: regardless of whether this is intentional or not, contestation by secondary powers results in weakening a hegemon or at least limiting the ways in which that hegemon can exert power. The concept of contestation does not exclude any particular means of power politics. Neither do its adherents argue that a particular means must be applied so that we can talk about contestation. Hence secondary powers may opt for geo-economics, geopolitics or a combination of both in their contestation. The fact that they apply economic and/or military means of power to a specific region makes their contestation a geostrategy.

As noted, Huntington and Luttwak argued that military-based power politics would not matter in the post-Cold War world. Luttwak's famous essay from the *National Interest* begins with the words 'the waning of the Cold War is steadily reducing the importance of military power in world affairs' (1990, p. 17). Thus national power now derives from 'disposable capital in lieu of firepower, civilian innovation in lieu of military-technical advancement, and market penetration in lieu of garrisons and bases' (1990, p. 18). Or, as Huntington wrote, 'in a world in which military conflict between major states is unlikely, economic power will be increasingly important in determining the primacy or subordination of states' (1993, p. 72).

Some scholars have taken up this sharp distinction between geo-economics and geopolitics, usually without referring to Luttwak (e.g. Blackwill and Harris 2016; Cowen and Smith 2009; Hsiung 2009; Leonard 2016; Mattlin and Wigell 2016; Mercille 2008). Yet others point out that geo-economics and geopolitics overlap. In his contribution to this volume, Baev shows that Russia has referred to economic and military means so as to project power to the rim of the Pacific Ocean (Chapter 6). The mix of geo-economics and geopolitics in Pakistan's anti-Indian balancing is addressed by Pattanaik (Chapter 14). Rivlin stresses that a military option was crucial for Western sanctions to be effective against Iran (Chapter 8).

In his study of the competition between China and India, Scott (2008) points out that the control over sea-lines of communication is essential to geo-economics and geopolitics; so is access to vital resources. In both cases, economic means such as giant infrastructure projects tend to co-occur with military protection thereof – China's famous 'String of Pearls', for instance (Scholvin 2016). Grosse (2014) analyses China's domestic capital accumulation and broader economic development, arguing that increasing economic bases of national power enable the People's Republic to change the structures of the global economy according to its preferences. He proposes that geo-economics is the merger of economic and geopolitical goals and implies that there are hybrid strategies of economic and military power projection. Somewhat confusingly, Baru argues that Japan turned into an economic power in the 1980s but 'it never became a geo-economic power, having failed to convert its new-found economic clout into military and political power' (2012, p. 51).

The purpose of the following empirical section of this chapter is to find out whether – and if so, how – secondary powers in sub-Saharan Africa combine geo-economics and geopolitics in their contestation against South Africa. As noted, Angola, Ethiopia, Kenya and Nigeria have been identified as secondary powers in some of my previous publications. Given the lack of space in a short book chapter, I will not repeat the assessment of national power in sub-Saharan Africa here.

The geo-economics and geopolitics of sub-Saharan African secondary powers

Angola

Until the end of the domestic war against the National Union for the Total Independence of Angola (União Nacional para a Independência Total de Angola, or UNITA) in 2002, Angola's foreign policy was directed at beating UNITA. Other objectives were of marginal relevance. This is not surprising considering that UNITA posed an existential threat to the survival of the ruling People's Movement for the Liberation of Angola (Movimento Popular de Libertação de Angola, or MPLA). To support the efforts of domestic warfare, Angola pursued a geopolitical course of action: it sought to reshape its direct neighbourhood by intervening in the Democractic Republic of Congo (DRC) in 1996 and in 2002 and, already in the 1970s and 1980s, by militarily supporting the struggle against the apartheid regime in South Africa and the South African occupation of Namibia (Malaquias 2000, 2002).

Angola's military intervention – along with Namibia and Zimbabwe – in the DRC in 2002, which thwarted attempts to overthrow the Congolese government, was the first major incident of friction vis-à-vis post-apartheid South Africa. It occurred at a time when South Africa's president, Thabo Mbeki, was pushing for a diplomatic solution. Yet Angola's intervention was – just like its earlier intervention in the DRC in 1996 – a key component in its fight against UNITA, especially UNITA's supply lines in the neighbouring country and the need to protect oil installations in the enclave of Cabinda, which financed the domestic war efforts of the MPLA. In addition, the Angolan government apparently hoped that, as a consequence of its intervention, the government of the DRC would become less inclined to allow UNITA access to Congolese territory (Scholvin 2013; Turner 2002).

For South Africa, meanwhile, the DRC and the whole of Central Africa was (and still is) an area of economic opportunities, which could only be exploited if violent conflicts in the region ended. From the perspective of the Mbeki government, the best way to achieve this objective was to mediate between the Congolese government and the insurgents (Adekeye, Adebayo and Landsberg 2007, Landsberg 2008). The purpose of Angola's intervention in the DRC was not to confront South Africa. South Africa's economic objectives in Central Africa were, at that time, irrelevant to policymakers in Luanda. However, Angola's actions worked against South Africa's chosen course, meaning that the 2002 intervention in the DRC was a case of unintended contestation and – given that South Africa had clearly voiced its preference for how the conflict should be resolved – a grave disregard for South Africa's regional leadership.

In recent years, Angola has opted for geo-economics instead of geopolitics. The secondary power has remained a reluctant participant in regional economic integration initiatives. Most importantly, it has not joined the free trade area established by the Southern African Development Community (SADC). Exporting to Angola and investing there remain difficult for South African enterprises. Whilst the Angolan government argues that it cannot join the SADC free trade area because its post-war economy is in a process of restructuring, Redvers (2013) points out that this argument appears to apply only to South African competition: Brazilian, Chinese and Portuguese firms have been granted relatively easy market access. By objecting to integration on terms mostly set by South Africa, Angola is pursuing a strategy of contestation. If one believes the declarations made by the government, this strategy is aimed at reducing the economic gap with South Africa. Redvers, however, argues that those who benefit from market protection are mostly so-called *empresários de confiança* – business people who have close personal links to the government, military and ruling party.

Angola's contestation strategy is not only defensive. The state-owned oil company, Sonangol, has played a crucial role in geo-economics. It has invested in infrastructure and mining in the regional neighbourhood, as summarised by Roque (2013). For example, Sonangol has carried out joint oil exploration projects with the Republic of the Congo, a move facilitated by the signing of tax and trade agreements in 2011. The port of Buba and a bauxite mine in Guinea-Bissau are of interest to subsidiaries of Sonangol. The company will probably venture into Zambia if oil is found in the country's Western Province. Plans are already in place for an extension of the Benguela Corridor, a railway line from the Angolan coast to the Congolese–Zambian Copperbelt. The Angolan government is looking to rehabilitate the port of Lobito at the end of that corridor to facilitate the export of minerals. Moreover, Sonangol has obtained concessions on the main port in São Tomé e Príncipe and on the expansion and modernisation of the country's airport. It is partnering with the local power and water company and the local oil company, the latter already being 70 per cent owned by Sonangol.

The Sonangol Group is thus much more than a mining company. It has become one of the most important enterprises in sub-Saharan Africa. In addition to its core activities (exploration and exploitation of oil resources, including deep-water drilling and seismic studies), the group has diversified into air transport, banking, real estate, shipping and telecommunications. Its most successful subsidiaries include two full-service banks, the telecommunication provider MSTelcom and the airline Sonair. These are also involved in Angola's economic expansion into the near cross-border region. In mid-2012, Sonair became the majority shareholder in the national air carrier of São Tomé e Príncipe, STP Airways. Banks owned by the Sonangol Group are interested in securing stakes in banks in Cape Verde and Guinea-Bissau. The DRC and Namibia are being considered for future expansion.

By expanding its economic influence in sub-Saharan Africa, Angola is seeking to increase its own economic power, narrowing the gap with the regional hegemon. Contestation against South Africa is also the result of Angolan ports being positioned as alternatives to South African ports: the minerals extracted in the Congolese–Zambian Copperbelt are, at present, mostly exported via Richards Bay, which is South Africa's largest harbour. Lobito may become a vital alternative, as the think tank Stratfor (2012) suggests. On top of that, Angolan and South African companies compete for markets in sub-Saharan Africa, with the status and position of Angolan companies being reinforced by the political support that they receive.

Ethiopia

Ethiopia's *Foreign Policy and National Security Strategy* (Federal Democratic Republic of Ethiopia, 2002) identifies economic backwardness and the desperate poverty in which the majority of Ethiopian people live as critical threats. It argues that foreign policy should contribute to the acceleration of national economic development by promoting investment and trade, arguably together with the objective of advancing democracy. Considering that Ethiopia is landlocked, rail and road corridors to Djibouti, Kenya and Sudan are a vital component of the country's economic strategy and foreign policy. Somaliland is another potential transit territory, given its relative stability in comparison with the rest of Somalia. Ethiopia's relations with these states are cooperative. South Sudan appears to be seen as a potential client state (Abbink 2013), particularly if it becomes dependent on Ethiopia as a security provider and as a transport hub.

Geo-economics is critical to Ethiopia. It has invested heavily in infrastructure, especially in relation to energy and transport, so as to boost its role as subregional hegemon. The airport of Addis Ababa has become a major hub for flights within Africa and from Africa to other continents. Rail and road corridors are being upgraded, most importantly the LAPSSET Corridor, which will connect Ethiopia, South Sudan and Uganda to the Kenyan port of Lamu by rail, road and pipeline (more on this later). Up to 27 new dams, with hydropower stations generating almost 25 gigawatts of electricity, are projected to become operational by 2027 (Cuesta Fernández 2015). High-voltage transmission lines to Kenya are expected to generate additional export earnings of US$1 billion by the end of the current decade (African Development Bank 2012).

Similar to the case of Angola, one might argue that Ethiopia appears to be pursuing a strategy of contestation through geo-economics: by fostering domestic growth, the gap between Ethiopia and South Africa will shrink, thereby limiting the latter's chances of reinforcing its political vision for sub-Saharan Africa against Ethiopia's will. However contestation against South Africa does not appear to be the motivation driving Ethiopian policymakers. Unlike in the case of Angola, Ethiopia's geo-economic project does not create competition for South Africa. Competition between Ethiopian and South African firms in regional markets is marginal and Ethiopia's regional trade remains extremely low; so is the potential of this trade growing (Scholvin and Wrana 2015). The transport corridors that Ethiopia seeks to build will not divert traffic from South Africa and the export of electricity does not work against South African interests either.

The curious thing about Ethiopia is that its geo-economic project co-occurs with a geopolitical one: the secondary power has deployed troops to Somalia, where they are fighting al-Shabaab. Almost 4,500 of the 22,000 troops that comprise the African Union Mission in Somalia are Ethiopian. The Ethiopian troops are in charge of the Bakool, Bay and Gedo regions, which border Ethiopia.[3] Furthermore Ethiopian troops in considerable numbers are involved in peacekeeping missions in Darfur (Sudan), in South Sudan and along the disputed border of South Sudan and Sudan (United Nations 2017). This commitment to regional security does not, however, mean contestation against South Africa. Ethiopia projects its influence – both economically and militarily – mostly into a sub-region that is distant from, and of limited interest to, South Africa.

The minimal overlap between Ethiopia's and South Africa's foreign policy interests is probably best demonstrated by the key topic on Ethiopia's foreign policy agenda: the right to use the water of the Nile River and its confluents. The river's basin is shared by Burundi, the DRC, Egypt, Eritrea, Ethiopia, Kenya, Rwanda, South Sudan, Sudan, Tanzania and Uganda. The 1929 Nile River Treaty – signed by Britain, being the colonial power at that time, and Egypt – has not been replaced and remains a contentious issue for the riparian countries because it means that they cannot use the waters of Lake Victoria and the Nile without the acquiescence of Egypt. Other privileges were granted to Egypt: most importantly, it is able to monitor the river flow in the riparian countries and veto upstream engineering projects that would affect the flow of the river. This apparently limits opportunities to use water for agriculture, industrial production and (especially) electricity generation in countries other than Egypt (Arsano 2007; El-Fadel *et al.* 2003).

Ethiopia's relations with Egypt reached a low point when the Ethiopian president, Meles Zenawi, suggested in 2010 that Egypt was backing rebels in Ethiopia because of the dispute over access to the Nile. He added that 'if Egypt went to war with upstream countries over this issue, it would lose' (quoted in Abbink 2011). An Egyptian delegation later went to Ethiopia to discuss cooperation in terms of dams under construction in Ethiopia, apparently easing tensions. The dispute over the Nile also demonstrates the interrelatedness of geo-economics and geopolitics: military means – threatening war with Egypt – are essential, at least for the rhetoric of the Ethiopian government. Using the water of the Nile and its confluents is vital to Ethiopia's aforementioned geo-economic project of national development and subregional powerhood.

Kenya

Subregional integration in East Africa was given fresh momentum in 2000, when the East African Community (EAC), which had been dissolved in 1977, was relaunched. Burundi and Rwanda joined the founding members – Kenya, Tanzania and Uganda – in 2007. South Sudan became a member in 2016. The EAC allows for the free movement of capital, goods and services and labour. It is looking to establish a currency union by 2024. Kenya, which plays a central role in the EAC, promulgated a new foreign policy strategy in 2015, which set the tone for a markedly assertive turn in the conduct of foreign relations. The new framework specifies that Kenya's foreign policy rests on five pillars: peace diplomacy with a focus on Africa; economic diplomacy, which means efforts to increase foreign investment and trade; diaspora diplomacy, directed at contributions by Kenyans abroad to Kenya's development; environmental diplomacy; and cultural diplomacy (Republic of Kenya 2014).

In a speech held during the 2013 election campaign, President Uhuru Kenyatta pledged to turn Kenya into a country with a highly favourable business environment so as to make it an 'African Lion economy' (quoted in *Kenya Today* 2013). Mabera (2016) points out that this secondary power is intent on becoming a newly industrialising, middle-income country in accordance with its *Vision 2030*. The quest for economic diversification, infrastructure development and macro-economic stability, but also human capital and technological progress, has become the centrepiece of Kenyan politics. The present government has placed particular emphasis on economic development, which it associates with indigenous capital formation and indigenous control of the economy. This form of economic nationalism is linked to regionalism: Kenya attaches great importance to Africa and, even more so, East Africa. Projects linked to regional integration have been fast-tracked in a coalition of the willing with Rwanda and Uganda. Cooperation with Ethiopia and South Sudan has also intensified – first in the context of the aforementioned LAPSSET Corridor but also in respect of the security policies of Somalia and South Sudan (Kagwanja 2014).

The LAPSSET Corridor consists of the yet-to-be built harbour of Lamu; a yet-to-be-built oil refinery at that harbour; a rail, road and pipeline network from there to Ethiopia, South Sudan and Uganda; and agricultural growth zones and export processing zones along the corridor. There is no clear time frame for the completion of the corridor. As Browne (2015) notes, it appears that in various public forums officials from all participating countries focus on achievements from the past and have only a vague vision of what still needs to be done, instead of ensuring that concrete plans with measurable milestones are in place. Considering the instability of South Sudan, it is unlikely that the LAPSSET Corridor will become a reality in the near future, at least not in the way it was initially envisaged. A more modest version of the corridor, focussing on Kenyan and Ugandan oil resources, may be pursued. Even this depends on the oil price recovering from its current low level. At present it appears that even Kenyan officials who are responsible for the corridor project cannot tell whether the project is dead or alive.

Beyond transport infrastructure, Kenya has been a driving force behind the Tripartite Free Trade Area (TFTA), which aims to bring together the 26 countries of the Common Market for Eastern and Southern Africa, the EAC and SADC in a commercial bloc. Kenya's interest in the TFTA is economic development through trade. It appears, however, that Kenya's free trade approach has been constrained by South Africa's reluctance to embrace trade liberalisation. South Africa rather sees the TFTA as a means by which to export its trade-restrictive, import-substituting policies to a wider region or – in other words – to promote regional instead of global value chains (Scholvin and Wrana 2015).

Looking at Kenya's economic initiatives from the perspective of contestation, it is plausible to argue that Kenya stands somewhere between Angola and Ethiopia. Boosting domestic economic development is motivated by domestic objectives. As noted, foreign policy has become subordinated to economic development. The LAPSSET Corridor does not work against South African interests. It may even help South African enterprises to also access regional markets. Nonetheless Kenya constitutes a counterweight to South Africa in a regional economic integration context, as conveyed in different opinions expressed about the TFTA. The economic nationalism of the Kenyatta government will lead to friction if Kenya fears that South African firms will outcompete Kenyan companies in East Africa, which is a possibility if economic integration between the EAC and SADC proceeds (Scholvin and Wrana 2015). Unlike Ethiopia, Kenya is potentially prone to contestation against South Africa. Compared with Angola, Kenya has not unleashed this potential yet.

The second factor that is shaping Kenya's foreign policy is its location in an insecure neighbourhood, with armed conflicts raging in the Great Lakes Region, Somalia and South Sudan. Humanitarian crises, including refugee movements, and cross-border hostilities by insurgents, pirates and terrorists all pose a threat to Kenya, which has reacted with military means, meaning by conducting geopolitics. In 2011, Kenya launched a military operation – involving 3,000 troops – into neighbouring Somalia, mainly in response to cross-border kidnappings by the Islamist militant organisation al-Shabaab. The operation was aimed at creating a buffer zone of about 100 kilometres on the Somali side of the border to prevent any further incursions into Kenyan territory. It was complemented by extensive swoops on districts in Kenyan towns suspected to have an al-Shabaab presence, especially Nairobi. The Kenyan government claimed that it had been asked by Somalia's transitional government to deploy the troops but this claim was rejected by the Somalis (Cheeseman 2011).

Furthermore Kenya is involved in the Intergovernmental Authority on Development, which has played an important role in Somalia, and the International

Conference on the Great Lakes Region, which serves as a forum for regional cooperation in stemming violent conflicts. The planning centre and secretariat of the multi-dimensional Eastern Africa Standby Force is located in Nairobi, demonstrating Kenya's subregional leadership role in terms of security policy.

Intervening in Somalia is not only a means of stopping the cross-border activities of al-Shabaab. It is also vital for building the LAPSSET Corridor and realising Kenya's *Vision 2030*. However unlike Angola's intervention in the DRC in 2002, Kenya's intervention in Somalia in 2011 did not constitute a case of unintended contestation against South Africa. South Africa does not play a major role in Somalia. Its reactions to the Kenyan intervention have been supportive: President Jacob Zuma pledged his support to Kenya's policy on Somalia at a Commonwealth summit a few months after the intervention began. The same applies to Kenya's commitment to security policy in the Great Lakes Region.

Nigeria

As reinforced over the years by successive governments, there is a strong conviction about Nigeria's manifest destiny as the champion of Africa (Bach 2007). When Nigeria attained its independence, the first president, Tafawe Balewa, declared that 'we belong to Africa and Africa must claim first attention in our external affairs' (quoted in Ubi and Akinkuotu 2014, p. 418). As Fawole (2012) argues, early Nigerian nationalists had a sort of messianic conception of their country's role in Africa. According to Agwu (2013), they pursued an altruistic foreign policy because of their own experiences with colonial oppression.

This is not the right place to examine whether Nigeria's pan-Africanism is altruistic or rather a legitimisation of the pursuit of Nigerian interests. What matters here is that the secondary power used to be committed to regional affairs, arguably in a different form to that demonstrated by Angola and Kenya and certainly to a greater extent than that displayed by Ethiopia. Yet Nigerian policy advisers and scholars have lately suggested that foreign policy should serve domestic interests by first contributing to the welfare of the Nigerian people (e.g. Ubi and Akinkuotu 2014). These often influential people argue that 'uneconomic matters [should not] predominate in [Nigeria's] external calculations' (John 2010, n.p.). Such recommendations are based on a critical interpretation of security interventions in West Africa, which occurred mostly in the 1990s, and the earlier support for African states that were fighting apartheid and colonialism. These efforts are seen as benevolent acts from which others benefited. Nigeria's economic presence in the countries that its military was purported to have stabilised has remained limited, as have economic benefits for Nigeria (Ojeme 2011).

These various thoughts are reflected in Nigerian policy planning and it appears that geopolitics is not on the Nigerian agenda anymore. Nigeria remains a key player in UN legitimised security interventions. It has contributed a significant number of troops to missions to Liberia, Mali and Sudan (United Nations 2017). Yet it is hard to see how this commitment would fit into a larger Nigerian geostrategy. The National Planning Commission (2012) now states that the effectiveness of the nation's foreign policy ought to be measured by foreign direct investment, foreign trade flows and the relocation to Nigeria of vital financial institutions. *Vision 20:2020*, which was proclaimed in 2008, aims to make Nigeria one of the world's 20 largest economies by 2020. The *Transformation Agenda*, formulated under the administration of President Goodluck Jonathan, underlines the need to foster international ties that serve the economic development agenda of Nigeria, including trade as well as issues such as education and technological cooperation. Bi-national commissions have been established with Canada, Germany, South Africa and the United States, whilst the steps involved in fostering business ties with China have been discussed at Nigerian foreign policy think tanks. Most of Nigeria's diplomatic representations abroad now have to justify their economic usefulness (Ubi and Akinkuotu 2014).

It would be wrong to conclude that Nigeria has shifted to a geo-economic strategy. Economics has become critical to its foreign policy but, unlike in the cases of Angola, Ethiopia and Kenya, the regional level hardly matters. The logic behind Nigeria's economic diplomacy is domestic economic development, particularly poverty reduction, through global partnerships. This also means that Nigeria's economic diplomacy qualifies, at best, as unintended contestation against South Africa. The extent of contestation remains modest because Nigeria's economic diplomacy is focussed at the global level. South Africa does not compete with Nigeria in global markets because the two countries export different products.

Nevertheless there have been isolated cases of diplomatic friction. Nelson Mandela's criticism of human rights violations in Nigeria – the execution of Ken Saro-Wiwa and eight other civil society activists in 1995, to be precise – and the blunt rejection of this criticism by Nigeria have become major points of reference in studies on South Africa's post-1994 project of regional leadership (e.g. Schoeman 2003; Scholvin 2013). The election of South Africa's former foreign minister, Nkosazana Dlamini-Zuma, as chairperson of the African Union (AU) caused severe friction, because the most powerful member states of the AU do not usually nominate their own nationals as candidates for chairpersonship.

Nigeria and South Africa furthermore disagreed on how to react to the crisis in Côte d'Ivoire in 2010. Nigeria backed the military intervention against President Laurent Gbagbo, whereas South Africa did not (Lynch 2011). Nigeria also supported the introduction of a no-fly zone over Libya in 2011, which led to massive airstrikes that allowed rebel forces to topple the Gaddafi regime. South Africa, meanwhile, sought a negotiated solution, using the framework of the AU (Fabricius 2015). It had initially voted in favour of UN Security Council Resolution 1973, which authorised the enforcement of a no-fly zone, but soon criticised Western powers for abusing that resolution and called for an end to military strikes. Nigeria did not voice any such criticism. The secondary power hence undermined South Africa's leadership, although its actual intentions, particularly in relation to contestation, remain unclear.

What is more, in 2008 the Nigerian government and the national Parliament stated that Nigerians living in South Africa were victims of xenophobia, which also manifested as physical violence against them. President Umaru Yar'Adua raised this issue during a state visit to South Africa. Despite this diplomatic effort, the deportations of Nigerians living illegally in South Africa continued (Bergstresser 2009). Tensions increased in 2012 when South Africa deported 125 Nigerians for allegedly failing to provide genuine yellow fever vaccination documents. The Nigerian authorities reacted by denying 126 South Africans entry into Nigeria on the same grounds a few days later (Bergstresser 2013).

Conclusion

There are few states in sub-Saharan Africa that possess sufficient economic and military power to contest against South Africa, the regional hegemon. From the individual perspectives of the secondary powers, contestation, at least in an intended and very pronounced form, tends to be an exception. What is more, geo-economics and geopolitics are sometimes interrelated strategies that complement each other but they also appear as features of different era in the foreign policies of the secondary powers.

Angola exemplifies how geo-economic strategies can replace geopolitics. The refusal of this secondary power to join the SADC free trade area and Sonangol's activities abroad constitute intended contestation. They form part of a geo-economic strategy. Geopolitics such as Angola's intervention in the DRC appears to be a long gone military approach to regional affairs. Nigeria also pursued a geopolitical strategy in West Africa in the 1990s but has become reluctant to apply military means in pursuit of strategic objectives. It concentrates on economic diplomacy instead. This may count, at maximum, as unintended contestation against South Africa. Yet only sporadic incidents of diplomatic friction indicate that Nigeria does not accept a subordinate position vis-à-vis South Africa. Because Nigeria's current foreign policy lacks a regional focus, one cannot call it geo-economic.

The interrelatedness of geo-economics and geopolitics, meanwhile, is demonstrated by Ethiopia and Kenya. The former pursues the objective of domestic economic development through case-specific cooperation with regional states, especially in terms of infrastructure development in the energy and transport sectors. There is no friction with South Africa, largely because South Africa is not substantially involved in the economics and politics of the Horn of Africa. Kenya's economic and security policies have become relatively more ambitious since the beginning of this century, although the LAPSSET Corridor reveals a sizeable gap between project objectives and outcomes. There is potential for contestation against South Africa because Kenya's envisaged outcomes of the TFTA are hardly compatible with those of South Africa. Higher levels of investment by South African enterprises in East Africa may also create challenges for Kenya's economic development strategy.

In both cases, it appears that geo-economic projects – domestic economic development through energy and transport corridors and, with regard to Kenya, regional integration – need a geopolitical backing. Would a purely geo-economic strategy work for Ethiopia considering that Egypt has considered using its air force against Ethiopian dams that interfere too much with the Nile (Kelley and Johnson 2012)? How would Ethiopia possibly deal with al-Shabaab if it were to apply economic means of statecraft only? In the case of Kenya, one may also convincingly argue that a rather conflict-laden region imposes the use of military means on the secondary power. The LAPSSET Corridor, being a role model geo-economic project, cannot prosper in an environment marked by cross-border raids of Somali militants and civil war in South Sudan.

This finding leads to the question of whether states are free to choose either geo-economics or geopolitics. At least the cases studied in this chapter imply that this choice is forced upon states by the conflict dynamics of their respective neighbour-hoods: only if there is no need to refer to military means of power politics, geo-economics will prosper as a stand-alone approach. Taking this thought a bit further, one should wonder whether the 'unfortunate parts of the world where armed con-frontations or civil strife persist', as Luttwak called them (1990, p. 17), are rather the rule than the exception in the early twenty-first century. This implies that the triumph of geo-economics that Luttwak had in mind remains limited to inter-national relations in some but not even all parts of the Global North.

Notes

1 The empirical section of this chapter is drawn from two earlier publications (Scholvin 2017a; 2017b).
2 I study Angola, Ethiopia, Kenya and Nigeria as secondary powers. The number of pub-lications on Nigeria's foreign policy has somewhat increased during the last few years. In particular, the topic of economic diplomacy and the question of how Nigeria can benefit from its foreign political commitments have been assessed. Few studies have been carried out on Angola's and Kenya's foreign policies. There is practically no associated research on Ethiopia.
3 For further information see http://amisom-au.org.

References

Abbink, J. (2011) 'Ethiopia', in Mehler, A., Melber, H. and van Walraven, K. (eds), *Africa Yearbook: Politics, Economy and Society South of the Sahara in 2010* (Leiden: Brill), pp. 337–338.

Abbink, J. (2013) 'Ethiopia', in Mehler, A., Melber, H. and van Walraven, K. (eds), *Africa Yearbook: Politics, Economy and Society South of the Sahara in 2012* (Leiden: Brill), pp. 325–336.

Adekeye, A., Adebayo, A. and Landsberg, C. (eds) (2007) *South Africa in Africa: The Post-Apartheid Era* (Scottsville: KwaZulu-Natal University Press).

African Development Bank. (2012) 'Ethiopia–Kenya Electricity Highway: Project appraisal Report', *African Development Bank*. Available at: www.afdb.org/fileadmin/uploads/afdb/Documents/Project-and-Operations/Ethiopia-Kenya_-_Ethiopia-Kenya_Electricity_Highway_-Project_Appraisal_Report_.pdf, accessed 26 May 2017.

Agwu, F. A. (2013) *Themes and Perspectives on Africa's International Relations* (Ibadan: University Press).

Anderson, D. M. and McKnight, J. (2015) 'Kenya at War: al-Shabaab and its Enemies in Eastern Africa', *African Affairs*, 454, pp. 1–27.

Arsano, Y. (2007) *Ethiopia and the Nile: Dilemma of National and Regional Hydropolitics*, unpublished PhD thesis, University of Zurich.

Bach, D. C. (2007) 'Nigeria's "Manifest Destiny" in West Africa: Dominance without Power', *Africa Spectrum*, 42, 2, pp. 301–321.

Baru, S. (2012) 'Geo-economics and Strategy', *Survival* 54, 3, pp. 47–58.

Bergstresser, H. (2009) 'Nigeria', in Mehler, A., Melber, H., and van Walraven, K. (eds), *Africa Yearbook: Politics, Economy and Society South of the Sahara in 2008* (Leiden: Brill), pp. 145–160.

Bergstresser, H. (2013) 'Nigeria', in Mehler, A., Melber, H., and van Walraven, K. (eds), *Africa Yearbook: Politics, Economy and Society South of the Sahara in 2012* (Leiden: Brill), pp. 157–173.

Blackwill, R. D. and Harris, J. M. (2016) *War by Other Means: Geoeconomics and Statecraft* (Cambridge, MA: Harvard University Press).

Browne, A. J. (2015) *LAPSSET: The History and Politics of an Eastern African Megaproject* (London: Rift Valley Institute).

Cheeseman, N. (2011) 'Kenya', in Mehler, A., Melber, H. and van Walraven, K. (eds), *Africa Yearbook: Politics, Economy and Society South of the Sahara in 2010*, pp. 345–357.

Cowen, D. and Smith, N. (2009) 'After Geopolitics?: From the Geopolitical Social to Geoeconomics', *Antipode* 41, 1, pp. 22–48.

Cooper, A. F., Higgott, R. A. and Nossal, K. R. (1991) 'Bound to Follow? Leadership and Followership in the Gulf Conflict', *Political Science Quarterly*, 106, 3, pp. 391–410.

Cuesta Fernández, I. (2015) 'Mammoth Dams, Lean Neighbours: Assessing the Bid to turn Ethiopia into East Africa's Powerhouse', in Scholvin, S. (ed.), *A New Scramble for Africa? The Rush for Energy Resources in Sub-Saharan Africa* (Farnham: Ashgate), pp. 93–110.

Ebert, H., Flemes, D. and Strüver, G. (2014) 'The Politics of Contestation in Asia: How Japan and Pakistan Deal with their Rising Neighbors', *Chinese Journal of International Politics*, 7, 2, pp. 221–260.

El-Fadel, M., El-Sayegh, Y., El-Fadl, K. and Khorbotly, D. (2003) 'The Nile River Basin: A Case Study in Surface Water Conflict Resolution', *Journal of Natural Resources and Life Science Education*, 32, pp. 107–117.

Fabricius, P. (2015) 'What Ended Zuma's Mediation in Libya?', *Institute for Security Studies*, 28 May. Available at: https://issafrica.org/iss-today/what-ended-zumas-mediation-in-libya, accessed 26 May 2017.

Fawole, A. W. (2012) 'Nigerian Foreign Policy: The Search for a New Paradigm', in Imobighe, T. A. and Alli, W. O. (eds), *Perspectives on Nigeria's National and External Relations: Essays in Honour of Professor A. Bolaji Akinyemi* (Ibadan: University Press), pp. 150–169.

Federal Democratic Republic of Ethiopia. (2002) *Foreign Affairs and National Security Policy Strategy* (Addis Ababa: Ministry of Information).

Flemes, D. (2009) 'Regional Power South Africa: Co-operative Hegemony Constrained by Historical Legacy', *Journal of Contemporary African Studies*, 27, 2, pp. 153–178.

Flemes, D. and Castro, R. (2016) 'Institutional Contestation: Colombia in the Pacific Alliance', *Bulletin of Latin American Research*, 35, 1, pp. 78–92.

Grosse, T. G. (2014) 'Geoeconomic Relations between the EU and China: The Lessons from the EU Weapon Embargo and From Galileo', *Geopolitics*, 19, 1, pp. 40–65.

Hsiung, J. C. (2009) 'The Age of Geoeconomics, China's Global Role, and Prospects of Cross-strait Integration', *Journal of Chinese Political Science*, 14, 2, pp. 113–133.

Huntington, S. P. (1993) 'Why International Primacy Matters', *International Security*, 17, 4, pp. 68–83.

International Crisis Group. (2012) 'The Kenyan Military Intervention in Somalia', *International Crisis Group*, Africa Report No. 184. Available at: www.crisisgroup.org/africa/horn-africa/kenya/kenyan-military-intervention-somalia, accessed 1 February 2018.

John, I. (2010) 'Rethinking Nigeria's Economic Diplomacy', *Vanguard*, 6 May. Available at: http://community.vanguardngr.com/profiles/blogs/rethinking-nigerias-economic, accessed 12 February 2017.

Kagwanja, P. (2014) 'Kenya's Foreign Policy: The Return of Geopolitics and the Revenge of the Liberal Order', *Observatoire des grands lacs en Afrique note*, 2.

Kelley, M. B. and Johnson, R. (2012) 'STRATFOR: Egypt is Prepared to Bomb all of Ethiopia's Nile Dams', *Business Insider*, 13 October. Available at: www.businessinsider.com/hacked-stratfor-emails-egypt-could-take-military-action-to-protect-its-stake-in-the-nile-2012-10?IR=T, accessed 17 January 2018.

Kenya Today. (2013) 'Jubilee Manifesto Launch: Uhuru Kenyatta Speech', *Kenya Today*, 3 February. Available at: www.kenya-today.com/politics/uhuru-kenyatta-manifesto, accessed 10 September 2017.

Landsberg, C. (2008) 'An African "Concert of Powers": Nigeria and South Africa's Construction of the AU and NEPAD', in Adebajo, A. and Abdul Raufu, M. (eds), *Gulliver's Troubles: Nigeria's Foreign Policy after the Cold War* (Scottsville: University of KwaZulu-Natal Press), pp. 203–219.

Leonard, M. (2016) 'Introduction: Connectivity Wars', in Leonard, M. (ed.), *Connectivity Wars: Why Migration, Finance and Trade Are the Geo-economic Battlegrounds of the Future* (London: European Council on Foreign Relations), pp. 13–30.

Luttwak, E. N. (1990) 'From Geopolitics to Geo-economics: Logic of Conflict, Grammar of Commerce', *The National Interest*, 20, pp. 17–23.

Lynch, C. (2011) 'On Ivory Coast Diplomacy, South Africa goes its Own Way', *Foreign Policy*, 23 February. Available at: http://foreignpolicy.com/2011/02/23/on-ivory-coast-diplomacy-south-africa-goes-its-own-way, accessed 26 May 2017.

Mabera, F. (2016) 'Kenya's Foreign Policy in Context (1963–2015)', *South African Journal of International Affairs*, 23, 3, pp. 365–384.

Malaquias, A. (2000) 'Angola's Foreign Policy since Independence: The Search for Domestic Security', *African Security Review*, 9, 3, pp. 34–46.

Malaquias, A. (2002) 'Dysfunctional Foreign Policy: Angola's Unsuccessful Quest for Security since Independence', in Adar, K. G. and Ajulu, R. (eds), *Globalization and Emerging Trends in African States' Foreign Policy-Making Process: A Comparative Perspective of Southern Africa* (Aldershot: Ashgate), pp. 13–33.

Mattlin, M. and Wigell, M. (2016) 'Geoeconomics in the Context of Restive Regional Powers', *Asia Europe Journal*, 14, 2, pp. 125–134.

Mercille, J. (2008) 'The Radical Geopolitics of US Foreign Policy: Geopolitical and Geoeconomic Logics of Power', *Political Geography*, 27, 5, pp. 570–586.

Miyandazi, L. (2012) 'Kenya's Military Intervention in Somalia: An Intricate Process', *African Centre for the Constructive Resolution of Disputes*, Policy and Practice Brief. Available at: www.accord.org.za/publication/kenya-s-military-intervention-in-somalia, accessed 25 May 2017.

National Planning Commission [of Nigeria]. (2012) 'Annual Performance Monitoring Report', *National Planning Commission*. Available at: www.nationalplanning.gov.ng/images/docs/MonitoringandEvaluation/NPCAnnualPerformanceMonitoringReport.pdf, accessed 26 May 2017.

National Planning Commission [of Nigeria]. (n.d.) 'The Transformation Agenda: 2011–2015', *National Planning Commission*. Available at: www.nationalplanning.gov.ng/images/docs/Transformation.pdf, accessed 26 May 2017.

National Planning Commission [of Nigeria]. (n.d.) 'Vision 20: 2020', *National Planning Commission*. Available at: www.nationalplanning.gov.ng/images/docs/NationalPlans/nigeria-vision-20-20-20.pdf, accessed 26 May 2017.

Ojeme, V. (2011) 'Economic Diplomacy: A Paradigm Shift in Nigeria's Foreign Policy', *Vanguard*, 21 August. Available at: www.vanguardngr.com/2011/08/economic-diplomacy-a-paradigm-shift-in-nigeria%E2%80%99s-foreign-policy, accessed 12 February 2017.

Redvers, L. (2013) 'Angola, the Reluctant SADC Trader', *South African Institute of International Affairs*, Occasional Paper No. 152. Available at: www.saiia.org.za/occasional-papers/angola-the-reluctant-sadc-trader, accessed 1 February 2018.

Republic of Kenya. (2014) 'Kenya Foreign Policy', *Republic of Kenya*. Available at: www.mfa.go.ke/wp-content/uploads/2016/09/Kenya-Foreign-Policy.pdf, accessed 26 May 2017.

Roque, P. C. (2013) 'Angola's Crucial Foreign Policy Drive', *German Institute for International and Security Affairs*, SWP Comment No. 15. Available at: www.swp-berlin.org/en/publication/angolas-crucial-foreign-policy-drive/, accessed 1 February 2018.

Schoeman, M. (2003) 'South Africa as an Emerging Middle Power, 1994–2003', in Daniel, J., Habib, A. and Southall, R. (eds), *State of the Nation: South Africa 2003–2004* (Cape Town: HSRC Press), pp. 349–367.

Schoeman, M. and Alden, C. (2003) 'The Hegemon that Wasn't: South Africa's Foreign Policy towards Zimbabwe', *Strategic Review for Southern Africa*, 25, 1, n.p.

Scholvin, S. (2013) 'From Rejection to Acceptance: The Conditions of Regional Contestation and Followership to post-Apartheid South Africa', *African Security*, 6, 2, pp. 133–152.

Scholvin, S. (2016) 'Geopolitics: An Overview of Concepts and Empirical Examples from International Relations', *The Finnish Institute of International Affairs*, FIIA Working Paper No. 91. Available at: www.fiia.fi/en/publication/geopolitics, accessed 1 February 2018.

Scholvin, S. (2017a) 'Secondary Powers vis-à-vis South Africa: Hard Balancing, Soft Balancing, Rejection of Followership, and Disregard of Leadership', *German Institute of Global and Area Studies*, GIGA Working Paper No. 306. Available at: www.giga-hamburg.de/de/system/files/publications/wp306_scholvin.pdf, accessed 9 February 2018.

Scholvin, S. (2017b) 'South Africa and Secondary Powers: Contestation in Sub-Saharan Africa', *South African Institute of International Affairs*, SAIIA Occasional Paper No. 270. Available at: www.saiia.org.za/occasional-papers/south-africa-and-secondary-powers-contestation-in-sub-saharan-africa, accessed 1 February 2018.

Scholvin, S. and Wrana, J. (2015) 'From the Cape to Cairo? The Potential of the Tripartite Free Trade Area', *South African Institute of International Affair*, SAIIA Occasional Paper No. 221. Available at: www.saiia.org.za/occasional-papers/from-the-cape-to-cairo-the-potential-of-the-tripartite-free-trade-area, accessed 1 February 2018.

Scott, D. (2008) 'The Great Power "Great Game" between India and China: "The Logic of Geography" ', *Geopolitics*, 13, 1, pp. 1–26.

Simon, D. (ed.) (1998) *South Africa in Southern Africa: Reconfiguring the Region* (Oxford: Currey).

Stratfor. (2012) 'The Geopolitics of Angola: An Exception to African Geography', *Stratfor*. Available at: www.stratfor.com/sample/analysis/geopolitics-angola-exception-african-geography, accessed 8 August 2012.

Turner, T. (2002) 'Angola's Role in the Congo War', in Clark, J. F. (ed.), *The African Stakes of the Congo War* (Basingstoke: Palgrave Macmillan), pp. 75–92.

Ubi, E. N. and Akinkuotu, O. O. (2014) 'Nigerian Foreign Policy and Economic Development, 1999–2013', *International Area Studies Review*, 17, 4, pp. 414–433.

United Nations. (2017) 'Troops and Police Contributors Archive (1990–2016)', *United Nations*. Available at: www.un.org/en/peacekeeping/resources/statistics/contributors_archive.shtml, accessed 16 February 2017.

Wigell, M. and Vihma, A. (2016) 'Geopolitics versus Geoeconomics: The Case of Russia's Changing Geostrategy and Its Effects on the EU', *International Affairs*, 92, 3, pp. 605–627.

16 Conclusion

Sören Scholvin, Mikael Wigell
and Mika Aaltola

Findings of this book

Debates about the future world order, in particular the question of whether armed conflict will once again become a feature of great power relations, have been catalysed by Russia's annexation of Crimea and its ongoing involvement in the low-intensity conflict in eastern Ukraine. Some scholars argue that these developments mean a return to the military-based logic of geopolitics in Europe – the continent that used to be the role model of the liberal order (e.g. Mead 2014). Britain and France have recently agreed to deepen their military cooperation. More defence spending is a demand of Germany's conservative party in its coalition talks with the Social Democrats, who remain sceptical on this issue. The Swedish government has reintroduced the distribution of millions of leaflets to private households, providing its citizens with instructions of what to do in the case of war.

In the Far East, which has become the world's second major theatre of power politics, the United States has threatened to wage war against North Korea because of that country's weapons of mass destruction programme. President Trump went so far to announce in front of the United Nations that the United States is ready to 'totally destroy' North Korea if forced to defend itself or its allies (White House 2017). Further south, China is projecting its military power so as to claim sovereignty over disputed seas and protect its maritime trade. Friction with Japan and Southeast Asian states – and, in the Indian Ocean, also with India – is increasing. It is not a mere coincident that Australia's defence budget rose by 6 per cent last year and is to reach 2 per cent of gross domestic product by 2021 (Gady 2017).

Yet unlike Russia, China is not so much a challenger of the liberal order because of its military activities. The People's Republic has proven capable of establishing institutions that create alternatives to those dominated by the West. As Mikko Huotari analysed in Chapter 10, China has been advancing crisis liquidity provision through financial institutions that circumvent the International Monetary Fund and the World Bank. It has provided targeted investment funds, which are active in numerous developing countries. The internationalisation of the renminbi is another means that the People's Republic could use for strategic purposes.

On the regional level, geo-economics appears to trump geopolitics, too. Pavel Baev argued in Chapter 6 that economic means characterise power politics in East and Southeast Asia, in spite of considerable conflict dynamics. The regional states, first of all China, have concentrated on domestic economic growth and modernisation for several decades. By now, economics is what makes them powerful – not their military capabilities, at least not in the first place.

The People's Republic is not, of course, the only state in the Far East that refers to geo-economics. In Chapter 11, Mikael Mattlin and Bart Gaens analysed how China and Japan use foreign aid and their respective roles in the Asian Development Bank and Asian Infrastructure Investment Bank so as to meet political objectives. When Japanese companies started setting up production facilities in East and Southeast Asian countries and importing resources from there in the 1970s and 1980s, foreign aid served as a means to compensate for negative side effects such as environmental degradation. In particular, infrastructure projects became a way for Japanese companies to enter local markets. China's foreign aid is also very much about infrastructure projects, tied closely to special economic zones, as it is in the case of Japan. It comes along with a strong rhetoric of self-sufficiency and South-South cooperation. Yet the People's Republic does not clearly distinguish between export credits and development assistance, which probably best demonstrates its self-interest driven foreign aid practices. What is more, so called tied aid – that is, aid granted on the condition that the beneficiary country will purchase the goods or services from suppliers in the donor country – is common for China and Japan.

As the previous paragraphs indicate, the contributions to this volume have shown that power politics in the early twenty-first century is not a simple return to Cold War geopolitics. In today's world, national prosperity and security depend on flows of capital, data, goods and people that are crisscrossing the globe. Aaltola *et al.* (2014) suggest that this new geography of flows penetrating sovereign state space renders traditional territory-based foreign and security policies ineffective.

In his contribution to this book, Christian Fjäder emphasised that states are increasingly dependent on various cross-border flows (Chapter 3). This dependency, which is often asymmetric in the sense that one state has more control over a particular type of flow than another, has become a leverage in power politics. Corresponding means range from economic sanctions to cross-border migration (as in the case of Turkey and the European Union) to currency manipulation (for example by China, which has been criticised for keeping the value of the Renminbi low so as to boost exports). Critical infrastructures – not only pipelines and power stations but also telecommunication networks – are further assets that matter for power politics through interdependence.

Chapter 4 by Mika Aaltola and Juha Käpylä looked at the role of logistical flows in the unfolding rivalry of China and the United States in Central Asia. The authors argued that what they called 'functional control' over man-made environments (for example, critical infrastructures) provides concrete means of asymmetric power exertion as well as a novel kind of territorial control for states empowered by their position in the overall structure of key logistical flows and infrastructures. As such, the way in which cities and regions, for instance, are linked through the global flows of data, goods and people is starting to play an increasingly important role in geostrategic scenarios. These linkages and networks – the hub-and-spoke systems of airports, data cables, railway lines and roads as well as sea-lines of communication – can be rerouted and rewired, with major consequences for power politics.

It appears that in situations of interdependence, economic power is often more consequential than military power in the pursuit of strategic goals (Blackwill and Harris 2016; Wigell and Vihma 2016); and economic concerns more relevant than military concerns for national security (Brattberg and Hamilton 2013). For instance, the Australian government published its *Critical Infrastructure Resilience Strategy* (Australian Government 2010). As Fjäder pointed out in his contribution, Canada and the European Union have strategies to protect critical infrastructures across national borders. It comes as no surprise that, in 2014, the World Economic Forum changed the name of its Agenda Council on Geopolitical Risks into Agenda Council on Geo-economics.

Geo-economics appears to be such an attractive form of power politics that it can even be found as a component of conflicts usually understood as driven by military logics. Chapter 14 by Smruti Pattanaik accordingly revealed that India refers to economic means so as to extend its influence in Central and South Asia. Pakistan, meanwhile, seeks to block India's increasing interaction with Central Asia and even more so with Afghanistan. It tries to build a sphere of influence of its own, also by geo-economic means. Pattanaik's contribution moreover highlighted that traditional geographical factors – Central Asia and Afghanistan are landlocked and India heavily depends on Pakistan as a transit country – have not ceased to matter.

Niklas Rossbach's analysis of the shale gas revolution and US foreign policy boosts the idea that traditional geographical factors – resource endowment in this case – still matter (Chapter 9). A general conclusion that can be drawn from Rossbach's text is that states that possess economic power benefit from a wider array of policy options. Their strategic choice is far greater than that of less powerful states. Apart from providing technical aid to allied states interested in exploiting their own unconventional oil and gas resources, the United States is now in a position to deliver energy supplies to its allies, for example to decrease the corresponding dependence of European countries on Russia. As an alternative, the superpower could try to reduce its global commitment, especially in the Middle East, because some policy advisers, whose judgement Rossbach calls into question, maintain that the United States is on a path towards energy independence. All this cannot be understood without knowing the details of unconventional hydrocarbon resources in North America, in particular their amount and cost of exploitation.

As soon as one recognises that traditional geographical factors remain essential to geo-economics, it does not sound odd to say that geo-economics is not a totally new type of foreign policy strategy. It has been with us for more than a century, as Braz Baracuhy pointed out in Chapter 2. Scholars of classical geopolitics such as James Fairgrieve and Halford Mackinder elaborated on issues that are, if one follows the definition from the introduction of this volume, geo-economics. For these scholars, geopolitics did not mean the pursuit of strategic objectives by military means. This understanding rather derives from Cold War foreign policy practices associated with Zbigniew Brzezinski and Henry Kissinger. Fairgrieve, Mackinder and their contemporaries understood geopolitics as a science about the impact of geography (independent variable) on politics (dependent variable) (Scholvin 2016). Hence much of what counts as geo-economics in our understanding of that term, was labelled geopolitics in the first half of the past century.

Taking up a point made by Blackwill and Harris in *War by Other Means* (2016), Baracuhy furthermore argued that economic and military aspects of power are always somehow interrelated: economic prosperity is the basis of defence expenditures; military power and (geo)political events usually have economic impacts. This means that 'geo-economics and geopolitics are distinct yet related [...] types of geostrategy' (this book, p. 18). Thus a finding of this volume is that geo-economics has not replaced geopolitics – to the contrary of what Luttwak (1990) and others predicted almost 30 years ago. Sören Scholvin has confirmed this in Chapter 15, where he demonstrated that secondary powers in sub-Saharan Africa – Angola, Ethiopia, Kenya and Nigeria – refer to a mix of geo-economics and geopolitics in their foreign policies, thus trying to shape their respective near abroad.

The mix of geo-economics and geopolitics applies to the Indian–Pakistani rivalry as well. As Chapter 14 in this volume has shown, Pakistan makes use of violent attacks – carried out by Islamist insurgents – to prevent India from increasing its economic and political footprint in Afghanistan. In his analysis of economic sanctions imposed against Iran since the revolution of 1979 (Chapter 8), Paul Rivlin concluded that sanctions would not, probably, have been successful if it were not for the latent military threat to Iran posed by the United States. Rivlin's excurse on Libya, in which he hinted at the fact that the willingness of the Gaddafi regime to give up its weapons of mass destruction led to its downfall, implies that economically weak states may use military power politics as an effective leverage against economically stronger opponents.

From a broader perspective, Kari Möttölä also reasoned that geo-economics and geopolitics can co-occur (Chapter 7). The key idea that he advanced is that even in co-occurrence, geo-economics and geopolitics follow different logics and have different effects on the international system. In the case of the United States during the Obama administration, geo-economics was about the Trans-Pacific Partnership and the Transatlantic Trade and Investment Partnership – not only two giant trade blocs under US hegemony but also two pillars of the world-wide liberal order. Geopolitics, meanwhile, appears to fragment the international system into distinct regions with security orders of their own. Möttölä pointed out that the United States has shifted its own military focus towards the Asia Pacific region (Far Eastern theatre), supports their European partners militarily against Russia (European theatre) and builds partnerships with regional countries and major European powers in the Middle East (Middle Eastern theatre).

Yet there is disagreement on the suitability of a mixed approach of geo-economics and geopolitics: whereas Baracuhy suggested that states ought to combine geo-economics and geopolitics, Baev reasoned that the simultaneous pursuit of geo-economic and geopolitical strategies weakens Russia's position in the Far East. In another publication, Wigell and Vihma (2016) similarly draw the conclusion that the mix of geo-economics and geopolitics is not conducive for Russia vis-à-vis the European Union. Moreover, it would be difficult to imagine, for example, that the government of Greece starts supporting armed militants in order to make the European Central Bank and the German government offer better conditions for the repayment of the Greek debt. At least in this case, Europe demonstrates how useless military force may be.

This leads us to Hans Kundnani's text on Germany as a role model of 'liberal geo-economics' (Chapter 5). Kundnani's contribution is particularly helpful to overcome the misguided association of geo-economics with economic nationalism and some sort of neo-mercantilism. Being a strong proponent of economic liberalism, Germany has used its financial power to enforce far-reaching reforms on south European countries, pushing through a strict course of austerity. In conflicts with Russia and also elsewhere, the German government has opted for economic sanctions and limited its military commitment to a minimum.

Liberal geo-economic powers can influence markets through their dominant role in international financial institutions, through economic sanctions – both applied against Iran because of its nuclear programme (Chapter 8) – and by creating zones of economic cooperation and free trade (Chapter 7e). The specific means in liberal geo-economics are different from what most readers will associate with geo-economics because Germany does not have sovereign wealth funds or large state-owned companies, which are the geo-economic means of states that have much more direct control over their respective national economies.

However even states that do not fall into the category of liberal geo-economics pursue geo-economics as a rather covert and indirect approach towards their strategic objectives (Vihma and Wigell 2016). Mikael Wigell and Ana Soliz Landivar and, to a lesser extent, also Martha Márquez brought geo-economics together with the concepts of soft balancing and soft power (Chapter 12 and 13). The authors have shown how geo-economics often works in a subtle way, through building and supporting interest groups in target countries – for example businesspeople and politicians in Latin America who personally benefit from Chinese investments.

China also builds diplomatic networks, including with intergovernmental institutions such as the Union of South American Nations, and invests in infrastructure to facilitate its regional investments and trade. Venezuela, meanwhile, has created an economic and political alliance with Central American and Caribbean countries as well as Bolivia. Both the People's Republic and Venezuela aim at reducing US influence in Latin America but they do not confront the United States directly. It is their economic cooperation with third countries that relatively weakens the superpower.

What is more, being passive or, even worse, pursuing policies that contradict what a sound geo-economic approach would look like may have significant consequences for the state in consideration. By not fostering economic ties with Latin America, by pursuing a course of economic nationalism and by policies and rhetoric that Latin American governments and people consider offensive and racist, the Trump administration virtually paves the way for China to expand its influence southwards of the Rio Grande. In the case of Venezuela meanwhile, it appears that an overly ambitious geo-economic project has been pursued: the costs of regional leadership were too high to be sustainable even prior to the collapse of the global oil price.

Questions for follow-up research

In addition to the findings summarised above, the contributions to this volume have also raised questions for follow-up research. First of all, it appears to us that it is not always easy to draw lines between economic and military means of power, although doing so would be essential to distinguish between geo-economics and geopolitics, following the definition that we advanced in Chapter 1. For instance, Baev discussed Russia's efforts to export military equipment to East and Southeast Asia. Are they part of a geo-economic strategy that seeks market control and strategic leverage through interdependence (on Russian spare parts for that equipment)? Or could this better be understood as a geopolitical strategy that is about changing the regional military balance of power by strengthening Russia's partners?

Related to this, Wigell and Soliz Landivar have shown that it can be difficult to tell whether a specific policy is geo-economics: China's quest for markets and resources in Latin America also aims at economic objectives. At this stage, it remains unclear to what extent increasing investment and trade will help the People's Republic to pursue political objectives, or, indeed, whether its foremost intention is the pursuit of political objectives. It is sensible to assume that the People's Republic pursues various objectives in Latin America, some of which are economic, others political, and only some fitting into the framework of geo-economics.

What is more, we need a better understanding of different types of geo-economics. Comparing Márquez's analysis of Venezuelan petro-diplomacy with Kundnani's study of German power politics in the Eurozone, it becomes clear that there are significant differences between, on the one side, states that conduct geo-economics through state-owned enterprises and, on the other side, states that refer to their overwhelming power in intergovernmental institutions. One particular type of geo-economics that merits a better conceptualisation is geo-economics through financial institutions. In order to do so, it appears worthwhile to bring geo-economics and approaches from Institutionalism and International Political Economy together. We think that adherents of geo-economics who concentrate on institutions in their own research should stress the value added by the geo-economic perspective. They should explain how geo-economics enriches the two established schools of thought.

As noted, Mattlin and Gaens have shown that infrastructure is central to Chinese and Japanese foreign assistance. They also argued that this largely serves the interests of China and Japan respectively. At the same time, what follows at least implicitly from their analysis is that the recipient countries benefit considerably from their relations with the two East Asian powers. We think that this hints at another key question: is geo-economics about zero-sum-games or are there ways of creating mutual benefits? Whereas many chapters in this book are based on the conviction that international relations are, in general, about zero-sum-games, this might not be true. If they are not, more attention must be paid to the chances for and probability of geo-economics as a mutually beneficial form of relations amongst states.

The chapters of this book dealt with geo-economics as part of international relations. Not many of them provided insights on the role of domestic issues. However national economies obviously constitute the very fundament of geo-economic strategies. For geo-economics, being powerful depends much more on domestic growth and modernisation than it does for military-based power politics. Whilst Baev sheds light on decisions taken by the Russian presidents and prime ministers so as to explain Russia's rise as a geo-economic player in East and Southeast Asia, one should also ask whether some states are less likely to pursue geo-economics for the simple reason that they lack corresponding assets of national power. As suggested above with regard to the cases of Libya and Pakistan, such states may refer to military power politics because they consider themselves relatively more powerful in this arena.

If one accepts that states may choose power politics based on either economic or military assets, it becomes critical that the distribution of economic power does not necessarily equal the distribution of military power, as Baracuhy remarked. Whereas the early post-Cold War era was characterised by unipolarity in the two dimensions, today's world is still dominated by the United States in terms of military power but economic power is spread more evenly amongst a group of states. Further research would be necessary so as to determine what this means for power politics: Could the United States, in the near future, use military pressure as a last resort not only against minor powers such as Iran and North Korea but also in order to slow down the economic rise of its challengers, in particular the BRICS? Will economically powerful states – not only the BRICS but also Europe's major powers – increase their military power, making use of their economic prosperity this way? Or will they concentrate on economic power politics?

Even if states stick to geo-economics and refrain from using military means, we think that there is need for a more thorough measurement of economic or geo-economic power. Baracuhy pointed out that factors such as institutions, markets and resources serve as the basis of geo-economic strategies because they are assets from which national economic power derives. It remains unclear though how national economic power can be calculated. Chapters 14 and 15 provide inroads into this topic but more systematic research should ideally come up with a list of measurable assets that matter to geo-economics and then apply this list so as to advance global and regional hierarchies. Taking up debates on the 'fungibility of power' (e.g. Art 1996; Baldwin 1979),[1] it should also be figured out which assets of power – institutions, markets, resources and others – are of use to which type of geo-economic challenges.

Another issue that merits more attention is failed geo-economics. Most chapters in this book analyse how states achieve their geostrategic goals through economic means. This is not surprising for a book that aims at showing that geo-economics is a foreign policy paradigm on the rise because of its suitability to present-day international relations. Yet, for example, Russia appears to have miscalculated the benefits and costs of its policy on the Far East, in particular with regard to its relationship with China. A costly geo-economic strategy has brought little strategic gain, as Baev argued. This weakens Russia's overall position and implies that more suitable policy options have been foregone. It even backfires because a misguided geo-economic strategy weakens the power base of the state that pursues such a strategy. The same applies to Venezuela. Follow-up studies on Márquez's contribution to this volume should seek to answer the questions whether and how an overly ambitious project of regional powerhood has contributed to the country's domestic crisis.

Then there is also an area of investigation that transcends the usual realm of International Relations: Márquez remarked – rather as a side note – that 'oil has been a driver of Venezuela's domestic and foreign policies since 1922, when major findings began providing the state with a stream of oil rent' (this book, p. 182). Generalising this idea, we find it intriguing to ask to what extent and how geographical conditions, resource endowment in the case of Venezuela, shape states and the policies that the respective governments pursue. Rossbach's contribution on the shale gas revolution could also be extended in this way, although the author does not hint at resource abundance pushing the United States towards a specific grand design of foreign policy. We do not suggest a new form of geographical determinism but it may be worthwhile to take up an idea formulated by one of the few present-day scholars who stand in the tradition of classical geopolitics: 'the political behavior of a country is the reflection of that country's history; and that country's history is in great part (though certainly not entirely) the product of its geographical setting' (Gray 1988, p. 43).

Note

1 Fungibility is convertibility: means of power that can be applied in issue-area A are not necessarily of use in issue-area B. For example, China may use its US dollar reserves to manipulate the exchange rate of the renminbi or to provide credits for infrastructure projects to its allies. The same means can be applied for different purposes and in different contexts. Weapons of mass destruction, meanwhile, served the Gaddafi regime as a deterrent against the West. They did not help in any way to make African states submit to Gaddafi's claim of continental leadership.

References

Aaltola, M., Käpylä, J., Mikkola, H. and Behr, T. (2014) *Towards the Geopolitics of Flows: Implications for Finland*, FIIA Report No. 40 (Helsinki: The Finnish Institute of International Affairs). Available at: www.fiia.fi/en/publication/towards-the-geopolitics-of-flows, accessed 10 January 2018.

Art, R. J. (1996) 'American Foreign Policy and the Fungibility of Force', *Security Studies*, 5, 4, pp. 7–42.

Australian Government. (2010) 'Critical Infrastructure Resilience Strategy', *Australian Government*. Available at: www.tisn.gov.au/Documents/Australian+Government+s+Critical+Infrastructure+Resilience+Strategy.pdf, accessed 9 February 2018.

Baldwin, D. A. (1979) 'Power Analysis and World Politics: New Trends Versus Old Tendencies', *World Politics*, 31, 2, pp. 161–194.

Blackwill, R. D. and Harris, J. M. (2016) *War by Other Means: Geoeconomics and State-craft* (Cambridge, MA: Harvard University Press).

Brattberg, E. and Hamilton, D. (2013) *Global Flow Security: A New Security Agenda for the Transatlantic Community in 2030* (Washington, DC: Center for Transatlatic Relations).

Gady, F. S. (2017) 'Australia to Increase Defense Budget', *The Diplomat*, 11 May. Available at: https://thediplomat.com/2017/05/australia-to-increase-defense-budget, accessed 25 January 2018.

Gray, C. S. (1988) *The Geopolitics of Super Power* (Lexington: University Press of Kentucky).

Luttwak, E. N. (1990) 'From Geopolitics to Geo-economics: Logic of Conflict, Grammar of Commerce', *National Interest*, 20, pp. 17–23.

Mead, W. R. (2014) 'The Return of Geopolitics: The Revenge of the Revisionist Powers', *Foreign Affairs*, 93, 3, pp. 69–79.

Scholvin, S. (2016) 'Geopolitics: An Overview of Concepts and Empirical Examples from International Relations', *The Finnish Institute of International Affairs*, FIIA Working Paper No. 91. Available at: www.fiia.fi/en/publication/geopolitics, accessed 2 February 2018.

Vihma, A. and Wigell, M. (2016) 'Unclear and Present Danger: Russia's Geoeconomics and the Nord Stream II Pipeline', *Global Affairs*, 2, 4, pp. 377–388.

White House. (2017) 'Remarks by President Trump to the 72nd Session of the United Nations General Assembly', *The White House*. Available at: www.whitehouse.gov/briefings-statements/remarks-president-trump-72nd-session-united-nations-general-assembly, accessed 25 January 2018.

Wigell, M. and Vihma, A. (2016) 'Geopolitics versus Geoeconomics: The Case of Russia's Geostrategy and Its Effects on the EU', *International Affairs*, 92, 3, pp. 605–627.

Index

Page numbers in **bold** denote tables, those in *italics* denote figures.

230   *Index*

Printed in Great Britain
by Amazon